University of Plymouth
Charles Seale Hayne Library
Subject to status this item may be renewed
via your Voyager account

http://voyager.plymouth.ac.uk
Tel: (01752) 232323

US Foreign Policy and the Iranian Revolution

US Foreign Policy and the Iranian Revolution

The Cold War Dynamics of Engagement and Strategic Alliance

Christian Emery

Lecturer in International Relations, School of Government, University of Plymouth, UK

First published 2013 by
PALGRAVE MACMILLAN

Palgrave Macmillan in the UK is an imprint of Macmillan Publishers Limited, registered in England, company number 785998, of Houndmills, Basingstoke, Hampshire RG21 6XS.

Palgrave Macmillan in the US is a division of St Martin's Press LLC, 175 Fifth Avenue, New York, NY 10010.

Palgrave Macmillan is the global academic imprint of the above companies and has companies and representatives throughout the world.

Palgrave® and Macmillan® are registered trademarks in the United States, the United Kingdom, Europe and other countries.

ISBN 978–1–137–32986–8

This book is printed on paper suitable for recycling and made from fully managed and sustained forest sources. Logging, pulping and manufacturing processes are expected to conform to the environmental regulations of the country of origin.

A catalogue record for this book is available from the British Library.

A catalog record for this book is available from the Library of Congress.

To my parents, Nick and Janet, and partner, Anna

Contents

Acknowledgements

I am indebted to Professor Scott Lucas. It was truly a life-changing event when I walked into Scott's US foreign policy class as a final-year undergraduate student at Birmingham in 2002. During my journey from graduate student to early career academic, I have been incredibly lucky to work with some fantastic colleagues. Dr Steve Hewitt has been a friend and supporter ever since he trusted me to cover his teaching back in 2007. Professors Ben Rosamond and Kim Hutchings have been supportive and inspirational heads of department at Warwick University and the London School of Economics (LSE), respectively. I spent three wonderful years at the LSE and extend my sincere thanks to all those colleagues and students who offered invaluable feedback during research seminars, classes, or over a drink at the George. I must single out Dr Toby Dodge, who has been a mentor, sounding board, and true friend. Special thanks also to Dr Roham Alvandi and Dr Bryan Gibson for sharing their friendship and expertise in US–Iranian relations.

This project has frequently taken me to the US, including an unforgettable summer as a visiting scholar at the University of Virginia (UVA). It is with regret that space does not permit me to extend my personal thanks to the many academics and former practitioners in the US who were generous with their time. Nevertheless, I would like to specifically thank Ambassador Nathaniel Howell, who not only sponsored me as a visiting scholar at UVA, but was generous enough to offer his own personal insights from his time in government. I must also thank Malcolm Byrne at the National Security Archive and all the staff at the Jimmy Carter Library. I have benefitted enormously from the wisdom of many distinguished individuals, but it goes without saying that all errors of fact and judgement remain my own.

Without the support of my friends and family, this book would have been a far more painful undertaking. I thank my sisters, Catherine and Fiona, for their love and encouragement. This book is dedicated to my wonderful parents, Nick and Janet, as a small token of thanks for their support and unstinting belief in me. The book is jointly dedicated to my partner, Anna. Without her love, emotional support, and patience, this book would simply not have happened. Thank you for everything.

Introduction

America's post-revolutionary relations with Iran were born in the aftermath of a heavy snowstorm in Washington. As members of the Carter administration battled the bitter cold and snow-covered streets to reach their desks on 11 February 1979, they struggled to absorb the morning's news: Iran's senior generals had abandoned the Shah's last Prime Minister, Shapour Bakhtiar, and ordered their troops to return to barracks to avoid more bloodshed. A small number of the Shah's elite Imperial Guard mounted a desperate last stand, but most had either switched sides or disappeared. Bakhtiar, accepting the inevitable, had submitted his resignation to Mehdi Bazargan, the man designated by the Revolution's unassailable leader, Ayatollah Ruhollah Khomeini, to be the first Prime Minister of the Islamic Republic of Iran.[1] In a radio and television address, Bazargan appealed for calm and praised the army's support for the 'will of the people'.[2] History had been made; a revolution led by a 76-year-old cleric espousing a relatively obscure interpretation of Shia political Islam had succeeded in dislodging one of Washington's most powerful and loyal allies in the Middle East. It now posed one of the gravest challenges to post-war US foreign policy. At a stroke, Washington had lost its principal bulwark to Soviet expansionism in the Northern Tier, its largest customer for sophisticated weaponry, and intelligence facilities vital for monitoring Soviet missile testing in Central Asia.

Once a path had been cleared through the snow, senior US policy-makers assembled in the White House Situation Room to digest this calamity. With Carter's political opponents already lambasting his government's failure to protect the Shah, it was agreed that Iran was too important to ignore and that America must rebuild some kind of connection with whatever regime emerged there.[3] Soon after, President Carter told reporters that his government accepted the Revolution and was already in close consultation with the new Iranian leadership and hoped for 'a very productive and peaceful cooperation'.[4]

Behind these diplomatic niceties lay an uncomfortable reality: there simply was no plan for a post-Shah Iran. For 25 years the US had taken

1

for granted Iran's status as an ally and semi-client state. As noted by former US diplomat John Limbert, 'Despite misgivings about Pahlavi repression, corruption, economic mismanagement, and brutality, for official Washington the Shah remained the lynchpin of America's anti-Soviet efforts in the Middle East.'[5] Although some low-level analysts had long warned of a crisis looming in Iran, Carter's senior foreign policy advisors, distracted by what they considered to be more pressing foreign policy initiatives, had resisted any serious rethinking of US policy in Iran. Now they had no choice but to adjust to a completely new reality in Iran.

The central objective of this book is to examine the nature and legacy of that adjustment. It first examines how a plan to engage the new regime was developed and implemented. It then examines how US policy objectives in Iran were refashioned in light of three major and converging crises: the Iran hostage crisis, the Soviet intervention in Afghanistan, and the onset of the Iran–Iraq War. By re-examining the Carter administration's record in post-revolutionary Iran, it provides a fresh perspective on the origins of one of the most bitter and enduring confrontations in international relations.

America's acceptance of the Revolution: Contested narratives

When Carter declared his acceptance of the Revolution on 11 February, he had no sense that US–Iranian relations would not only transform his presidential legacy, but challenge every president who subsequently entered the White House. Nearly 35 years later, the confrontation between the US and Iran has become so ideologically entrenched and domestically vitriolic that it is easy to lose sight of the importance the US placed on reaching an accommodation with the nascent Islamic Republic. The view is far more obscured within the circles of power in Iran. Nearly all of Iran's senior leaders have stated their belief that American policy-makers never accepted the Revolution and immediately set about destabilising the new revolutionary government.[6] More critically for contemporary US–Iranian relations, current Supreme Leader Ayatollah Ali Khamenei maintains that America's conspiracy to undermine the Islamic Republic began as soon as the Revolution succeeded.[7] In 2008, for example, Iran's highest-ranking political and religious leader told an audience that 'there hasn't been a day in which America has had good intentions toward Iran'.[8]

In one important sense, the analysis presented in this book provides a vital corrective to Khamenei's narrative of American motives in Iran. It shows that there was no immediate conspiracy to undermine the Revolution. On the contrary, the Carter administration tried persistently, and in good faith, to rebuild relations with the new regime. Good faith was not enough, however, and this book highlights a number of factors that undermined Washington's attempt to demonstrate its acceptance of the Revolution. Any chance of a rapprochement, at least in the short term, was ruled out when Iran's first

Supreme Leader, Ayatollah Ruhollah Khomeini, refused to intervene when militant revolutionaries overran the US embassy in Tehran and held 53 Americans hostage for 444 days.

This cataclysmic event in contemporary US–Iranian relations, beginning 9 months after the Revolution succeeded, was not planned or executed by anyone with significant political authority in Tehran. Nor does it appear that the militants who seized the embassy had much in the way of a long-term strategy. True, Khomeini's prolonging of the crisis was a semi-calculated decision aimed to consolidate his vision of an Islamic Republic. Yet even this piece of political opportunism was ad hoc and eventually subsumed by a political process that was itself fluid and chaotic. As yet, nobody has been able to convincingly demonstrate that Khomeini had anything other than vague notions of what he hoped the crisis would achieve.

Whilst there is little evidence of a tightly choreographed plan, there has been a remarkably consistent justification for attacking the embassy in the first place. It is often assumed to have been a response to the decision to allow the Shah to enter the US for medical treatment. Indeed, it has been widely acknowledged that US embassy officials had predicted that they would come under attack should Carter decide to let in the Shah. Yet this act of purported provocation did not exist in a vacuum. The young Iranians who climbed the wall and overpowered the small Marine detachment guarding the embassy were not just engaging in an act of emotional revolutionary catharsis targeted on the symbol of America's presence in Iran. Nor was dubbing the embassy the 'Den of Spies' simply a rhetorical flourish. Those participating had convinced themselves that it was justified as a defensive action vital for consolidating the Revolution. The embassy really was considered the base for counter-revolutionary conspiracies.

Despite the irreparable damage the hostage crisis has inflicted on Iran's international standing, this remains the state-sanctioned version of events and a pillar of Iran's revolutionary identity. During one sermon at Friday prayers in 1998, Khamenei told his audience: 'From the beginning of the Islamic Revolution, they made the embassy a place for planning conspiracies, and these activities led the students to attack and take over the embassy.'[9] Despite several prominent Iranian politicians having expressed regret for the hostage crisis, including many of the students who led the attack, its essentially defensive nature remains the narrative presented by the state in school books and during periods of collective remembrance.

This book confirms that this claim is baseless. American diplomats were in fact rebuffing exiled Iranian groups seeking US assistance to destabilise the revolutionary government. Rather than conspiring to bring down the Iranian government, the documentary record indicates that US officials fretted over Iran's fragility and saw its destabilisation as the most likely precursor to Soviet adventurism in the Persian Gulf. Even as the Carter administration was leaving office, the advice offered to the incoming Reagan administration was to avoid exiled groups actively conspiring against the Islamic Republic. Even after the hostage crisis, the Carter administration consistently avoided actions that would rule out a future rapprochement. They advised the next government to do the same.

The purpose of this book is not to provide a one-sided account of Iranian paranoia and hostility in the face of American goodwill and best intentions. There were very good reasons why Iran's new leaders were suspicious of America's motives. The US had, after all, played a critical role in sustaining the authoritarian regime the revolutionaries had just shed blood to remove. In 1953 they had aided a coup that removed the legal Prime Minister Mohammad Mossadeq. Many of Iran's new leaders had suffered imprisonment and torture at the hands of the Shah's security services, which they knew the CIA had helped to train. As the US–Iran security alliance accelerated in the 1970s, a large and often culturally insensitive American presence had been established in Iran's major cities. It was American petrodollars that helped fuel the Shah's unpopular and catastrophically expensive modernisation binge. When the price of oil crashed in 1976, leaving a gaping hole in Iran's finances, it was the poor and lower middle classes who felt the greatest economic strain. Carter may have declared his acceptance of the Revolution, but it was also widely suspected that key members of his administration had favoured a military coup. From this perspective, at the very best, Washington had a long way to go before proving it had accepted the Revolution. At worst, America had Iranian blood on its hand and already firmly established itself as the enemy of the Revolution.

The American perspective was very different: principally because it lacked one. An Iranian preoccupation with America that bordered on an obsession was not reciprocated in the US. At meetings attended by senior government officials, questions such as 'what's an Ayatollah?' were raised. Analysts scrambled to understand the meaning of Khomeini's adherence to esoteric theories of Shia jurisprudence. Reading the communiqués from Washington to embassy officials in Tehran, one is struck by the constant requests for the most basic of information.[10] Unlike Iran's revolutionaries, who had a clear image of America's pattern of behaviour, the Americans lacked any real reference point for the new reality in Iran. Many ordinary Americans were unaware that there was a difference between Sunni and Shia, or that most Iranians spoke Persian, not Arabic. It would not be until the hostage crisis erupted in November 1979 that most Americans obtained a fixed, and sadly negative, image of Iran.

This lack of attention extended to the White House. Once Carter had instructed his diplomats to try and rebuild relations with post-revolutionary Iran, he provided almost no direction. National Security Advisor Zbigniew Brzezinski, having spent the preceding 2 months trying to persuade Carter to assist the military in crushing the Revolution, became disinterested in

Iran policy.[11] Henry Precht, who headed the State Department's Iran desk, described Secretary of State Vance as 'ambivalent' about Iran policy.[12] The Carter foreign policy had almost torn itself apart on what to do as the Shah's authority teetered and then collapsed. The battle scars were still raw; Henry Precht and Gary Sick, the principal White House aide for Iran, were barely on speaking terms. Relations between the White House and the US embassy in Tehran were abysmal. Ambassador Sullivan's visceral protests against Carter's refusal to ditch the Shah had not quite cost him his job but had cost him the President's trust.

This contrasting experience forms an important part of the background to the events discussed in this book. America entered this phase of relations with no meaningful historical baggage. Gary Sick would later note that events such as US complicity in the 1953 coup had 'all the relevance of a pressed flower'.[13] They considered it self-evident that America was genuine about wanting to rebuild relations and honestly believed they were negotiating in good faith. This 'year zero' approach had two main effects. On the one hand, it frustrated US diplomats who found themselves spending much of their time trying to convince their Iranian contacts that America had indeed accepted the Revolution.[14] On the other hand, the lack of any deep insight into Iranian political behaviour established an information gap into which American policy-makers could project their own pathologies. This brings us to the central contribution this book hopes to make in better understanding the origins of the 'new' US policy in Iran.

This book's contribution to the field

Why did the Carter administration attempt to engage a revolutionary movement that had just swept aside a powerful and loyal US ally? It was not an obvious decision. In his celebrated study of ideology and US foreign policy, Michael Hunt highlights the suspicion America's elite have historically exhibited towards foreign revolutions. This fear, first generated by the French and Haitian revolutions, and heightened by fear of revolutionary contagion in the second half of the nineteenth century, became a more pressing political imperative once the US acquired the military and economic capabilities to affect revolutions abroad.[15] Many activities by the new regime appeared to run contrary to US interests: ranging between support for the PLO, opposition to the Camp David Accords, hostility towards pro-American Gulf allies, and initial toleration of leftist groups. It would seem, therefore, that a policy of containment or downright confrontation could have been expected or even justified. Or the US could simply have sat the whole affair out and made no attempt to build a new relationship. So why did the US believe the new Iranian regime worth engaging and how did engagement emerge as a viable strategy? The first section of this book proceeds from this fundamental, yet largely ignored question.

Washington believed it had accepted the Revolution and adopted a highly pragmatic, realist approach to resurrecting US interests in the region. Good intentions were not enough, however, and this book argues that, although well meaning, many of the assumptions that guided Washington's 'new' policy were inappropriate for dealing with the new reality in Iran. Without doubt, the task of repairing America's position in Iran was hugely challenging. The situation in Iran in 1979 and 1980 was opaque and chaotic; it was clearly unrealistic to expect the US to understand all of the Revolution's internal dynamics. Iran's historical experience with America weighed heavily on elite and public attitudes, and at times pathological suspicion of America's motives clouded reasonable judgement. Ultimately, it was Khomeini's decision to prolong the hostage crisis for 444 days which finally ruled out any rapprochement in the short term.

For these reasons, the question of whether the US could have done better remains a contentious issue. The orthodox view is that conflict was inevitable once hardliners in Iran wrestled control of Iranian foreign policy. This view holds that nothing more could have been done to preserve a working relationship between America and Iran. This book acknowledges the dire problems facing US diplomats in Iran, but challenges the deterministic assumption that conflict was unavoidable. Whilst it is impossible to know whether the course of US–Iranian relations could have been altered had different decisions been taken by US officials, they could indeed have done better. Whether American–Iranian relations could have been saved is highly questionable, but it is not completely implausible. It was not just the patently poor decisions, such as not opening up contact with Khomeini prior to his return to Iran, not giving up on the Shah when it was clear he was lost, the Huyser mission, allowing the Shah to take asylum in the US, and sending Brzezinski to meet Bazargan in Algiers. US policy was undermined on a more conceptual level by an instinct that political change can be 'managed': that new elites could be identified and socialised into America's understanding of their country's national interest. The situation required a reassessment: a pause to observe the patterns as they emerged. American overtures would then have been more sympathetic to the context in which they were played out. Washington's failure was in identifying the counterproductive, which is the first criterion for conceiving good policy.

The grounds upon which US officials hoped a new relationship could be forged were not built on solid intellectual foundations. Despite Khomeini's victory suggesting that the Cold War was no longer the primary source of turmoil for the region,[16] the Revolution was categorised as a Cold War crisis. It thus required US policy-makers to identify, and help manoeuvre into influence, new elites who could protect the basic features of the previous US–Iranian relationship. In the search for understanding the new reality in Iran, the known Cold War paradigm was elevated above the more uncertain religious, political, and historical dynamics of the Iranian Revolution. US policy proceeded from the position that the Cold War dynamics underpinning the US–Iranian alliance remained more or less unchanged. Shortly after the Revolution, Ambassador Sullivan outlined the approach the US government should take towards the new regime in Tehran: 'We both start from a basic opposition to Soviet encroachment, and we must build a new relationship starting from there.'[17] When National Security Advisor Zbigniew Brzezinski met with senior members of the provisional government in Algiers in October 1979, he told them, 'We have a common enemy to the north. We can work together in the future.'[18]

Unfortunately, Washington's continued presentation of Iran as a critical theatre for superpower rivalry reinforced a paradigm for US–Iranian relations that the more radical elements of Iran's post-revolutionary polity were dedicated to dismantling. It undermined Washington's claim that it had accepted the Revolution and projected America's concerns and orthodox understanding of geopolitics onto a transitional regime operating in a febrile political environment. More broadly, the US defined its 'mutual interest' with Iran in terms that smacked of protecting the status quo, rarely a welcome notion to revisionist revolutionary movements. Cold War dogma still blighted US policy. Various leftist groups had contributed to the Revolution and had used their momentary toleration by the regime to expand and organise. Perhaps unsurprisingly, repeated warnings were subsequently issued of a potential 'leftist takeover' should Khomeini's grip on the Revolution slip.[19] Very often these reports used 'the Left' interchangeably to describe disparate left-orientated secular and religious groups, as well as the official Iranian communist party (the Tudeh) and other real or imagined communists. A more important problem was that those, mostly sitting in Washington, raising the spectre of a united leftist front capable of challenging either the government or Khomeini ignored the enormous obstacles to coalescing one, with or without Soviet encouragement. Few US officials inside Iran, or closely watching the situation from outside, were preoccupied with either the internal or external communist threat.

US Cold War strategy dictated that security vacuums in areas of strategic importance and superpower competition could not be tolerated. If the US did not move to fill this vacuum, then the field would be left open to the Soviets.[20] In reality, however, America had almost no ability to stabilise Iran and its attempts to do so were counterproductive. If the US wanted urgently to repair an anti-Soviet strategic alliance according to orthodox diplomatic lines, then that would be perhaps understandable, but it should have been aware of the extreme risks of how this would be presented to hard-line elements. Khomeini had spoken in March 1979 of the US relationship with the Shah as simply designed to 'to protect itself and its bases from the Soviet Union'. Khomeini described this iniquitous relationship as high treason to the homeland.[21] This and many other similar statements were freely available to US policy-makers. It was not particularly surprising that the fundamentalists viewed with extreme suspicion any suggestion that the provisional government was forming a strategic alliance with America.

Many policy-makers hoped Iran's ideological and revolutionary zeal would be tempered by geopolitical realities and its leaders would conform to the version of 'realism' understood by US decision-makers. This perception also drove the assumption that Western-educated secular groups would eventually emerge once it became apparent that unworldly clerics could not run a modern country. It was an approach that implicitly imposed America's view of Iran's needs. When Iran's leaders did not conform to these expectations, they were relegated to residual cognitive categories such as 'irrational'.[22]

US policy was clumsy and at times too activist. Embassy officials and CIA officers followed assiduously the State Department's instruction that 'We should not feel inhibited about seeking contacts or making our views known'.[23] Rather than attempting to cultivate leaders of a coalition of westernised political liberals, at a time of intense and fractious power struggles, a more wise strategy would have been to keep a low profile in Iran and to avoid being associated with one group. Paradoxically, although US diplomats inside Iran were active inside Iran, they received little support from senior leaders in Washington. When acting head of mission Charlie Naas rotated back to Washington, nobody in the White House requested a briefing. Naas' replacement, Bruce Laingen, did not speak to Carter until as a released hostage in January 1981. The lack of significant policy coordination was exasperated by a lack of trust between the State Department and Brzezinski's staff on the National Security Council. The result was that the people on the ground offering sensible advice, such as establishing links with Khomeini before the Revolution, not allowing the Shah into the US for medical treatment, and not sending Brzezinski to Algiers to meet Bazargan, lacked sufficient authority and access to the President.

According to Henry Precht, one of the key advocates of engagement, US strategy was to shape a pro-American regime in Iran.[24] However, some of the more covert activities in support of this aim were ill advised and counterproductive. The effort to solicit covert relations with prominent moderates, as well as liberal clerics such as Ayatollah Shariatmadari, would ultimately contribute to their downfall.[25] The intelligence briefings the US provided Iranian leaders demonstrates the lengths the US went to repair relations, but the fact that the Iranians were unable to pass on the intelligence to Khomeini's circle for fear of being associated with US intelligence speaks to America's misreading of the balance of power in Iran. The situation required caution, patience, and measured confidence-building. In their absence, the US allowed itself to be put in the position whereby it became an effective tool to marginalise or even criminalise those most likely to limit the ascendancy of the most radical elements in Iran. US activism in Iran fostered paranoia and unnecessarily raised the stakes for those who supported US–Iranian engagement.

At the same time, given the importance placed on repairing relations, more effort could have been put into strategies that would provide tangible benefits. This included resolving the issue of the spare parts Iran had paid for before the Revolution and now asked to be delivered. Given the byzantine manner in which the arms sales pipeline had developed over the past three decades, and the fact that certain US firms had lodged claims against Iran for terminated contracts, this was an extremely complex issue. Whilst acknowledging the unrealistic expectations of some in Iran that this mechanism could be instantly repaired, it seems reasonable to suggest that more resources and political pressure could have been mobilised in support of an issue that US embassy officials described as the 'acid test' of America's acceptance of the Revolution.[26] During the Shah's era, a staff of hundreds had been dedicated to maintaining the military sales delivery pipeline. After the Revolution, the number of US officials responsible for this system was cut to single figures. It was also a far more tangible demonstration of America's respect for Iran's independence than empty statements that US officials accepted the realities of the new regime. Unlike intelligence sharing or any proposed anti-communist alliance, it would enable Iran to confront security concerns independent of those which correlated with American strategic priorities. Embassy staff put a lot of effort into the issue but received little support from Washington.

Despite the intelligence communities' failure to predict the Revolution, the problem was not simply a lack of reliable information. In fact, much of the reporting from inside Iran was commendably accurate, but at critical points sound advice was ignored in Washington. This was as much the result of the dysfunctional bureaucratic environment in which information was processed as the actual substance of the analysis. Because of these intellectual, organisational, and tactical failings, avoidable mistakes were made. The result was that, even if we acknowledge the scale of the challenge facing US policy-makers, engagement was almost certainly doomed to failure by the manner in which it was pursued. Some may remain deeply sceptical to any suggestion that any opportunities were missed on the US side in 1979 or 1980. Yet, even this view should not obviate any analysis of misperception or faulty thinking.

The book's coverage of the period after the hostage crisis until the last days of the Carter administration is more sympathetic. The hostages were held according to a timetable dictated by an internal Iranian political process, and Carter faced no good alternatives in how to respond to a crisis that posed huge domestic problems. The extent that the hostage crisis was also a Cold War crisis has been underestimated, particularly as it became embroiled in transatlantic tensions and the two defining regional wars of the period. At a time of intense confrontation between Iran and America, Cold War concerns led the US to become paradoxically preoccupied with preserving Iran's stability. One of the foreign policy instruments shown to reflect this tension was the multilateral economic sanctions levied against Tehran. They are often assumed to have been relatively ineffective, primarily due to a lack of cooperation by America's closest European allies. The analysis presented here takes a different view. Rather than focus on whether the multilateral sanctions succeeded as an instrument of economic coercion, it is more useful to examine how they were refashioned by Cold War and transatlantic dynamics. This approach reveals the multiple objectives their adoption supported on both sides of the Atlantic. For example, such was the fear that a destabilised Iran would pose an attractive target for the Soviets, the European allies were quietly reassured that they were looking for a primarily symbolic commitment. The US did not seek 'crippling' sanctions. As one US official put it, the US was after 'form and not substance' from its allies.[27] Because of this wider utility, judgements of their effectiveness based solely on their coercive effect or economic scope are misleading.

Under pressure from both his national security team and re-election campaign, and after receiving extremely poor advice from his military advisors, Carter eventually ordered a doomed rescue mission in late April 1980. When the bodies of dead servicemen were publically gloated over by Iranian revolutionaries, he did not retaliate with a military escalation his advisors warned would not just endanger the hostages, but also alienate US allies, destabilise the region, and push Iran towards the Soviet Union.[28]

When Iraq launched a surprise attack on Iran in September 1980, Iran's leaders assumed it to be acting in collusion with the US. This claim remains central to the Iranian narrative of America's nefarious intentions towards the Revolution. When in 2009 newly incumbent President Barack Obama used the occasion of the Iranian New Year to offer the Iranian nation a 'new beginning' of engagement to end nearly 30 years of animosity, Ayatollah Khamenei referenced the so-called 'green light' conspiracy in his public rebuttal of Obama's overture. Reciting the litany of American sins against the Iranian people, Khamenei reminded his citizens that this was the same America that was responsible for inflicting the greatest calamity in Iran's modern history:

> They showed Saddam a green light. This was another measure by the American government to attack Iran. If Saddam did not have the green light from the Americans, he would have not attacked our borders. They imposed eight years of war on our country. About 300,000 of our young people, our people were martyred in this eight-year war.[29]

Evaluating all the available sources, this book debunks the suggestion that America issued a 'green light' for Saddam Hussein to invade Iran in September 1980. It unpacks the origins of Washington's response to the Iran–Iraq conflict by charting US assessments of deteriorating Iran–Iraq relations. In light of allegations of America's collusion with Iranian opposition groups, which undoubtedly encouraged Iraq to attack the Islamic Republic, it reappraises the nature of this relationship. It then addresses the question of what the US understood to be Saddam's intentions.

Scope and structure

This book provides a brief historical survey of post-war US policy in Iran, but it is not concerned with reappraising the US–Iranian relationship prior to the Carter administration. It is not even primarily concerned with reappraising Carter's policy before the Revolution, although it includes a chapter on this period. The main intellectual endeavour here is to examine what happened next. It examines in unprecedented detail the development and execution of US policy in Iran from January 1979, when the Pahlavi regime finally collapsed, to the end of the Carter presidency in January 1981. Although this scope is purposefully narrow, close attention is paid to the wider development of America's post-war relations with Iran. The book also orientates US objectives in Iran around Carter's evolving foreign policy and the myriad of domestic and international crises his administration grappled with. It stresses the convergence between US policy in Iran and evolving US–Soviet relations.

The book is divided into three parts. Part 1, entitled 'The origins of engagement', explores the assessments, pathologies, and interactions that guided US attempts to engage Iran. Chapter 1 traces the development of Carter's Iran policy during the first 2 years of his presidency. It emphasises the lack of attention that was paid to Iran during this period. Chapter 2 examines how US policy-makers interpreted the implications of the Iranian Revolution for the balance of power and superpower relations. It shows how perceptions of the internal and external communist threat in Iran and the wider region influenced US policy. Chapter 3 shows how US–Iranian elite interactions provided the pull for America's choice of cooperation over confrontation. This chapter also introduces some of the key perceptions that guided America's engagement policy. Of these, three were particularly critical: first, moderate elements, and not clerics, would take over the reins of Iran's post-revolutionary foreign policy. Second, these moderates, loosely based around the nationalist opposition to the Shah, appeared to exhibit orthodox assumptions about diplomacy and international relations. Third, these new elites were wary of the Soviet threat inside and outside Iran. In the immediate aftermath of the Revolution, these perceptions were brought into sharper relief by increasing leftist activity in Iran and concerns that the Soviet Union would take advantage of political vacuum in Iran.

Part II, entitled 'The dynamics of engagement', examines how US diplomats attempted to put engagement into practice. The main purpose of Chapter 4 is to analyse how US diplomats tried to demonstrate their acceptance of the Revolution and some of the practical steps they took to try and repair US–Iranian relations. It demonstrates how, after months of vicious bureaucratic infighting, the State Department, the most vocal of advocates of engaging the Iranian revolutionaries, achieved a virtual monopoly over Iran policy. It shows how US policy understood and reacted to changing political and security conditions in Iran. As bilateral relations rapidly began to unravel, Chapter 5 re-examines a highly secretive and until now largely misunderstood attempt by the State Department and CIA to kick-start engagement through a series of highly secret intelligence-sharing initiatives. It also reflects on some of the CIA's other activities in Iran, including its contact with various groups inside Iran.

Part III, entitled 'Engagement held hostage', examines how US objectives were re-fashioned by three convergent crises: the hostage crisis, the Soviet Union's intervention in Afghanistan, and the Iran–Iraq War. Chapter 6 begins by reappraising the two disastrous decisions that contributed to, though of course did not justify, the attack on the US embassy. The first was the decision to admit the Shah for medical treatment, against the advice of senior embassy staff. The second was the decision to send Brzezinski to meet Prime Minister Bazargan in Algiers. It then examines how Carter balanced the conflicting demands of domestic and geopolitical expediency in his response to the hostage crisis. A key tool of US policy that reflected this tension, examined in detail here, were the economic sanctions levied against Iran by the US and its allies. Chapter 6 also details Washington's reading of leftist and Soviet attempts to benefit from the hostage crisis.

Chapter 7 explores the linkage between the Soviet invasion of Afghanistan and Iran policy. It argues that the Soviet intervention had two principal effects on US policy. Initially, it was seen as an opportunity to resolve the hostage crisis. Paradoxically, given the extremely visible failure of US engagement, the Soviet intervention represented to Washington the perfect demonstration of the value of the strategic relationship it had attempted to rebuild. Second, President Carter would consistently resist punitive actions that might jeopardise the strategic objectives America defined in Iran and the wider region.

The final chapter of Part III reappraises the Carter administration's response to Iraq's invasion of Iran in September 1980. It provides evidence that, despite being aware of an increased likelihood of war between Iran and Iraq, US officials were in fact caught by surprise when hostilities broke out. The administration's initial hope was for Iraqi forces to make limited gains, almost exclusively because of the leverage it could offer the US on the hostage crisis. By October 1980, however, Brzezinski was counselling President Carter to oppose the Iraqi occupation of Iran because of the danger that it would encourage Soviet penetration.

The conclusion pulls together the main arguments of the book and attempts to illustrate the key lessons that emerge from US policy towards the nascent Islamic Republic. US policy failed not because of an instinctive hostility to the Islamic Republic or any attempt to undermine it, charges levelled at it by the Iranian government then and now. Nevertheless, an effective policy was undermined by a number of conceptual flaws and counterproductive actions. Several of these flaws persist and continue to frame the current debate on whether to engage Iran. The book finishes by reflecting on the legacy of this critical period in US–Iranian relations.

Current state of the literature

Most studies of the Carter administration's record in Iran focus either on Washington's floundering policy as the Shah's regime collapsed[30] or on the US embassy hostage crisis 10 months later.[31] In both cases, scholars have often focussed on the organisational and bureaucratic forces at work in the decision-making process.[32] Other studies have looked at the systemic failure of US intelligence to predict the Revolution.[33] The foreign policy analysis literature that has not stressed bureaucratic factors during the planning of the hostage rescue mission has generally focussed on cognitive factors or the use of historical analogies.[34] Several scholars interested in Carter's human rights policy, which was the centrepiece of his 1976 presidential campaign, are critical of Carter's failure to live up to these ideals by continuing to support the Shah. Joshua Muravchik, for example, eviscerates his record on human rights and soft approach to key allies such as the Shah.[35] Robert Strong is more generous, praising Carter for doing a 'good job' in privately conveying to the Shah his concerns about human rights without embarrassing a critical ally or failing to recognise the progress he was making.[36]

Most analysts are critical of Carter's management of Iran policy during the actual Revolution, with the critics emphasising a common theme: Carter's failure to reconcile the contradictory advice he was being offered by his National Security Advisor, Zbigniew Brzezinski, and Secretary of State, Cyrus Vance. As the Revolution began to gain momentum after November 1979, Carter is accused of failing to either back the Shah to the hilt, which meant inevitable bloodshed, or committing the US to a strategy that recognised the Shah was finished as a political force in Iran. The result, as Alexander Moens argues, was that the Shah was left unsure whether the US was urging him to either crush the opposition or accelerate political liberalisation. These two prescriptions reflected the views of Brzezinski and Vance, respectively. Moens lambasts Carter for not addressing the contradictions amongst his key advisors. Whilst Carter dithered, Washington lost a potentially crucial opportunity to establish links with the opposition.[37] The main problem, according to Moens, was that the lowest common denominator between the two warring camps in the Carter's foreign policy bureaucracy was continued support for the Shah. The Vance camp held onto the Shah to achieve stabilising reforms, while Brzezinski held onto the Shah to get him to call in the army. In the end, Carter was left with no policy other than the sub-optimal choice of sticking with the Shah even when it was clear he was irrecoverably weakened.

An attendant consequence of these bureaucratic tensions was the failure to develop any real plan for a post-Shah Iran. Scott Kaufman, a specialist of the Carter foreign policy, criticises a lack of leadership from the Oval Office in preventing the administration from making contingency plans for the Shah's fall. Although Kaufman does not hint at what such plans might have looked like, he insists that a 'differently organized bureaucracy would have made it easier for the administration to confront this crisis'.[38] James Bill and Richard Cottam, both Iranian specialists with links to the Carter administration, are extremely critical of Carter's failure to drop the Shah and establish contact with Khomeini's entourage. Bill supports the view that 'the administration stubbornly and stupidly persisted beyond all reasonable limits in backing the Shah'. Bill concludes that Carter ignored the advice of State Department officials who had tried to warn him for some time of the Shah's vulnerability and instead placed too much value on the Soviet-centric views of his National Security Advisor.[39] Moens, Gary Sick, and James Bill show that the decision to ostracise Khomeini was the result of an intervention by Brzezinski, who considered approaching Khomeini almost an act of treason. Moen shows that Brzezinski was able to manipulate the decision-making process by excluding those who had given up on the Shah and advocated an approach towards Khomeini from senior meetings attended by Carter. Brzezinski then used his personal access to Carter to persuade him to veto at the last minute an initiative by the State Department to send emissaries to meet Khomeini in Paris. Given the preoccupation with the bureaucratic politics of the Carter administration in the existing literature, one of the interesting aspects of this book is that it shows how the bureaucratic environment changed after the Revolution had succeeded. Brzezinski became disinterested in Iran policy and the open warfare that had previously characterised US policy ended. The relief was, however, relatively short-lived and the same bureaucratic schisms would reopen as Carter's senior advisors clashed over how to respond to the hostage crisis. One of the more curious aspects of the period is why policy-makers failed to digest more accurate appraisals of the Shah's deteriorating position that were produced by key allies such as Israel or Britain. The diplomatic assessments of both counties, which were undoubtedly shared with their US counterparts, indicate timely and broadly accurate predictions of when trouble might emerge for the Shah. This leads Ali Ansari to conclude that the key unknown was not the nature of the opposition, but the behaviour of the Shah himself. To Ansari, the question of who lost Iran in Washington ignores the central point that the author of the Revolution was the Shah himself. 'Not so much because of what he did but as a consequence of both a fatal inaction and an inability to lead at the critical juncture when leadership was most earnestly required.'[40] This is also broadly the view of Gary Sick, then the principal White House aide for Iran and part of Brzezinski's staff. Sick's work joins a relative abundance of memoirs written in the early to mid-1980s by former Carter officials.[41] Twenty-five years later, Sick's account remains one of the most widely read and respected books on the Carter policy in Iran. His frank appraisal of the bureaucratic tensions that undermined Washington's ability to respond to the crisis in Iran makes it, however, one of the most valuable. Yet, for Sick, the most important actor was the Shah. He was ultimately responsible for his own decision-making and could not make up his mind on how best to restore order in a manner that secured a legacy for his son. That said, Sick is broadly critical of the State Department's Iran team, and particularly Ambassador William Sullivan, who he charges with not adequately preparing the White House before delivering the shock news in early November 1979 that the Shah was likely finished.

An alternative perspective is provided by Ofira Seliktar in one of the few books focussed exclusively on the Carter era not written by a former official. Seliktar attempts to establish a systematic analysis of predictive failure in foreign policy at the paradigmatic, policy, and intelligence levels. As such she is mostly concerned with US policy failure before the Revolution's triumph. Seliktar argues that the US could and should have prevented the fall of the Shah. It did not because a group of bleeding heart liberals within the State Department, operating under the influence of a few liberal academics, hijacked Iran policy and forced it away from the *realpolitik* instincts advocated by the likes of Brzezinski. This group of so-called *moralpolitikers* promoted a benign image of Khomeini's intentions and exaggerated the liberal credentials of his supporters. By implication, Seliktar asserts that the notion of engaging individuals who were in fact irrational fanatics was based on a pernicious fantasy.

Seliktar's work has attracted criticism for a number of reasons, not least because she refused to interview any former US officials. Moreover, her claim that external rather than internal factors best explain the collapse of the Pahlavi regime rests on a degree of omnipotent power the US simply did not possess. Subsequent research has confirmed that the Iranian Revolution reinforced the sense that America lacked the ability to project power in the region. This sense of vulnerability, accelerated by the hostage crisis and Soviet intervention in Afghanistan, would ultimately lead the Carter administration to begin a strategic pivot towards the Gulf that would ultimately transcend the Cold War.[42]

The disproportionate emphasis Seliktar places on a small group of officials, who only gained prominence after the Shah's authority had already suffered enormous damage, belies the far deeper historical origins of the Revolution.[43] Nor does she explain how unwavering support for the Shah could have been sustained over the longer term; indeed, she offers little in the way of alternative policy prescriptions. Seliktar's conclusions are thus highly dubious. Yet, she is right in one key respect: once the Revolution succeeded, the US failed to appreciate the duality of power between the official Iranian government and radical clerics. Seliktar blames this on the residual thinking of the same individuals who had abandoned the Shah. In fact, as this book shows, much deeper pathologies about the nature of clerical rule existed. In any case, if one accepts that a more 'realist' stance in Washington could not have saved the Shah, Seliktar's argument is mostly rendered moot.

There has been surprisingly little scholarly attention given to US policy between the collapse of the Shah and the hostage crisis. Of the few studies that come closest to filling this gap, most are now at least 25 years old.[44] The dominant narrative is that Iran was a lost cause once those who considered a resumption of ties ideologically inconceivable came to dominate the Revolution.[45] John Limbert, a political officer at the embassy who later endured 444 days of captivity as a hostage, asserts that 'the idea of friendship or a correct relationship in some ways was more threatening to them than outright hostility'.[46] Bruce Laingen, head of the US mission at the time of its seizure by militants, rejects any notion that 'subtlety and discretion' were absent in US dealings with the revolutionary regime. Laingen phrases the breakdown of relations in simple terms: 'those who took power in Tehran simply did not want us around.'[47] William Daugherty, one of three CIA officers taken hostage, agrees: 'With hindsight, it is easily arguable that, if the militants had not used the admission of the Shah as a pretext to take the Embassy and break relations, some other unacceptable act would have occurred to sever the relationship.'[48] President Carter himself portrayed the US as a bystander to uncontrollable events and famously wrote of Ayatollah Khomeini: 'It's almost impossible to deal with a crazy man.'[49]

Many scholars agree. Barry Rubin argues that Khomeini's political dominance made it 'by definition' impossible to 'maintain friendly, or even indifferent, bi-lateral relations'.[50] Kenneth Pollack notes that 'Khomeini simply refused and blocked every effort at reconciliation. Khomeini redefined the goal of the revolution as the total cleansing of American influence from Iran'.[51] Richard Cottam argues that the prevailing trends in the Revolution simply favoured the radical clergy. Cottam notes that at the time American policy-makers felt powerless to arrest trends in Iran they clearly viewed as favouring those who were intensely hostile to the US.[52]

The question of whether the US could have done better or whether post-revolutionary relations with Iran were doomed by events outside America's control was revisited during a 2008 conference in Musgrove, St Simons Island, Georgia. The conference was focussed on the period during the Iran–Iraq War (1980–1988), and of those participating, only former CIA analysts Bruce Riedel and Chuck Cogan had any responsibility for Iran policy during the Carter administration. In a sad reflection of academic relations, and the political environment in Iran, the organisers could not entice any Iranian participation. Nevertheless, former US officials and academics compared their experiences and insights with declassified documents in an attempt to better understand the process by which Iran and the US became enemies. Four years later, this resulted in a highly original book that combines the transcript of the conference proceedings, a thoughtful theoretical reflection on the origins of the US–Iranian conflict, a selection of primary documents, and a summary of the conference's main findings.[53] The book shows that, during the final act of the conference, the participants sought to identify 'missed opportunities' that, if they could have been grasped, might have led to a better outcome. There was no specific reflection on the development of US policy, although both Cogan and Riedel strenuously refuted any suggestion of an organised conspiracy to undermine the new government.

The discussion on whether opportunities were squandered in 1979 revolved around the decision to allow the Shah entry into the US. The participants were split, with some changing their minds during the conference. David Newton, who in 1979 was deputy chief of mission in Damascus, contended that in retrospect things could have been different if Carter had listened to the advice of Bruce Laingen, who in July 1979 had informed his superiors that it was a matter of 'utmost importance' to avoid 'any premature gesture toward the Shah'. Laingen was actually being diplomatic. John Limbert, who would spend 444 days as a hostage, is rather more robust in characterising the strength of feeling amongst those in the US embassy who knew the dire consequences of failing to heed Laingen's advice.[54] David Newton provides a compelling explanation for why Laingen's advice was ignored: because he was only acting head of mission, he simply lacked the gravitas or access to power enjoyed by previous US ambassadors in Iran, such as Richard Helms.[55] Bruce Riedel, who had led the CIA's task force on the hostage crisis, went further, describing the decision to bring the Shah to the US as 'just a boneheaded, dumb mistake'. He characterised the whole episode as a 'paradigm for Carter's way of making decisions through the entire Iran crisis. He reluctantly, after agonizing, comes around to making the decision that his aides have been pushing him to make.' Riedel also notes that Laingen was not the only one warning against bringing the Shah to America. The head of the Iran team in the Defense Intelligence Agency at the time was Tom Braman, who had been in the US embassy when it was first overrun in February 1979. Based on this traumatic experience, Braman's analysis was clear: 'if you bring in the Shah, they will take over the embassy.'[56] Chuck Cogan, a CIA analyst later immortalised as the cautious foil to Senator Charlie Wilson in the film *Charlie Wilson's War*, added that he had met Laingen numerous times and come to chare his concerns about the consequences of admitting the Shah.[57]

A notable dissenter at the conference was Iran specialist Mark Gasiorowski, who categorically denied that there were any missed opportunities and insisted that 'the Iranians in the leadership were just too radical in this period to even contemplate a different kind of relationship with the

US'. As such, Gasiorowski aligns himself with the body of work already mentioned that argues that regardless of anything the US might have done differently, the radicals would have found 'some other reason to go after the "Great Satan" '.[58] Several of the other participants disagreed with Gasiorowski, insisting that a confrontation of the scale that occurred was not inevitable: that opportunities had indeed been missed. MIT scholar John Truman, for example, argued that it was the act of letting in the Shah that 'undermined the credibility of all but the most radical elements'. Thomas Pickering, a former Carter-era diplomat with significant experience of the Middle East, began the conference by expressing his view that a confrontation with Iran was inevitable, but ended it having been persuaded by his former colleagues that this was a view 'at least questionable'.

The Musgrove conference had focussed on two main controversies during the Carter administration: the decision to admit the Shah to the US, and whether Saddam Hussein had been given a 'green light' to attack Iran in September 1980. Carter was heavily criticised in the first case but completely exonerated on the second. Whilst all participants had agreed that his administration had attempted to engage Iran immediately after the Revolution, little attention had been given to the actual dynamics of that engagement. This broadly reflects the current state of literature. One notable exception is Professor Gasiorowski's recent article 'US Intelligence Assistance to Iran, May–October 1979'.[59] Gasiorowski's core argument is that senior Iranian leaders were provided with warnings of advanced Iraqi invasion plans, which if acted upon could have potentially prevented Iran's devastating war with Iraq. The analysis presented in this book complements Gasiorowski's research by putting the intelligence briefings he focuses on into the wider context of the policy they supported. Nevertheless, it will present a slightly different assessment of the US–Iranian intelligence liaisons. Whilst it is fairly clear that Iran would have benefitted from maintaining these contacts, the notion that the US actually possessed intelligence indicating advanced Iraqi plans for an invasion runs contrary to the balance of evidence available from both the documentation and testimonies of other US officials.

Reviewing the literature, three main observations emerge. First, scholarly reflection of Carter's Iran policy has focussed on purported key decisions: the decision to not attempt a military coup; the decision to allow the Shah into the US for medical treatment; the decision to try and rescue the hostages; and whether a decision was made to encourage Saddam to attack Iran. Few studies provide a detailed account of the context in which all these decisions were made. Fewer still explain why and how the US attempted to actually engage the new regime in Iran.

Second, the issue of whether the US could have done better in its earliest dealings with the nascent revolutionary regime is very much an unresolved and to some extent stifled debate. Whilst there has been significant criticism of the Carter record before the Revolution, once it succeeded, the common feeling is that the damage had been done; the only question remaining is whether the Carter administration inherited an intractable situation or not. Preoccupied by US failures prior to 1979, not much attention has been given to how his administration attempted to rescue the situation. Criticism of Carter's handling of the hostage crisis then becomes polarised. Some, as we have seen, see the decision to allow the Shah into the US as a major strategic error. Others suggest that Carter put too much personal investment into the crisis, thereby consuming his entire administration and guaranteeing the Iranian radicals daily publicity. Others complain that he never induced a sense amongst Iran's leaders that this was an act of war that would soon result in devastating reprisals. These positions are heavily inflected with observations about Carter's personality: that he was borderline pacifist or simply indecisive, and/or put particular emphasis on domestic sources of foreign policy. What this book stresses is that the Carter administration's response to the hostage crisis was also heavily constrained by external factors, that is, the international environment and particularly the perception that Iran remained the strategic choice that must not be allowed to collapse or fall under Soviet influence. It also focuses on US perceptions of events and groups that have mostly been studied in isolation. So, for example, there are studies of Soviet–Iranian relations but there are no detailed studies of how the US perceived them.[60] Equally, there are studies of the Iranian leftist groups, but none examines how the US assessed their position in Iran or relationship with the Soviet Union.[61]

Third, popular and academic attention interest in US policy in Iran has never been higher than now. We can also see how Iran's contested narrative of American policy in the immediate aftermath of the Revolution remains a critical factor in both its internal and international behaviour. All of these factors, as well as newly available primary sources, compel a fresh look at this early and critical period in US–Iranian relations.

US policy in Iran since 1945

Every US president since Truman had viewed close ties with Iran as based on a broad range of unchanging mutual strategic and economic concerns, to prevent Iran's resources, and the oil fields of the Persian Gulf that straddled its southern border, from falling into Soviet hands. The experience of 1953, when the Shah had briefly fled Iran before a US-assisted coup succeeded in removing the legal Prime Minister Mossadeq, fed the Shah's instinct to consolidate all real power in his own hands. Most accounts of US–Iranian relations have tended to depict consistent support for the Shah from this point until 1979. Several recent studies have questioned this simplistic narrative by emphasising the extent to which US officials in the Eisenhower and Kennedy administrations had grown concerned about the sustainability of the Shah's increasingly dictatorial and unpopular regime.[62] Having witnessed the fall of pro-US dictators in Iraq in 1958 and Cuba in 1959, US policy-makers started to encourage reform in Iran lest the Shah suffer the same fate. One official even suggested the US should be attempting to persuade the Shah to 'retire to the role of a constitutional monarch'.[63] That may have been going too far, but the Kennedy administration concluded that the Shah was wrong to emphasise military expansion at the expense of political liberalisation.[64] The perceived connection between instability and communism led US policy-makers to encourage economic development and political reform in Iran. In particular, Kennedy officials brought a new emphasis on modernisation, which – according to Michael Latham – was a means 'to promote a liberal world in which the development of "emerging" nations would protect the security of the United States'.[65] US officials had since the 1950s identified Dr Ali Amini as a potential prime minister capable of carrying out a programme of political reform. Amini, a popular former cabinet minister from a prominent landowning family, had greatly impressed US officials during a 3-year stint as the Iranian ambassador in Washington. In 1961, the Shah finally relented to US pressure and appointed Amini Prime Minister.

In urging the Shah to support Amini, Kennedy emphasised that 'national leaders must identify themselves with the common people'. Yet, political reform continued to be narrowly defined in Washington.[66] With regard to free elections, for example, the US remained noncommittal. Washington feared that elections would trigger social agitation and force Amini to resign. Furthermore, despite some in Washington welcoming Amini's appointment as a victory for modernisation, other more traditional hands in Iran policy, including US ambassador Edward Wailes, fundamentally doubted that anyone in Iran was capable of delivering genuine reform.[67] Ambassador Julius Holmes, who replaced Wailes in June 1961, went even further by arguing that the Iranian people were by character suited to authoritarian government and that 'the most likely and probably the most suitable form of government for this country is one where the people are firmly and resolutely guided by a central authority not subject to the daily whims of representatives of the disunited, highly individualistic, and uncooperative people of this nation'.[68]

Given this assessment, the US foreign policy bureaucracy appears to have come to two conclusions. The first was that Amini would fail to transform Iran into a genuine democracy. The second was that the Shah was never going to be a modernising force, but was the only show in town. The result was that the Kennedy administration eventually accepted that they had little choice but to stick with the Shah. In July 1962, Amini, aware that he lacked any real support from the US, resigned and was replaced by Asadollah Alam.[69] Whilst Amini was staunchly pro-American and independent minded, Alam owed his patronage only to the Shah and actively supported his domination of Iran's political life.

The Shah now had the space to initiate his own ambitious programme of land reform and modernisation known as the 'White Revolution'. The immediate consequence of land reform, according to Ali Ansari, was the alienation of the landed aristocracy and the *ulema*. Both groups had previously been vital to the sustenance of the institution of the monarchy.[70] The radical shift in the Shah's political position was described by John Bowling, the head of the State Department Iran desk:

> Whereas in the past the Shah was allied and supported by the Army and the elite versus the middle class and students, he has now through his reform programs allied himself with the Army, the peasantry and the urban proletariat versus the traditional elite, students and middle class.[71]

With Amini gone, the US appeared to have little choice but to support the Shah's White Revolution. Andrew Warne provides a more damning explanation for Washington's abandonment of Iranian political reform. Highlighting the increasing role of psychological profiling in American political analysis, Warne argues that the potential middle-class leaders of a democratic Iran were considered too irrational and unstable to rule, with US officials attributing their volatility to 'an identity crisis in which they were torn between the traditional world and the modern one'. At the same time, they widely speculated that 'the Shah suffered from severe emotional insecurity, an inferiority complex, and a compulsive attachment to military aid, concluding that any attempt to reduce his power might cause him great anxiety and lead him to turn to the Soviets'. The resulting belief, according to Warne, was that the Iranian people were psychologically unprepared to rule, and that the Shah was psychologically unprepared to give up power.[72] Warne thus concludes that that in building a psychological portrait of Iran, US analysts relied on many of the stereotypes of orientalism.

Inside Iran, senior clerics, often landowners in their own right, regarded land reform as violating Shia religious principles.[73] At the forefront of the protests was a previously unremarkable *mujtahid* named Ruhollah Khomeini. His arrest in June 1963 provoked major riots across Iran that the Shah's security forces brutally suppressed, killing hundreds of dissidents, including religious students in the holy city of Qom.[74] After spending 2 months in prison, Khomeini would be released, only for him to resume his opposition activities with increasing rigour. Arrested again, precipitating further riots, he would confirm his position as a politically astute opposition leader with his opposition to the proposed 'status of forces' agreement. Khomeini's uncompromising attacks on this agreement, which exempted US personnel from the jurisdiction of Iranian courts, catapulted him into the forefront of the opposition to the Shah. Arrested for the fourth time, he was finally exiled to Turkey in October 1964. The US embassy considered this a poor decision that gave 'more currency to nationalist propaganda over the Status Bill than anything else'.[75] Reports of Khomeini's activities and eventual exile, however, went largely unreported in Washington, where the Johnson administration was increasingly preoccupied by Vietnam.

In June 1965, the Shah made a state visit to Moscow, laying the foundations for major commercial and military purchase agreements in 1966. At the same time, the Pahlavi government signed agreements dramatically increasing commercial trade with a variety of other communist countries. The Pahlavi government was turning to Moscow in an effort to pressure the US to increase supplies of sophisticated arms.[76] The improvement of relations between Iran and the Soviet Union refocused Washington's attention on Iran, but, with the election of Richard Nixon in 1968, the Shah would no longer need to apply such leverage.

Most scholars agree that the nature of the US–Iran relationship shifted during the Nixon administration. The shift reflected wider changes in the American political landscape and also the dynamics of the Cold War. US forces were bogged down in Vietnam, and the incoming Nixon administration faced a domestic political environment hostile to the deployment of US manpower in far-flung Third World countries. The resulting Nixon Doctrine was thus both a specific strategy for American disembarkation from Vietnam and a general philosophy governing US security policy in the Third World. It also reflected the perception of ascendant Soviet power and sought to harmonise the necessity of containing that new reality with the imperative of post-Vietnam American strategic retrenchment.[77] In concrete terms, as a security strategy, it asked US allies to take more responsibility for their own security. At a more structural level, it sought to regulate the Cold War and forge a new 'structure of peace' – a stable international equilibrium that reflected the complexities and exigencies of the post-Vietnam epoch.[78] At the very point that America was rolling back its global commitment, two factors were increasing the West's vulnerability in the Persian Gulf. The first was Britain's withdrawal 'East of Suez'. The second was the West's increasing demand for oil. The result was a redefined role for the Shah as the West's strongman in the Persian Gulf.

By 1972, Nixon had achieved two major foreign policy triumphs that seemed to suggest that his ambitious attempt to stabilise superpower relations was achievable. The first was the President's landmark visit to China in February, which marked a decisive reorganisation of the diplomatic chessboard. Beyond the specific regional and economic benefits offered by his opening to China, the Nixon–Kissinger policy was an exercise in bipolar strategic management.[79] With the Kremlin now concerned by the spectre of a potential Sino-American alliance, Nixon obtained the necessary leverage for Moscow to yield to his vision of détente.[80] This led to Nixon's second triumph when, in May, he became the first US President to travel to Moscow. There he proclaimed with Soviet General Secretary Leonid Brezhnev a new era of 'peaceful coexistence', which included a strategic arms limitation treaty and an agreement on 'Basic Principles of Relations'.[81]

The US relationship with Iran after 1969 embodied both the local and paradigmatic application of the Nixon Doctrine. Tellingly, Nixon flew directly from his meeting with Brezhnev in Moscow to Tehran, but his administration had long viewed Iran as the ideal model for the application of the Nixon Doctrine. In July 1969, Kissinger had instructed National Security Council (NSC) staff to conduct a review of US interests in the Persian Gulf. The paper was to discuss the implication of the British decision to withdraw from its strategic role east of Suez. The NSC report concluded that the Shah, militarily and economically supported by the US, could fill the vacuum left by the British. Yet, the Shah's oil wealth also gave him a degree of spending power, and as the US–Iran relationship shifted from grant aid to credit purchase in the late 1960s, the Shah was initially able to strike a more independent tone. His general opposition to superpower influence in the region was seen when he opposed the continuation of America's military presence in Bahrain for fear that it would provoke a more activist Soviet policy in the region. The Shah's vision was to establish Iran as a regionally preponderant and militarily self-sufficient power.[82]

The Shah's vision was not incompatible with the devolutionary principle embodied in the Nixon Doctrine. He remained hostile to Soviet expansionism in the region, allocated favourable oil quotas to the US, and signed highly lucrative purchasing agreements for US military equipment. It was the perception of a more assertive Soviet policy in the region, however, that helped cement the close personal affinity between Nixon and the Shah. The Treaty of Friendship Iraq signed with the Soviet Union on 6 April 1972 substantially heightened the Shah's anxieties and provided the direct security context for Nixon's visit to Tehran in May of that year. According to Gary Sick, the principal White House aide responsible for Persian Gulf affairs during the Carter administration, it was at this meeting that the US–Iranian relationship was radically restructured.[83] In a two-and-half-hour meeting, Nixon agreed to substantially increase the number of US personnel living and working in Tehran and guaranteed unrestricted access to the most sophisticated weapons in the US arsenal short of nuclear weapons (later known as the 'blank cheque' agreement). In return, the Shah agreed to take on a principal role in protecting US interests in the Persian Gulf.

Although the US–Iranian military relationship continued to escalate both in the volume and sophistication of arms and equipment supplied, some of the Shah's policies were troubling to Western leaders. The Shah sought to take advantage of Nixon's delegatory foreign policy, and the skyrocketing price of oil, to fuel his ambition to transform Iran into a genuine world power.[84] Nor was he a mere pawn in the game of great powers. Resentful of the West's access to cheap oil whilst Iran was forced to pay top-rate for expensive Western technology, he announced his intention to quadruple the price of oil. The audacious move marked a re-balancing of relations between the US and Iran. For the first time, the livelihoods of ordinary US workers were affected by the conduct of US–Iranian relations.[85] At the same time, increased Soviet involvement in the Third World and the continuing political and economic fallout of the 1973 Arab–Israeli War reinforced how critical the Shah was to Nixon's reordered geopolitical structure. The Shah's relationship with the US had been transformed from one of reliable ally to indispensable regional policeman. The Shah increasingly appeared a leader with genuine international stature.

Roy Mottahedeh describes the period between 1964 and 1973 as the 'golden autumn' of Pahlavi rule.[86] During this period, the economy often grew at over 10 percent a year, a rate matched by few countries. Iran's oil revenues grew from $1.1 billion in 1970 to a staggering $17.4 billion in 1974.[87] The Shah took advantage of this extra revenue to purchase more than $9 billion worth of sophisticated weaponry between 1972 and 1976 alone.[88] The Iranian economy struggled, however, to absorb the sheer scale of the cash injection the Shah put in. The frantic speed at which the Shah was attempting to establish Iran as a modern industrialised and militarised state was also creating tensions in what remained a largely traditional Iranian society. The recent work of Andrew Scott Cooper has emphasised the lack of consideration Nixon and his primary foreign policy advisor Henry Kissinger gave to oil politics specifically and economic affairs generally. Cooper demonstrates that for a long time Washington remained ambivalent to the Shah's determination to mobilise higher global prices and squeeze Western oil companies, a malaise Cooper attributes to Nixon and Kissinger's desire to see the Shah maintain his military spending power and general lack of expertise in energy policy.

Kickbacks and rigged defence contracts became commonplace as Iran's new-found oil wealth inspired greed and political corruption inside and outside the country. Meanwhile, the high price of oil was crippling the Western economies. By the mid-1970s, Washington's patience was fraying. Cooper identifies 1976 as the watershed; faced with a stagnant economy and a possible collapse on Wall Street, the new US president, Gerald Ford, secretly conspired to break OPEC and slash the cost of oil. With the Shah counting on the high price of oil to avoid economic collapse, his co-conspirators would be the Saudis, then (as now) the pre-eminent swing producer. In the fall of 1976, Ford made the critical decision to sell advanced weaponry to the Saudis. In exchange, the Saudis opened the spigots, breaking OPEC's pre-eminent position and flooding the market with cheap oil. The Iranian economy, massively imbalanced and predicted upon ever-rising oil prices, collapsed completely. Increasingly debilitated by cancer and detached from the social dislocation wrought by his modernisation policies, the Shah saw his lofty ambitions for his country thwarted. So, Cooper argues, the stage was set for the Iranian Revolution.

By then, the inflow of US support personnel was exacerbating tensions in Iranian cities. This was not entirely ignored by the US intelligence community. Just 2 months after Nixon had met the Shah in May 1972, a paper disseminated by the State Department's Bureau of Intelligence and Research (INR) warned that 'a violence-inclined "youth underground" has taken root in Iran with possible serious consequences for the country's long term stability'.[89] By 1975, the effect of expanding arms sales and inflow of US support personnel were exacerbating tensions in Iranian cities. A CIA report warned that the unfulfilled expectations of an increasingly urbanised Iranian labour force, in visible contrast to the status of foreign workers brought in to support the Shah's modernisation programmes, were creating major societal tensions.[90]

These warnings registered, but by now the Iranian–American relationship was so politically intimate and lucrative that US policy-makers found it easy to find justifications for supporting the administration's position. If there was opposition to the Shah, US policy-makers remained confident that he was capable of suppressing it as he had in 1963–1964. They found it easy to ignore the domestic forces brewing inside Iran and gave little thought to the results of US policies on Iranian society itself. James Bill sums up the policy in Iran that Carter would inherit:

> The United States anchored its national interests to this small, non-Western, absolute monarchy on a scale unprecedented in American diplomatic history. The period between 1972 and 1977 saw the two countries increasingly fused, beginning at the top of their respective power structures.[91]

Part I

The Origins of Engagement

1
The Collapse of US Policy 1977–1979

For the first 2 years of the Carter administration, a series of complex diplomatic initiatives with allies and adversaries relegated Iran policy to the periphery of the foreign policy agenda. The SALT II talks and Arab–Israeli peace process were the most complex and time consuming of these negotiations, but talks over the repatriation of the Panama Canal, restoring diplomatic relations with China, and the deployment of a new generation of tactical nuclear weapons in Europe were all considered more pressing than re-evaluating Iran policy. No specific policy analysis on Iran was commissioned in the first few months of the Carter presidency.[1]

This did not mean, however, that the new government in Washington lacked voices calling for a re-appraisal of Iran's role in American strategic planning. In fact, concerns over US policy in Iran had been raised soon after Carter entered the White House. On 17 February 1977, newly incumbent President Jimmy Carter signed Presidential Review Memorandum 10 (PRM-10), initiating a comprehensive inter-agency review of America's military force posture and US–Soviet competition in the world. As part of this policy review, Brzezinski told Samuel Huntington, a Harvard political scientist who had recently come into the National Security Council (NSC), 'Go out and tell us how we are doing in the world vis-à-vis the Soviet Union'. Huntington, assisted by Brzezinski's military assistant, William Odom, started drafting a report entitled 'Crisis Confrontations', which proceeded from a simple question: 'Where is the most likely point for a US–Soviet confrontation?'[2] The pair developed a set of criteria that eventually eliminated all countries except one, Iran. In their analysis, the US lacked any credible deterrent to Soviet penetration in the Persian Gulf and had become dangerously reliant on the Shah for containing the Soviet threat.

Their warnings were driven by new assessments about the military balance of power and the realisation that the force structure that had been built to contain or deter the Soviets in the 1950s and 1960s was heavily dependent on nuclear weapons. By the late 1970s, the Soviets had achieved parity in strategic nuclear capabilities, collapsing these early Cold War deterrence strategies. At the same time, global economic power was more diffusely distributed, with key allies increasingly dependent on access to Persian Gulf oil. Britain's withdrawal 'East of Suez' further increased America's security commitments in the Gulf at the very point that Moscow's ability to project power into the region appeared to be growing. Finally, after consultations with NSC staff members (in particular, William Quandt, Robert Hunter, Paul Henze, and Gary Sick), Huntington noted the potential for the Soviet Union to exploit domestic problems in Iran.[3]

These factors led Huntington and Odom to conclude that 'in the regional areas of East–West competition, the largest strategic stakes and the most fragile situation was in Iran and the Persian Gulf area'.[4] Brzezinski concurred, and at a Policy Review Committee on 8 July 1977 recommended that the US substantially increase its capability to intervene militarily in the Persian Gulf region on a large scale and at fairly short notice. These conclusions were enshrined in Presidential Directive (PD) 18, signed by Carter on 24 August 1977. As part of this, the Pentagon was ordered to create a Rapid Deployment Force (RDF) for the Gulf region. PD-18 stipulated that the quick projection of US forces in the Gulf must be considered as high a priority as either the European or Asian theatre.

It has since been argued that PRM-10 thus laid the foundations for a new US-led security framework for the Persian Gulf region that would ultimately transcend the Cold War and culminate in the two US-led interventions in Iraq of 1991 and 2003.[5] In August 1977, however, the impetus for implementing PD-18 stopped outside the NSC. The Pentagon lacked the resources for creating any RDF for the Gulf, having experienced a 38 percent decline in its budget since 1968. It thus essentially ignored the PD-18 instruction to set up an RDF. The State Department also had its own reasons for being resistant to implementing PD-18. It was concerned by the radicalising effect of an increased military presence in the region, and made little effort to prepare US allies for its enactment. Furthermore, many of the senior officials in the State Department doubted that the balance of forces in the region had significantly shifted, or that Soviet behaviour indicated threatening intentions in the Persian Gulf. Odom subsequently claimed that Secretary of State Cyrus Vance 'did not believe the Soviets had any genuine strategic concept of projecting power into that region'.[6]

PRM-10 had also highlighted a politically sensitive reality; the Western alliance might be unable to hold back Soviets in Europe in the event of a conventional conflict. Given European reluctance to increase defence spending, and tight budget restrictions in the US, Carter's main advisors considered building a credible defence posture in Europe at the same time as an RDF capability in other regions to be an insurmountable challenge.[7] Increased Soviet involvement in the Horn of Africa added greater validity to some of PRM-10's analysis regarding superpower competition in the vicinity of the Persian Gulf. For the moment, however, Vance's argument that tensions in the Third World should not be linked to ongoing negotiations regarding strategic arms limitations prevailed.[8] Only after the Iranian Revolution would the US begin to seriously start the process of pivoting towards the Gulf, a move accelerated by the hostage crisis and Soviet intervention in Afghanistan.

As well as forlornly pushing PD-18, Odom and Huntington had spent much of 1977 and 1978 attempting, in Odom's words, 'to get people to do some real hardnosed analysis about the internal situation in Iran'.[9] They were concerned by reports that that Shah was losing confidence in America's air–land force projection capability and questioned Washington's political will to deter Soviet ambitions in the Gulf. They broadly sympathised with the Shah's concerns that two of Carter's major policy initiatives in 1977, a reduction in global arms transfers and the promotion of human rights, implied a downgrading of US–Iranian relations. The two NSC analysts warned that the Shah was having a dangerous crisis of confidence that could encourage instability in Iran or push Iran towards the Soviet Union.

As a presidential candidate, Carter had presented himself as a political outsider untarnished by the foreign and domestic scandals that had blighted the Nixon–Ford era. He had explicitly distanced his foreign policy approach from Nixon's realist/globalist version of world order and talked loftily of a new moralistic course in America's foreign relations and a movement away from outdated Cold War ideologies.[10]

Rolling back the central tenets of the Nixon Doctrine was generally understood to mean curbing the supply of sophisticated weaponry to pro-American dictators with dubious human rights records. Unsurprisingly, the Shah, an authoritarian leader who even the US embassy in Tehran admitted ruled his country with an iron fist, watched Carter's election with a high degree of trepidation.

The related issues of arms sales and human rights had become the defining political issues for US policy in Iran. The liberal wing of the Democratic Party had long assailed the Nixon–Ford administrations for excusing the Shah's increasingly repressive tendencies. Such criticism had been countered by the Shah's status as the darling of the Republican establishment, the very model of a loyal and stable ally. By 1975, however, this reputation was in jeopardy.[11] The cause was his abrupt decision to pull out of a joint US–Israeli–Iranian covert operation to support Kurdish separatists in Iraq. The aim of the mission had been to hurt the most radical Arab regime in the region, damage Soviet prestige in the region, and protect Israel by tying down Iraq's Soviet-armed military on its eastern border. For all three reasons it was hugely popular amongst the small but vocal neoconservative movement that was burgeoning around Senator Henry 'Scoop' Jackson. When in March 1975 the Shah unilaterally abandoned the Kurdish operation, closing the border and standing by as the trapped Kurds were massacred by Iraqi forces, Jackson and allies launched scathing attacks on his reliability as an ally.

There were in fact very sensible reasons for the Shah to end the Kurdish operation. In early 1975, Iraq had offered a favourable settlement to a long-running border dispute if Iran agreed to end its support for the Kurds. According to Andrew Warne, the Shah had already come to the conclusion that escalating a conflict with Iraq or provoking its benefactor, the Soviet Union, was contrary to Iranian interest. The Kurds had simply outlived their usefulness.[12] For having the temerity of pursuing a foreign policy focussed exclusively on Iran's national interest, Republicans now criticised the Shah's support for high oil prices and issued demands for the White House to curb arms sales and revisit plans to sell nuclear reactors to Iran. Fewer Republicans were now willing to defend the Shah's human rights record.

Increased Congressional criticism on the substance of US–Iranian relations dovetailed with a wider struggle in executive–legislative relations over the control of US foreign policy. Since the late 1960s, lawmakers, academics, and pressure groups had argued that the US presidency had exceeded constitutional limits on executive power and was dangerously out of control.[13] Congress was able to tap into public disillusionment with American foreign policy and a public perception that excessive executive power was at the root of America's failure in Vietnam. In the mid-1970s, a series of scandals emanating from the White House, ranging from Watergate to illegal CIA covert operations at home and abroad, further discredited the presidency. Congress began reasserting its influence on America's foreign relations, striking a major victory in 1976 by establishing the Senate Select Committee on Intelligence. Congress could now effectively scrutinise CIA activities, although the White House would find creative ways to circumvent this oversight. In the same year, Congress took aim at another tool of executive power lacking legislative scrutiny. In 1976, Congress radically overhauled the statutory framework governing arms exports with the passage of the International Security Assistance and Arms Export Control Act. From this point, arms contracts exceeding $25 million became subject to a stringent Congressional review process.

Many Congressmen saw the 'blank cheque' policy in Iran as summing up everything that was bad about the indiscriminate use of arms sales as a foreign policy tool. In July 1976, Senator Hubert Humphrey's Foreign Affairs Assistance Subcommittee characterised the foreign military sales programme in Iran as 'out of control'. By the start of the Carter administration, a chorus of public, media, and Congressional disapproval surrounded arms sales to Iran. Harold Brown explicitly acknowledged by commissioning a report on the state of the programme in April 1977. It generally noted improvements in how the programme was administered, but cautioned that 'Congress has interjected itself into the arms sales policy framework and does not appear likely to lose interest in the subject'.[14]

President Carter would thus have to expend significantly more political capital on the Hill than his predecessors if he wanted to force through large and controversial arms sales to Iran. His willingness to do so would represent the first major test of his commitment to rolling back the Nixon Doctrine.

Business as usual: The arms sales programme to Iran

Whilst there had been little or no high-level discussion of Iran policy in the hectic few months of the Carter presidency, PRM-10 and PD-18 had in theory acknowledged concerns regarding America's ability to project power into the Persian Gulf. The 'realist' analysis Odom and Huntington were developing in Washington was driven by changing assessments of the Soviet threat and concerns that regional allies may lose faith in America's ability to protect them. US diplomats at the embassy in Tehran were also concerned by America's ailing security guarantee. The difference was that they used this concern to push back against any attempt to downgrade bilateral relations or pressure the Shah on human rights. The ambitious strategic pivot advocated by the NSC would require a major bureaucratic battle and a huge relocation of financial and logistic resources. In contrast, the US embassy in Tehran used the same analysis to argue against any major shift on Iran policy.

The embassy's first major report on the state of the US–Iranian relations, delivered 2 months after Carter's inauguration, was a classic example of such reporting. It offered policy suggestions based on the assessment that the Shah believed the America's security guarantee was no longer commensurate to the rising Soviet threat. Whether the Shah's perception was correct was largely irrelevant to their presentation of an indispensable ally unsure whether Washington was committed to defending him. The report's author, Jack Miklos, had served as Iran country director at the State Department from 1969 to 1974 before moving to Tehran to serve as chargé d'affaires. Miklos moved amongst Iran's political elite and, like most non-Persian-speaking Americans in Iran, remained largely insulated from the lives of ordinary Iranians. He maintained an unshakable belief in the strength of Pahlavi regime matched only by his conviction that Iran's political system should not be held to Western standards of human rights. His report began by summing up a basic Cold War objective in Iran unchanged since the Truman administration. US policy was 'to maintain a stable, independent, non-communist and cooperative Iran which has the strength and will to resist Soviet aggressiveness, whether direct and indirect, and to continue its role for stability in the Persian Gulf, Middle East, and South Asia'.[15]

Miklos applauded the Shah's responsiveness to Washington's request for Iran to play a more prominent role in both regional and international arenas. He cited Iran's participation in the four-power commission in Vietnam and the aid and military equipment it had provided to South Vietnam. More recently, he noted, Iran had sent a military contingent to supervise peace on the Golan Heights and provided financial assistance to Egypt and other needy countries allied to the US. Miklos then praised the Shah for using his growing military power to assist Oman in putting down a communist insurgency, fulfilling the more muscular role of regional policeman assigned to him by Nixon. No mention was made of his abandonment of the Kurds 2 years earlier.

If the Shah held his side of the US–Iranian strategic bargain, Miklos warned that the credibility of America's security guarantee was a serious concern for Iran's leaders. The Shah was said to believe America's ageing security commitment 'no longer credible', and had decided he faced little alternative other than to embark upon a large-scale and expensive military modernisation programme aimed at attaining military self-sufficiency. It was thus eroding American power that now brought him into conflict with Carter's apparent desire to roll back on arms sales as a tool of foreign policy.

Miklos' view proceeded from an orthodox realist analysis. Iran's military policies were measured against rising security threats, and its leaders would be unlikely to adjust their threat perceptions to fit any normative or political agenda in Washington. Nor could the US unilaterally prevent other states in the region from building up their relative military power. Given that the Shah was under no illusion that he alone could deter Soviet aggression, there was a basic incompatibility between asking Iran to take more responsibility for defending the Northern Tier whilst severely moderating its arms purchases. Miklos argued that any attempt to drastically cut back arms sales would probably lead the Shah to approach the Soviet Union for arms, something he had already done on a limited scale. The only strategy likely to succeed therefore was to persuade Iran that Washington not only shared its threat perceptions but was willing to provide a credible deterrent against them.

Miklos' political antenna told him, however, that he needed to suggest strategies to curb the Shah's thirst for sophisticated arms. Between the extremes of unlimited supply and a total cut-off, Miklos suggested Washington establish a consultative process akin to the US–Israeli relationship, which would include a 'detailed examination of the regional political-military environment but also a methodical examination of Iran's financial and human resources'. His key recommendation was to remove those with a bureaucratic or financial self-interest in the arms pipeline and only include technically qualified personnel who were not committed at either the Washington or Tehran ends. Miklos was essentially reverse-engineering a solution from the problem. The problem was that this had already been tried. In late 1973, James Schlesinger became Secretary of Defence and resolved to push back against the Shah's spending spree. Schlesinger's view was that the Shah's problem was not a shortage of sophisticated weaponry, but rather the inability of his armed forces to absorb, maintain, or effectively use such advanced military technology. He worried that the net result would be the erosion of confidence in the Pentagon's ability to provide effective military assistance. Should the Shah become embroiled in a regional conflict not of Washington's choosing, Schlesinger also worried that he would rely on US technicians for repairing and in some cases operating his military hardware. Though this gave US policy-makers a strong say in Iranian foreign policy, it could also place them in the difficult position of either having to become actively involved in a regional war or visibly abandoning the Shah.

Schlesinger was also concerned by the corruption and vested interests that skewed objective assessments of what equipment Iran needed to defend itself. To this end he sent a retired army colonel, Richard Hallock, to act as an independent auditor of Iran's legitimate security needs. Schlesinger then commissioned a major study into reforming US–Iranian arms sales. Andrew Scott Cooper, author of a highly detailed book on US decision-making during the oil shock years of the 1970s, venerates Schlesinger as a visionary: an analyst who saw the rising danger of the highly visible American presence in Iran, worried about the Shah's ambitions to eventually acquire nuclear weapons, and understood the fragility of the Pahlavi regime. According to Cooper, in 1975, Schlesinger attempted to single-handedly persuade Ford to reassess the entire basis of America's policy in Iran.[16]

This brought him into a direct power struggle with Henry Kissinger, a turf war Schlesinger comprehensively lost. When Schlesinger was fired in November 1975, Kissinger ensured the report he had ordered on US military sales to Iran remained in bureaucratic no-man's-land until 1976, when the White House finally agreed to initiate a review of the US arms transfer policy. Gary Sick recollects that even this was framed within a broad and vaguely defined study into US policy in the Persian Gulf. Too late to make any impression on the Ford administration, it would be bequeathed to the incoming Carter administration, along with the inherent flaws in the US relationship with Iran it outlined.[17] Defense Secretary Harold Brown then commissioned his own report on the state of arms sales to Iran, but was less willing than Schlesinger to fight a bureaucratic battle over the subject.

Miklos' report concluded that the early decisions Washington took over the direction of the arms transfer policy would be critical to how the Iranian government would perceive the new US administration's attitude towards bilateral relations.[18] The first real test of Carter's genuine commitment to fundamentally altering an arms relationship that had clearly got out of hand came over the sale of E-3A AWACS aircraft. The Shah asked for ten aircraft; the US responded with an offer of five. After the Shah sent a personal letter to Carter, on 27 April 1977, Carter upped his offer to seven. This was in fact the number the Shah had first envisioned when he approached the Ford administration in 1976. Carter sent Leslie Gelb before Congress to argue for the sale of seven E-3A AWACS aircraft to Iran on the grounds that they would cost less than installing a ground-based radar network and would implicate fewer American personnel.[19] In another indication that it was business as usual, 4 months later Carter informed the Shah that the proposed US sale of F-16 military aircraft to Iran should also receive favourable Congressional review.

The Nixon–Kissinger 'blank cheque' policy would thus be only symbolically trimmed back. By the time Khomeini returned to Iran, the value of outstanding military contracts surpassed $11 billion. This included 160 General Dynamics F-16 fighters, 7 Boeing E-3A AWACS radar aircraft, 16 Phantom reconnaissance aircraft, two Tang-class submarines, and more than 14,000 missiles, including the advanced Phoenix air-to-air missile, Hawk surface-to-air missile, and the ship-mounted Harpoon surface-to-surface system.[20]

Business as usual: Human rights in Iran

Iran would test Carter's determination to redress the balance between American values and Cold War realism in areas of vital strategic importance. Nearly all of the senior figures in the State Department were unhappy with the Shah's human rights record, including Vance, his deputy Warren Christopher, United Nations ambassador Andrew Young, Under Secretary David Newsom, Director of Policy Planning Antony Lake, Assistant Secretary of State Leslie Gelb, and head of Iran desk Henry Precht. They were joined by Robert Hunter, Jessica Tuchman, and David Aaron in the NSC. Opposing this group were those that argued that Iran's centrality to the Cold War confrontation overrode its human rights record, including Brzezinski, Harold Brown, senior officials at the US embassy in Tehran, Under Secretary of State Harold Saunders, and the CIA Directorate of Operations.[21] Both sides often seized on the same reporting to provide compelling but contradictory prescriptions from their entrenched positions.

A wide body of literature has illustrated how Carter, faced with a divided bureaucracy, failed to address these tensions.[22] To most of these scholars, Carter's indecision reflected deeper problems in a decision-making process that often gave equal footing to opposing views from different policy centres. The result was that Carter praised the Shah as a bulwark of Western security whilst others in his government saw him as a tyrant destined to fall. According to John Stempel, a political officer at the Tehran embassy from 1975 until July 1979, the resulting contradictory statements and actions angered and encouraged the Shah's opposition at the same time, while leaving the Shah uncertain about US intentions.[23]

These tensions arose as much from divergent world views and ideological convictions as competing bureaucratic responsibilities, but they only really came to the fore when the Carter administration finally focussed on the Shah's dire position after November 1978. The fact that there was a high-level debate driven in part by differing conceptions of what constituted a 'moral' policy in Iran only after the Shah's position was all but lost anyway is illustrative of what was really driving Iran policy. In the late 1950s and early 1960s, US administrations had pressed for reform not out of genuine concern for democracy in Iran, but because they had recently witnessed the collapse of pro-American dictators. In 1977 and 1978, the Intelligence Community and US embassy reported that the Shah faced no significant challenge to this authority. This comparison offers a simple but compelling explanation for the lack of urgency on human rights in Iran.

As was also the case during the Kennedy administration, another factor was the US embassy's reporting on both the possibility of reform in Iran and the unintended consequences of pushing the issue too hard. Miklos' 1977 report had addressed the problems Carter's human rights policy would generate in US–Iranian relations. Like the arms sales programme, he cautioned against trying to push the Shah too hard and too quickly. According to Miklos, the repression of internal communist groups was conditioned by Iran's proximity to the Soviet Union and assessment of Moscow's intentions in Iran. Although the report did not explicitly make the link, the implication appeared to be that pushing human rights at a time when the Shah was increasingly questioning America's security guarantee was both unlikely to work and potentially damaging to US interests. Furthermore, according to Miklos, a 'large majority' of the thousands of political prisoners (they estimated at least 3,500 but acknowledged that Amnesty International put the figure at 200,000) had engaged or conspired in acts of violence. Echoing many of the traits Andrew Warne observes as prevalent in US embassy reporting since the 1960s, Miklos offered a psycho-socio-justification for not pushing reform in Iran. He posited a gap between Western and Iranian standards of ethics, arguing that the Iranian people were unprepared for Western norms regarding democracy. Iran's historical development, according to Miklos, meant that 'the concepts of democratic process are essentially alien to its tradition'. It was a view shared by several of the leading 'realist' voices in the Carter administration, including Brzezinski.[24]

Miklos advised against 'ex cathedra denunciations' or excessive support for critics of the Shah's record. US officials ought instead to work with the Iranian bureaucracy to identify areas of law or practice in which liberalisation would not undermine Iranian security. The best results would be achieved through frequent and high-level contact between the two governments, and adequate exposure of the Shah to the President.

The Shah's state visit to Washington in November 1977 would be the first opportunity for Carter to personally press the Iranian leader on human rights. The issue was hardly mentioned, drawing sharp criticism from the liberal wing of the Democratic Party and even some in the administration. Patricia Derian, the Assistant Secretary of State for Human Rights and Humanitarian Affairs, was one such critic. In a letter to Assistant Secretary Roy Atherton, Derian lamented Carter's failure to act on a recent Amnesty

International letter to the President urging him to discuss in some detail with the Shah concerns regarding human rights in Iran. Given the deteriorating situation regarding the Shah's treatment of dissent in Iran, Derian lambasted Carter's failure to act:

> In this climate, the official silence of the United States government, perceived everywhere as the Shah's closest supporter, is ever more deafening. This silence casts doubt on the president's commitment to the principle of advancement of human rights, not only in Iran but globally.[25]

The Shah had believed Carter's electoral pledge to end Washington's unwavering support for anti-communist dictators to be squarely aimed at America's relationship with Iran.[26] James Bill argues that in early 1977 the Shah was well aware of his critics in the new administration and responded by setting forth a new programme of liberalisation that was to include 'an end to torture, a selective release of political prisoners, an attempt to introduce legal reform, and a loosening of tight censorship controls'.[27] The Shah's pre-emptive strike led some in Washington to believe that Carter's moral influence was already having a moderating effect. This, in combination with the embassy's advice that a confrontational campaign would be counterproductive, helps explain why little was said about Iran's dreadful human rights record. This was a pleasant surprise for the Shah, who had been anticipating more tangible pressure, probably linked to arms sales. The absence of meaningful criticism was not lost on his opposition either. When the Iranian people observed an exchange of visits between Carter and the Shah, but little in the way of liberalising policies, they correctly concluded that little real pressure was being put on the Shah to reform. As 1977 moved into 1978, this strengthened the position of those arguing that the opposition's only recourse was to ramp up anti-government violence. It has thus been argued that Carter inadvertently encouraged an upsurge in opposition violence, which was inevitably met with increasing state repression.[28]

The view that it was US pressure in 1977 (anticipated or actual) that had persuaded the Shah to embark upon an ultimately unfulfilled programme of liberalisation is challenged by renowned Iranian historian Nikki Keddie. According to Keddie, the Shah's easing of restrictions may have resulted from pressures outside, or predating, the Carter administration's human rights policy. Keddie identifies the Shah's illness with cancer and concern over the succession of his son as one such factor. She writes that 'It seems logical to attribute some easing of dictatorship and ironclad restraints on opposition in 1977 to the shah's recognition that his designated successors would not be able to start their rule with this type of strong hand, but would have to enlist some cooperation from various elements of the population, including the increasingly vocal opposition'. Keddie also suggests that reforms in the judiciary and reductions in the use of torture may have been as much due to pressures from world opinion, and particularly organisations such as Amnesty International and the International Commission of Jurists, as to pressure from the US.[29]

Whatever motivated the Shah's short-lived reforms, the perception that Carter's purported moral turn had failed to moderate the Shah's behaviour had a lasting effect on leading figures in the post-revolutionary government. Abolhassan Bani-Sadr, the future first President of the Islamic Republic, later noted his initial hope that the American public was 'seeking a new spirituality, a new international morality' and that Carter was elected 'because he portrayed himself as a defender of human rights'.[30] Ayatollah Ali Montazeri, Khomeini's key lieutenant inside Iran and one-time designated heir, spoke of the sense of disappointment amongst the Iranian people that Carter had failed to fulfil his electoral mandate. Montazeri lamented that 'We didn't expect Carter to defend the Shah, for he was a religious man who has raised the slogan of defending human rights'.[31] It was a sad irony that Montazeri later fell from grace for criticising the post-revolutionary government's disregard for basic human rights.

The simple truth was that Carter's moralism was exaggerated. According to historian Scott Kaufman, 'Carter repeatedly demonstrated a preparedness to push aside morality in the name of protecting geopolitical or strategic interests'.[32] Whilst there was some political will in Washington to press for reform in Iran, it was bludgeoned into submission by parts of the bureaucracy committed to realist conceptions of US diplomacy. This faction's influence would later increase as fears of regional instability and a heightened Soviet threat increased in the second half of the Carter administration. Paradoxically, it was probably the lack of perceived threats to the Pahlavi regime that initially inhibited any serious push on human rights.

Growing dissent and bureaucratic conflict

Iran policy muddled on in much the same way. Senior State Department officials had little time for the Shah's brutality, but were distracted by more pressing diplomatic initiatives. Their colleagues in Iran on the other hand were generally sympathetic to his predicament and sceptical that Iranian society was ready for democracy. The CIA, having already outsourced most of its internal Iranian reporting to the Shah's security services, was more concerned about preserving facilities in Iran to monitor strategic arms agreements than about anticipating political instability. Harold Brown was not significantly interested in Iran and generally allied himself with the realist faction that argued for stability over reform.

A group of scholars were invited to brief William Sullivan, the newly appointed ambassador to Iran, shortly before he left for Tehran. The State Department's record of the meeting admits that most of the group left with the impression that it would be 'business as usual' for US–Iranian relations.[33]

To illustrate the lack of any significant change in Iran policy, Henry Precht recants the instructions Carter gave to Sullivan:

> We heard from Sullivan after his meeting with Carter, before he went to Iran, that he didn't want any pressure applied to the Shah on human rights. He wanted to continue the relationship the United States had always had with the Shah. We would sell him whatever arms we could, maybe being a little more cautious, but wouldn't press him on human rights.[34]

Others in the State Department, though not at the highest levels, were harbouring doubts as to the sustainability of the Shah's rule.[35] They re-circulated a 1975 National Intelligence Estimate, in which the State Department's Bureau of Intelligence and Research (INR) warned of the growing links between religious leaders and secular intelligentsia.[36] They also cited the concerns of prominent academics, most notably James Bill, Marvin Zonis, and Richard Cottam, who warned that the rise in the Shah's international and regional stature masked his failure to broaden his political base. Nobody was listening. The failure to contemplate any potential threat to this objective, or challenge thinking on Iran, was personified by a CIA report produced in August 1977 that began by noting the following basic assumptions:

1. The Shah will be an active participant in Iranian life well into the 1980s.
2. There will be no radical change in Iranian political behaviour in the near future.
3. Iran will not become involved in a war that would absorb all its energies and resources.
4. Oil will continue to dominate the Iranian economy.[37]

Only the fourth prediction turned out to have any basis in fact. Nevertheless, the CIA's position was clear: it considered that most of the major decisions, actions, and attitudes that would influence the next decade were already in place and observable in 1977. One year later, despite an upsurge in violence inside Iran, the CIA proclaimed that Iran 'is not in a revolutionary or even a pre-revolutionary situation'.[38] The same can be said of reporting in Afghanistan, the other country that would dominate the second half of the Carter presidency. For decades the US had implicitly accepted that Afghanistan was a Soviet buffer state; in other words, the Kremlin viewed it as part of its defences, not as a staging post for an offensive push into a sphere of influence that remained America. A National Intelligence Estimate written in 1954 stated that 'Soviet attention to Afghanistan is part of a general effort to counter recent Western (particularly US) gains in the Middle East–South Asia area'.[39] In the final year of the Ford administration, the State Department marked the continuation of this thinking by noting that the US 'is not, nor should it become, committed to, or responsible for the "protection" of Afghanistan in any respect'.[40] When the incoming Carter administration assessed the balance of power in region, they did not consider any significant threats to it emanating from Afghanistan.[41] In fact, they were impressed with President Daoud's improving ties with Iran. In January 1978, the US embassy in Kabul reported that the Afghan leader had 'made significant contributions to the improvement of regional stability – thereby helping to fulfil another principal US objective'.[42]

By the autumn of 1978, dissenters in the State Department were growing more alarmed by the increasing strength of the opposition and the Shah's increasingly erratic behaviour. These officials tried repeatedly to provoke Vance into rethinking many of the premises underpinning policy in Iran. Vance was however more unreachable than ever, preoccupied by the laboriously difficult peace talks between Egypt and Israel. They then lobbied his immediate-ranking assistants, Deputy Secretary Warren Christopher and Under Secretary for Political Affairs David Newsom, to impress upon Vance the urgency of the situation.[43] Both were unwilling or unable to do so.

The next most senior-ranking officials in the State Department with a remit covering Iran were Assistant Secretary for the NEA region, Harold Saunders, and Deputy Assistant Secretary, Bill Crawford. In the critical months of August, which saw mass demonstrations, the resignation of Prime Minister Jamshid Amouzegar, and the Shah's confidence finally collapse, Saunders was totally preoccupied with preparing for the Camp David conference. His immediate deputy, Bill Crawford, was an Arabist with little or no knowledge of Iran and was happy to delegate affairs to Precht. Precht was himself on the cusp of a sea change in his thinking on the Shah's position, having received an alarming report by Sullivan regarding the Shah's increasingly paralysing depression and self-doubt. Between Sullivan and Precht, a statement to the Shah was drawn up, expressing Washington's resolute support and confidence in him. The statement was packed onto a suitcase for those attending the Camp David talks and would remain unopened in that suitcase for the next 2 weeks.[44] By the time it was opened, the demonstrations in Iran had escalated and the Shah, on 7 September, announced martial law.

When security forces opened fire on demonstrators in Jaleh Square the next day, killing either scores or hundreds (sources differ), Precht came to the conclusion that at best the Shah would have to bring the opposition into a political settlement, thus surrendering some of his absolute power. By this time, the Shah had effectively removed himself from public life in Iran and ceased to provide any effective leadership. Precht, however, recognised that his opinion was shared by no one in Washington and would be seen as tantamount to a betrayal by Brzezinski. A week before the massacre at Jaleh Square, the latest Defense Intelligence Agency assessment was that the Shah would very likely remain in power going into the early 1980s at least.[45]

Conscious of his career prospects, Precht attempted slowly and cautiously to steer American policy into accepting the new reality in Iran. Meanwhile, Saunders only agreed to review for a staff meeting all of the different groups aligned against the Shah.[46]

By the start of November 1978, US officials were aware that the Shah was facing serious difficulties but most believed he was simply suffering from a crisis of confidence. It was not until Ambassador William Sullivan delivered his infamous 'thinking the unthinkable' memo on 2 November 1978 that the debate shifted from how to buck up the Shah to considering whether he would survive at all.[47] For the first time, some hard thinking about Iran had to be done at the highest level.

The combination of weak intelligence gathering, pressures to adhere to prevailing views, and a mindset that the Shah would be able to rule indefinitely had led to severe underestimates of the importance of the Shah's opponents, and particularly religious opponents.[48] The US did in fact have an enormous intelligence presence in Iran. Most of this effort was, however, focussed upon the facilities in northern Iran used to monitor Soviet activities across the border. The US also avoided meeting Iranian dissident figures for fear of offending the Shah and eventually relied on his own security services for reporting on the opposition. Such was the sensitivity of the Shah to American reporting on internal events inside Iran that Americans involved in such efforts risked being penalised by a non-career-enhancing re-assignment.[49] Consequently, American officials did not meet with Iranian dissidents, or indeed with many Iranian nationals. A 2004 working group report by the Institute for the Study of Diplomacy, at Georgetown University, singled out the implications of this failure:

> From the mid-1970s, the U.S. received its intelligence on Iranian internal dynamics from groups that supported the Shah, including SAVAK, and the country was viewed as stable as long as reassurances were given that 'communists' or other leftist organizations were being successfully repressed. As one participant who spent time in Iran in the mid-1970's commented, 'There were no sources of information that went though the [non-elite population] ... Everything was shut down.'[50]

Congress was so troubled by the apparent inability of the Carter administration to anticipate the seriousness of the crisis in Iran that in January 1979 the House of Representatives Select Committee conducted an evaluation of the performance of the US Intelligence Community. The report singled out poor methods of intelligence gathering but its main conclusion centred on the political environment that had been established within the American–Iranian relationship. The report concluded that America's reliance upon the Shah had become so entrenched that there was little incentive for analysts to provide candid reports concerning the monarchy.[51]

By November, the situation in Iran was reaching crisis point. The demoralised Shah appealed to Washington for help. The advice he received from different parts of the bureaucracy illustrates the state of disarray that characterised Washington's reading of the situation in Iran. In a telephone call from Brzezinski on 3 November, he was told the US would 'back him to the hilt', which he perceived as support for smashing the opposition.[52] The next day the US ambassador, William Sullivan, informed him that he knew of no such advice.[53] To make matter even more unclear, the next day Vance told reporters that the US considered political liberalisation to be the most effective way of restoring order and avoiding bloodshed.[54] Little wonder the Shah was paralysed by indecision.

In early December 1978, Henry Precht cut an isolated and frustrated figure in Washington. Precht had served as political-military officer in the Tehran embassy from 1972 to 1976, a period of massive arms sales to Iran. For this work he had been promoted and flown back to Washington to head the State Department's Iran desk. In May 1977, he was the drafting officer for President Carter's policy (PD-13) on conventional arms sales. In an early sign of his limited ability to influence thinking in the White House, Precht's version of a flexible policy was changed to a more rigid one. As it turned out, the eventual policy that emerged was more flexible than rigid, with only modest reductions in arms sales to Iran. Between September and November 1978, Precht came to the conclusion that the Shah could not survive. By early December he was convinced that the collapse was very imminent and Washington must, as he put it, 'prepare for a soft landing and transition to an unknown future by putting some daylight between the United States and his regime and by getting to know – and be better understood by – his opposition, who had been off-limits for a decade'.[55] Precht believed that the Shah should immediately abdicate and power should be transferred to an opposition government that was acceptable to both the US and, more critically, Ayatollah Khomeini. Precht took this argument to his immediate superior, Harold Saunders, who listened politely but disagreed that the Shah was lost. The political reality, Saunders told Precht, was that Carter had made the decision to support the Shah and he could not recommend such an abrupt reversal of US policy. Precht was undeterred and decided to take his objections to the seventh floor, the corridor of power in the State Department housing the offices of the Secretary of State, the Deputy Secretary, and the Under Secretary for Political Affairs.[56]

Precht received a sympathetic hearing from Antony Lake, the head of the policy planning group, and Arnold Raphel, who had served in Iran before becoming Vance's senior executive assistant. Both advised Precht that he should tone down his pleas and repackage them as objective analysis rather than emotional appeals. They were aware that Ambassador Sullivan's increasingly dramatic reporting from Iran, which contained much the same analysis and advice, had only harmed his argument. Nevertheless,

Precht's view was starting to gain traction at the highest levels in the State Department, with Warren Christopher and David Newsom both reportedly converted.[57] Brzezinski was, however, effective at controlling the information reaching Carter, and the National Security Advisor succeeded in barring Precht from high-level meetings in the White House. The only person who had the stature to reach Carter was Vance. In mid-December, however, Vance was negotiating with Sadat in Cairo; when the President summoned him home, it was to announce the normalisation of relations with China, an event that he knew would upset Moscow and postpone SALT II. This irked Vance, who considered détente to be the larger strategic prize, and resented how Brzezinski's emphasis on normalisation with China was undercutting US–Soviet relations at a point where progress on SALT II appeared to be made.

Vance returned to the stack of requests for him to immediately devote attention to Iran, written by Precht, Sullivan, Newsom, Raphel, and even Senator Ted Kennedy, who had been called in by the malcontents to try and refocus Vance on the perilous situation in Iran. Vance was stirred to put Iran on his list of priorities but he was firmly out of the information loop. When he telephoned the seasoned former diplomat George Ball, who had just returned from Iran to deliver his verdict that the Shah was in serious trouble and the status quo was not an acceptable US policy, Ball was struck by Vance's ignorance on events in Iran. Ball urged him to accept the Sullivan–Precht analysis and establish links with the opposition whilst encouraging the Shah to step down. He warned that Carter was listening only to Brzezinski and Brown, whose hawkish calls for the Shah to smash the opposition Ball considered detached from reality and certain to cause a bloodbath. Vance, for the first time, began to prepare himself to put his departments' view to the President. The stage was set for a bureaucratic battle which would have profound consequences for US policy in Iran.

As the Shah's authority haemorrhaged in late December 1978, a major policy chasm opened up between President Jimmy Carter's senior foreign policy advisors. Secretary of State Cyrus Vance, although not pushing as hard as some of his subordinates wanted by insisting the Shah step down, wanted the Shah to accelerate political form and expand his political base. If he could not establish a civilian government, as a last resort the Shah should form a military government or hand over control to a regency council. On the other side of the debate, Brzezinski, with the general support of Defense Secretary Stansfield Turner, wanted the Shah to break the protestors with force. If he could not, as Brzezinski would remark, the US would have 'no choice but to make the decision for him'.[58] The defining factor at this point was the President's belief system, characterised by Brzezinski as a 'fundamentalist belief in non-interventionism'.[59] Believing he had a mandate to restore America's moral credibility, Carter resisted Brzezinski's 'iron-fist' solution to crushing the opposition even when it was clear that the Shah could no longer stay in power by himself.

In early January, one of the representatives from the Queen's court asked for a meeting with Charlie Naas, the number two in the US embassy. The courtier asked Naas to assess the chances of the Shah returning if he left. Naas gave him 5 percent. The chances for the son coming back he put at 10–15 percent.[60] On 11 January, Ayatollah Khomeini announced his intention to return to Iran, and Shapour Bakhtiar, the Shah's last Prime Minister, announced that Mohammad Reza Pahlavi would leave Iran in the next few days. Brzezinski once again called for a military coup; Carter again refused. With the President unwilling to commit to Brzezinski's strategy, but equally unwilling to abandon the Shah or authorise official contact with Khomeini, Washington was a bystander as events unfolded in Iran. Once it became apparent that an Islamic revolution had succeeded in dislodging one of Washington's most powerful and loyal allies in the Middle East, US decision-makers were confronted with an uncomfortable reality; there simply was no plan for a post-Shah Iran. There was simply a grave Cold War crisis.

2
Framing the Revolution as a Cold War Crisis

Given Iran's long-standing importance to US Cold War strategy, and the worrying decline in US–Soviet relations, it was inevitable that the Iranian Revolution would be framed as a Cold War crisis. At the same time, Carter was being told by some of his advisors, including Secretary of Defense Harold Brown and Brzezinski, that 'the trend in strategic forces has favoured the Soviet Union since the mid 1960s'.[1] Richard Lehman, chairman of the National Intelligence Council, warned that 'Even without Iran, the power balance will be exceptionally delicate in the early to mid 1980s. In this period Soviet military strength will grow substantially relative to that of the US.'[2] The week before Khomeini landed in Tehran, Chairman of the Joint Chiefs of Staff David Jones stressed the danger of Soviet advances in strategic and conventional forces and asked Congress to support an increase in military spending. Presenting his military posture statement for FY 1980, Jones warned that the Soviet emphasis on military power threatened to upset the delicate balance of stability in the global power arena.[3]

Some policy-makers even suspected that the Soviet Union was somehow orchestrating the entire Iranian crisis, building up to an Afghanistan-style coup.[4] The Revolution immediately inflamed US–Soviet relations. On 15 February, the US issued a formal protest to the Kremlin about Soviet anti-American activities in Iran. The protest stated that such activities and the possible Soviet connection to the murder of Ambassador Dubs in Afghanistan could strain relations and delay the conclusion of SALT.[5] The purpose of this chapter, therefore, is to illustrate how US officials interpreted the implications of the crisis in Iran for the balance of power and Cold War strategy. It shows how perceptions of the internal and external communist threat in Iran and the wider region influenced the development of US policy during and immediately after the Revolution. Given that the formation of a united front of pro-Soviet leftists was seen as a central pillar of Soviet policy in Iran, US estimates of leftist activity in Iran were inextricably linked to estimates of Soviet policy and influence.[6] This chapter therefore includes a detailed narrative of how Washington viewed Soviet policy, and leftist activity in Iran, in both a historical and contemporary context.

Towards a Cold War crisis in Iran

Most commentators of the presidency of Jimmy Carter divide his foreign policy into two distinct periods. At the start of the Carter–Brezhnev years, much of the commentary emphasised a sense of optimism for renewed cooperation rather than increasing threat perceptions. In January 1977, Carter spoke of constructing a 'just and peaceful world that is truly humane' and instructed Cyrus Vance that his single greatest objective would be to work for a nuclear arms limitation agreement with the Soviet Union.[7] In the same month, Brezhnev told an audience at Tula that 'detente means willingness to resolve differences and disputes not by force ... but by peaceful means at a conference table ... We are prepared, jointly with the new administration in the United States, to accomplish a major advance in relations between our two countries.'[8]

Carter's hope that a major breakthrough in US–Soviet relations could be achieved in his first year was short-lived. The seeds of mistrust that would ultimately spiral into the collapse of détente and beginning of the period known as 'the Second Cold War' were planted almost immediately during Vance's very first trip to Moscow in March 1977. Vance travelled with two proposals: the first an ambitious proposal for deep cuts in intercontinental ballistic missiles (ICBMs), and the second a deferral option built on the 1974 Vladivostok summit. Vance, buoyed by Brezhnev's comments in Tula, was shocked when the General Secretary blasted both proposals as 'inequitable'.[9] The Soviets rejected both proposals, brought forth no proposal of their own, and organised a press conference at which Soviet Foreign Minister Andrei Gromyko lambasted Washington's new approach. Vance described his reception as like receiving a 'wet rag across the face' and lamented that the Soviets had 'missed the mother of all opportunities'.[10]

At a conference in Musgrove, Georgia, 17 years later, members of the US delegation and former Soviet officials reflected on what had gone wrong.[11] Anatolii Dobrynin, the long-standing Soviet ambassador to the US, put forward the Soviet perspective; Carter had gone too far, too quickly on arms limitation. Brezhnev, conditioned to the Kissinger approach to human rights, viewed its linkage to arms control as a personal affront.[12] What had particularly angered the Kremlin was that, from their perspective, they had clearly signalled their anxieties weeks before Vance's visit. Even Brezhnev's Tula speech had expressed concerns about 'adding new questions to those that are currently being discussed in SALT; attempting to teach us how to live according to rules that are incompatible with socialist democracy'. The Soviets considered the Carter administration to be bullying them into a new agenda.

US participants at Musgrove were aghast at how their Soviet opponents had so misread their good intentions, but the contemporary documents indicate that some officials had understood exactly what had gone wrong in Moscow. In August 1977, the State Department's Bureau of INR made an almost identical assessment to Dobrynin:

> For Moscow, the main issue is whether the US adheres to the détente formulas that shaped relations over the proceeding five-year period- acceptance of parity, moderation of differences, etc. – or whether the numerous US foreign policy initiatives, especially in the realm of arms control and human rights, signify a new set of priorities, with the US attempting to impose its view of these issues on the Soviet Union.[13]

The INR concluded that even a cursory glance at Soviet media commentary in the weeks before Vance's trip would have shown that Washington had been 'put on notice' that Moscow considered the new administration dangerously unaware of their legitimate security concerns and apparently not prepared to deal with the Soviets as equals. On their return from Moscow, a State Department team including Leslie Gelb and Soviet specialists William Shulman and Bill Hyland put together a more piecemeal proposal. In late April 1977, Vance met with Dobrynin to suggest a three-stage package: a treaty lasting until 1986, with a weapons ceiling reduced from Vladivostok; an interim agreement for 2–3 years on difficult questions such as cruise missiles; and an agreement to deeper cuts and limitations on weapons development in SALT II. Dobrynin responded positively, and much later lamented that 'everything would have been fine' had this more gradual and cooperative framework been proposed in March 1977.[14]

The State Department's three-stage proposal would ultimately form the basis of the SALT II agreement signed in Vienna on 18 June 1979, but the momentum and trust required to fulfil Carter's dream for a transformation of the competitive, adversarial US–Soviet relationship was never regained. In the time lost between Moscow 1977 and Vienna 1979, Vance and other former US officials later observed that the right wing in the US had time to mobilise in opposition to any arms control treaty with the Soviet Union. Without an early cooperative and empathetic framework for bilateral relations, the two superpowers were unable to manage increasing friction in the Third World by remaining focussed on the core objectives of their relationship.[15] By the time of the Iranian Revolution, groups such as the Coalition for a Democratic Majority (CDM), and the Committee on the Present Danger (CPD) were mounting fierce attacks on US' handling of relations with the Soviet Union.[16]

The second phase of Carter's foreign policy was characterised by what John Dumbrell describes as 'more orthodox anticommunist containment, exemplified by Washington's reaction to the Iranian Revolution and to the Soviet invasion of Afghanistan'.[17] As Odom and Njølstad have shown, it was at this point that the Carter administration decided to start projecting more US power in the Persian Gulf.[18] Détente survived the Iranian Revolution, but the 'discovery' of a Soviet combat brigade in Cuba in September 1979 led Carter to ask the Senate to delay SALT II's ratification. Joint Cuban–Soviet ventures had been growing concern, particularly in the National Security Council (NSC), since the Soviet airlift of Cuban troops into the Ogaden region of North Africa in 1977. Brzezinski's particular distress was heightened by joint Soviet–Cuban operations in North Yemen in December 1978 and involvement in Nicaragua, Grenada, and El Salvador in early 1979.[19] This chain of events would contribute to the NSC's reaching the mistaken conclusion that Moscow had recently introduced troops into Cuba, when in fact they had been present since the Missile Crisis of October 1962. Brzezinski would later admit that the response to the Cuban brigade was the 'worst handled' episode in US–Soviet relations during the Carter administration.[20] There were some brief hopes of bringing the ratification of SALT II to a vote in the Senate later in 1980, but this was abandoned as the situation in Afghanistan deteriorated and the US presidential election approached.[21]

As the Shah's regime teetered and finally fell, Washington surveyed a complicated map of superpower competition in the Persian Gulf, partly because in strategic terms this extended to much of the eastern half of the Indian Ocean and up to south-central Asia. It was within these parameters that Brzezinski would define his 'arc of crisis', with the Middle East forming its central sector.[22] During the 1970s, the Soviets had signed friendship treaties with eight countries in and around the periphery of the Gulf: Egypt (1971), India (1971), Iraq (1972), Somalia (1974), Mozambique (1977), Ethiopia (1978), Afghanistan (1978), and South Yemen (1979). Moscow's 1977 tilt towards Ethiopia in the Ogaden War cost the Soviets its access to naval facilities in Somalia, once the most important client in sub-Saharan Africa. Moscow, however, quickly replaced this loss by accessing ports in Aden, Ethiopia's Dahlak Islands, and an anchorage near the South Yemeni Island Socotra. To reinforce the Ethiopian military effort, the Soviet overflew Turkey, Syria, and other states without permission, landing nearly two divisions of Cuban troops plus tanks and artillery. Soviet advantages in South Yemen and Ethiopia were particularly egregious. Between these two Marxist-dominated states were the strategically vital straits of Bab-el-Mandeb: the strategic link between the Indian Ocean and the Mediterranean and the gateway to the Suez Canal.

It was America's passivity in the face of these developments that had prompted Huntington and Odom to single out the Gulf as the soft spot in America's strategic planning. Brian Auten notes Carter's own broader concerns regarding America's strategic posture. To illustrate Carter's hardening position, Auten cites Carter's increased defence budgeting, his commitment to the MX missile and 'countervailing' nuclear strategies, as well as shifts in American strategic policy for the North Atlantic Treaty.[23] According to Auten, Carter simply woke up to the burgeoning nature of the Soviet threat – something that had been obscured by the image of the Vietnam War and by the politics of détente.

The Iranian Revolution thus formed part of a continuing pattern of problems for US–Soviet relations at the end of a decade which had seen superpower confrontation in the Third World reach its height.[24] These developments altered Carter's perception of the Soviet threat, which shifted the bureaucratic advantage towards his more hawkish advisors.[25] None were more hawkish than Brzezinski, who fretted over the myriad dangers facing America's strategic alliance network. In early December 1978, Brzezinski drafted a secret memorandum to Carter summing up his sense that a threatening shift was occurring in the region's strategic balance. The current crisis in Iran, he noted, came on the back of a communist coup in Afghanistan in April 1978 and political instability in Pakistan and Saudi Arabia. In his analysis, America's regional allies no longer considered the US capable of protecting them and any power vacuum in the region could be filled by elements more sympathetic to Moscow.[26] Brzezinski characterised an 'arc of crisis' spreading from Bangladesh, through Pakistan, Iran, and Saudi Arabia, to the Horn of Africa. He warned that, due to a combination of internal weakness and external pressures, 'There is no question in my mind that we are confronting the beginning of a major crisis, in some ways similar to the one in Europe in the late 40's'.

If by late 1978 Carter had already experienced a major epiphany regarding the Soviet threat, as Auten suggests, this did not translate into a more coherent Iran policy. Nor was he unwilling to ignore his National Security Advisor's advice. Whilst Brzezinski and his allies were pushing for an augmented military and diplomatic presence in the 'arc of crisis', Carter and Vance still saw negotiations with the Soviet Union and peace between Egypt and Israel as the best way of stabilising that region. In December 1978, just as it became clear that the Shah had lost the will to resist the large array of protestors seeking his removal, Carter and Vance were heavily invested in these negotiations. Having failed to win the argument for smashing the Shah's opposition, Brzezinski shifted his strategy towards saving the Middle East peace process. Drawing on a recent study by James Schlesinger, Brzezinski argued that the loss of Iranian oilfields to a hostile regime would deprive Israel (as well as other key allies) of its main supply of oil. Given that Carter had asked Israel to give up the oilfields it occupied in Sinai in return for peace with Egypt, Brzezinski predicted that the loss of Iranian oil could threaten the entire peace process. Moreover, Brzezinski pleaded, how could Anwar Sadat and Menachem Begin take pledges of support from Carter at face value if the US dropped the Shah, a key sponsor of the peace process, at the first sign of trouble?

Vance had finally been stirred by his aides into giving his full attention to the crisis in Iran and was prepared with a counter-argument. His central argument was that the point where Washington could save the Shah had already passed. To counter the concerns Brzezinski had raised over Iranian oil supplies, he pointed out that ongoing strikes and labour unrest in Iran's oilfields had already decimated production. It was, therefore, the lack of a political solution that included the Iranian opposition that was preventing Iranian oil from reaching markets. Vance added that Israel had already started looking for alternative suppliers, with the option of signing a supply contract with Mexico.[27]

Faced once again with conflicting advice from his principal advisors, Carter's eventual decision was a typical fudge. He rebuffed Brzezinski's demand for a coup, but equally refused Vance's advice that he should ask the Shah abdicate. Carter then acquiesced to Vance's request to send an emissary to Khomeini before reversing this order at the last minute after being convinced by Brzezinski that it would undermine the Iranian military and damage confidence amongst other regional leaders. With the President unwilling to commit to Brzezinski's strategy, but equally unwilling to abandon the Shah or authorise official contact with Khomeini, Washington was a bystander as events unfolded in Iran.

The loss of the Shah

The Shah's flight from Tehran 6 weeks after Brzezinski's memo dramatically raised the stakes for US strategy in the region. At a Special Coordination Committee (SCC) meeting on 11 January 1979, representatives from the State Department, Pentagon, CIA, and Joint Chiefs of Staff finally agreed on the new conventional wisdom in Iran: the Shah was finished and Khomeini would return to dominate the process of establishing an Islamic Republic. The secular nationalists would have considerable freedom in pursuing a pragmatic foreign policy. Brzezinski reported the SCC's findings:

> Khomeini will revert to his role as venerable sage, establishing the parameters of political action but not involving himself in the details. The National Front will operate carefully within those general limits, but will have considerable freedom of manoeuvre for their own moderate foreign policy and military objectives, though they will have to tread carefully on the domestic scene.[28]

Brzezinski was unconvinced by the new thinking. The reality, he warned Carter, was far different: the National Front was weak and divided, Khomeini was stubborn, and a resurgent Left would pose a serious threat in the resulting scramble for power. The US would have to do what it could to restore its position in Iran, but he was not optimistic. Carter, however, was conscious of accusations that he had 'lost Iran' and aware that some kind of modus vivendi with moderate elements in Iran would be supported by the majority of his party, particularly the new internationalists. To emphasise his support for the 'new' thinking on Iran, he wrote a rebuke in the margin of Brzezinski's memo: 'Zbig – After we make joint decisions, deploring for the record doesn't help me.'[29] Five days after the SCC meeting, the Shah departed Iran. The following day, Assistant Secretary Harold Saunders outlined US objectives to the House Foreign Affairs Committee:

> We want to maintain a close and friendly relationship with an independent, stable and secure Iran. We believe the interests of Iran and [those] of the United States are closely intertwined and we seek an environment of mutual respect and positive cooperation.[30]

The State Department warned that another major setback, such as the ousting of Sadat, the collapse of the Arab–Israeli peace process, political instability in Saudi Arabia, or another slump in US–Turkish relations, could 'put the region dangerously out of control'.[31] Henry Kissinger warned of an 'adverse geopolitical momentum', which he blamed on America's failure to discourage Soviet adventurism or adequately support key allies such as Turkey, Pakistan, or Saudi Arabia.[32] For others the problem ran deeper: to détente itself and the concessions Moscow exploited in its pursuit. In an article in *Foreign Affairs*, the Middle Eastern specialist George Lenczowski argued that the emphasis on human rights and the decrying of arms sales, alongside détente, had 'accentuated' Soviet behaviour in the Middle East. 'One does not have to be Saudi Arabian', wrote Lenczowski, 'to view this increased Soviet presence – direct and indirect – as an encircling movement stretching in a broad arc from Afghanistan to the southern reaches of the Red Sea.'[33] The *Economist* weighed in, portraying a 'crumbling triangle' extending from Kabul to Ankara to Addis Ababa, and opined that 'previous neutrals may become pro-Russian' and 'former pro-westerners...nervously neutral'.[34]

Brzezinski recommended to Carter that the dramatic increase in US military capabilities and offshore presence in the Persian Gulf region that PD-18 had called for 2 years earlier should now be enacted.[35] He also called for a two-step diplomatic offensive. First, a close consultative security relationship should be established with Egypt, Saudi Arabia, and Jordan, which together with Israel would form an informal 'inner cooperative core'. Second, security-oriented consultations could gradually be formally developed also with Sudan and Turkey. If stability could be restored in Iran, Brzezinski proposed bringing Iran into the inner core.

As the Shah had been charged with defending the Northern Tier from Soviet encroachment, his demise portended increased Soviet-instigated instability in the region. Analysts became jittery. When Moscow supported

South Yemen's moves against North Yemen in February 1979, it was contrasted with the restraint it had shown the previous autumn. A CIA estimate suggested this indicated an 'increased Soviet perception of the area's vulnerability and a willingness to exploit it'.[36] The State Department observed that 'US security guarantees to the region will have to be more extensive and perhaps more formal than those currently in existence'.[37] Relations with Turkey, only starting to recover from a serious slump, also assumed a far greater importance in containing the Soviet threat: not least because it would assume Iran's previous role as the most important US base for surveillance of the USSR. In a memo to Brzezinski on 15 December 1978, NSC staffer Paul Henze stressed that the Turks should be left in no doubt that 'We intend to keep their corner firm'.[38] Two weeks later, Henze made US aims explicit: 'A major effort in military and economic assistance to Turkey must be initiated.'[39] The US went on to supply $11,837,100 of military aid to Turkey during the fiscal year 1979.[40]

Regional instability, coming on the back of perceived Soviet gains in the Horn of Africa, the failure of the US to protect the Shah, and existing American arms embargoes against Turkey and Pakistan, led to concerns that elites in the region would reorient their foreign policies if America did not provide a credible commitment to their protection. In February 1979, Secretary of Defense Harold Brown embarked on a high-profile trip to the Middle East. Although ostensibly there in support of the upcoming Camp David negotiations, his pronouncements were particularly intended to assuage local anxieties in the face of a perceived mounting Soviet threat. Almost a year before the Carter Doctrine was announced, Brown specifically warned the Soviet Union that the US would not tolerate any future threat to vital Western interests in the Gulf; emanating from either a direct Soviet incursion or Soviet-supported communist coups.[41]

Even the State Department, which had been broadly resistant to enacting PD-18, now called for a visible 'display of American military capabilities and intentions' and possible covert operations in North Yemen. It also called for diplomatic approaches, not just to Iran, but to states historically closer to the Soviet orbit such as Iraq and Syria.[42] It was well understood that Moscow would see this increased purposefulness as hostile to their interests and likely to escalate their own countermeasures. The State Department advised that 'Whether we like it or not, we shall probably be forced by pursuit of this strategy to take steps in US–Soviet bilateral relations that call into question the cooperative elements of those relations'.

Détente had already suffered considerable setbacks, and the Revolution placed further political and technical obstacles in its path. The demise of the Pahlavi regime resulted in the loss of seven electronic intelligence facilities in Iran that constituted a vital part of the technical means of verification necessary to monitor Soviet compliance with the SALT I. The Tacksman I and Tacksman II stations at Kabkan and Behshahr were supposed to play an even larger role in verifying Soviet compliance with the more controversial and complex SALT II treaty. The Tacksman sites looking down from high above the Iranian plateau were located close to Soviet ICBM, intermediate-range ballistic missile (IRBM), anti-ballistic missile (ABM), and cruise missile test ranges in the plains of Central Asia. The significance of these losses to America was not lost on the Iranian ambassador to Moscow, Mohammad Mokri, who noted in July 1979 that one of the key benefits the Revolution had brought the Soviet Union was that they had 'destroyed the spying stations and military bases' vital to US intelligence.[43] In the short term, Washington's only recourse was to demand assurances that Moscow would not encrypt telemetry data from missile tests. Although an understanding was reached, the reliance on Moscow's good faith meant the verification issue remained controversial in the American domestic debate over SALT II.[44]

Khomeini's victory not only jeopardised détente, but it also threatened Carter's historic achievement of a peace deal between Israel and Egypt. Khomeini was long known to oppose the Camp David negotiations, and US intelligence predicted that Iran would adopt hostile relations with Israel and Egypt. [45] Post-revolutionary Iran would provide moral and political support for anti-Israel militant groups, specifically the Palestinian Liberation Organization (PLO).[46] Again, the US considered these implications also in terms of superpower rivalry. The following assessment was made in a May 1979 intelligence report:

> The Soviets must be gratified by the current polarization in the Middle East and their own identification with the overwhelming majority of the Arab states on a major policy issue – opposition to the Egyptian–Israeli peace treaty. On balance, the signing of the treaty has thus far worked to Soviet advantage as has the fall of the Shah of Iran.[47]

If this was not enough, another roadblock was thrown in front of détente when, on 17 February 1979, China invaded Vietnam. Formal relations between Beijing and Washington had only resumed the previous month, and the Soviet leadership immediately accused the Carter administration of being complicit in China's intervention.[48] Believing that Washington's diplomacy with China was aimed at pressuring the Soviet Union, Gromyko criticises Washington for 'playing the China card' during his Supreme Soviet election speech.[49]

US perceptions of Soviet involvement in the Revolution

> When the revolution in Iran occurred, it became clear from the very start – at least for me, and I think to most of us in the Foreign Ministry – that this was the kind of Revolution we would dream about.[50]

This was how Vice Foreign Minister Gregory Kornienko described the Soviet reaction to the Iranian Revolution at an academic conference in 1995. Such was the scale of the damage to American interests, several voices instinctively looked for a hidden Soviet hand driving the Iranian revolutionaries. In December 1978, Brzezinski began circulating an obscure and fallacious article entitled 'Who's Meddling in Iran' written by the Australian journalist Robert Moss. The article outlined Moss' belief that since Moscow's interests were so well served by subverting the Revolution, it could be safely assumed, despite a lack of reliable intelligence, that they were doing so.[51]

In December 1978, the CIA reported 'no evidence to substantiate the claim voiced periodically by moderate opposition leaders and members of the government that behind the pattern of events lies the guiding hand of "foreign elements," "leftists," or more specifically, the Tudeh Party'.[52] In February they repeated this judgement in a specific report entitled 'Soviet Involvement in the Iranian Crisis', concluding that 'the Soviets have not had a substantial influence in the past year's developments in Iran'.[53] Vance also advised embassy staff that 'We have no evidence to support voluminous allegations that the Soviets are supporting the religious or leftist dissidents. Reports of Soviet troop movements on the Iranian border and of smuggling arms into Iran are unsupported by our evidence.' The State Department was actually surprised by 'Moscow's reticence regarding what was happening in Iran'.[54]

Concerned by instability on their vulnerable southern border, Moscow's preferred scenario appeared to be a significantly weakened Shah facing considerable domestic opposition to his relationship with America.[55] Moscow's lack of support for the opposition was not lost on Khomeini, who declared: 'The Soviet Union, though it cannot be regarded with as much hostility as the US, has nevertheless failed to condemn the Shah. Instead, it has supported him and has misrepresented the sacred Islamic movement of Iran.'[56] Rather than forging links with Khomeini, Moscow's primary concern was a potential American military intervention or Iranian military coup. In November 1978, Brezhnev had written to Carter, claiming: 'Information is also coming in about even a possibility of military interference by the US in Iran. We would not want to believe it.'[57] After General Huyser was dispatched to Iran to assess the Iranian military's capacity to mount a coup, US intervention in Iranian affairs became an almost daily theme in the Soviet media. One *Pravda* article warned that 'A military coup, on the Chile model, is by no means inconceivable'.[58] The Soviets also used the clandestine radio station National Voice of Iran (NVOI) to relay the message into Iran. One broadcast warned that 'Huyser is constantly in touch with pro-Shah elements and is preparing a military coup just in case'.[59]

In mid-January, US embassy staff in Moscow observed a change in Soviet thinking. The head of the Soviet Iran desk office asked a US official 'to agree that the role of the Shah was over, or at least, so limited that as to be only a negligible factor in the future Iranian scene'. The Russian, identified as Kovrigin, confided that 'Bakhtiar has little chance for survival'.[60] By late January, Soviet officials and clandestine media began speaking favourably of Khomeini and against Prime Minister Shapour Bakhtiar, who they described as a tool of the Shah and dependent on American support.[61] A week later, the Soviets crossed the Rubicon, voicing support for Khomeini and calling for the overthrow of Bakhtiar.

Once the Revolution was judged to have succeeded, the Kremlin's strategy was to re-position itself as the Revolution's protector whilst reinforcing America's image as its main threat. This fitted in with America's perception of Soviet strategy in the Middle East. A CIA estimate in June 1979 described Moscow's ambition to 'undermine US credibility and upgrade their own image as defender of Arab interests'.[62] Deputy Head of International Department Karen Brutents noted that 'We tried to make overtures to the Iranians at this point. We even proposed considerable economic aid, you know. These activities were stepped up as we received reports that the United States intended to take military action.'[63] As one Soviet clandestine radio broadcast stated: 'During the Iranian people's struggle against the monarchy the USSR...did everything to prevent outside interference in Iran's affairs and to block plans for armed intervention against the Revolution.'[64]

Although Soviet ambitions to break out into the Indian Ocean were seen as long-standing, in the immediate aftermath of the Revolution, few in the Carter administration predicted naked Soviet military aggression in Iran to this end. US estimates sought instead to assess Moscow's capability to both influence and subvert the government in Iran. The CIA warned that 'the new regime's inherent weakness and its withdrawal from regional security role have created power-vacuums both within Iran and in the area generally that they would like to exploit'.[65] The US observed that almost all of the Soviet's major successes since 1945 stemmed from its ability to exploit purely internal developments for its own purposes after the fact.[66] This was the case with the arms deal with Nasser in 1955, the overthrow of the Hashemite monarchy in Iraq, and the Libyan coup. In other words, despite the fact the Soviets were understood to have played no role in the Revolution, the Kremlin would still do its utmost to hijack it for its own ends. Iran shared a land border with the Soviet Union that extended for over 1,000 miles. It also had one of the oldest communist parties in the region, which, although not a significantly powerful party in its own right, appeared to have that potential and had entered a tactical alliance with Khomeini. The existence of ethnically similar populations on both sides of the common border provided another distinct opportunity.[67] This would become a particular concern following serious and sustained ethnic conflict during 1979.

The Cold War dynamics of US engagement

As the Pahlavi regime appeared close to collapse, Brzezinski had warned Carter that 'the resulting political vacuum might well be filled by elements more sympathetic to the Soviet Union'.[68] Brzezinski had, however, lost the argument that US policy should aim to prevent any such vacuum by smashing the revolutionary movement. On the opposite side of the argument, the State Department had argued that the Iranian Left would only be a threat if the Shah stayed on and 'the present situation be permitted to continue'.[69] Although it is common to contrast the world view of Carter's two principal foreign policy advisors, Brzezinski and Vance, both viewed US policy through a Soviet-centric lens. John Limbert, a Persian-speaking diplomat in the State Department, later recollected how it was 'unthinkable' to anyone that Washington would abandon more than three decades of anti-communist policy.[70]

In its own words, the Carter administration 'determined shortly after the success of the Revolution to attempt to establish a new relationship based on the changing realities in Iran'.[71] Behind Carter's apparently pragmatic acceptance of 'new realities' in Iran lay the deeply entrenched assumptions that Iran was a key prize in the 'great game' of great power competition; this coincided with an increasing emphasis on containing Soviet-inspired communism in the later 2 years of the Carter administration. Stabilising relations with Iran, and a desire for internal stability inside Iran, was thus a policy in tune with America's conventional approach of keeping the Soviets out of the Persian Gulf, which was fundamental to the global balance of power. This inescapable Cold War logic would ultimately persuade Brzezinski, who had been most reluctant to abandon the Shah and hostile to engaging Khomeini, that Washington must form a rapprochement with the post-revolutionary Iran. Henry Precht, who headed the State Department's Iran desk, put it simply: 'Brzezinski, I believe, wanted to make a fresh start with Iran after the Revolution and to engage them on our side in the Cold War.'[72]

The continuity between America's pre- and post-revolutionary objectives in Iran was outlined again and again by US officials. Six weeks after the Shah fled Tehran, Ambassador Sullivan was still furious that his plan to abandon the Pahlavi regime and open up relations with Khomeini had been vetoed and would soon retire from the Foreign Service. Had his plan been approved, a core part of the message US diplomats would have taken to the Ayatollah was a mutual interest in ensuring an orderly political transition that would prevent communists taking advantage of any collapse in state authority. Now Khomeini had returned victorious, and with the CIA reporting increased communist activity, Sullivan still advised that 'Above all else, we wish to see the sovereign integrity of Iran to remain intact and the country to remain free from Soviet domination'.[73] Bruce Laingen, the head of the US mission in Tehran, would later explain the linkage between engagement and enduring geopolitics to Prime Minister Mehdi Bazargan and his deputy Ebrahim Yazdi in August 1979: 'On our side we regarded the territorial integrity, the independence, and the stability of Iran as important to us before the revolution and just as important to us in its aftermath.'[74]

As will be developed in the next chapter, a limited number of interactions with members of the Shah opposition had convinced several key State Department officials that the new regime in Iran would want to maintain a security relationship with America to some degree recognisable to the pre-existing framework for US–Iranian relations.[75] Vance himself had also come to believe that the new regime would recognise their main external threat as being the Soviet Union. Shortly before he left Iran, Sullivan outlined to Vance a 'realist' engagement strategy that stressed a mutual interest in containing the Soviet threat:

> Our major objective is to develop a sound working relationship with Iran. We accept the Revolution. We know the Shah is not coming back. We realise there is a legacy of past history that must be overcome. But we think that Iran–US relations are too important to remain as they are today. Iran is important to the US and we believe we have much to offer the new government. We both start from a basic opposition to Soviet encroachment, and we must build a new relationship starting from there.[76]

The CIA was warning of increased leftist activity amidst the turmoil in Iran. US Cold War strategy dictated that security vacuums in areas of strategic importance were highly dangerous.[77] If the US did not move to fill the vacuum, then the Soviets would exploit Iran's instability. The communist threat was both external and internal, with its long and permeable border with the Soviet Union rendering Iran seemingly vulnerable to 'a campaign of infiltration and subversion of the sort that the Russians were often thought to excel at'.[78] For this reason the activities of the Iranian Left, historically seen as potential or active Soviet proxies, were inextricably tied to perceptions of Soviet potential in Iran.

How Washington deciphered the Iranian Left in Iran

Washington's Soviet-centric approach to Iranian affairs muddied the waters of internal dynamics in general, but was particularly unhelpful for understanding the ideological and tactical changes that had occurred within a broad and fractious political spectrum. But Cold War dogma was not the only factor contributing to Washington's shallow reading of the Iranian Left. An institutional and analytical culture unsuited to monitoring complex social and cultural transformative movements, a breakdown in the US intelligence cycle in Iran, and an over-reliance on the Shah for monitoring the opposition all contributed to this malaise.

The ideological and political complexities of the Iranian Left were thus all but impenetrable to US analysts. In partial mitigation, the Left was chaotically diverse and showed an almost limitless capacity for factionalism and internecine conflict. Reflecting on this, Roy Mottahedeh writes that 'Every division in the Communist world, from the birth of Maoism on, was repeated tenfold in the Iranian left'.[79] Even now, typological analysis of the Left and its discourse is an arduous scholarly undertaking.[80]

The role of the Left in the Iranian Revolution became further complicated as its history quickly became subject to multiple distortions by the Revolution's winners and losers. The intellectual and popular narratives of Marxism in the mass uprising against the Shah were erased by Ayatollah Khomeini's revisionist history of the 1979 Revolution, which dubbed it a solely Islamic uprising. Then, equally unconvincingly, the Marxist Left held for many years after 1979 to the belief that it had 'made' the Revolution, only for its achievement to be stolen by Khomeini and the clergy. Between these two versions, another separate narrative existed: the problematic label of 'Islamic Marxism' and the tactical and philosophical interaction between the Left and Islamists. Within this analysis, scholars pointed to the philosophical path of intellectuals such as Ali Shariati and Jalal Al-e-Ahmad and their influence on the Revolution. Some scholars pondered whether Shariati had been the critical ideological bridge that delivered the Left into the hands of Khomeini.[81] Others questioned whether Khomeini adopted an opportune class-based and populist analysis in an effort to occupy the ideological space of the Left.[82]

Of all the leftist groups in Iran, the Tudeh was by far the most well known to Americans. Washington had a file on its activities going back to its creation in 1941. It was the oldest communist party in the Middle East and had been one of the largest outside Europe. Unlike other groups, it had a formal party structure, a leadership for some time based in Eastern Europe, a widely distributed body of literature, a broadcasting capability, and a comparatively conventional communist ideology.

The two largest CIA studies of communist and leftist activity in Iran, both produced in February 1979, devoted less than 2 pages out of a combined 21 to groups other than the Tudeh. Although Washington was aware of several distinct communist or leftist groups, surveys of US communiqués, intelligence assessments, policy studies, and media reports often reveal the portrayal of a vaguely defined and monolithic political 'Left'. They were aware that Khomeini's followers vastly outnumbered the communists and other leftists.[83] Nevertheless, US officials repeatedly warned of a potential 'leftist takeover' should Khomeini's grip on the Revolution slip.[84] Sometimes the 'Left' appears to have been used as an interchangeable term for the radical Left (secular or religious), the Tudeh, or other undefined communists. Reporting lacked a clear sense of the tensions and fissures within the various leftist groups. Those that raised the spectre of a united leftist front capable of challenging either the government or Khomeini ignored the enormous obstacles to coalescing one, with or without Soviet encouragement. The Tudeh were widely discredited for their association with both the Soviet Union and the Marxist government in Kabul. There was also disquiet within the ranks over the party's support for Ayatollah Khomeini. The two primary leftist guerrilla groups, the People's Strugglers of Iran (Mojahedin-i Khalq-i Iran – known henceforth as MEK) and the Iranian People's Sacrificing Guerrillas (Charik'ha-yi Fada'i-yi Khalq-i Iran – known henceforth as Feda'i), were hostile to each other and far from united internally. Although the MEK and Feda'i were recovering from severe state repression, they remained ideologically factionalised and unsure how best to exploit the post-Revolution environment.[85] A secular faction of the MEK, the Pekyar, had broken away from the MEK leadership in 1975. Another splinter group, the Mojahedin of the Islamic Revolution, went in the opposite direction, demanding a greater emphasis on religion in politics. The Feda'i would soon split into two main factions: one supporting Khomeini, the other opposing him.

This gap in American understanding would become increasingly damaging as the radical Left would go on to represent a far graver challenge to Khomeini's leadership than the Tudeh. Analyses of Khomeini's attitude to the Left equally lacked nuance, with the Ayatollah observed at times to be either 'concerned by leftist activities' or 'likely to suppress the left'.[86] CIA and State Department reporting consistently and correctly indicated that efforts to get Khomeini to embrace the Tudeh, rather than simply tolerate them, had been rebuffed. But Khomeini's attitude to individual leftist groups was seldom clarified, despite his clearly distinct policy towards the Tudeh, MEK, and Feda'i.[87]

Viewing communist activities in a historical context

Following the major disturbances of 1978, particularly those in the oil plants, more attention was paid to the Tudeh. Brzezinski summed up the prevailing view on the Tudeh: 'In its entire 37 year history it has been a faithful and reliable tool of Soviet policy in the country.'[88] Washington's perception of the Tudeh from 1978 was in many ways framed by its understanding of its activities in the 1940s and 1950s.

Marxist intellectual thought and communist activities in Iran had a long history stretching back to the late nineteenth century. From the start, Washington had viewed this development as closely associated with an agenda set by Russian Bolsheviks and the Soviet Union. The CIA dated communism in Iran to 1917: 'when Iranian workers returning from the Caucasus oilfields – with encouragement from Soviet agents – formed the Justice Party, which in 1921 formed the Communist Party of Iran.'[89] In fact, a casual reading of Fereydoun Adamiyat's book on social democracy in the constitutional Revolution era, widely available in US academic libraries, would have revealed that figures such as Mammad Amin Rasulzade, arguably Iran's first Leninist, had been active at least 10 years prior to 1917.

The CIA portrayed a Soviet hand in every stage of communism's development in Iran, next noting that communist groups supported by Soviet troops tried unsuccessfully to form a separatist republic in northern Iran in 1921. Moscow was again seen as instrumental in the formation and expansion of the Tudeh Party in 1941, a period when Soviet troops occupied northern Iran. This point was made in the introduction of a 1949 CIA report, entitled 'The Tudeh Party: A Vehicle of Communism in Iran':

> The Tudeh (Masses) Party represents the culmination of a Revolutionary movement extending as far back as the first decade of the twentieth century, when Russian radicals began to use the liberal Iranian press then in existence to attack the Czarist regime and to prepare Iran for radical government.[90]

The Tudeh had lent their considerable support in facilitating the creation of the Azerbaijan People's Republic (APR). Supported by the physical occupation by Soviet troops, the Iranian government and most Iranians, as well as clearly the West, saw the formation of the APR as a brazen Soviet attempt to annex the parts of northern Iran that they had occupied since August 1941. The separatist Azerbaijani Democratic Party (ADP) had itself been formed at the behest of Moscow, as Stalin sought an appropriate means for securing a firm hold over northern Iran.[91]

The withdrawal of Soviet troops from northern Iran and collapse of the Soviet support for Kurdish and Azeri republics marked the start of Tehran's steady movement into the American orbit. The coinciding decline in Soviet–Iranian relations was confirmed by the Majlis' rejection of the 1947 Soviet oil agreement that offered Moscow lucrative concessions in Iran's northern oilfields. The US ambassador to Moscow cautioned that 'It must not be thought, however, that the Kremlin will resign itself to this humiliating reverse'. The CIA began to view Soviet designs on Iran less in terms of military action. Instead, they reported that Moscow was more inclined to 'intensify its efforts to build up subversive forces within Iran'.[92]

The Tudeh were seen as the primary mode for this effort. Its support for the oil concession and role in the separatist revolts had, however, eroded much of the considerable support they had built up within Iran. An attempt to assassinate the Shah in 1949 led to its prescription throughout Iran and prompted a campaign of repression by the Pahlavi state, which culminated with its effective crippling by 1949. The party moved underground, but re-emerged in 1951, and combining its support of Prime Minister Mossadeq with xenophobic slogans appeared to be gaining it more supporters.[93] By 1952, the CIA estimated the party had 20,000 hard-core members, 8,000 of whom were in Tehran, and that its rank and file were predominantly proletarian.[94] The Tudeh's appeal was judged to be greatest amongst students and civil servants, both large constituencies in Iran. It was also believed to have successfully penetrated the professional and trade union groups and even the military.[95]

It appears that by 1953, Washington viewed the Tudeh's strength with such alarm that its potential to be a Soviet proxy government formed the larger part of the rationale for ousting Mossadeq. In an analysis that would be repeated in 1979, the fear was that, should the charismatic leader fall, the communists could exploit the resulting power vacuum. At an NSC meeting in March 1953, Secretary of State John Dulles conceded that Mossedeq was no communist, but should he fall, 'The communists might easily take over'. If that happened, he warned, 'not only would the free world be deprived of the enormous asset represented by Iranian oil production and reserves, but... in short order the other areas of the Middle East, with some sixty percent of the world's oil reserves, would fall into Communist hands'.[96] Documents unearthed by the *New York Times* in 2000 suggested that the joint British and US-sponsored coup in 1953 was justified primarily by the judgement that the nationalist government would inevitably collapse and the Soviets, through the Tudeh, would be in a position to move Iran into the Soviet camp.[97] Even the threat to Western oil interests posed by nationalisation was presented as secondary to this. Decades later, several US diplomats and CIA agents responsible for monitoring the Tudeh in the early 1950s admitted that the Tudeh's power was routinely exaggerated by higher-level US officials.[98]

After the Shah's triumphant return from Egypt, the Tudeh suffered its most damaging suppression. According to the CIA, over 1,000 members were arrested and most of the leadership fled to Eastern Europe.[99] Most damaging, stated a much later CIA intelligence estimate, the Tudeh's presence in the military was crushed, with approximately 500 pro-communist officers arrested. By the mid-1950s, the Tudeh's network in Iran was decimated, and many of its cadres had been arrested, executed, or forced to flee the country. Its leadership, now in exile in Leipzig, East Germany, attempted to refine its structure and keep alive at least a symbolic presence in Iran via radio, press, and covert communications. US intelligence believed that the expatriate community consisted of 400 members, including senior leadership and their families. The Central Committee convened in Moscow and the Executive Committee and Secretariat were based in East Germany. Leaders, the CIA reported, received a stipend from local communist parties whilst members supported themselves.[100]

Moscow's relationship with the Tudeh continued to be shaped by the ebb and flow of Soviet–Iranian relations. Moscow, though upset by the Tudeh's suppression, proceeded to work with the Iranian government on matters of mutual concern. Soviet policy shifted towards deterring Iran from joining the Central Eastern Treaty Organisation (CENTO), a policy that was not aided by the appearance of Soviet support for the Tudeh. Instead, it focussed on normalising economic relations, compensating Iran for supplies provided to Soviet troops during WWII and even returning 11 tons of gold previously sequestered.[101] None of this could prevent the Shah from signing the Baghdad treaty in October 1955. America's commitment to assist Iran was further strengthened: first by the declaration of the Eisenhower doctrine in 1957 and then a bilateral defence agreement signed in 1959.

The Soviets initially vented their fury via a massive propaganda campaign, utilising the National Voice of Iran (NVOI), a pro-Tudeh radio station, but then began to explore a thaw in Soviet relations. The Tudeh again became of little value to the Soviets, who quickly reversed their opposition to the Shah's land reforms no sooner had the Shah announced a ban on stationing nuclear missiles on Iran. The Tudeh then failed once again to support a major anti-Shah movement, this time led by Khomeini and the clerics in 1963. Despite a general upsurge in leftist activity in the 1960s, connected to the failure of the National Front to establish an effective counterbalance to the Shah, the Tudeh became further marginalised. They faced attacks by both the more radical secular left and Ali Shariati, who seemingly combined Islamist and Marxist ideologies.[102]

Moscow's rapprochement with the Shah continued to provoke deep rifts in Iran's leftist and communist movements, but most of the Tudeh's leadership continued to follow Moscow's lead and support the Shah's land reforms.[103] Despite this, the Kremlin increasingly had little confidence in the Tudeh's leadership and opted to preserve relative stability on its southern border. The party ceased to be a particularly relevant or effective asset for the Soviet Union. Nor did the exiled or domestic Tudeh leadership manage to emulate Khomeini, exiled since 1963, and establish themselves as anything equating to a cult of personality. In fact, the opposite was the case; they appeared unable to control the vicious infighting and idly watched various factions break away. By the mid-1960s, the US State Department estimated the party membership to be approximately only 1,500.[104]

The Shah's security forces found it easy to infiltrate, disrupt, and destroy the violent splinter groups of the Tudeh which had sprung up in the 1960s. By 1971, the Tudeh's attempts to reorganise inside the country had come to nothing.

Misreading the Tudeh–USSR relationship

US reporting of the Tudeh had all but ended in the mid-1960s, by which time it was assumed that the Shah's repression had broadly succeeded in crushing it. When Zbigniew Brzezinski came to advise Carter about its state in late 1978, he had to caveat his summary by admitting 'the party has been nearly unreported for more than a decade'. Despite this, he remained confident in his assessment that its services were entirely at the disposal of the Soviet Union. The questions not adequately addressed in US estimates were the extent to which Moscow consulted the Tudeh in its formulation of policy and the strategic effects of their relationship.

The Tudeh were, as Brenda Shaffer astutely observes, an asset in providing information and limited political leverage, but also a liability in that they reinforced the image of the Soviet Union as an intruder in domestic Iranian affairs.[105] The Soviet instinct to improve state-level relations with Iran meant that it rarely criticised the repression of communists in Iran.[106] Moscow had no qualms in abandoning the aspirations of Iranian communists for the sake of geopolitical expediency. In 1921, Moscow withdrew its support for the short-lived Soviet Republic in Gilan in return for a 'Treaty of Friendship' with Iran, which granted the Soviet Union a discretionary right to intervene militarily in Iran should it feel hostile forces were using it as a base for attacking Soviet territory.

The alternate favouritism or displeasure Moscow displayed towards various factions in the Tudeh encouraged the endemic distrust that existed between hard-line and moderate groups. Feruyden Kishawarz, a leader of the moderate faction, criticised the Soviets for promoting hardliners such as Abdul-Samad Kambakhsh and future party secretary Noureddin Kianouri. Kishawarz accused Moscow of pushing their favourites through the ranks until they reached high party posts and 'gradually changed the Tudeh party of Iran into a tool of the Soviet Union's policy in Iran'.[107] Maziar Behrooz' study on Tudeh factionalism during the 1953 coup shows how competing attitudes to Soviet interference and ideological direction, and confusion regarding Soviet policy, contributed to the Tudeh's anti-Mossadeq stance in 1951–1952. Although the party reversed this policy and supported Mossadeq's oil nationalisation programme, Behrooz identifies intense intraparty factionalism as the cause of its failure to support him during the coup that ousted him in 1953.[108] He connects this to a lack of clear guidance emanating from Kremlin, which was itself in the grip of an intense power struggle and ideological reorientation following the death of Stalin.[109] This would ultimately provoke a split in the Tudeh, as 'The Revolutionary Organisation of the Tudeh Party of Iran' (ROTPI) split from the main party in protest at Khrushchev's de-Stalinisation policies.[110]

The CIA's 1979 backgrounder of Tudeh–Soviet relations during the Mossadeq era was far less complex; it simply stated the Tudeh played a 'key role' in supporting Mossadeq by 'inciting mob violence on the streets of Tehran'.[111] Of course, what it failed to mention was that CIA agent provocateurs, posing as Tudeh activists, had played a key role in the coup's success. The Tudeh's paralysis during the crisis is also testament to a wider US misreading at the time. The party was very far from the well-organised and unified pro-Soviet government in waiting.

Global changes in international communism further factionalised the Tudeh. The Sino–Soviet dispute led to the defection of three leaders in support of China, who formed a party called the Organization of Marxist-Leninists. After the death of Mao, this faction allied with Albania, while another, the ROTPI, continued to support China.[112] The rift was discussed briefly in a 1977 CIA report but not in either of the two large reports on communist activity produced in 1979:

> Ever since its formation, the Tudeh has been an instrument of Soviet policy in Iran. A dozen years ago the improvement in relations between Tehran and Moscow led to the Tudeh Party softening its attacks on the Shah and the government. This, in turn, created a rift in the party that led the hard-liners to split off into a pro-Chinese faction. The effect was felt primarily by Iranian activists abroad.[113]

Ideological shifts in the Soviet Union had left the Tudeh's own theoretical orientation confused. Washington assumed that the Tudeh's slowness to call openly for the Shah's exit simply reflected Moscow's wishes. Yet they did so based on assumption rather than a close understanding of Moscow's policy direction. Where the Tudeh actually stood on this policy was never fully interrogated. The Tudeh Party languished in an ideological rut of their own creation with some, citing Lenin, believing that the objective conditions did not exist for revolution in Iran. They repeatedly denounced their rival leftist factions who did call for conflict with the Shah, with no evidence of Soviet encouragement, and even made overtures to the Shah's government as a 'responsible' party of opposition.[114]

The Soviet relationship with the Tudeh was also a contributing factor to the disillusionment of Iran's intellectuals with the party. As the Tudeh emerged in 1941 as the first major progressive party in 20 years of Reza Shah's rule, its appearance as a genuinely modern and increasingly radical movement gained either the sympathy or membership of most Iranian intellectuals. Negin Nabavi demonstrates that the term *rawshanfekr*, which indicates the 'modern' intellectual, seems to have become more prevalent in 1941, which saw both the abdication of Reza Shah and the emergence of the Tudeh. As a consequence of this association, the very notion of the 'intellectual' came to have Marxist connotations, 'embodying the belief in the idea of revolutionary struggle against the status quo'.[115]

The defining intellectuals of the post-war era, including Ali Shariati, Jalal Al-e-Ahmad, Khalil Maleki, and Ali Asghar Hajj Sayyed Javadi, all joined the Tudeh at the height of its influence in Iran.[116] All had by the early 1950s rejected it; denouncing, amongst other things, its policy towards Mossadeq and subservience to the USSR.[117] The intellectual development of the Iranian Left, its interaction with Islam, and its effect on the rise of revolutionary Shi'ism would proceed from a point of hostility towards the Tudeh. Their initial association with communism did little, however, to dissuade the convenient assumption by the Pahlavi state that to be an intellectual was to be a communist.

Washington did not comprehend the extent to which internal tensions inside the Soviet Union, and even world communism, were detrimental to Iranian communism. US officials tended to see the Soviets as consciously and expediently turning its support up or down as it pursued specific goals in its state-level relations with Iran. The danger of the Tudeh's relationship with Moscow was that it was not just subject to radical shifts in Moscow's policy towards Iran, but also internal tensions and preoccupations inside the Kremlin and wider ideological changes and geopolitical tensions in the communist world. These factors in and of themselves contributed to the Tudeh's poor showing during the Revolution, regardless of Soviet efforts to limit its role for fear of damaging bilateral relations. When, after the Revolution, Washington asserted that the Soviets were attempting to form a united and pro-Soviet leftist front, this should have been an important footnote to the long-term feasibility of this strategy.

US assessments of leftist activity during the Revolution

In August 1978, the embassy in Tehran had reported on de facto ties between the Khomeini camp and the Tudeh.[118] In October 1978, members of the Tudeh living in Moscow commented that the Soviets had ordered leftist pro-Soviet elements to participate in opposition activities, though they did not promise to provide any material help. The CIA later reported that the purpose was to align the Tudeh with the religious opposition, but concluded they had been rebuffed.[119] At best, Khomeini refrained from harshly criticising the party for the most part of 1979. Only in mid-January 1979 did the Carter administration perceive an official Tudeh policy of supporting armed struggle to remove the Pahlavi regime. Washington assumed, in this case correctly, that this reflected the Kremlin's final judgement that the Shah's exit was certain.

There was a broadly shared opinion, therefore, that there was no evidence of Tudeh involvement in the disturbances prior to November 1978 and, in any case, the Tudeh's role through early 1979 appeared 'relatively insignificant'.[120] Nor had they managed to infiltrate the military or key areas of the economy such as the central bank, customs, oil refineries, Iran Air, and the Tehran Water Board. The Tudeh had even by its own account little organised presence in Iran.[121] Several Soviet officials and academics were quoted as acknowledging Tudeh participation in the anti-Shah agitation as being 'very weak'.[122]

This generally sober analysis of communist activities in Iran was not mirrored in the analysis of some sections of the media. In late January 1979, the conservative French newspaper *La Figaro* reminded its readers that 'Some three years ago the Shah stated that there were only 3,000 communists in Iran and explained they were all or practically all in prison'. The harshly anti-leftist paper now noted that the communists were not just recovered and active but they were 'making a fine job at the moment of infiltrating and recruiting a people's movement'.[123] The paper warned its readers not to be fooled; Islam and communism could be reconciled, and 'the communists have always known that their own chance here was to get on the Ayatollah's bandwagon'. Khomeini was a communist Trojan horse, out of which pro-Soviet hordes, disguised as Islamists, would open the gates to Soviet expansion into the Persian Gulf. It was no coincidence, the paper noted, that when the Tudeh Party wanted the Shah assassinated in 1949, it had armed a religious fanatic. It was also clear, apparently, that many of the 30,000 striking oil workers were communists. This was obvious, *La Figaro* postulated, when Khomeini himself asked those workers to resume work to meet the country's internal consumption and they refused.[124]

The article was picked up and disseminated within the US government by the Foreign Broadcasting Information Service (FBIS), the open-source intelligence component of the CIA's Directorate of Science and Technology. It was unlikely, however, to have cut much ice. Even whilst some ideologues, notably Brzezinski, suspected KGB involvement in the opposition, multiple reports by the CIA and State Department continued to discount the role the Tudeh played in politics. The CIA reported that the Tudeh's operations had largely centred on communications, principally through its clandestine radio programme the National Voice of Iran and its weekly newspaper, *Norvid*. The Shah's people still consistently charged that 'communists' had played a major role in the disturbances since 1978. With the Shah's people still offering 'little convincing evidence' for this allegation, US intelligence remained un-persuaded.[125] In any case, the CIA no longer considered SAVAK (Sāzemān-e Ettelā'āt va Amniyat-e Keshvar – the Shah's feared security and intelligence service) to have any effective capability for reporting in Iran, noting that 'The current unrest, however, has rendered SAVAK nearly impotent'.[126]

Deciphering Tudeh activities in early 1979 was complicated by a coinciding change in the party's leadership. On 4 January, Iraj Eskandari, who had been party secretary since 1971, was replaced by Nur-ed-Kianuri. Feruyden Kishawarz, the former Tudeh minister who as noted earlier had been criticising Kianuri as a Soviet stooge since the 1950s, wasted no time in pointing out the significance of his accession. In an interview with the increasingly communist-obsessed *Le Monde*, Kishawarz again described Kianuri as an 'unconditional supporter of the Soviet Union'. His appointment as leader was now seen as an 'indication of the Soviet Union's designs'.[127] Eskandari meanwhile went on the offensive inside Tehran, giving two prominent interviews in which he decried most of the party history and called for independence from the USSR.

Brzezinski's caricature of the Tudeh as a long-standing and faithful tool of Soviet foreign policy was based on a profound misreading of Moscow's historical involvement in Iranian communism. Nor was it based on any up-to-date assessments. Ironically, however, with the ascent of Kianuri, Moscow did obtain a solid ally. The CIA admitted ignorance to the circumstances of him obtaining the leadership and whether it represented a policy shift, a personal power struggle, or simply the passing of an old leader unable to retain control of the party. All that was reported was Kianuri's insistence on cooperation with the Islamists and his warning against counter-revolutionary threats. Kianuri did in fact differ from his predecessor in his tactical approach to securing political advantages for the Tudeh. He was far more supportive of Khomeini than his predecessor and generally loyal to the Kremlin, despite some public attempts to distance the Tudeh from the USSR. Other party members who actually did make attempts to limit the influence of the Soviet Union quickly fell afoul of the new leadership.[128] Kianuri would remain in communication with the Soviet embassy, though it appears he received little policy direction, largely because the Soviets were unsure what direction to give.

More by luck than judgement, Kianuri's outlook still fitted the general perception in Washington that the Tudeh was pursuing pragmatic policies, which took account of its limited popular appeal and organisational strength and its need initially to cooperate with other groups within the wide spectrum of the opposition. In his first interview with a Western journalist as the new leader of the Tudeh, Nur-ed-Din Kianuri expressed total identification with Khomeini's outlook and claimed his support was not a 'temporary tactic' and that there were no great differences between scientific socialism and Islam's social ideas.[129] The party recognised Khomeini's popularity and vocally offered to help consolidate and defend the Islamic Revolution. The Tudeh's leadership increasingly also avoided grandiose statements of admiration for the communist Democratic Republic of Afghanistan (DRA). In return, Khomeini mostly refrained from publicly criticising the party.

The US correctly judged that, much like the National Front, the Tudeh's alliance with Khomeini proceeded from a position of weakness. They also believed, correctly again, that this reflected Moscow's judgement that Khomeini was an individual they could do business with. In early 1979, the Tudeh was judged by US analysts to have played a relatively minor role in the Revolution, but there appeared to be the space and opportunity for it to expand under a Khomeini-dominated regime. For the first time in over 30 years, it was able to operate legally and openly. A CIA estimate for February 1979 warned that the Tudeh 'over the past weeks has increased its activities in Tehran and in the oil fields'. Moreover, Washington was aware that 300,000 small arms captured or looted from the Iranian military were now in the hands of extremist groups on both the religious and leftist sides. Aware that Khomeini was only tolerating the Tudeh, the CIA warned that the Tudeh probably hoped for a 'period of chaos and continued economic paralysis which would allow them to gain more influence among workers and to allow them to infiltrate the government and its security forces'.[130]

Washington was blissfully aware, however, that the Tudeh's ability to influence Iranian society extended into the mainstream Iranian press. By early 1979, Rahman Hatefi, a high-level member of the Tudeh inside Iran, had successfully penetrated the editorial leadership of *Keyhan*, the largest Iranian daily. Hatefi fortuitously became editor-in-chief when the paper's founder, Mostafa Mesbahzadeh, was forced to flee Iran. From this position, Hatefi was able to shift *Keyhan*'s reporting in line with Tudeh objectives. To this end, *Keyhan* emphasised the party's support for Khomeini, whom the paper glorified, and produced a constant flow of reports describing US-inspired 'counter-revolutionary' plots. During this period, the Tudeh began to suspect that the provisional government (PGOI) appointed by Khomeini was trying to improve relations with the US. In February, the Tudeh Party Central Committee called for abandoning 'class struggle' until the US was driven out of Iran.[131] Its radio broadcasts became increasingly hostile towards the PGOI, emphasising that the only truly anti-imperialist groups were Khomeini and the Tudeh.

US diplomats in Iran complained that a hostile press was whipping up anti-American feelings in Iranian society. Ambassador Sullivan had even warned his superiors that the Left had tried to take control of the media, a concern apparently shared by some of the religious opposition. It appears that even some of the Islamists were becoming suspicious. On 21 January, a group of pro-Khomeini activists occupied the premises of the *Keyhan* newspaper and demanded that the paper print a 21-page article to counteract the excessive space it had given 'leftists'.[132] Little did they know that the editor of Iran's largest daily newspaper was a Tudeh member working towards a pro-Soviet agenda.[133] Hatefi was eventually ousted during a purge of journalists in the spring of 1979. In 1983, he was arrested, along with most of the Tudeh leadership, and died in prison shortly after, probably under torture.

Conclusion

US policy-makers anticipated Soviet subversion and opportunism as the Shah's regime collapsed; they then expected the Kremlin to exploit the security vacuum created by Iran's chaotic revolutionary transition. Brzezinski informed Carter in March 1979 that the Soviet Union 'could become the major strategic winner in the Persian Gulf as a result of the downfall of the Shah. In a prolonged period of change in Iran, the Soviet would be increasingly inclined to provide backing for those forces which they considered sympathetic to their own interests.'[134] It was simply assumed that the US was seeking a much more prominent role in the region.

For decades Iran had been central to the Cold War confrontation, and it was inevitable that the development of a new US policy was guided by considerations of power and material interests. This Soviet-centric organising principle for US policy was the point of departure, but there is little evidence of a pattern in US foreign policy that shows a predisposed inclination towards revolutionary movements that have swept away client regimes in regions central to the Cold War confrontation. Thus, although US policy-makers believed that they were compelled to take a strategic, broadly realist approach to Iran policy, this alone is an inadequate analytical framework to examine US decision-making. We need to explore how US decision-makers understood the nature of the Islamic Revolution, not just the Cold War crisis it provoked. The next task therefore is to understand why the Iranians were considered worthy of engaging.

3
US–Iranian Elite Interactions and the Pathologies of Engagement

A large strand of the theoretical literature concerning revolutions examines the dilemma that emerges when revolutionary movements achieve statehood and are faced with the pressure to conform to the conventions of international society. David Armstrong observes that the revolutionary state commonly finds itself in a situation where 'the belief system on which its revolution was founded and which legitimized the assumption of state power by the revolutionary elite is certain to run counter to the prevailing political doctrines of most other states'.[1] At this point, scholarly opinion divides; there are those, such as Armstrong and Kenneth Waltz, who believe that revolutionary states are unable to resist external pressures to conform and eventually assume more moderate and pragmatic foreign policies. In contrast, scholars such as Raymond Aron and Fred Halliday argue that the process of socialisation is never fully accepted by revolutionary elites.[2] Foreign policy then becomes a battleground in which radical and pragmatic strands compete, resulting in policies that mix ideological conditioning and *realpolitik*.

The notion of a fundamental tension between two poles, extremist and pragmatic, pulling Iranian foreign policy in opposing directions remains a predominant theme in the scholarship.[3] The vast majority of the scholarship has thus rejected neo-realist claims about the international system conditioning revolutionary behaviour and instead argues that the moderation of revolutionary ideology depends on changes at elite levels. Steven Walt finds no evidence to support the neo-realist assumption that revolutionary states are eventually socialised into more pragmatic practices. Walt believes that revolutionary ideology continued to influence new Iranian elites to pursue internationalist and radical foreign policy despite significant military and economic costs.[4] Many scholars, however, draw a distinction between Ayatollah Khomeini's founding term as Supreme Leader (1979–1989), and the more pragmatic approach to foreign policy his death made possible. Some go so far as to suggest that Khomeini's ideological pan-Islamist world view explicitly denigrated the concept of secular national interest and rejected the Westphalian nation-state concept, espousing Islam as a force cross-cutting national boundaries and binding all Muslims states together.[5] The period after Khomeini's death, however, beginning with the Rafsanjani presidency (1989–1997) and accelerating under Khatami (1997–2005), heralded a visibly less ideological foreign policy.[6] The mainstream view, at least in academia, now seems to be that the politics of survival have consistently circumscribed ideology and few hold that Iran is conveniently irrational.[7] Anoush Ehteshami, for example, argues that 'Post-revolutionary Iran succumbed to the practical geopolitical forces that were at the heart of the monarchy's foreign policy making and its strategic thinking'.[8]

All of these studies start from the premise that it is the state's top leadership, not the state, which defines the national interest and constructs foreign policy accordingly.[9] Other states appear to recognise this by seeking access and influence to new elites and displaying extreme sensitivity to internal power struggles within revolutionary states. By interacting with new elites, decision-makers can ascertain their likely foreign policy orientation and establish channels through which mutual interests and threats can be shared. Any actor seeking to engage a new one along lines of perceived mutual interest thus needs to interact with other elites in order to accurately construct and project an image of what constitutes another state's national interest.[10] When these interactions are limited, stifled by domestic pressures, or unrepresentative of the broader political body, decision-makers are unable to achieve what Ralph K. White describes as 'realistic empathy'. White, a former US Information Agency official, later a political scientist and psychologist, defines empathy as 'the great corrective for all forms of war-promoting misperception...It [means] simply understanding the thoughts and feelings of others.' To achieve it means 'jumping in imagination into another person's skin, imagining what it might be like to look out at his world through his eyes, and imagining how you might feel about what you saw'.[11] Without realistic empathy, it is difficult to appreciate an opponent's fears, vulnerabilities, or anger. In the absence of empathy, sustained through elite interactions, policy-makers rely more on pre-existing pathologies and images. At the very least, they find it difficult to challenge their preconceptions.

US policy during the early phase of the Iranian Revolution illustrates the role of elite interactions and realistic empathy. The previous chapter explored the international power dynamics that pushed Washington towards a cooperationist policy towards the post-revolutionary regime. This chapter explores the bilateral dynamics of America's engagement strategy. It examines the inter-elite interactions, both before and after the Revolution, which served as critical pull factors in Washington's favouring of a cooperative solution. According to Henry Precht, a key proponent of engagement, the Carter administration attempted to preserve America's position in Iran by 'securing access to the Iranian new political elite and shaping a pro-US regime in Tehran'.[12] These interactions enabled the Carter adminis-tration to construct an organising framework for Iran's post-revolutionary orientation which, when combined with pathologies relating to the ability of clerics to rule a modern country, established an organising framework for engagement.

In 1978 and early 1979, a group of US diplomats held a series of meetings with opposition leaders, many of whom would emerge as the early technocrats of the post-revolutionary regime. These meetings rein-forced the assumption that the principal organising concept for Iranian foreign policy-making would be the Cold War logic of 'spheres of influ-ence'; Iran's proximity to the Soviet Union would caution that, either through Soviet instigation or in the event of a leftist political ascen-dency, Iran was susceptible to being drawn into the Soviet orbit. There was some optimism, therefore, that a relationship could be forged that retained core elements of the pre-existing strategic relationship. Although elite interactions laid the intellectual and interpersonal foundations for US engagement, they were only very partially successful in achieving 'realistic empathy'.

Laying the foundations: Elite interactions prior to the Revolution

In February 1979, Carter's chief of staff Hamilton Jordan wrote: 'For better or worse, the US now had a stake in trying to build relations with the new government.'[13] Following the appointment of the moderate Bazargan provi-sional government and the withdrawal of Khomeini to Qom, there was some optimism that the situation looked hopeful for them to do so. Secretary of State Vance and Ambassador Sullivan outlined an engagement strategy based on the enduring geopolitical and economic features of US policy in Iran. On this basis, US officials emphasised a mutual interest in containing direct Soviet aggression, deterring Soviet proxies such as Iraq, and undermining Iranian leftist groups. There was no indication that Iran would cease supply-ing oil to the US and its Western allies once stability and productivity had been restored to the oilfields.

Although Washington had a new set of elites to deal with in Iran, the process of securing access to them had begun long before the US set out any new policy on a post-Shah Iran. The appointment of Bazargan was in itself a positive development; he was leader of the Liberation Movement (LM), whose senior leaders had been meeting with John Stempel, Henry Precht, Warren Zimmerman, and Richard Cottam since May 1978. Stempel had been introduced to Bazargan and Liberation Movement of Iran (LM) co-founder Yadollah Sahabi through Mohammad Tavasoli, another high-ranking member of the LM whom Stempel had met in Tehran in May 1978.[14] Mark Gasiorowski writes that 'Tavasoli was soon designated the LM's main contact with the embassy'. In the following months, Stempel met regularly with Tavasoli and other LM leaders to discuss the evolving situation.[15]

Bazargan's choice as foreign minister, Karim Sanjabi, had also been in contact with US embassy officials and was understood to be a moderate secularist.[16] The position of deputy PM went to Abbas Amir-Entezam, a Berkeley graduate who had lived in America on and off for over 20 years. Entezam had even conducted negotiations with US diplomats at the tender age of 21 and, in 1953, was personally selected by Mossedeq to approach US officials as a representative of the Liberation Movement. During this time, Entezam had become acquainted with Richard Cottam, then a CIA officer in Iran who later become an academic who advised the State Department on Iranian affairs. Whilst still politically active inside Iran, Entezam had maintained infrequent contact with US officials, including CIA agent George Cave, and the pair would strike up their relationship again after the Revolution. Entezam replaced Tavasoli as the head the LM's political office in October 1978 and met Stempel, on Cottam's recommendation, in January 1979. The two met frequently over the following weeks, with Entezam keeping Stempel abreast of the important political manoeuvrings between Bakhtiar's government and the opposition movement.[17]

The other three prominent moderates, either in the cabinet or soon to join, were Sadegh Ghotbzadeh, Ebrahim Yazdi, and Abolhassan Bani-Sadr. Robert Mantel, a staff member for the Senate's Foreign Relations Committee, had met with Ghotbzadeh, then one of Khomeini's chief aides, in November 1977. On 17 January 1979, Mantel sent a memo to Precht recalling that Ghotbzadeh did not seem 'ideologically anti-American'. In fact, 'he and his organisation were admirers of the US and ideals for which it stood'.[18] Bani-Sadr, Khomeini's other political aide and rival of Ghotbzadeh, had been approached, unwittingly, by CIA agent Guy Rutherford in Paris during 1978. The two had developed a cooperative relationship that would later see Rutherford travel to Tehran in August 1979 to try and 'turn him over to an embassy officer'.[19] Rutherford reported that although Bani-Sadr, who was by this time a member of the Revolutionary Council, respected Khomeini, he did not 'regard him infallible'.[20] The final prominent moderate was Yazdi, who was well known to embassy officials and had met with Henry Precht in Washington, DC.

More information on Iran's new elites came through the shadowy figure of Rahmatollah Moghaddam-Maraghei, a former Majlis deputy and founder of the Radical Movement, a liberal opposition party. Moghaddam advised US officials on his interactions with other leading members of the opposition, including Sanjabi, Bazargan, and Dariush Forouhar (who would become Minister of Labour). US embassy official George Lambrakis met with Moghaddam at least three times in 1978 to receive background information on the composition and internal character of the Shah's opposition. Moghaddam in return frequently complained of the Shah's human rights record and implored Lambrakis to do tell his superiors to do something about it.[21] He did not wish the Shah to leave Iran, but he passionately wanted the people to regain a share of power. He summed up the position of the opposition to Lambrakis as 'not anarchists, not communists, and not anti-American'.[22]

After the Revolution, Moghaddam became both a vocal opponent to clerical influence in government and a CIA informant (code-named SDProbe). He was a valuable source for a number of reasons. First, he was Governor General for East Azerbaijan and could thus report on the ongoing ethnic tensions that encompassed also a bitter power struggle between Khomeini and Ayatollah Shariatmadari. Second, he was close to Shariatmadari, who the CIA would later attempt to court as a possible leader of a more Western-orientated coalition. Third, he was a member of the Assembly of Experts and thus had contact with many of the key clerical and political leadership. This included the extremely influential Ayatollah Beheshti, with whom embassy officials had also some contact.

Mobilising the communist threat

The provisional government of Iran (PGOI) comprised people the US felt comfortable dealing with. This first cabinet included five ministers with dual Iranian and American citizenship. Stempel had taken from his meetings with senior members of the opposition that both the nationalists and clerics feared a Marxist takeover and were willing to work pragmatically to avoid splitting the non-leftist opposition. In August, Tavasoli warned that the nationalists needed close ties with the religious movement precisely because the choice was now between Islam and communism. Despite Stempel's sceptical response to Tavasoli's claim that the clergy 'merely wished to measure conformity of religious law with civil law', he did not dispute that the nationalists viewed their alliance with the clerics as important to preventing Iran being split between the Marxists and Islamists.[23] Even when Ambassador Sullivan sent the White House his infamous cable 'thinking the unthinkable: Iran without the Shah' on November 9, he suggested that Khomeini's anti-communism could form the basis of an accommodation with the military.[24] There was even a hypothesis, put forward by Vance in late November 1978, of a potential Soviet awareness that the non-leftist opposition feared the 'spectre of a Red Menace'.[25] Vance posited that this might lead the Soviets to encourage the communist party of Iran (Tudeh) to cooperate with the Islamists in order to diminish this perception. Vance's prediction proved largely correct.

Former CIA officer turned academic Richard Cottam had met Khomeini in December 1978 and told State Department officials that Khomeini's advisors were keenly aware of the Soviet threat, would move cautiously to avoid actions that would benefit the communists, and would continue to look to America to deter Soviet aggression.[26] Cottam described Khomeini's circle as 'afraid of the Soviet Union and desirous of relying on the US for Iran's defence'.[27] According to Cottam, they did not seek a formal defensive relationship, but did want US backing against the Soviet threat. Precht added that Khomeini's followers felt the Soviets would feel threatened by an Islamic government on its border capable of radicalising its own Muslim population. The State Department, from Vance downwards, was equally quick to dismiss claims made by the Shah's advisors and state-controlled media that Khomeini's inner circle was under the influence of the Soviet Union.[28]

Whilst the meetings with opposition members had confirmed some anti-communist anxieties, much of it seemed to be short-term fears that communists could take advantage of a messy revolutionary transition. US officials ignored information that contradicted the inherent plausibility that a new relationship could be forged on Iran's apparently self-evident fear of Soviet encroachment. One US intelligence report cautioned that 'Khomeini has consistently said that Islam requires a "neutrality" or "non alignment" '.[29] One individual who broadly discounted the communist threat was Ebrahim Yazdi. Yazdi was a green card-carrying 48-year-old medical researcher who had been working in Texas since the early 1960s. Yazdi would become foreign minister and one of the most reliable contacts the US embassy had within the provisional government.[30] In mid-September, Richard Cottam had suggested to Gary Sick that he meet with Yazdi whilst he was passing through Washington on his way to join Khomeini's entourage in Paris.[31] Sick felt it unwise for such a senior member of the NSC to meet with a prominent member of the opposition and he recommended Precht take his place. Although Precht readily agreed, Warren Christopher vetoed the idea in line with the current policy of avoiding official contact with the opposition. The two would get the opportunity to talk informally during a dinner in a Washington restaurant in the next month, but it would not be until December that the State Department decided to establish direct contact with opposition members.[32] Precht had kept Yazdi's number and he became a reliable opposition contact for the US, meeting Warren Zimmerman, the political counsellor for the US embassy in Paris, or simply talking with Precht on the phone.[33] On December 12, Precht and American academic Marvin Zonis met with Yazdi to discuss Khomeini's current plans. At that meeting, Yazdi unequivocally 'dismissed the communists as unimportant politically in Iran'.[34] Yazdi similarly dismissed the threat of Soviet intervention and was only concerned that the Iraqis might take advantage of unrest in Iran.

Nevertheless, mobilising the communist threat now neatly fitted the US embassy's strategy of trying to encourage the formation of a government led by the Shah's last Prime Minister, Shapour Bakhtiar. Bakhtiar, a long-standing member of the National Front, had been appointed by the Shah as a last attempt to placate the opposition. In January 1979, US officials in Tehran were trying to get members of the secular and religious opposition to enter

into negotiations with Bakhtiar. In order to do so, and encourage a political process that included Khomeini, they decided to play on the opposition
concerns of communist influence to encourage a peaceful transition during Khomeini's return. This echoed Cottam's claim that 'All oppositionists
agree that continued disorder will open way for communist organisations to
play greater role'.[35] The effort was twofold: to convince the opposition that a
chaotic transition would lead to Soviet and communist meddling, whilst also
trying to foster a degree of cooperation between the anti-communist military and the opposition. Both efforts failed in their primary aim: to persuade
Khomeini to support the Bakhtiar government.

As a contingency should Bakhtiar fall, Carter agreed to send General
Robert Huyser to Tehran to contact the Iranian military elite and, at least
from Brzezinski's perspective, sound out their ability to affect a military
coup as the last resort.[36] More importantly, Brzezinski no longer trusted the
US embassy's reporting from Iran. It was only when Charlie Naas eventually asked Huyser directly that his orders were known to US officials in Iran.
Naas later described the instructions he described as typical of Carter's habit
of constructing policy 'by committee'. In a concession to Brzezinski, Huyser
was to scout out the possibility of a coup; his main effort, however, was to
support Vance's aim of encouraging the military to switch their support to
Bakhtiar and a new constitution. The Huyser mission can be usefully understood as an example of bureaucratic dysfunction operationalised as strategic
planning. More importantly, it was a critically ill-timed tactical error that
was widely understood in Iran to be a part of a conspiracy to drown the
Revolution at birth.[37]

Vance was still determined to negotiate with Khomeini and told Carter
that he wanted to warn Khomeini that if Bakhtiar failed, the communists
would benefit. After being heavily lobbied by Sullivan, Vance had already
instructed Theodore Eliot, a recently retired senior diplomat, to travel to
Paris to meet Khomeini. The plan was to elicit Ayatollah Khomeini's consent
for a coalition between the Iranian military and internal religious leaders.
It would later emerge that Sullivan had secretly begun conducting unautho-
rised talks with the opposition, even agreeing on names of senior military
figures who would accompany the Shah into exile. Despite Sullivan having briefed the Shah on the possible meeting, Brzezinski remained opposed
to any action which might weaken Bakhtiar and the military. Brzezinski
felt that any action that validated or encouraged an opposition he saw
as dedicated to eroding America's position in Iran would be playing into
Soviet hands. As a scholar of Polish origin with expertise in nineteenth- and
twentieth-century revolutions, he was particularly conscious of the Kerensky
model, wherein a reformer holds power for just long enough to be removed
by the most radical alternative. He persuaded Carter to veto the meeting.[38]
Carter opted for a compromise, asking the French to communicate to
Khomeini the need for him to stop his opposition to Bakhtiar.

Carter's veto left Sullivan incandescent with rage. On the 10th of January, he sent a message to Vance:

> You should know that the President has made a gross and perhaps irre-trievable mistake by failing to send emissary to Paris to see Khomeini as previously agreed...General Huyser has already asked sec Brown to ask President to reconsider, in view of urgent appeals from Iranian military that we arrange relationship between them and Khomeini.[39]

Sullivan's outburst would have cost him his job had Vance not persuaded Carter that it would be ruinous to change ambassadors at such a critical juncture. His attempt to construct a policy that accepted Khomeini's general guidance over a post-Shah Iran was, in retrospect, analytically credible and persuasive. It was not taken up, however, because Carter, under the strong influence of Brzezinski, had not yet accepted the Shah's exit as inevitable. More importantly, he did not trust Sullivan with the competency to initi-ate such a high-stakes reorientation of US policy.[40] It is impossible to judge whether an engagement strategy that included Khomeini would have suc-ceeded, yet it is reasonable to suggest that deliberately not engaging him under the belief that it would weaken more pro-American groups was mis-guided and ultimately counterproductive. It would, however, remain the guiding principle for US policy in Iran even after Khomeini's authority was accepted as absolute.

On 14 January, Carter finally authorised a meeting between the politi-cal councillor at the US embassy in Paris, Warren Zimmerman, and Ebrahim Yazdi, marking the first official meetings between US officials and Khomeini's entourage. Zimmerman's brief was a holding mission: Yazdi was to be per-suaded that the time was not ready for Khomeini to return to Iran. The aim was thus to give Huyser the time for an arrangement to be made between the military and Bakhtiar and clerics such as Ayatollah Beheshti. Again, the communist threat was emphasised as the basis for coopera-tion, but also tactically in order to establish space for the Huyser mission. The threat posed by the Left, particularly if Iran descended into serious instability, was by this time firmly entrenched as mutually appreciated amongst the moderate opposition, despite Yazdi's previous meeting with Precht.

During their third meeting in five days, Zimmerman presented Yazdi with a lengthy statement stressing the need for caution amongst the Khomeini camp. The Left, the statement asserted, 'would be the only force to gain from a religious-military clash'.[41] The other element of this strategy was to leave Yazdi with the impression that America was doing all it could to pre-vent a military takeover and that Khomeini's continued caution was vital to this effort. Yazdi noted the Tudeh threat and informed Zimmerman that Khomeini had asked his supporters in Tehran to contact the army. Yet, he remained broadly unconvinced that the communists had the capability to take advantage of any scenario. The Islamic movement was simply 'too strong'.[42] The next day, Yazdi outlined his guiding principles for a nonaligned and non-interventionist foreign policy. Relations would be cordial with the Soviet Union, Yazdi confirmed, yet a negative historical experience, Soviet atheism, and Moscow's hostility towards its own Muslim population would remain significant obstacles to close relations. By noting that 'At least Americans believe in God', Yazdi hoped to demonstrate what was his genuine commitment to retaining ties with the West.[43] Yet he gave no indication that a strategic anti-communist alliance would be the primary basis for US–Iranian relations.

Mehdi Bazargan, who, unlike Yazdi, was inside Iran, had meanwhile visited the striking oil workers with the aim of resuming the necessary production needed to provide the daily needs of the people. Bazargan had been astonished at the strength of the leftist workers there, an observation not lost on Gary Sick.[44] It is impossible to know whether the decision to respond to Zimmerman's pressing for greater coordination between the opposition and the military was influenced by this fear of communist opportunism. Yet by 22 January, Entezam was telling embassy staff that the LM urgently wanted talks with the military in order to effectively and peacefully choreograph Khomeini's return to Iran.[45] Entezam made it clear that America could convince the military that Khomeini's return was 'good idea'.

On 24 January, Bakhtiar agreed to Khomeini's return to Iran, and the US embassy even reported that he approved of Khomeini's initial programme. Bakhtiar's negotiations with members of Khomeini's entourage continued, but Khomeini considered the Prime Minister tainted by his association with the Shah. After Khomeini landed in Tehran on 1 February, he demanded Bakhtiar's immediate resignation. US officials were made aware through intermediaries that Khomeini had decreed that the only acceptable solution was a temporary Islamic government to supervise a referendum that would decide Iran's transition to an Islamic Republic.[46] On 4 February, Khomeini appointed Bazargan as Prime Minister of a provisional government.

By the time Khomeini triumphantly returned to Tehran and swiftly made Bakhtiar's position untenable, the utility of appealing to the new regime on the basis of a mutual threat of communist and Soviet opportunism was a firmly established tactic. The extent to which Washington perceived this threat was less important than the extent to which the new regime understood this threat and was receptive to the notion that cooperation with America was vital in resisting it. In this regard, there were indications that the moderates, as James Bill observed, believed 'the fledgling Revolution as under siege and surrounded by enemies; thus, a number of the moderates believed US support to be essential'.[47]

The question now was whether Washington should recognise the Bazargan government or maintain its support for Bakhtiar. At a meeting of senior US officials on 11 February, State Department officials Warren Christopher and David Newsom argued that the US must recognise a government led by Bazargan. Brzezinski questioned this, arguing that an accommodation between the military and the Bazargan government would lead the armed forces to eventually disintegrate 'with major domestic and foreign implications'.[48] Carter, however, sided with those advocating engagement, concluding that the US had no choice but to work with the Bazargan government. After contacting General Robert Huyser, who was in Iran to lease with the Iranian military, Brzezinski was informed that a coup was not feasible without a 'massive US commitment'. With that, Brzezinski finally abandoned the idea.

The period between a Special Coordination Committee (SCC) meeting of 11 January and 11 February marked the State Department's reclaiming of Iran policy. There was now broad consensus that Washington's support for a new government backed by Khomeini was essential. The prevailing view was that Khomeini would quickly move aside and moderates would provide the natural source of leadership for the new regime. Elite interactions established the anti-communist credentials of the opposition. A mutually reinforcing misperception was that the clerics were unequipped and uninterested in running the actual instruments of state.

US assessments of clerical authority in Iran

Guided by what Bill Beeman describes as a 'technocratic US belief system' running through US foreign policy, it was inconceivable that a modern nation-state could be run by clerics.[49] At an SCC meeting on 11 January 1979, representatives from the State Department, Pentagon, CIA, and Joint Chiefs of Staff had agreed that Khomeini would limit his role to that of a 'venerable sage'.[50] The perception that Khomeini would have only a distant influence on policy was less the product of a close reading of the Shia tradition of quietism and more a reflection of America's ignorance of political Islam. Robert Jervis hypothesises that misperception is most likely to occur when an actor is not just miscategorised according to existing typologies, but when no such category exists in the minds of leaders.[51] Khomeini's doctrines, a complex amalgamation of esoteric Shia jurisprudence situated within Iranian political and intellectual historical development, were beyond categorisation for US officials. Political Islam, even broadly defined, was a force that Brzezinski admitted to Carter 'America doesn't have much experience of dealing with'.[52] Other elites within the Iranian revolutionary movement, due to their Western education, orthodox understanding of international relations, and perceived concern for Iran's vulnerability to Soviet penetration, were easily categorised. US diplomats would look to facilitate a smooth transition of power to this group.

In partial mitigation, the Pahlavi regime had for years presented the view that mullahs were unworldly stooges, instead focussing American leaders on the communist threat. It was also an image Khomeini had partly cultivated. Following extensive media training from Bani-Sadr and Ghotbzadeh, Khomeini promoted an image of political reticence that obscured the dictatorial and dogmatic persona that emerged swiftly after his return to Iran.[53] Khomeini responded to their calls for a softening of his rhetoric, placing greater emphasis on freedom, independence, democracy, and women's rights in Iran.

These strategists recognised the need to maintain the support of the middle classes, frightened by the notion of theocracy, and thus Khomeini maintained that he would 'fulfil no government position'. Instead, Khomeini vaguely declared that he was 'content, as in the past, to be my nation's guide'.[54] Nikki Keddie writes that 'Whether sincerely or not, Khomeini made several publicly recorded statements that neither he nor the *ulama* would hold direct power in a new government, and he never before or shortly after coming to power referred to *veleyat-e faqih*'.[55] What role the 'guide' would play, beyond setting out the ideological parameters that the politicians could operate within, was unclear. Indeed, these parameters themselves were largely unknown in the West. Khomeini went to significant lengths, however, to insist Iran would not be a theocratic state. In another comment published by the Italian paper *L'Espresso*, Khomeini stressed that 'The Islamic Republic can only be based on the people's will, in other words, universal suffrage'.[56] Richard Cottam, one of the very few Americans to ever meet Khomeini, further convinced the State Department that the Ayatollah had little ambition to dominate the political system and was fundamentally a democrat concerned by the communist threat. On 3 February 1978, Ambassador Sullivan reported that his embassy's assessment was that the religious movement would probably not be able to avoid making 'some accommodations with westernised ideas of government held by many in the opposition movement'. He added that the religious movement dominated by Khomeini was 'far better organized, enlightened and able to resist communism than its detractors would lead us to believe'.[57]

Yet there were signs that strongly hinted at the hold Khomeini's authority would later command over secular politicians. One such indication was the political homage nationalist leaders paid him whilst in exile and the Ayatollah's ability to bend these secular leaders into adopting his line on key issues such as the nature of Islamic government and the ruling out of any accommodation with the Bakhtiar government. On 8 November 1978, the Shah's most prominent secular opposition leader, Karim Sanjabi, the leader of the National Front, visited Khomeini in France and promptly acquiesced to his insistence on there being an 'Islamic government'.[58] The leader of the other main secular faction, the Freedom Movement, led by Mehdi Bazargan, had in October already pledged his allegiance to Khomeini. By this time, Khomeini's support from the urban and rural working classes, and oil workers, was indisputable.

Khomeini's refusal to contemplate any compromise other than the immediate exit of the Shah and the establishment of Islamic government, rather than the full implementation of the 1906–1907 constitution, became the unassailable position of the revolutionary movement. Popular and higher-ranking ayatollahs, such as Taleghani or Shariatmadari, who advocated the restoration of the 1906–1907 constitution ignored by Reza Shah could not match Khomeini's resolute and uncompromising stance.[59] The moderate clerics were bound to lose influence to the more uncompromising Khomeini in revolutionary circumstances. The middle classes, represented chiefly by the revived National Front, had little choice but to join forces with Khomeini and acknowledge his leadership, despite some of their private reservations.[60] In recognition of Khomeini's moratorium on compromise of any nature with the Shah, a succession of former nationalist opponents of the Shah refused the prime ministership. When Shapour Bakhtiar finally accepted the invitation on December 28, he was immediately expelled from the National Front and ostracised by the entire opposition.[61]

The US ignored the fact that the moderates had embraced Khomeini from a position of weakness; their alliance was the result of some common ideological stances on the role of Islam, but more importantly the moderates' lack of revolutionary credentials and first-class political leaders after years of suppression by the Shah [62] Khomeini's ability to dictate the Revolution's ideological path was overlooked, and Brzezinski dismissively advised Carter that 'Religious institutions rarely succeed in dominating the political systems of Muslim countries'.[63] A January 1979 intelligence memorandum reported that Khomeini 'seems bored with political strategy' and 'apparently allows his aides to work out the details on specific foreign policy issues'.[64] It followed, therefore, that Khomeini could restore order and allow a transfer of the everyday running of the country to non-clerical politicians. These assumptions were initially reinforced by the fact that Khomeini did, as predicted, swiftly leave Tehran and take up residence in Qom. Although events in Iran after the Revolution would reveal the true extent of Khomeini's political ambition, the Carter administration would never shed their belief that clerical rule was unsustainable and sooner rather than later they would be forced to hand over the reigns of government to secular technocrats.[65]

By February 1979, international pressures, elite interactions, and a lack of experience with political Islam led US diplomats to look to facilitate a smooth transition of power to a group of 'moderates', who by their Western educational background and perceived concern for Iran's vulnerability to Soviet influence offered the hope of continued and useful relations. This objective was brought into sharper relief by assessments of increasing leftist activity in Iran and concerns that the Soviet Union would seek to take advantage of the political vacuum in Iran.

US concerns of a leftist takeover

On 4 February, Khomeini appointed a provisional government led by Mehdi Bazargan which deliberately excluded any communists. Khomeini refused to meet any leftists, though he seldom criticised the Tudeh by name.[66] The Tudeh still publicly expressed total confidence in Khomeini and by extension had little option other than to recognise the government he supported. Though Kianuri publicly denied that this was a temporary tactic, US officials suspected that the party, encouraged by the Soviets, was pursuing a holding policy. Since it had gone underground in the 1950s, the CIA had considered the Tudeh's long-term aim as 'to install an elite party apparatus consisting of a cadre capable of moving rapidly once the Shah's hold on absolute power weakened'.[67]

The chaotic security situation in Iran and obvious weakness of the provisional government brought this analysis into even sharper relief. On 14 February, the leftist guerrilla group Feda'i had briefly occupied the US embassy. On 15 February, the CIA reported that Tudeh activity had increased markedly. A few weeks later, Director of Central Intelligence (DCI) Stansfield Turner warned that 'Marxists' would be the main beneficiary of any conflict between Khomeini and Bazargan. Turner warned that 'Should the situation degenerate into open civil war, the Soviets are likely to funnel covert support to these elements that then appear most favourable to their interests, while professing non intervention and continuing to warn the US against intervention'.[68] Sullivan argued a similar line, warning that the communists sought to take advantage of the Iranian military's disintegration.[69] Before the Revolution, Brzezinski had long been concerned by Iran's fragmentation, having been told by the Iranian Ambassador prior to the Revolution that a Khomeini victory would lead the Kurds and other ethnic groups to go their separate ways.[70]

Industrial action was another major source of instability that offered the Tudeh specific opportunities. Continued economic paralysis, the CIA cautioned, 'Could allow [the Tudeh] to gain more influence among the workers and to infiltrate the government and its security forces'.[71] There were more questions about Tudeh participation in the continuing oil strikes. An intelligence estimate reported some sources as indicating that the Tudeh was behind the radical strikers in the oilfields who had resisted Khomeini's efforts to restore oil production to meet domestic needs. The CIA added a note of caution to this assumption, noting that an unnamed Eastern European diplomat had attributed the disruption on the oilfields to extreme Islamic rightists.[72] Islamic extremists, however, seem less likely to have the capability to pull off such a strike; they also seem much more unlikely to countermand a direct order from Khomeini. The conservative American think tank Heritage Foundation and the *Washington Post* both published articles in February stating that not only had the Tudeh recently exerted a radicalising influence in the oilfields, but that the leftists approached their support in that sector as their chief tool for extracting more influence from Khomeini.[73] The State Department estimated that between 1,000 and 2,000 party members worked in the oilfields. The CIA was more circumspect, and reported that the strikes would have occurred whether or not the Tudeh had participated.[74] To partially offset the Iranian shortfall and stabilise the volatile world oil market, the Saudis produced a spectacular 3 MBD production, bringing Saudi production up to 10.5 MBD by mid-January. Other supplementary output boosts came from Kuwait, Nigeria, and Venezuela.[75]

It has been strongly argued by Professor Mohsen Milani that the 'Tudeh policy was intended to immobilise the PGOI as a preliminary step toward taking over the state and pushing Iran into the Soviet orbit'. Milani, who seems to be motivated by a desire to uphold Bazargan's reputation, argues that Tudeh tactics included 'exaggerating the possibility of an imminent counter-Revolutionary conspiracy, intensifying the atmosphere of fear and demanding fundamental change'.[76] Central to this strategy was an effort to force a wedge between the Bazargan government and the fundamentalist clique by constantly portraying the PGOI as reformist and closely linked to the Americans.

The Tudeh, Milani asserts, actively radicalised the Revolution in order to ostracise a government they suspected of being pro-American and make Iran effectively ungovernable. Milani's case is certainly buttressed by an examination of pro-Tudeh NVOI broadcasts at the time. Throughout 1979, these broadcasts pursued a strategy of defending the Soviet Union, spreading hysteria surrounding US encouragement for counter-revolutionaries, and professing loyalty to the Revolution. Notable by their absence in any NVOI broadcasts were any statements of support for the Bazargan government. All these elements can be seen in the following broadcast from May 1979, which was translated by the CIA:

> The Soviet Union always sincerely supported the national, progressive and anti-despotic movement of the Iranian nation under the leadership of the Ayatollah Khomeini ... how can fabricating lies, malicious accusations and completely false and damaging slogan, even contrary to neighbourliness, be defined other than as a counter-Revolutionary conspiracy begun by remnants of the former regime, SAVAKISTS, and masked and unmasked agents of imperialism.[77]

In a creative example of propaganda, the NVOI portrayed this tactic as the modus operandi during the US–Pahlavi era of cooperation and its continuation thus a threat to the Revolution:

> In the past, the former Shah's regime, the SAVAKist torturers and their mercenary writers, by following their teachers and inspirers across the

ocean in the US Central Intelligence Agency, used the bogey of communism to crush any anti-despotic movement. Regrettably there are still some people who resort to the same ugly and indecent methods.

Broadcasts such as these reinforced Washington's perception that the NVOI represented a joint Soviet–Tudeh effort to derail US–Iranian relations, which, at that time, were showing tentative signs of improvement. There was no real sense that this was part of a joint Soviet–Tudeh strategy of destabilising the entire foundations of Khomeini's authority in order to take over the entire state. A memo from the NSC's situation room in March described an upcoming meeting between Soviet officials and representatives from regional communist parties and claimed that one aim was 'making rule by Khomeini impossible'. But the writer of the memo admitted that the main purpose of the conference between Soviet officials and neighbouring communist organisations was to coordinate support for the Tudeh Party in anticipation of persecution by Khomeini.[78]

Rather than pursuing a realistic strategy for political domination themselves, it appears that in early 1979 the Tudeh's ambitions were limited to preventing the Islamists from dominating other political groups. Khomeini's advisors and supporters may have insisted that political parties would be able to operate freely, but the CIA suspected that this might not last. Independently from the NSC, they suggested that the Tudeh's immediate goal was to gain enough influence simply to prevent future repression. Indeed, Kianuri would later admit that the Tudeh hoped to come to power, but only if the Islamic Republic had already collapsed. He, like other senior members, dismissed the Tudeh's capability to affect its collapse and explained that his priority was the party's survival and preventing a counter-revolutionary coup.[79]

The real extent of Soviet–Tudeh coordination was largely unknown. Vance had cautioned back in November 1978 that 'we have no information on the extent of control the exiled leadership has over its members still in Iran but believe it is far from absolute'.[80] The CIA admitted in February that 'it can be assumed that Tudeh policies have at least tacit Soviet backing, but reporting on actual Soviet involvement is not extensive'.[81]

Communist or leftist influence in general was seen much more in terms of a potential rather than immediate threat. The fragility of the government was seen in Washington as the product of its struggle with multi-tiered clerical power centres. Few really considered the Tudeh as a major factor in exacerbating a tension they viewed as inherent to the competing world views of these two competing authorities. The gravest threat to Khomeini was probably seen in terms of the ethnic violence, which was not seen as Tudeh infiltrated or instigated, and probably the imam's own health. Henry Precht, the head of the State Department's Iran desk, offers the following recollection:

I don't think anyone in the US government took seriously their threat to Khomeini and the winning Revolutionaries. I very much doubt that they were capable of driving 'a wedge' between the PRG and his inner circle. It is possible that they tried to do so, but I don't believe that they were a significant factor.[82]

For the most part, it seems, the Kremlin took a similarly realistic attitude to the limited influence of the Tudeh in Iran as Precht.[83] Even the Tudeh leader, Nur-ed-Kianuri, admitted in June 1979 that he had no contact with Khomeini. Kianuri was forced to admit the Tudeh's political isolation was a major obstacle to establishing closer relations between Iran and the Soviet Union.[84] The US had grown to understand by the end of October that the Tudeh were lying low, small in number, discredited, fragmented, and lacking in charismatic leaders.[85]

Soviet propaganda in Iran

In late May, an intelligence estimate judged that Moscow was generally gratified by the situation in Iran and their position in the Middle East in general. This was drawn into sharper relief by the downturn in US–Iranian relations following the Javits resolution.

US analysts acknowledged opportunities for the Soviets from Sadat's alienation and the new Iranian regime's weakness, but they also observed contradictions in Soviet tactics. Two apparently irreconcilable motives were limiting Soviet policy in Iran: the Kremlin continued to want proper relations with the new regime in order to protect the Tudeh and discourage an anti-Soviet posture. This required a degree of stability within the Iranian regime. On the other hand, instability in Iran established a political vacuum that could be filled by pro-Soviet leftist groups. Moscow recognised an interest in both a weak Bazargan government, which was ostensibly amenable to good relations with America, and a weak clerical movement, which was more interested in exporting radical Islam and hostile to communism. In pursuit of these complex and conflicting goals, the CIA predicted a Soviet effort to improve relations with the Bazargan government as long as it was backed by Khomeini. At the same time, it was also encouraging the formation of a united front of leftists, with the Tudeh at its core, which could at once penetrate the Iranian regime in order to 'ultimately subvert it'.[86] What the CIA did not make clear was whether the Soviets were aiming to first split the Bazargan government from Khomeini as the first step to this goal.

Moscow's dual-track strategy required a flexible tool for subverting American interests, defending criticism of the Soviet Union, and demonstrating its sympathies or condemnation for various groups or actions as and when it appeared prudent. The use of a third-party broadcasting instrument, such as the NVOI, was therefore seen as an important tool for Soviet policy, and Brzezinski asked to be regularly provided transcripts of its content. The specific day-to-day nature of Soviet control of NVOI's content remained a largely unknown factor in early 1979. However, it was judged 'clearly an asset of the USSR'.[87] The Center for Strategic Studies reported that although formally controlled by the Tudeh, the NVOI was 'actually thought to be a Soviet propaganda station based in Baku'.[88] As noted, the consistent aim of NVOI broadcasts was to reinforce the wide public perception in Iran that the CIA would strive to restore the Pahlavi dynasty, as they had in 1953. US intelligence reported in August that broadcasts were seizing upon recent demonstrations and assassinations as 'evidence' of a continuing CIA threat to the revolution.[89] At the same time NVOI was a platform to refute allegations of Moscow's involvement in the ethnic rebellions, though this suspicion remained amongst Iranian leaders.

The NVOI facilitated Moscow's dual track of cautiously engaging the Bazargan government whilst also discreetly pressing the case for the Tudeh. CIA director Turner noted this strategy on 1 March 1979:

> While the Soviets have maintained a cautious and conciliatory line toward Barzagan in most respects thus far, clandestine radio has tacitly supported his leftist opponents on one key issue – their insistence that they be allowed to retain the arms which enable them to force concession from him. Moscow is likely to increase covert efforts to broaden its contacts among the leftist factions while gradually becoming more open in support for Tudeh's claim to a role in the new power alignment.[90]

Washington protested to Moscow and tried to develop American counter-broadcasting capabilities in Iran, but pro-Soviet propaganda remained a severe irritant that contributed to the poisonous atmosphere in which America sought to repair its position in Iran.[91]

Summary: Why engagement?

By 10 February, the Revolution had unequivocally succeeded and Washington was publically committed to building a new relationship with the Bazargan government. The Carter administration remains the only US government to genuinely attempt to engage post-revolutionary Iran without preconditions. All subsequent US administrations have asserted that engagement can only follow the cessation of a wide range of activities by the Iranian government believed to threaten stability in the Middle East. In 1979, however, the US government did not explicitly link the possibility of rapprochement to the moderation of any of Iran's wider regional or domestic policies, as has been the case ever since. In fact, it was the Iranians who eventually managed to extract an American obligation not to 'intervene, directly or indirectly, politically or militarily, in Iran's internal affairs'.[92]

But why was the US so determined to rebuild relations with a regime in charge of a country gripped by a frenzy of anti-American violence? US military officials were stuck in facilities all across the country and facing serious threats to their safety. They would eventually be taken to the embassy in Tehran by Deputy Prime Minister Ebrahim Yazdi. Outside the sprawling embassy, thousands of protestors gathered to shout anti-American slogans. So much tear gas was used that the embassy compound became almost un-livable. Hunkered down in the embassy, US diplomats read the daily butcher's bill of executed Pahlavi loyalists, recognising many of the names as social acquaintances.[93]

On a more macro level, there is little evidence of a pattern in US foreign policy that shows a predisposed inclination towards revolutionary movements that have swept away client regimes in regions central to the Cold War confrontation. In fact, the historical record seems to indicate that American leaders are far more likely to be hostile towards foreign revolutions than seek to accommodate them.[94] A policy of engagement seems even more counterintuitive when weighed against some of the known characteristics of the new regime. Ayatollah Khomeini had made his hostility to the Shah's relationship with the US the centrepiece of his revolutionary discourse. The banner 'death to America' was quickly established as a pillar of Khomeini's revolutionary identity. Washington was clearly aware of the extreme anxieties Iran's Islamic Republic provoked amongst its allies in the Arab world. Iranian broadcasting called for the spread of Islamic Revolution and the overthrow of several 'despotic' US allies. Khomeini was known to oppose the Camp David negotiations, and US intelligence predicted that Iran would adopt hostile relations with Israel and Egypt.[95] It was also clear that post-revolutionary Iran would provide moral and political support for anti-Israel militant groups, specifically the Palestine Liberation Organization (PLO). The CIA would soon report that the PLO, considered a terrorist organisation supported by the USSR, was playing a role in training Iran's Revolutionary Guard.[96]

Although the regional implications of the Revolution were troubling, the development of a 'new' Iran policy was shaped by concerns regarding the balance of power between the US and the Soviet Union. Yet 'realist' considerations alone are unable to explain why the US decided upon a policy of engagement, or how that was pursued. This chapter has shown how inter-elite interactions, both before and after the Revolution, served as pull factors in favouring cooperative solutions. Close inter-elite relations had been the hallmark of the US–Iranian relations during the Shah era. Nixon and the Shah, Kissinger and Zahedi, Brzezinski and Oveisi: such was the centrality of these close personal ties that Ali Ansari argues that the entire US–Iranian relationship was based on 'personalities rather than states'.[97] Inter-elite relations had insulated US policy-makers from the reality of state–society relations in Iran. After the Revolution, the US would rely on an even narrower base in Iran's political landscape to rescue America's position in the Persian Gulf. Engagement was based on the assumption that clerics could not rule and moderates would place security above ideology and construct foreign policy cognisant of Iran's geopolitical situation. It was presumed that Iran in the post-Shah era would conform to America's criteria of a rational actor; at worst, it would avoid a confrontation with the US, but there was some optimism that a relationship could be forged that retained core elements of the strategic relationship that had existed during the Shah's regime. Resisting the self-evident external and internal communist threat would, according to the American mindset, require stable relations with the West.

Part II
The Dynamics of Engagement

4
Putting Engagement into Practice

Washington believed it had accepted the Revolution and set out a highly pragmatic approach to resurrecting US interests in the region. This chapter shows how US policy-makers placed their hopes in a small group of elites who seemed capable of defining Iran's geopolitical interests in the terms understood by US officials. It shows how US diplomats tried to demonstrate their acceptance of the Revolution and some of the practical steps they took to try and repair US–Iranian relations. It also shows how US policy understood and reacted to changing political and security conditions in Iran. US diplomats in Iran had also to cope with a changing domestic situation in America, where the excesses of the Revolution had provoked virulent criticism of the new Iranian government. Equally, the ebb and flow of US–Soviet relations and the collapse of détente would affect assessments of the Soviet threat in Iran (and indeed Soviet estimates of US policy in the region).

Despite these pressures, the construction and execution of the 'new' thinking in Iran suffered from a number of deficiencies. US policy-makers could not resist the urge to try and 'manage' the crisis in Iran. It has been an American tendency to choose favourites and try to anoint them as the new elites of a country. Washington tends to prefer secular, Western-educated politicians, who appear to be congenial to US interests.[1] This was as much the case in Iran in 1979 as it would be in Iraq in 2003. This chapter will show that policy was unsympathetic to the duality of power that existed between the provisional government of Iran (PGOI) and the clerical authority, even when all the indicators suggested that clerical rule was far from a transitory influence in Iran and the clerics had out-manoeuvred the official government. US officials were equally unsympathetic to the historical context in which many Iranians were reading their intentions. In the final analysis, US policy proceeded not from a strong understanding of local dynamics, but as how best to respond to the Cold War crisis it provoked. Washington ignored sufficient signs that this would not be a profitable way of repairing relations and continued to read the situation through the lens of US–Soviet competition, which was often unhelpful to reading local dynamics.

As bilateral relations rapidly began to unravel, the section re-examines a highly secretive attempt by the State Department and CIA to kick-start engagement through a series of highly secret intelligence-sharing initiatives. The final chapter in this section analyses the two disastrous decisions that contributed to, though of course did not justify, the attack on the US embassy. The first was the decision to admit the Shah for medical treatment, against the advice of senior embassy staff. The second was the decision to send Brzezinski to meet Prime Minister Bazargan in Algiers. Both decisions reflected the structural and intellectual failings in US policy.

The State Department 'running the show'

The period after 11 February marked the State Department's reclaiming of Iran policy. Officials in the State Department had previously seen their advice to establish links with the opposition ignored by Carter, who preferred to listen to Brzezinski's advice that such activities would undermine the Shah.[2] The crisis in Iran had occupied the highest attention of US policymakers for hardly more than 3 weeks. Once the decision to engage post-revolutionary Iran had been taken, the US embassy in Tehran would be left to pursue this goal with minimal supervision or support from Washington. In the words of Henry Precht, Vance became 'ambivalent' about Iran and emerged himself in reviving the SALT II negotiations.[3] Negotiations between the US and the Soviet Union were at a critical point. On 10 January, Brezhnev told a group of visiting senators that he wanted to sign the SALT II accord quickly.[4] Four days later, Carter had announced that he wanted to send SALT II to the Senate as a Treaty rather than as an Executive Order.[5] In order to achieve this, Vance entered a series of meetings with the Soviets in order to finalise key technical issues such as limits on missile testing and the allowable number of multiple independently targetable re-entry vehicles (MIRVs).[6] The loss of US facilities in Iran vital for monitoring Soviet missile testing increased the pressure on these talks. The aiming of SS-20 Soviet missiles at Western Europe in late January further inflamed domestic opposition to détente and provoked NATO to consider deploying new intermediate-range US missiles.[7]

Iran had not made it onto the agenda title of a National Security Council (NSC) meeting until early January 1979; it would then disappear again until October, when the White House agonised over whether to allow the Shah into the US for medical treatment.[8] Nobody at a policy-making level would visit Iran once Ayatollah Khomeini returned. One of the last requests made by the acting head of the embassy, Bruce Laingen, was for an official at undersecretary level or above to travel to Tehran to assist their effort to persuade Iran of Washington's serious intention to adjust to the realities of a post-Shah Iran. Laingen wrote: 'We would welcome the allied support in our efforts to enhance our credentials with the new Iranian leadership that a senior visitor could bring to bear.'[9]

The flip side of this was that the open warfare that had previously characterised US policy ended. In the words of Gary Sick, his superior, Brzezinski, 'walked away from policy'.[10] As a result Sick himself was isolated, and had to lobby his disinterested boss just to get access to certain meetings. Not that much in the way of high-level policy development or supervision was going on anyway. Soon after Khomeini's return to Iran, Charlie Naas and John Stempel briefly returned to Washington and made themselves available on the political circuit. Naas recollects that the atmosphere was one of 'resignation'. Even in the State Department, 'nobody wanted to know what had happened in Iran'. Little effort was being made to get to grips with the Islamic Revolution; concepts such as *velayat-e faqih* were entirely unknown to even normally well-informed individuals. At one meeting, Naas was stunned when Vice President Walter Mondale slapped Naas' CIA companion on the back and asked him if the Shah can come back! When Naas was invited to the White House, he was not granted an audience with Carter. He left Tehran without receiving any formal instructions.[11] Gary Sick recollects that the White House was in the 'initial stages of grief', a stage often associated with denial.[12]

The lack of high-level interest in Iran policy reduced Henry Precht to running what Gary Sick called a 'one-man show' in Washington.[13] Precht's relationship with Brzezinski and Sick had completely broken down over the preceding 6 months on account of their perception of Precht's anti-Shah views and (unfounded) suspicion that he was leaking his opinions to the media. Having been at the sharp end of the bitter infighting that had characterised US policy in Iran, Precht found his new-found freedom enormously liberating:

> I no longer felt the tension with the White House. They weren't playing a role, as far as I could tell, leaving Iran to the State Department. No voice from Brzezinski or Sick came down. I pretty much had my own way.[14]

When interviewed for this book, Precht stated that 'Following the success of the Revolution the open warfare between the White House and State came to an end. We [the State Department's Iran desk and the embassy in Tehran] were left pretty much on our own to implement the Presidential decision to try to build a new relationship with Iran.'[15] Precht's immediate superiors were Assistant Secretary Harold Saunders and Deputy Assistant Secretary of State for Near East and South Asian affairs Bill Crawford. Neither Saunders nor Crawford had any expertise on Iran and generally deferred to Precht on Iranian matters. Precht described his own knowledge as inadequate, and, reading the communiqués from Washington to embassy officials in Tehran, one is struck by the constant requests for the most basic of information. Seven months after the Revolution, Harold Saunders admitted, 'We know very little about Iranian groups' and 'We need to know more'.[16] On 29 June 1979, Deputy Secretary of State Warren Christopher cabled a wish list to embassy staff, including CIA officers, outlining all the information they lacked. The list was illustrative of the level of reporting available to policy-makers.

1. Political relationships within the Revolutionary leadership

    a) Who are the potent figures within and without official positions? Whom should we watch as comers? We need bios.
    b) What are the political alliances and strengths of Amir-Entezam and Sabaghian? We know relatively little of either.

2. What is the popular impression of Bazargan? How is he regarded by various key groups? Does he have any rivals?
3. We do not have a very good fix on Taleghani, his entourage and his links to others in the religious and secular establishments.
4. Designation of specific political and economic areas to watch.
5. How is the US perceived? What actions or inactions since mid-February have hurt us? What could we do better?
6. Reports of military conversations are most helpful. From time to time it would be useful to summarize, depicting trends, for each of the services. Police and gendarmerie info also valuable
7. We appreciate extremely valuable economic reporting. Regular coverage of market basket prices and shortages. How are the unemployed making ends meet?
8. What are the activities, strengths, plans of liberal democrats (Matin-Daftary), National Front (Sanjabi), left guerrillas (Fadeyeen), various mujahdeen groups, pro-Shah elements?
9. How fare the provinces, particularly harvest, food availability?
10. What is [the] status of efforts to close down, sell off or ship out military facilities or equipment?
11. What can you gather of perceptions of key embassies? What are the Soviets up to?
12. What is the situation with the Universities, NIRT, other media?
13. Status of planning for the constitution and elections
14. What have PGOI/Khomeini done on amnesty for military policy, others.[17]

Regardless of historical baggage, cultural bias, or faults within the analytical mindset of US officials, there were some significant practical obstacles to answering these questions. Before the Revolution, approximately 1,400 official staff had been attached to the embassy. Nearly all the senior Iranian staff had a green card and left Iran shortly before or after the Revolution.

By November 1979, security concerns and political uncertainty had reduced personnel to about the mid-1970s. Even this represented a substantial increase, with the number of personnel having dropped to about 40 in the wake of the first embassy seizure in February 1979. This modest expansion of the American diplomatic community was described by William Philips as a 'direct outgrowth of the Carter administration's decision to rapidly improve relations with the embryonic Islamic Republic'.[18] The US had made only very limited inroads into staffing the embassy with Persian speakers, repeating a major failure of the Pahlavi era.[19] If a full-strength embassy had failed to grasp adequately the changing realities in Iran in 1978 and early 1979, it was difficult to see how an ever-shrinking one could do much better.

Following attacks on US officials in Tabriz, the consulates in Shiraz and Tabriz were manned by Iranian employees in partial contact with Americans. Movement around Tehran was extremely restricted; the embassy compound was subject to regular demonstrations and until August inhabited by a band of ill-disciplined militants. Although senior US officials at the embassy had few troubles accessing the PGOI, they had little contact amongst the clerics. The vast majority of time spent by the overwhelmed embassy staff was spent doing mundane consular work: processing visas, resolving contractual disputes between US and Iranian companies, arranging visits for private and public American citizens, and seeking clarifications from various parties in Iran's dysfunctional bureaucracy. Even by November 1979, the State Department described the embassy's primary occupation as 'cleaning up the residue from our relationship with the previous regime'.[20]

Mixed signs and the beginning of intelligence sharing

February saw chaotic scenes in Iran's cities. Clashes between military units and various revolutionary forces were endemic, and staff inside the US embassy slept to the sound of automatic gunfire punctuating the night. Those suspected of ties to the former regime were rounded up and often subjected to summary and brutal justice. Ethnic tension flared up as Kurdish, Arab, and Azeri groups all tried to establish positions of strength that they presumed would be advantageous when dealing with a central authority that was yet to emerge. Looting was widespread and various military units simply opened up their arsenals. Amidst the chaos, the need to protect sensitive military material superseded any diplomatic priorities. To this end, Major Neil Robinson, working for the Defense Intelligence Agency, was tasked with preventing surveillance equipment used to monitor Soviet facilities from falling into unfriendly hands. At the same time, navy Commander Donald Sharer was trying to locate and destroy instructional manuals for F-14 defence systems amongst the abandoned US and Iranian military facilities.[21] Vance instructed US diplomats to remind the Iranians of a shared interest in protecting the 'security and integrity' of this equipment, and their accompanying manuals, from access 'by those who may be working for unfriendly foreign powers'.[22] According to some reports, it was too late; extremely sensitive manuals for the Phantom training jet were stolen by a Tudeh sympathiser and passed to Moscow.[23]

Yet amongst these tumultuous scenes, some positive signs emerged from the Bazargan government. On 7 February, Bazargan was asked by a Greek journalist: 'One way or another you will depend on the United States since you must obtain arms from somewhere.' Bazargan's response again hinted at his own general belief that it was ultimately in Iran's interest to restore good relations with America. 'Up to a point you are right', he responded. 'In establishing an era of equal relations with the United States, I do not see why we should not buy weapons from it.'[24] Requests for food supplies and spare parts gave succour to the belief that the US could, as it hoped, make the best out of a difficult situation.[25] A succession of promising announcements soon followed. Bazargan's promise that US technicians, including military advisors, would be re-invited to their old jobs seemed to suggest that a degree of continuity, even in potentially sensitive areas, was still possible. Khomeini, whose move to Qom had further inspired confidence in Washington, seemed to confirm this by sending a personal representative to Vance in order to express a spirit of cooperation and, more importantly, seek assurances that the US would be supportive of a stable government.[26]

Soon after, Yazdi, repeating in public what he had told Precht and Cottam in private, announced that relations with the Soviets would be cordial at best and that Iran desired improved relations with America as long as they reflected the changes in Iran. The US construed even the traumatic but brief seizure of the US embassy by left-wing militants on Valentine's Day as a positive development. The embassy's swift and effective rescue by forces loyal to Khomeini and under the personal command of Yazdi was seen as a positive statement of the new regime's intent to preserve sound relations. So much so that Carter publicly declared these positive developments at a press conference on 27 February, declaring that the new government 'desires a close working and friendly relationship with the US'.[27] Yet it was not all good news; on 21 February, Iran announced that the US would not be permitted to continue operating its secret surveillance installations in northern Iran. Nevertheless, the fact that the Iranian government allowed these operations to close quietly was evidence of some of moderation. 'They didn't make a big stink about it', wrote Henry Precht.[28]

About this time, Naas began making the rounds of the PGOI's ministers, although he made the conscious decision to leave Bazargan to last, recognising his preoccupation with trying to extend his control over the new government. Naas' pitch to the new ministers illustrates both his personal sincerity in accepting the Revolution, but also the orthodox Cold War lines upon which the 'new' beginning for US relations was to be drawn.

Naas began his meetings with all the new ministers with the same opening gambit:

> We understand that the kind of relationship we had with his majesty, will be quite different, we still believe that there are sufficient common interests between the two countries that over time we can develop a new relationship, we hope you share the same hope. The Soviet Union is still there, the Tudeh are still there; regarding these great problems of security, if we can be helpful, fine, but we know life has changed.[29]

It was the internal security situation, however, that worried many of Iran's new leaders. Khomeini's authority was being tested by ethnic groups and rival groups, most notably Ayatollah Shariatmadari and the Muslim People's Republic Party (MPRP). Iran's descent into chaos and even civil war, as the intelligence community had consistently asserted, would establish the ideal conditions for Soviet meddling. As Barzagan's government continued to struggle to assert its authority, Sullivan added his concerns:

> We doubt that Bazargan, as distinct from the larger Islamic Revolutionary movement, will be able to assert his government's authority or to see its program through to successful completion. Rather, it seems more likely that the coming months will be dominated by potential contenders for power preparing themselves for the possibility of eventual armed confrontation.[30]

The threats facing the provisional government reinforced some of the more negative perceptions it held of American intentions. As ethnic violence spread amongst the Azeris and in Khuzestan and Kurdistan, some strongly suspected US encouragement. The US looked to intelligence sharing as a tangible demonstration of America's goodwill towards the new regime whilst refocussing the government on the Soviet threat. On 23 March 1979, Thomas Blanton, a member of the NSC responsible for South Asian affairs, informed deputy National Security Advisor David Aaron of this intention. Blanton reported that he had tasked the CIA and State Department with preparing a presentation that Ambassador Sullivan would give to Bazargan highlighting their mutual concern for Afghanistan. Blanton reported thus:

> We have also tasked State and CIA to develop a presentation for Bill Sullivan to give to Barzagan which will highlight our concern about Afghanistan, brief him on what we know of Soviet activities, and in the process point out to him how much of this information is obtained and the need we have for Iranian cooperation in that regard.[31]

It seemed an opportune moment to establish a foundation for cooperation. In mid-March, Persian-speaking Afghan Shias in Herat, close to the Iranian border, had risen in revolt. The rebels slaughtered those members of the Afghan army who did not defect to their side, killed dozens of Soviet advisors, and held the city for a week. Kabul accused Iran of encouraging the revolt because of a speech made by Ayatollah Shariatmadari and an attack on the Afghan consulate in Mashad.[32] The pro-Soviet Afghan government mounted a sustained propaganda campaign, alleging some 4,000 Iranians disguised as Afghan migrant workers had crossed the border to aid the revolt, whilst also using the allegation of external meddling to appeal to Moscow for military assistance. Relations between Tehran and Kabul had plummeted to an all-time low. In May 1979, Naas met Bazargan, with the Prime Minister asking for US intelligence assessments of issues relevant to Iranian interests. A few days later, Naas sent Deputy Prime Minister Amir Entezam, whom the US had the most productive relationship with amongst the PGOI, a letter containing two US reports. The topic of both was Soviet activities in Afghanistan.[33]

The sharing of intelligence was not just a strategy to reinforce their common sense of purpose in confronting the communist threat. The US aimed to convince the Iranian leadership of the value of retaining the signals intelligence (SIGINT) capability it had built up in northern Iran. The satellites, spy planes, and listening posts that were dotted in these isolated locations were vital to the US, not only to monitor Soviet intentions in Afghanistan and Iran, but also to ensure it was complying with the SALT II treaties. There was also, as Bruce Laingen stated in a memo, a 'principle involved in our continuing inability to gain access to what is ours'.[34]

Blanton wanted to convince the Iranians that these facilities were equally vital to Iran's national security. It was not entirely undesirable for the Iranians to believe that their cooperation with the US was relying to some extent on Iranian cooperation. This would massage the egos of the vehemently anti-imperialist Iranians. Blanton showed a rare appreciation that the US should avoid giving the Iranians the impression of being pawns in America's Cold War strategy. Blanton reported to Aaron that

> The Soviets have indeed run afoul of resurgent Islam. There is nothing that we need do to emphasize the fact and, indeed, it would be taken amiss if we appeared to be exploiting the Islamic angle for 'Cold War' purposes.[35]

The timing of these overtures was in fact poor. Emphasising Iran's vulnerability to the Soviet threat at a time when the regime was preoccupied by the much graver ethnic disturbances did little to persuade the Iranians that America shared similar strategic priorities. Although the US offered to provide intelligence on 'external' support for these disturbances, in reality US intelligence had little knowledge of the groups involved. Gary Sick saw first-hand the limited interest of the Iranians in Soviet movements in Afghanistan when he met with Bazargan's nephew, Morteza. It was testament to Washington's desperation for contacts that Morteza, a young man of limited influence, was considered of sufficient importance to receive a briefing from a senior member of the NSC.[36] Sick spent most of the meeting denying US involvement in the disturbances whilst reiterating that US intelligence could be helpful in providing intelligence on external support for internal subversion as well as Soviet activities in Afghanistan and along the northern Iranian border. Bazargan's response was disappointing. He acknowledged the offer of intelligence sharing but 'showed no interest whatsoever in Soviet military activities across the border'. Bazargan was also 'absolutely convinced that the Soviets are not involved in the Kurdish, Khuzestan activities which were foremost in his mind'.[37]

April 1 saw the official declaration of the Islamic Republic (IRI). The announcement followed approval by a huge majority in a nationwide referendum. Many Azeri, Kurdish, and Turkoman areas had boycotted it, however, and the establishment of the IRI did little to diminish Iran's ethnic strife. The White House was also distracted, still firmly focussed on implementing the peace deal that had been signed between Egypt and Israel on 14 March. Embassy staff in Tehran still lacked any real direction from senior State Department officials as it responded to Iran's two main concerns: visas for Iranian students and, more importantly, the resumption of supply of military spare parts Iran had paid for but were yet to be delivered. Things were made harder when Ambassador Sullivan, who was felt to be too closely associated with the previous regime, left Tehran on 6 April. It was at this point that Naas, now head of the US mission, finally met with Prime Minister Bazargan. He began the conversation by explaining that he had not yet called on Bazargan because he respected that he had been very busy. Naas knew that the Prime Minister would have heard about his meetings with the other ministers, where he had emphasised the mutual Soviet threat, and hoped that he had been able to use this time to think about the new US–Iranian relationship. That relationship, Naas understood, would be different, but that the two countries still maintained significant overlapping interests. Bazargan agreed but cautioned that his life would become very hard if Carter ever allowed the Shah to live in the US. Naas would only meet Bazargan three more times, preferring to conduct business with Deputy Prime Minister (and then Foreign Minister) Yazdi; he established a good working relationship with some. As the political environment became more febrile, and the moderates became more anxious of appearing too close to the Americans, Yazdi and Naas learnt to communicate indirectly and informally. Naas learnt the signals he was being sent without Yazdi having to exceed the safe parameters in which their discussions often had to operate.[38]

Washington still lacked an ambassador in Tehran and soon identified and designated Walter Cutler to replace Sullivan. Cutler seemed well suited to the job; he had experience of Iran, having served as the US consul in Tabriz in the mid-1960s, but was not closely associated with the Shah. Cutler had been a political officer in Saigon at the height of the Vietnam War, acting as special assistant for the State Department during the negotiations that ended the conflict there. He was thus used to directing embassy work and conducting careful negotiations in a difficult security environment.

Events inside Iran were, however, conspiring against the US. Ayatollah Motahhari, one of the most vocal clerical critics of Marxism, was gunned down by apparently leftist assassins on 1 May. Motahhari's assassination had, in the view of one biographer, been caused by the publication of an article entitled 'Materialism in Iran', in which he strongly criticised those Islamic groups who were influenced by Marxism.[39] Motahhari had himself predicted his assassination and cited his article as the primary cause. The attack by the militant leftist group did not encourage the clerics to seek any assistance from the US in security matters; instead, it convinced them that the increasingly bloody campaign by Furqan and Feda'i was being directed by the US. Khomeini himself used the term 'The American Left' in his denouncements of these terrorist groups.[40]

US officials considered it self-evident that undermining the new regime would not be in America's interests and found such conspiratorial attitudes infuriating. Yet, the reason that allegations of US collusion with leftist groups gained traction was because it had precedent, a fact that pro-Soviet propaganda radio broadcasting was quick to repeat. In 1953, CIA agent provocateurs had posed as rioting members of the Tudeh in order to rally hard-line opposition to a simulated communist threat in Iran. In an interview with Lebanese newspaper *Al Mustaqbal*, leading cleric Ayatollah Montazeri claimed that the US had not accepted the Revolution and was supporting counter-revolutionary groups who posed as leftists:

> We believe that not all communists and leftists in Iran are what they claim to be. We believe that many of them are communists and leftists created by the United States. As was the case under the Mossadeq Administration when the 'oil Tudeh' was created to strike at the movement of Dr Mossadeq, the United States is now creating these leftists to frighten the people against communism. Fearing the Iranian Revolution and its impact on the neighboring countries, the United States has resorted to creating (counter-revolutionary) organizations.[41]

The implication of Montazeri's analysis was as significant as his specific allegation of American collusion with leftist terrorists. It was a signal that the clerical elite would reject any US engagement that emphasised the communist threat: not just on the basis that the threat was an artificial construction, but that it was ultimately a strategy aimed at subverting the Revolution. Any approach on this basis could not, as the US suggested, represent an interest in Iran's security or an acceptance of the Revolution. This attitude would also have serious ramifications for the Bazargan government's efforts to repair relations with the US. In an interview published in the Kuwaiti newspaper *Ar-Ra'y al-'Am*, Montazeri accused Bazargan of not supporting the Revolution and claimed he had 'struck up a friendship with the United States to fight communism'.[42]

The US underestimated the extent to which anti-communist engagement would run up against Iranian historical memory. US diplomats were if anything too visible and failed to take account of the climate of anti-Americanism. Shaul Bakhash, a journalist working in Iran in 1979, remembers one clumsy attempt by a US diplomat to contact him.

> He had just come in from the United States and said can you come over and see me at the embassy. I said I can't come near the embassy. And he says well I'll come over and see you. I said don't come near my house. Don't telephone. But I was astonished that he didn't sense how much hostility there was in Iran towards the US and how risky it would be for any Iranian to show up at the embassy or to have an embassy car drive up to an Iranian's house.[43]

To try and lessen the damage, Vance sent a letter to Foreign Minister Yazdi restating his country's desire to restore relations on an equitable basis based on mutual respect. Unfortunately, Vance's work was entirely undone when on 17 May the US Senate passed a resolution condemning the Iranian regime's persecution of political opponents.

The Javits resolution

Since February 1979, the American media's presentation of the new regime had become increasingly problematic for those attempting to build confidence in Tehran. Having been broadly critical of the Shah during his final months and cautiously supportive of Khomeini, the summary executions and the brutal suppression of minorities had quickly turned the media anti-Khomeini. By May, the excesses of the Revolution were the object of sustained criticism in the US media.[44] On 17 May, a Congressional resolution sponsored by the Jewish American Senator Jacob Javits, a close friend of the Shah's sister, was harshly critical of the persecution of the Iranian Jewish community. It was predictably seen by hard-line elements as evidence of a 'Zionist' conspiracy against the Revolution.[45]

Whilst the PGOI was less concerned with conspiracy theories, they certainly shared the radicals' resentment of the naked hypocrisy of the resolution. Yazdi lodged his formal complaint through a letter to Vance, noting that 30 years of the Shah's detention, torture, and murder of the opposition had warranted not a single Senate resolution. Yazdi warned that resolutions 'concerning the penalization of the former regime's criminals' did not conform to Vance's own claim that his government had 'no intention to interfere in Iran's internal affairs'.[46] In view of this, Yazdi warned, the Iranian government, 'under strong pressure from the nation's public opinion', had felt compelled to make 'revisions in its ties with the United States government in the direction of limiting them'. Following the Iranian media's announcement of the resolution, again skilfully manipulated by the pro-Tudeh radio broadcasts of the National Voice of Iran, there began a series of large demonstrations against the embassy.[47] The chancery's flag was torn down and the walls riddled with anti-American graffiti.

The State Department was aware of the damage the resolution would cause to its efforts and had lobbied strongly against its passing. Charlie Naas laments that 'the Javits resolution was the coup de grace to my efforts in Tehran'.[48] Having believed he had been making some progress, towards engagement, including an agreement for a new ambassador (to be Walter Cutler), Naas' will was broken. Having endured months of psychological stress, including being threatened with execution during the Valentine's Day embassy seizure, with frenzied crowds again massing outside the embassy, Naas requested a transfer.[49]

US embassy officials tried, though with little success, to 'explain the complexities of the Iranian Revolution to the congress and press'.[50] To some extent, this was a case of the Carter administration's human rights policy coming home to roost. It was difficult for the State Department to persuade moralpolitikers within the Democratic Party that the politically expedient engagement with Iran should override criticism of the human rights situation there. Once Khomeini was informed of the Senate's decision, he instructed Bazargan to reject Washington's nomination of Cutler. This only exacerbated the situation further by making the Senate more hostile to Tehran and resistant to any further attempts to send an ambassador. After several weeks, it was decided to send Bruce Laingen as chargé, but with the rank of ambassador. In Laingen's own words, this was to convey the message that he was 'a senior type, sent out there to resume the discussions with the authorities'.[51]

Another interpretation of Cutler's rejection was voiced by Iranian state-controlled radio, one that demonstrated how the hardliners' political mobilisation of conspiracy was grounded in elements of historical reality. Just as Montazeri's allegation that leftist guerrillas were actually American agents, the allegation that Cutler was one of Washington's 'international experts on plots' was a distortion. But again it gained some traction because there were elements of reality within the allegation. In this case, it was Cutler's previous assignment as ambassador to Zaire that was presented as evidence of America's instinctive counter-revolutionary tendencies and support despotic rulers. Despite Carter's emphasis on human rights, Zaire's brutal and corrupt dictator, Mobutu Sese Seko, continued to receive nearly half the foreign aid allocated to sub-Saharan Africa.[52] When Mobutu was challenged by separatist fighters in Shaba province, during Cutler's assignment, Carter repeated Mobutu's erroneous claims of Soviet involvement and Washington provided transportation and logistical support to the French and Belgian paratroopers that were deployed to aid Mobutu against the rebels.[53] It did not take a master propagandist to take advantage of the situation. Radio Tehran declared that

> The US government, which did not want or cannot accept the reality and originality of the Islamic Revolution in Iran, wanted this time also to plan for its ambitions by sending Cutler, one of its international experts on plots to Iran under the guise of ambassador to carry our special missions in Iran. Specialists in political affairs know well that Cutler played a main role in the Zaire plot.[54]

After Cutler's rejection, it was clear that re-nominating an ambassador would be problematic even if diplomatic conditions in Iran improved. Warren Christopher was forced to instruct embassy officials in Tehran that, even if the government managed to convince Khomeini to accept a new nomination, they should 'discourage speculation on [the] timing of any arrangement'.[55] Christopher warned that 'it may be some time until the Senate is receptive to another nomination'. The situation was particularly frustrating as Christopher at the same time asked Laingen to convey Washington's deep appreciation of a favourable statement made by Entezam shortly before the resolution was announced.

Bruce Laingen's assignment at the embassy was supposed to be temporary and not anticipated to run for more than 6 weeks. As such Laingen never met with President Carter, but received the following instructions from senior officials in the State Department. First, he was to try and enhance the security arrangements at the embassy compound, with the removal of the 30-man squad of Revolutionary Guards a priority.[56] In charge of this group was Mashallah Kashani, a disagreeable and ill-disciplined individual who treated the compound as his own fiefdom, using parts of it for interrogating a variety of unfortunate alleged enemies of the Revolution.[57] Laingen was also tasked with improving morale amongst the beleaguered and socially isolated embassy community, though upon his arrival in Tehran he was surprised to find morale remarkably high. Laingen was also charged with rehabilitating the consular function. A third responsibility was to continue Charlie Naas' work putting 'some order into sorting out our military supply relationships with this new regime'.[58]

By June, Washington was seriously concerned by the limited progress being made in improving its position with the Iranian regime. Henry Precht was asked by Vance to draft a letter of instruction to the embassy in Tehran. The memo asked senior officials to convey to either Entezam or Yazdi, considered the strongest supporters of engagement within the PGOI, the following message:

> We are disturbed by the deterioration in recent weeks in our relations. We had hoped to set our relationship with Iran on a course of steady, gradual improvement. Ambassador Cutler's appointment was planned as a significant stage in this process.[59]

Gary Sick argues that his opposite number in the State Department, Henry Precht, 'never wavered' in his opinion that the Bazargan government was steadily gaining strength.[60] Sick adds that Precht's optimism was questioned by many others, even in the State Department. Ambassador Sullivan, in his final report, gave the grim assessment that neither the US nor PG had any hope of influencing Khomeini: 'Even the cabinet has great difficulty in getting his undivided attention. Directly influencing him, in sum, is virtually impossible.'[61] Sullivan gloomily predicted that in the months ahead Iran 'will be a virtual dictatorship' led by a man 'untutored in world affairs' firmly convinced that 'we are interfering and attempting to undo the Revolution'. John Stempel was equally pessimistic, informing his superiors in Washington that Khomeini would 'probably welcome a complete break in diplomatic relations with the US'.[62]

The CIA and State Department's Bureau of Intelligence Research's assessment, however, was that no group had yet to emerge from the power struggle as dominant, and that Khomeini faced many threats, especially from rival Ayatollah Shariatmadari. The US political officer in Isfahan, David McGaffey, who had himself been beaten up by a mob in late January, predicted increasing violence and chaos, with the result being theocracy ruling over a 'diminished Iran' or a 'leftist takeover'.[63] In light of this, both Sullivan and Naas opined that it was in America's interest that Khomeini, whose health was failing, remained in power.[64]

By mid-June, however, Khomeini and the Islamic Republican Party made further political gains.[65] The PGOI's authority had just been dealt another severe blow through the establishment of the Revolutionary Guard.[66] Gary Sick describes this as a 'political masterstroke', enabling the fundamentalists to bypass the PG and rule the country through an alternative system.[67] This built on the system of *komitehs*, or revolutionary councils, that had already been established for the same purpose. The PGOI increasingly found that its directives were ignored, were nullified, or had to be 'negotiated with each local group'.[68] Washington's faith in the ability of the PGOI to manage foreign policy, something the US had pinned their hopes to, was rapidly eroding. In one episode, Charles Naas reported back to Washington that

Sadegh Ghotbzadeh, managing director of National Iranian Radio and Television, 'may have been making foreign policy' without the knowledge of the office of the Prime Minister.[69]

Reaching out to Khomeini

In his widely read examination of US policy in this period, James Bill rails against the failure to establish relations with Khomeini as symptomatic of a wider failure to accept or acknowledge the Revolution.[70] It is both fair and accurate to point to a gross underestimation of Khomeini's intentions and more importantly capability to take an active role in the day-to-day running of the country. As noted earlier, this was a widely held view within the State Department and was also the assessment Brzezinski had provided Carter in January 1979.[71] This was also, according to the CIA, the expectation of many of Iran's Arab neighbours.[72] At a meeting convened by the State Department at the end of March, Cottam repeated his earlier judgement that Khomeini's undeniably hostile attitude to America would remain only a theoretical influence on Iran's foreign policy.[73] Gary Sick's view is that Henry Precht's overly optimistic view of the Bazargan government, which was accepted by Vance and Saunders, obstructed the true picture of the duality of power in Iran.[74] According to Babak Ganji, the State Department was slow to acknowledge the emergence of Khomeini, and only in late August did Laingen report that 'Khomeini and his entourage called the shots'.[75] Laingen was writing in the immediate aftermath of the election of the Assembly of Experts; thus he had structural evidence of institutions capable of extending Khomeini's authority.

Yet the suggestion that Laingen's report marked an epiphany in US assessments is misleading. The State Department was not particularly slow to recognise that the Bazargan government would struggle to impose its control over the reins of power. As early as mid-March, Sullivan had himself expressed grave doubts that the Bazargan government would be able to 'assert his government's authority or to see its program through to successful completion'.[76] Naas had in June described the government as 'beholden to Khomeini, who dictates the Revolutionary committee system'.[77]

In the same month, Vance noted: 'We are under no illusions about the difficulty of developing a better relationship with the PGOI. Until the PGOI has a better grip on the political and economic systems, there is little prospect that we can deal effectively with the leadership on the many problems on our agenda.'[78] Charlie Naas reported in July his impression that the 'Government is composed of essentially decent men, but they have little or no power; they are beholden to Khomeini'.[79] Khomeini himself was in poor health but Naas advised that policy should be based around the expectation that he would be around for a while. In fact, given America's fear of instability, it was hoped that Khomeini's health would endure. Naas admitted that

'His death now could throw this country into deeper turmoil; his charisma is one of the few elements keeping the society from complete anarchy'.

The problem was that even when the US knew fully well that Khomeini was the dominant figure in Iranian politics, it was the Bazargan government they turned to for advice on the practical steps Washington could take to improving America's standing with more radical elements. They did not recognise that this strategy weakened the moderates' position with the hard-liners. To that end, Warren Christopher advised the embassy to 'welcome the views of the prime minister and foreign minister on the practical steps which we and the government of Iran might take to convince Khomeini and other key leaders that these repeated charges of US interference are not only false but are contrary to our mutual interest in building a new relationship'.[80]

The State Department's urging of the US not to give up on the PGOI did not reflect an unawareness of the severe limits placed on its authority. It reflected their belief that the PGOI was capable of influencing Khomeini and thus Washington's only realistic link to the Ayatollah. The US did also make some belated attempt to establish links with Khomeini. By April, senior officials in the State Department, aware that Khomeini had met with representatives of many other countries including the Soviet Union, resolved to make their own diplomatic overture. As a first step, Naas was asked by Henry Precht to request an audience with Khomeini, which Naas did not relish but nevertheless approached Bazargan and Yazdi to set up. The second step was supposed to be a special message to be carried to Khomeini by a newly appointed ambassador.

Bazargan was successful in persuading Khomeini to receive a US delegation, and agreed to accompany Naas to the meeting. The Javits amendment then led to Khomeini rejecting Cutler's nomination, cancelling the meeting with Naas, and placing a moratorium on any cleric meeting embassy staff.[81] Despite this setback, the State Department pondered the idea of appointing a special emissary to establish a working relationship with Khomeini's office. On 1 June, they asked the embassy to sound out 'whether this would be an appropriate moment for such a mission' and how such an emissary would be received.[82] In one of Naas' final reports as head of the US mission in Tehran, he informed Vance that 'I do not favour the despatch of an emissary to Khomeini unless PGOI takes the initiative, an emissary would have little or no opportunity nor chance of affecting his mind-set and would it be seen as further knuckling down to his brand of extremism'. Naas added: 'We should not become identified with the kind of state and policies Khomeini is creating and which are unlikely to endure over the long term.'

The deeper misread was not an underestimation of clerical opposition to the Bazargan government; it was the belief that fundamentalist influence in Iran's foreign relations was transitory and thus it was dangerous to erode the confidence of the secular leaders by pursuing a parallel track with the clerics.

Although Khomeini's ultimate authority on policy matters was accepted by summer 1979, the notion that Khomeini's hard-line view was unsustainable in the longer term remained widely held. Harold Saunders, just weeks before the US embassy was seized on November 4, predicted that sooner or later the clerics would have to 'compromise their Islamic principles to meet popular needs' and this would inevitably mean they would seek help from westernised officials.[83] This suggested that it would be wiser to enhance links with more moderate forces that would inevitably wrestle control of Iran's foreign policy. 'The main modernizing thrust of Iran's development will inevitably over time weaken Khomeini and the clerics', predicted Saunders. He therefore advised against appearing to 'embrace Khomeini and the clerics at the expense of our secular friends'. There were also worries at how such a meeting would play in the US. The embassy was eventually cautioned not to request a meeting with Khomeini and, if it was suggested, they should seek instruction first.[84]

It appears that rather than being unaware of the duality of power in Tehran, the US actually directed policy in recognition of it. The concentration of America's diplomatic effort on the Bazargan government was partly the inevitable result of the impossibility of reaching Khomeini.[85] It also seems reasonable to suggest that there were few Americans suitably qualified to connect with Khomeini in a manner cognisant of his cultural or religious world view. Yet, in the absence of any evidence suggesting that these 'unworldly' clerics would eventually lose power, US support for the PGOI must be equally located within a secular, technocratic, and modernist belief system institutionally and educationally entrenched within America's political elite. As much as Khomeini clearly had little interest in meeting US officials after the Javits agreement, two points should be weighed against this. First, calls for greater contact with Khomeini had been impeded since late 1978, and only in May 1979, almost 5 months after the US accepted the Ayatollah's return to Iran was inevitable, was an approach mooted. Second, US officials were being told that shunning the clerics in favour of the moderates was a tactical error.

America's failure to reach Khomeini was considered a major error by former MP Rahmatollah Moghaddam-Maraghehie. Moghaddam was balancing the conflicting demands of his role as Governor of East Azerbaijan, member of the Assembly of Experts, opponent of clerical rule, and CIA informant. In late October, Moghaddam met Henry Precht, who was on a fact-finding mission in Tehran, and strongly urged a US representative to call on Khomeini as soon as possible 'no matter what the difficulties'.[86] Should Khomeini suddenly die before meeting the US, he warned, 'Even moderates who do not fully support Khomeini will criticize the US and say that the lack of a meeting was because of the US' lack of acceptance of the Revolution'. Richard Cottam was also urging talks with Khomeini's clerical clique. Precht proceeded to meet the two senior clerics closest to Khomeini, ayatollahs Montazeri and Beheshti. Both had refused to meet the US head of mission, Bruce Laingen, but now met Precht presumably because they interpreted Khomeini's edict on meeting Americans to extend only to embassy staff. Beheshti was considered by Precht to be 'wise', and when Precht asked if exiled Iranians could return, he replied they would be welcome as long as they accepted the Revolution. Montazeri struck Precht as less wise; he informed Precht that he had been happy when Carter had been elected as he was in prison and had heard he was interested in human rights. According to Precht, he blamed the un-fulfilment of that ambition on 'the Jews'.

Back in Washington, the Carter administration was still trying to manage the fallout of the discovery of a Soviet combat brigade in Cuba. In a memorandum to Carter, Brzezinski writes that 'you may not want to hear this, but I think that the increasingly persuasive perception here and abroad is that in US–Soviet relations, the Soviets are increasingly assertive and the US more acquiescent. State's handling of the Soviet brigade negotiations is a case in point.' Brzezinski recommended that 'in the future, we will have to work for greater White House control'.[87] In this context, it was perhaps inevitable that the State Department's handling of Iran policy, and US–Iranian relations more broadly, was compared to Iranian–Soviet relations. What a retrospective analysis reveals, however, is that US assessments of Moscow's policy in Iran bore little resemblance to Brzezinski's characterisation of an assertive Soviet policy in areas of vital strategic importance.

Comparing US–Iranian relations to Soviet–Iranian relations

Despite complaints about Soviet anti-American propaganda in the early days of the Revolution, many US analysts, particularly those inside Iran, seriously doubted the ability of the Soviets to ingratiate themselves with the new regime. In early March, the US embassy in Tehran admitted that 'Undoubtedly, political turmoil in Iran presents a temptation to the Soviets to fish in troubled waters'. Nevertheless, Moscow would face significant obstacles in translating this into real political gain:

> There is greater historical precedent for suspicion of Russian motives in Iran than there is ours. The fundamental conservatism of Iranian society and the hold of Islam on much of the popular, too, are factors which work against rapid growth of Soviet influence here. The Soviets might try to gain a foothold through support of dissident ethnic minorities, but nothing could be better calculated to unite the Persian majority against them.[88]

The CIA also listed an impressive list of constraints on Moscow's policy, not only in Iran, but also in the wider region.[89] Chief amongst these were a desire to avoid a political or military confrontation with the US, the preference of most states for Western hard currency and technology, and the general anti-communist outlook of virtually all Arab nations – even those with close ties with the USSR. There was also a contradiction between Moscow's use of arms sales to build relations with Iran's Arab neighbours (and mortal enemy, Iraq), and its efforts to seek stable relations with the Iranian regime. The CIA also observed a major tension between the desire to avoid a major confrontation in the region and the need for tension to produce a market for the military sales it could use to cement links. Managing these tensions and exploiting the opportunities arising from instability, without it infecting Soviet territory or diplomacy, were thus perceived to be the key to Soviet success.

Initial fears of Tudeh activity also subsided. The judgement was that the Tudeh did not pose a significant political threat to the PGOI, and much less to the Khomeinists, who could be relied on to exclude from power any group with links to the Soviet Union. It appears the Kremlin took a similarly realistic attitude to the limited influence of the Tudeh in Iran.[90] Even the Tudeh leader Nur-ed-Kianuri admitted in June 1979 that he had no contact with Khomeini.[91] The US embassy had grown to understand by the end of October that the Tudeh were 'lying low, small in number, discredited, fragmented and lacking in charismatic leaders'.[92]

Despite the general view that Khomeini and the PGOI were unlikely to forge close relations with the Soviets, Moscow's relations with the new regime were inevitably compared to Washington's. In this regard, the Soviets were perceived to enjoy several advantages over the Americans.[93] Khomeini's first meeting with a foreign envoy was with the Soviet ambassador Vladimir M. Vinogradov, on 25 February 1979. Khomeini's selection of Mohammed Mokri in May 1979 as his ambassador to Moscow coincided with his rejection of the American ambassadorial nomination, Walter Cutler. Mokri, who was a consistent advocate of strong bilateral relations, travelled back to Tehran shortly after the Senate passed the resolution condemning human rights abuses in Iran.[94] Mokri compared Moscow's commitment to non-intervention and strong fraternal support for the Revolution with the Senate's interference in Iranian affairs. Mokri had been described by the CIA in February 1979 as a member of Khomeini's entourage who had 'spent many years defending the Tudeh Party'.[95]

In Mokri, the Soviets had a close ally. On 9 June, he gave an interview to *Pars*, where he declared: 'We shall have no difficulty with our northern neighbour and relations between Iran and the Soviet Union will become more constructive and more fruitful day by day.'[96] Also repeating the theory that leftist terrorists were inspired by the US, Mokri stressed that Moscow had 'no connection with the secessionist groups that attach themselves to the left or pretend to be leftist, and who are probably the agents of the SAVAK or Israel'. The day after his interview, Mokri met with Khomeini and reportedly held discussions on Iranian–Soviet relations including Caspian shipping, trade, and cultural and political exchanges.[97] The next day, the Soviet ambassador in Tehran was granted an audience with Khomeini himself, with the discussion, extraordinarily, relayed on Tehran Domestic Service. Despite Mokri's groundwork, the meeting soon turned into a bruising affair as Khomeini issued withering attacks on Soviet activities in Iran and Afghanistan.

Khomeini: I do not wish it to be shown that you interfered in Khuzestan. Your policy should be such as to remove misunderstanding. May events not prove that arms are being imported in Iran from the Soviet Union. And, if this is the case, then I have a complaint against you.

Afghanistan is an Islamic country and we are desirous to see that its problems be solved in Islamic ways. Soviet intervention in that country will have an impact on Iran too, and we ask the Soviet Union not to interfere in Afghanistan

Vinogradov: The Soviet people do not understand why the Soviet Union is ranked together with the Western countries. Of course, we know that some people are not informed about certain political issues; they ought to be guided and told which country is a friend and which is a foe. For example, some young people say: the Soviet hand ought to be curtailed; or that the Soviet Union and the United States are both our foes.

I can say with assurance that the Soviet Union does not give arms to anyone in Iran, and we never interfere in the internal affairs of any country

Khomeini: The fact that our young people say neither east nor the west means that neither should interfere in Iran. You ought to prove that the Soviet-made arms are not imported from your country into Iran.

Vinogradov: We do not say that we should be granted privilege, but it is discomforting for our country to be identified as an enemy. Regarding Afghanistan, I would like to ask: is there not a counter-Revolutionary movement in existence against the government?

Khomeini: It appears that you are not much informed about the situation in Afghanistan. I would like to say in general that those in Iran and Afghanistan who act in the name of communists, their works are not beneficial for the Soviet Union. Their activities are more important for the United States than for the Soviet Union.

The present regime in Afghanistan puts great pressure in the name of communism on the people, and we have been informed that about 50,000 people have been killed in Afghanistan, and they have arrested Islamic Ulema there. If Taraki insists on his way, his fate will be like that of Mohammed Reza, and I do not wish the Islamic countries and their relations with the USSR to become unfavourable.[98]

A series of further developments over the summer of 1979 hinted at increasingly strained relations. In June 1979, two members of the Islamic-leftist group Mojahedin-i Khalq (MEK) were arrested for spying for the USSR. One had apparently smuggled a suitcase full of arms through Lebanon and intended to smuggle out two Iraqi communists. The other apparently confessed to having contact with an official at the Soviet embassy. The veracity of this report was undermined somewhat by the unlikely allegation that one of the suspects had arranged introductions between CIA spies and USSR officials.[99] Nevertheless, Iranian officials continued to view Moscow's relationship with leftist and separatist groups with deep suspicion.

There were also signs of Moscow's growing concerns about resurgent Islamic fundamentalism inside the Soviet Union. This was communicated to US officials by a British NATO delegation. The UK considered the likelihood of the Soviet Muslim population being infected by the Islamic revival in Iran as small, principally because of the different social conditions in the USSR and the fact that Shiites accounted for only a small minority of Soviet Muslims.[100] However, their memo cited reports that Radio Tehran's Arabic service had begun broadcasts hostile to the Soviet Union and its treatment of Muslims. It also pointed to allegations of Soviet jamming speeches by Khomeini broadcast in Soviet Azerbaijan as evidence of growing uneasiness in Moscow.[101] The British also noted Soviet attempts to mobilise state-controlled religious authorities against the possible effects of the Islamic revival.

A CIA memorandum written in mid-August outlined a still cautious Soviet policy that recognised the limitations of its influence in Iran. It described relations between Moscow and Tehran as 'cool at best'. According to the memo, the Soviets had accepted as early as May that 'there was little they could do to improve relations or temper Khomeini's anti-Soviet stance'.[102] The CIA concluded that the Soviet's aims were now fourfold:

1. Stabilising the situation on the USSR's southern flank
2. Encouraging the new regime's anti-Western leanings
3. Ensuring the survival of sympathetic, leftist elements, especially the pro-Soviet Tudeh
4. Protecting the USSR's economic interest.

The CIA indicated that the prospects for achieving these goals were mixed. Their analysis concluded that the Soviets had made 'no progress' in economic relations, reporting an overall slowdown in bilateral commercial relations. There seemed little the Kremlin needed to do to encourage the anti-Western leanings of the radical Left or clerics, but the CIA observed that Moscow probably recognised that 'a sizeable pro-US element remains in the government, military and elite'. In regard to preserving the Tudeh, on 20 August, the Revolutionary Guards sealed off both the editorial office of its newspaper *Mardom* and the secretariat of the party central committee.[103]

The CIA analysed that a shift in Soviet policy in Iran had occurred over the summer of 1979. In particular, it observed a greater willingness within Moscow to criticise Khomeini and defend the Tudeh. This shift was the result of Moscow's realisation that such was the limited returns their engagement had achieved, Moscow had less to lose. In this context, the intelligence memorandum noted harsh criticism of Khomeini in the Czech media, which they assumed must have been sanctioned by the Kremlin. For the main part, however, they perceived a holding policy: 'Moscow's activities are probably more aimed at influencing the present regime's policies and at preparing for a post-Khomeini situation than at actually undermining or subverting the government in Tehran.'[104] The lack of evidence for subversive Soviet activities was frustrating to some in the NSC. Paul Henze railed against both the CIA and the State Department for reporting that there was no evidence for Soviet support for Kurdish separatists in Iraq and Iran. Despite having no particular expertise on the region, he denounced the report as 'typical of the flaccid naiveté we have been observing for months in both State and CIA reporting and analysis of this subject'. Henze complained that 'because clear-cut, court admissible evidence does not drop into our laps we smugly maintain that we have no evidence!'[105]

Soviet–Iranian relations continued to decline, lending credence to the assessment that the Soviets were largely giving up on engaging the new regime. *Pravda* quoted a report in *Keyhan* that alleged 'Soviet aircraft had made night flights over Kurdestan and dropped weapons and equipment for the rebels'.[106] Khomeini himself repeated a similar allegation soon after. Following further harsh condemnations of Soviet policy in Afghanistan and continued allegations of support for Kurdish rebels, Soviet media started to become critical of the Iranian government. Reporting of the revolt in Kurdistan became more favourable towards the Kurds. *Pravda* quoted Tehran's *Iran Week* as saying the main cause of the 'fratricidal conflict' was the 'central administration's stubborn reluctance to resolve the problem of granting national and cultural autonomy to the Kurdish population, which took an active part in the overthrow of the monarchy'.[107] On 16 September, Radio Moscow carried a story condemning Iranian reactionaries and religious obscurantists for 'striving to undermine the progressive anti-feudal and anti-imperialist regime in Afghanistan' and 'constantly slandering socialism'.[108]

Relations further soured in September after Iranian radicals purged Iranian universities of leftists. At the same time, the ongoing dispute over the price and delivery of Iranian natural gas was deadlocked, with the Iranians demanding a higher price and the Soviets demanding compensation for the interruption in deliveries earlier in the year. Perhaps most significantly, in early September, well-connected writer Alexander Bovin wrote an article in *Nedelya* describing the Revolution as a 'disaster' whilst also blasting Khomeini's fanatical anti-communism and theocratic vision.[109]

In mid-September, the State Department sought the counsel of its embassy in Moscow as to whether these developments did in fact mark a shift. The response was that 'recent speculation about a shift in Soviet policy towards Iran appears premature. The Soviets are rapidly backpedalling in an effort to disassociate official policy from critical press commentary on Iran.'[110] The embassy cited a number of Soviet messages to support this assessment. Shortly after the Bovin article was published, Soviet Premier Alexey Kosygin issued a message of support to both Bazargan and Khomeini. More importantly, the American embassy reported that the Main Political Authority's Iran desk officer, Kovrigin, had flatly denied any speculation that there had been any change in policy. The US also noted that within a few days of the Bovin article, *Izvestiya* carried a long article from its Tehran correspondent implicitly contradicting most of the objections Bovin had raised and reiterating Soviet support for the revolution and desire for cooperation.

Bovin, the US embassy cable added, had told an American journalist that his opinions were his own and not reflective of government policy. Despite this, they cautioned that embassy officials did not automatically take Bovin's back-pedalling at face value. Bovin was one of Brezhnev's speech writers and the embassy surmised that his article, though not representing a shift in Soviet policy, was an accurate reflection of the Kremlin's increasing irritation at some Iranian policies. They cited the use of force against the Kurds, suppression of the Tudeh and other leftists, support for the Afghan rebels, defaulting on gas delivery contracts, and accusations of Soviet meddling in Iran.[111]

On the whole, the embassy in Moscow described a Soviet analysis of events in Iran which was remarkably similar to Washington's. In their view, the Kremlin would prefer a more secular-orientated Iranian government, but recognised that Khomeini and the clergy would remain dominant in the short term. They also viewed the provisional government as weak. Critically, like the State Department and CIA, the Soviets believed that clerical dominance was transitory, with the elderly Khomeini without an obvious successor.

Resuming military sales: The acid test

After denouncing the Shah's arms build-up as wasteful and inconsistent with the policy of non-alignment of the newly installed Islamic Republic, Ayatollah Khomeini quickly and unilaterally abrogated more than $11 billion of arms contracts.[112] Written into many of these contracts were termination costs, whereby in the event of cancellation the US government agreed to either absorb or redistribute arms built but not delivered. US companies thus were insulated from the immediate damage of Iran's cancellation, and in many cases the US was able to find other buyers, commonly the Israelis and Saudis. In the longer term, however, the loss of America's largest recipient of sophisticated military hardware posed a major blow to Carter's already doubtful goal of reducing America's record 1978 trade deficit of $28.5 billion by up to $8 billion in the year ahead.[113]

All that was retained were contracts covering spare parts and support for weapons systems Iran had already purchased. As noted earlier, Bazargan had immediately recognised the basic reliance of the Iranian armed forces on American hardware and had anticipated the resumption, though on an unknown scale, of this arrangement. The Revolutionary Council was reluctantly forced to accept the need to resolve the issue of spare parts only after sending armed irregular and regular forces to quash the ethnic rebellions in Khuzestan and Kurdistan.[114] With the need for American spares now self-evident, the PGOI attempted to use its access to the US as leverage in its attempts to improve its standing with the radical elements of the Revolutionary Council. Negotiating the resumption of military spares made a strategic case against the continued erosion of the PGOI's authority. It was also a far more tangible demonstration of America's respect for Iran's independence than empty statements that US officials accepted the realities of the new regime. Unlike intelligence sharing or any proposed anti-communist alliance, it would enable Iran to confront security concerns independent of those which correlated with American strategic priorities.

The importance of this issue was never fully understood in terms of the power dynamics between the PGOI and the fundamentalists, but the urgency the PGOI put into resolving the military sales issue was quickly noted by the embassy. Bruce Laingen would note in July 1979 that this had become the 'acid test' of America's commitment to good relations in the eyes of the Iranians.[115] One of the major challenges for embassy staff was responding to the urgency with which the government, untutored in the idiosyncrasies of complex and now defunct payment systems, demanded delivery of the spare parts Iranians had paid for.

On 15 April, Deputy Prime Minister Entezam had complained to Charles Naas, deputy chief of mission in Tehran, of the urgent need for spare parts for Iran's fleet of helicopters. Although most in the embassy supported this, and resumption of military sales generally, the rejection of the Cutler ambassadorship and negative attitudes in the press and Congress made the policy problematic. Naas advised Vance to limit his comments on Iran, but to quietly supply spare parts to the extent permitted by US Congress.[116] Congressmen, especially in the liberal wing of the Democratic Party, were already pushing back against the policy. In late August 1979, the Democratic senator for Wisconsin, William Proxmire, wrote a personal letter to the President voicing his concerns over the resumption of arms sales to the new regime in light of its repression of the Kurds. Proxmire expressed his opposition on the grounds of human rights and not supporting repression of minorities:

> I have noted that there is increasing speculation that the United States may be entertaining the resumption of significant arms sales to Iran. I personally oppose such sales as an instrument of US policy on many grounds, but I want to bring to your attention just one factor that seems to be forcing the issue at the moment. The Iranian regime is seeking renewed arms sales in order to provide military equipment and supplies for the campaign against the Kurdish minorities in Western Iran.[117]

The resumption of arms sales appeared, therefore, to be running up against key commitments Carter had made whilst campaigning for the presidency in 1976. Senator Proxmire, in warning that the resumption of arms sales to Iran would not 'well represent US traditions', was calling Carter on this commitment.

Proxmire need not have worried. The small army of staff that had administered the Shah's military sales had left in the aftermath of the Revolution. Only a skeleton staff of less than a dozen remained. The head of the Military Assistance Group, Maj. Gen. Philip Gast, had stayed on and was doing his best, but Laingen was instructed to put added impetus behind the process 'to get it moving a little faster'.[118] By July, the Carter administration had resolved to resume the sales of 'non-sensitive' military hardware.[119] It was seen by Vance as evidence that relations were 'slowly improving'.[120] Bruce Laingen met with Yazdi on 16 July to discuss military sales. Yazdi had three issues: spare parts Iran had already paid for, parts it wished to order under a new account, and 747 repairables which had been sent to the US but not returned. US officials had long predicted that the symbiotic nature of the US–Iranian arms trade would dictate the terms of any relationship with any Iranian government. It would establish considerable leverage for the US, but under extremely trying conditions.

US officials reported that the reality of Iran's reliance on US equipment had had a marked effect on the Bazargan government. The day after meeting Yazdi, Laingen reported that Yazdi had claimed to be learning to 'temper his Revolutionary idealism required by the exigencies of his job'.[121] Laingen realised that the US would have to both educate the new regime and then act quickly to retain its confidence:

> I am convinced that we are going to have to make an even greater effort than we have heretofore in educating the new Iranian leadership on the intricacies of their country's foreign military sales relationship with US. We must be prepared to provide them with as much detail as they can possibly absorb and then some, and we must be prepared to provide it in a timely fashion.[122]

Because the Iranians did not fully understand the complexities of the payment and delivery systems, they perceived the Americans to be dragging their feet more than they actually were. Nor could they understand why the US government took a 5 percent handling fee on arms sales.[123] Because of the leverage Yazdi felt the issue offered against the fundamentalists, he began pushing the US aggressively. Recognising this urgency, Laingen advised that 'Prompt action on the Interservice or Interagency Support Agreement (IISA) 5.5 million dollar Equipment and Military Supplies (EMS) case and an early resumption of flow of whatever may be left in the pipeline will provide the tangible proof needed that we are not attempting to create obstacles in the path to resolution of outstanding military sales problems'.[124] The Iranians were still impatient for tangible results and, when they were not forthcoming, they complained that the US was only paying 'lip service' to improving relations. Barzagan complained to Laingen that 'Not even a date when we might expect delivery has been given us'.[125] Yazdi started dropping subtle hints that American obstructionism in general might force the Iranians into close cooperation with the Soviet Union.

One explanation may be that the repression meted out by the new regime to those it perceived as opponents made it difficult to make favourable statements about the Revolution. Various domestic voices, including many in Congress, clearly took a dim view of delivering spare parts or resuming any arms sales. This was actually also the case during the previous era. In 1977, Carter, forgoing his own commitment to make arms sales the exception rather than rule amongst his foreign policy tools, had overridden Congressional opposition to sell the Shah seven AWAC airplanes.[126] Domestic politics had presented only limited impediments to US arms sales to Iran during the Shah era, and what opposition there was Carter was willing and able to withstand. The US clearly had to weigh up the wider benefits it received from the Shah: support for the Arab–Israeli peace initiatives, the use of military and intelligence facilities, his insatiable appetite for US technology, generous oil concessions, and support for the other pro-American Gulf monarchies. Yet, the observation still remains that in the Shah's era, strategic imperatives silenced criticism of the regime's behaviour. This was not the case after the Revolution, despite the hard-headed realist approach the US had apparently committed itself to.

5
The CIA and Engagement

Overall, the State Department's assessment of the prospects for engagement was not particularly optimistic by the start of July 1979.[1] The provisional government of Iran (PGOI) was seen as having 'little flexibility in its rough attitude' towards the US. Against a backdrop of strong anti-Americanism led by Khomeini and the Left, foreign minister Yazdi and others were widely accused of being CIA agents. Ironically, the CIA station in Iran was not functioning in any effective sense. The entire CIA detachment had flown out following the first embassy takeover on 14 February. It was not just personnel that were evacuated; many embassy safes and files had been flown to storage in Frankfurt. They would be returned to Tehran in July, in itself a fateful decision given the events that would transpire following the embassy's seizure in November. From March 1979, the Tehran station consisted of several case officers and communicators rotating in and out of Iran on a 'temporary duty' basis.[2] The Directorate of Operations Near East Division, however, quickly began looking ahead to the time when the station could again be staffed with permanently assigned personnel and functioning as a station should – recruiting agents and collecting intelligence.[3] By May, Thomas Ahern had been assigned in Tehran as permanent station chief.

The Shariatmadari connection

One of the first tasks Ahern was given was to continue cultivating links with Khomeini's biggest clerical rival, Ayatollah Shariatmadari. The State Department had followed the competition between Shariatmadari and Khomeini since as early as August 1978.[4] In a memo for Vance describing the political scene in Iran, Harold Saunders advanced the following observation of their rivalry:

> The Shah's strongest opponents come from the Shia religious leadership, split in two apparently cooperating factions, one an ultraconservative

group headed by Khomeini (exiled in Iraq) and the other by the more moderate Shariatmadari of Qom, Iran.[5]

US embassy staff had met Ayatollah Shariatmadari in January 1979 and been pleasantly surprised by his amiable disposition towards America; more encouragingly, he had remarked upon the need for the US to protect Iran from the USSR. Shariatmadari seemed to suggest that American support was necessary to preserve Iran's sovereignty from communist infiltration. Shariatmadari's anti-communist credentials had been further bolstered after he had been singled out by the Afghan government as encouraging the revolt by Shia Afghans in Herat. In April, the CIA had used various contacts, including Iranian-American businessmen travelling in Iran, to meet Shariatmadari and assess what influence he had in Iran.[6] The CIA also gained contacts with the Shariatmadari through Rahmatollah Moghaddam-Maraghehie, who claimed to be close to the Ayatollah. In at least one of these meetings, in early May, it appears that Shariatmadari complained about a lack of information available to him and expressed an interest in receiving US intelligence on not just internal affairs, but of events in the wider region. Ahern reported on 8 May that he believed this offer represented 'excellent potential' and should be followed up.[7] As it became increasingly dangerous for Iranians to be seen with embassy officials, following the sharp deterioration of US–Iranian relations in May, a space opened up for the CIA to pursue engagement through more covert channels.

On 12 May, DCI Turner confirmed to Ahern that US policy in developing relations with Shariatmadari was 'not to split the Islamic Movement but rather to expand the moderate forces within it to the point where they become dominant'.[8] He gave little indication that this would happen soon and urged that any approach to Shariatmadari must be 'as secure as possible'.[9] At the same time Turner added that 'While the goal is simple to define, we are still in search of the mechanism to obtain it'.[10] In attempting to find that mechanism, Ahern looked to identify and cultivate a broad coalition between westernised political liberals, Western-orientated military figures, and moderate religious figures. The glue that was perceived to bind this coalition would be a general suspicion of the Soviet threat, opposition to clerical dominance, and a sense that some kind of modus vivendi with the United States was necessary for intelligence and security purposes. Ahern identified Shariatmadari as the 'most likely catalyst for such as coalition'.[11]

One of five Grand Ayatollahs and a vocal opponent of Khomeini's principle of *velayat-e faqih*, Shariatmadari appeared the best-placed cleric to check Khomeini's gradual consolidation of power. Beyond his theological authority, Shariatmadari enjoyed the support of the Muslim People's Republican Party (MPRP). Although less prominent than the other major moderate party, the Freedom Movement, the MPRP stood for democracy, Muslim-orientated nationalism, and non-clerical rule, as well as ties with the West.[12]

The MPRP was strongest in Azerbaijan and, like large numbers of Azeri, many of its members looked to Shariatmadari as their spiritual leader. In June 1979, his support from the middle classes, the Azeri, the opponents of Khomeini, and by much of the religious establishment in Qom had seen him successfully force Khomeini to live up to his promise for a representative constituent assembly for ethnic minorities. Shariatmadari was at the time attempting three things: to protect his followers centred in Tabriz, to limit Khomeini's constitutional power to vet the popularly elected president, and to see a strong candidate from his supporters contest the presidential election.[13]

Effort was therefore made to establish profitable links with Shariatmadari and his supporters, in particular those inside and associated with the MPRP. The CIA was poorly placed to do so, and the result was a risky, rushed, and arbitrary operation. Several contacts apparently close to Shariatmadari provided extremely questionable information and on several occasions the CIA indicated a heavy degree of scepticism that they were reliable or would not compromise CIA activities. One high-risk contact was a former SAVAK agent identified as Brigadier General Farazian, code-named Janus/13. The CIA considered Farazian a 'political animal' and suspected that he was positioning himself as a possible high-ranking intelligence chief in a possible Shariatmadari coalition. Ahern recognised the danger of such an association and rejected any direct contact between Farazian, the CIA, and Shariatmadari. It was also far from clear exactly what relationship Farazian had with Shariatmadari or another senior cleric, Ayatollah Reza Zanjani, with whom he urged the US to establish links. Although ultimately rejecting Farazian as a direct channel, the CIA continued to view Farazian as a useful source of information and as an indirect channel to both Shariatmadari and the MPRP. That a relationship existed at all is testament to the risks the CIA, and Washington, was prepared to take to regain influence in Iranian politics and build up its intelligence portfolio.

Another individual of whom the CIA was sceptical but continued to meet was Ali Eslami, described by the CIA as a prominent *bazari* and claiming to be close to Shariatmadari. Eslami made the implausible claim that he was able to bring 30,000 supporters onto the streets at 2 hours' notice for marching to protest against Khomeini. 'According to Eslami', the CIA reported on 24 July, 'the time is particularly ripe to move against Khomeini'. Yet, Eslami doubted that any political leader or 'dictator', even Shariatmadari, was capable of filling the power vacuum.[14] A more reliable contact, Rahmatollah Moghaddam-Maraghehie was manoeuvring to change this and position Shariatmadari as a genuine alternative to Khomeini. Moghaddam was tentatively attempting to form a new political front group to be composed of the old nationalists and Ayatollah Shariatmadari's Muslim People's Republican Party. This was entirely the kind of coalition Ahern and Washington had hoped could be forged.

That it could not be forged was due to a combination of the CIA's incautious effort to establish links with a coalition it erroneously considered could challenge Khomeini, Shariatmadari's tactical naivety, and Khomeini's political acumen in the wake of the hostage crisis. By late 1979 and early 1980, the MPRP was engaged in active conflict with Revolutionary Guards and other irregular Khomeinists.[15] In another example of the political utility of the developing confrontation with America, Khomeini used the revelations surrounding the apparent contacts between the US and the MPRP to rid himself of the two major challenges to his authority: Shariatmadari and the Azeri activists. After the US embassy documents identifying US efforts to cultivate relations with the MPRP and Shariatmadari were captured and published by the students occupying the US embassy, the radicals eventually had all the ammunition they needed to eliminate Shariatmadari as a political threat. It was also clear that Shariatmadari had miscalculated; in June 1979, his attempt to hold Khomeini to his promise to establish a regional assembly had broad support amongst the clergy. His demand that Khomeini amend the constitution that had already been adopted by an elected assembly enjoyed minimal support.[16] Resorting to a familiar tactic, Khomeini used a day of religious significance to mobilise support against his opponents. That occasion was the beginning of the 40-day commemoration of the Shia martyr Imam Hussein's death, on 9 January 1980.[17] Millions of Khomeini's followers marched in Qom, Tabriz, and Tehran, the MPRP's offices were ransacked, and its leaders beaten and even killed. The MPRP was dissolved and Shariatmadari was silenced and placed under virtual house arrest until his death.[18]

In the notes that accompanied the published captured US documents, the Students of the Imam's Line wrote that 'their reason for seeking refuge in the devilish embrace of the USA was that the American scarecrow could be used as a weapon against the paganism of communism and the USSR'.[19] Much of volume 55 of the series is dedicated to discrediting Shariatmadari for his links with US officials and the CIA. The hardliners were of course primarily eliminating a dangerous political rival, but they were also pushing back against the threat they believed US anti-communist policy posed to Iran's sovereignty.

There is no doubting that Iran in 1979 was one of the most challenging environments for intelligence operations in the world, yet the CIA chose not to assign seasoned veterans as the first permanently assigned case officers. Instead, in September, the CIA elected to send two agents, Malcolm Kalp and William Daugherty, who spoke no Persian nor had any prior experience of Iran. Daugherty was on his first assignment and had already been earlier rejected by the previous acting head of station for lacking the necessary experience. In order to establish cover for their clandestine activities, it is conventional for CIA case officers to pose as ordinary embassy officials when not active. With such drastic cuts in the number of embassy officials present in Tehran, the risk of CIA agents having their cover blown was far greater. Bruce Laingen was understandably concerned and stressed the importance of elaborate and watertight cover for CIA operatives. Laingen also argued that the number of agents be limited to four.[20] In fact, there were only three, including Ahern, in the 8 short weeks before the embassy was seized. Before themselves becoming hostages, Kalp and Daugherty unsurprisingly failed to cultivate any truly valuable contacts.[21]

Intelligence sharing as diplomacy: George Cave enters the fray

As the CIA made some tentative attempts to foster links with elements outside the PGOI, a joint CIA–State Department plan looked to kick-start engagement with the official government through a series of highly secret intelligence-sharing initiatives. The US hoped that by sharing more sensitive intelligence with selected individuals in the PGOI they could enhance this effort. Intelligence briefings had begun in March when National Security Council (NSC) officials had asked the CIA to provide an intelligence presentation for Ambassador Sullivan to deliver at a meeting with the newly appointed Prime Minister Bazargan. Deputy Prime Minister Yazdi had raised the possibility of receiving US intelligence briefings with Charlie Naas. Yazdi also showed some interest in the workings of an 'intercept network', which he had apparently become aware America had been establishing in 'all parts of Iran'. Yazdi was probably referring to Project Ibex, a large-scale signals intelligence (SIGINT) operation designed to provide intelligence on Soviet missile testing. The Iranians had kept most of these facilities in impeccable condition, placing guards on the doors, and even keeping the air conditioning and lights switched on. Such was the apparent activity around these sites that they appeared to be in operation, despite the Iranians having little or no idea of how to operate the facilities. Having observed all this activity, two US journalists from the *LA Times* and *Washington Post* called on Naas in early spring to check whether he was aware that the sites had reopened. Naas sternly informed the reporters that they were neither manned nor operational and any reports to the contrary would 'destroy' the US–Iranian relationship. On this occasion, his advice was heeded and no story emerged in print.

Shortly afterwards, on 6 May, Bazargan and Entezam met with Naas and John Stempel to discuss a range of security threats they were increasingly concerned with. Bazargan requested information that would 'help Iran defend its independence from its enemies'.[22] This was not the first time the US had prepared an intelligence briefing for members of the PGOI. Back in March, Thomas Blanton, a member of the NSC responsible for South Asian affairs, had tasked the CIA with developing an intelligence briefing highlighting Soviet involvement in Afghanistan for William Sullivan to deliver to Bazargan.[23] Despite that briefing receiving a lukewarm reception, US officials were still keen to stress the Soviet threat. A few days after the 6 May meeting, Naas sent Entezam a letter containing two US reports. The topic of both was Soviet activities in Afghanistan.[24] Entezam curiously thanked the US embassy for the report, which Mark Gasiorowski described as 'rather innocuous', but requested that the government really needed intelligence on internal security threats.[25] The US had lacked any such information, illustrating the mismatch between Washington's desire to mobilise Iran's vulnerability to external Cold War threats, and a preoccupation with internal insecurity amongst Iran's leaders.

The one exception was Iraq. Entezam, Yazdi, and Bazargan had all made requests for information on possible threatening Iraqi intentions in Iran.[26] In July, Bruce Laingen persuaded Harold Saunders to set up a more formal intelligence sharing channel. Laingen had recognised that the Iranians were particularly receptive to intelligence on internal and Iraqi threats.[27] The aims of these briefings were fivefold. First, to support attempts to forge at least informal strategic alliance by emphasising the threat posed by Soviet and Soviet proxy (i.e. Iraqi) activities in the region. Second, to demonstrate Washington's desire to work productively in areas of mutual concern and thus America's acceptance of the Revolution. Third, to help stabilise the Bazargan government and give both sides a stake in maintaining cordial relations. Fourth, to persuade the new regime of the value of an intelligence relationship and in doing so make the case for the resumption of reconnaissance operations in northern Iran. Finally, to promote contacts with a variety of sources who, though not receiving particularly sensitive information, responded positively to being privy to it.

It appears that Laingen, unlike his superiors in Washington, considered the starting point of US–Iranian relations to be the mutual threat of Iraq and not the Soviet Union. The 'sticky relationship' between Persian Iran and Arab Iraq was, in Laingen's view, a good starting point for security cooperation:

> We were prepared to cooperate with them in providing them our judgment, to some degree our military intelligence estimates of Iraqi intentions and movement vis-a-vis Iran at that time. And some very, very sensitive classified conversations occurred at the level of the Prime Minister, where I talked to him and talked about how we saw Iraq as a force in the Middle East and particularly as we judged the provisional regime's concern that Iraq had malice of forethought vis-a-vis Iran.[28]

Laingen's request to Saunders seems to have galvanised senior figures in the State Department to embrace intelligence sharing as a means of kick-starting engagement. A few weeks later, Under Secretary of State David Newsom asked John Stempel, by then a professor at the US Naval Academy, and CIA agent George Cave, until recently station chief in Saudi Arabia, to meet with Entezam in Stockholm. Entezam, who had recently become

Iran's ambassador to Sweden, remembered Cave as a young case officer in Iran during the late 1950s and early 1960s.[29] According to Cave, Entezam had approached the US ambassador in Stockholm and specifically requested Cave be sent to see him.[30]

On 5 August, Cave and Stempel travelled to Stockholm and met Entezam, who had taken up the position of ambassador to Sweden. During the four-and-half-hour meeting, Entezam reiterated his primary interest in intelligence on internal threats to the regime, particularly any threats which had external support.[31] 'We were only trying to prevent further chaos and instability', Entezam would later explain of these meetings, which he also, somewhat vaguely, claimed the Revolutionary Council had sanctioned 'in principle'.[32] Cave proposed giving regular intelligence briefings to top PGOI officials in Iran every 3–6 months, with more time-sensitive intelligence passed on as and when required.[33]

The first of these briefings occurred in Tehran on 21 August and was provided by Robert Ames, a CIA officer serving as the National Intelligence Officer for the Near East. The US delegation included Laingen and Victor Tomseth with Bazargan, Yazdi, and Entezam the only Iranians present.[34] The first briefing was apparently well received; in a long memo outlining the state of US policy in Iran, Harold Saunders reported that 'Iranians were most interested in Iraq, Palestinians; Afghans, and Soviet dangers to the PGOI. They asked for a repeat briefing in two months.'[35] When back in Washington, Cave met with Precht, and over the course of lunch the two discussed the state of mind of the Iranian secular leadership. Cave shared his perception of a deep sense of inadequacy amongst the leadership: 'a desire for help, but an inability to ask for or even accept it'. Cave also spoke of their concern regarding the strength of clerical influence but, like US officials, noted a broad sense of optimism that in the longer term this would diminish. In the short term, however, they feared the upcoming Majlis election would result in further gains for the mullahs. Interestingly, Cave reported their view that Khomeini was also troubled by this development, which saw Iran's political demographics moving further from his intended vision. In their opinion, Khomeini did not have an answer to resolve the situation.[36] On 30–31 August, Cave once again travelled to Stockholm. This time, Cave brought up the IBEX system, informing Entezam of its potential for intercepting SIGINT without the need for American assistance. He even provided the names of Iranian technicians who had been trained to use the equipment. Entezam requested an overview of IBEX' capabilities to be included in the next briefing in October. Cave agreed but in return asked for Entezam's help in gaining access for US personnel to the Tacksman sites in northern Iran. Unlike IBEX, these sites could not be operated without American supervision, but Cave stressed that the intelligence they provided could be mutually advantageous.[37]

On 13 September, Laingen again received guidelines from Precht for an upcoming meeting with Yazdi which included offers of inter-governmental cooperation and intelligence gathering; it was stressed again that the US was extremely interested in restoring the listening facilities.[38] Henry Precht described the intelligence briefings during this period as an effort by the CIA to 'get a foot in the door' in Iran.[39]

Laingen received another communiqué from the CIA in mid-September providing him with some additional intelligence the US had received regarding the Soviets expanding their presence in Afghanistan. The CIA urged Laingen to build on the intelligence briefings CIA officials had provided in August. Langley now hoped to establish a regular supply of intelligence on Afghanistan that would be cabled direct from Langley to the US embassy in Tehran for Laingen to deliver orally to Bazargan or Yazdi. The CIA, reassuring Laingen that the State Department was aware of and supported this initiative, hoped that this would become a two-way dialogue and urged Laingen to seek corroboration from the Iranians on the intelligence they provided. The first intelligence they offered was hardly incendiary; the CIA reported that a four-star Soviet General, accompanied by 12 generals and 6 colonels, had visited Kabul on 17 August. The delegation was there to 'study the insurgency' and the CIA predicted would stay for 25 days.[40] The memo also declared that the agency had unconfirmed reports that a brigade of Soviet troops was stationed in Kabul and had reliable information that 400 Soviet troops were stationed in Bagram airport. Whilst the Kabul allegation was unfounded, and very possibly deliberately alarmist, an airborne battalion of Soviet troops, disguised as technical specialists, had been in Bagram since July.

Newsom instructed George Cave to travel to Tehran on 15 October to provide Yazdi and Entezam with a comprehensive intelligence briefing.[41] US energy specialist Ron Smith delivered a lengthy and rambling presentation on Soviet energy problems. The implication was clear: the Soviets coveted Iran's abundant energy supplies. Yazdi described the briefing as 'a bunch of nonsense'.[42] The Iranian participants still seemed to be under the impression that the US was in some way aiding some of Iran's enemies, either monarchists abroad or ethnic groups inside the country. James Bill, in his widely celebrated history of post-war US–Iranian diplomacy, provides a decidedly unflattering account of the second intelligence briefing. It was his version of events that became the standard version of events. Yet, in the following years, there were some hints that more had been achieved in October than had previously been thought. They centred on the intelligence Cave had provided on the nature of the Iraqi threat. Laingen confirmed that Iran had been provided with high-level intelligence on Iraqi intentions and movements vis-à-vis Iran and the Iranian response had been very favourable. In his judgement, it was, alongside the military spares issue, 'as important a signal as I was able to make that summer that we really meant business about rebuilding a relationship'. The documentary evidence indicates that

Entezam had requested more information on the Iraqi threats in the weeks following the briefing.[43]

A far more startling account of the October briefing has recently emerged. According to this version, provided by Mark Gasiorowski, George Cave provided the Iranians with detailed warnings of imminent Iraqi plans.

US warnings of an Iraqi invasion

Mark Gasiorowski's research is compelling because it is based on interviews with several of the protagonists. George Cave had only just ceased to be an employee of the CIA, and thus able to speak to researchers. Cave, who also provided information during this researching of this book, explains that 'The crux of briefing was that Iraq had begun planning the invasion of Iran'.[44] The presentation provided extensive evidence of Iraqi military exercises that could only be explained as major invasion plans. Cave also warned that Iraq was pre-positioning military material around the border and undertaking engineering projects to facilitate an invasion. The Iranians were informed of covert Iraqi operations designed to support an invasion, including the creation of an organisation called the Arab Liberation Front that would launch a coordinated uprising amongst the Arabs of Khuzestan as Iraqi troops attacked. Cave concluded that Iraq had not yet made any final decision to invade, but urged the Iranians to make use of the IBEX listening posts the CIA had constructed in northern Iran, largely paid for by the Shah, which could provide invaluable tactical information regarding Iraqi troop movements.[45]

The suggestion that at this time the US possessed intelligence indicating advanced Iraqi invasion plans has been greeted by a high degree of scepticism amongst other former Carter officials. Wayne White (Persian Gulf director State Department, INR) and Gary Sick believe that if the US were in possession of such evidence, then they would have been aware of it (they were not).[46] This is also the view of Henry Precht, who confirmed that 'I had no impression at the time that anyone believed Iraq was planning a major attack although we thought that Saddam might be stirring up the Kurds. At the time I did not think he would take on his larger and still probably more potent neighbour.'[47] Precht adds that he met both Yazdi and Entezam soon after and neither mentioned anything about Iraq.[48]

It is possible that such sensitive intelligence was probably withheld from senior State Department and NSC officials with a responsibility for Iran. This seems unlikely, however, given that withholding such crucial intelligence would render the entire INR unable to fulfil its high-priority 'Global Warning Function' and cut out some of the most senior analysts responsible for Persian Gulf affairs in the State Department and NSC. White had been covering the Iraq–Iran account in minute detail from September 1979, and recollects the situation thus:

Iraq army was doing little more than continuing its well-known annual schedule of primarily battalion & brigade level training exercises. We would watch units going out to their well-known exercise areas or firing ranges, conducting normal exercises, and returning to their garrisons. Very little of the Iraqi military was anywhere near the Iraqi–Iranian frontier.[49]

White's view is strengthened by the fact that even when sections of the Intelligence Community began issuing warnings of an imminent Iraqi threat in April 1980, they were still premature by 5 months. Though unverifiable at this point, there is some logic to the possibility that the Iraqi threat was being exaggerated or at least presented in its most severe light. Since at least March 1979, US officials had used intelligence briefings to ingratiate themselves with Iranian officials, demonstrate America's concern for revolutionary Iran's security, and highlight the mutual benefits of maintaining the intelligence facilities. Clearly, the US Intelligence Community was anxious to gain access to the SIGINT sites in northern Iran, and although Cave had suggested the Iranians could use IBEX without US assistance, in return he had pressed Entezam to negotiate American access to the Tacksman sites in northern Iran. If a body of purported evidence indicating Iraq was preparing to invade Iran was passed on to Iranian officials in mid- to late 1979, then this was intelligence that would have been heavily disputed by other parts of the US intelligence community. That may be the most likely explanation as to why it was not passed around.

Whatever the substance of the intelligence passed on to Iranians, the episode illustrates some of the factors undermining US policy on Iran. First, the US Intelligence Community, previously reliant on SAVAK for internal Iranian reporting, and configured to monitor the Soviet threat (and that of their proxy states), lacked intelligence on the internal threats that most concerned the Iranians. The briefings thus could only partially demonstrate Washington's acceptance of the Revolution; indeed, the Iranian participants used the meetings to repeat their allegation that America was supporting counter-revolutionary forces. Second, although the operation shows the lengths the US went to repair relations, the fact that the Iranians concerned were unable to pass on the intelligence to Khomeini's circle, for fear of being associated with US intelligence, speaks to America's misreading of the balance of power in Iran and the weight of history that burdened engagement. Third, the starting point that continued cooperation with America was vital to Iran's security, with clear linkage to the Soviet–Iraqi threat, represented a US-centric vision of strategic alliance that seemingly bypassed the reality of Khomeini's world view. Fourth, US officials chose to ignore the fact that these meetings had not been sanctioned by Khomeini and were thus extremely high risk. The political situation in Iran required caution and not the appearance of America favouring one faction over another. Above all, it needed to avoid any suggestion of CIA activity in Iran. Bruce Laingen understood this and had urged the CIA to keep a low profile. However, it was only after Laingen became aware that the White House was seriously considering admitting the Shah that he advised Cave to leave Iran. He had already suspected that Cave's presence had become known in Iran.

The intelligence briefings were unfortunately timed. The last CIA delegation arrived just 1 week before the Shah arrived in New York. The briefings also coincided with an internal political row inside Iran as some moderates attempted to persuade Khomeini to disband the Assembly of Experts. The Assembly of Experts had, to the dismay of the Bazargan cabinet, assumed control for writing a constitution which now concentrated huge amounts of power in the hands of the clerics. Many of the moderates, led by Entezam, had opposed the assembly's creation from the start and now saw its dissolution as pivotal to rescuing the democratic intentions and credentials of the Revolution. Entezam succeeded in having the majority of the cabinet sign a letter to Khomeini opposing the assembly. When the proposal for the dismissal of the assembly, and a suggestion for a public referendum on the question of writing the constitution, was presented to Khomeini, he angrily dismissed it and called it a conspiratorial act. Entezam later commented that the accusations of him being a CIA spy, based largely upon his participation with these intelligence briefings, were deliberate retribution for his attacks upon the assembly. He later noted that 'this was the Islamic Republic and Mr. Khomeini's revenge against me, because of my suggestion for dissolving the Assembly of Experts'.[50]

Entezam, given the code name SD PLOD-1 by the CIA, had by October 1979 become central to America's diplomatic efforts inside Iran. This and the fact that his personal phone number was passed to CIA agent George Cave made Entezam the focus of sustained attacks from the radicals. Over the next 30 years, he would spend 17 years in and out of jail. Future President Bani-Sadr, who had been courted even more aggressively by the CIA going back to his time in Paris, would be another to suffer after he was identified by his sister's phone number in CIA documents found by the militants occupying the embassy.[51]

Saunders justifies the risks taken to advance America's diplomatic position in Iran by noting that many of the moderates were desperate for the US to stay in Iran. What is most telling, however, is Saunders' speculation that this was because they were concerned by the Soviet threat.[52] Viewed in such zero-sum terms of the Cold War, Washington viewed the risks as entirely acceptable. Even when some, such as the embassy's public affairs officer John Graves, recognised a dangerous lack of caution and discretion, Washington ignored their warnings.[53]

At the end of October, CIA station chief Tom Ahern admitted that the US had developed almost no capability to influence events in Iran and no prospect of developing one in the near term. At this stage, the US could only take solace from their judgement that the 'Peculiar national and religious character is a temporary barrier to communist advances. Meanwhile its non material cast makes Iran an unlikely proliferation candidate for the medium term. Finally, it is an introverted Revolution.'

Part III
Engagement Held Hostage

6
Re-evaluating US Policy after the Hostage Crisis

At the end of summer 1979, some US embassy officials hoped that the worst of the backlash from the Javits amendment was over. Head of mission Bruce Laingen noted that security seemed to be improving with fewer roadblocks and roaming revolutionary *comités* allowing the Americans to get out of the compound and travel around the city with more ease. By August, Laingen was able to send US embassy staff out to the consulates in Shiraz and Tabriz, where consular facilities were closed but buildings were manned by Iranian employees.[1] John Limbert arrived as a Persian-speaking diplomat and enthusiastically and joyfully re-immersed himself in the country he knew and loved.[2]

Morale in the embassy was improving, particularly after the thuggish group 'guarding' the embassy was removed forcibly by other revolutionary elements. This was seen as 'very tangible evidence', noted Laingen, 'that the Provisional Government, at least, did want to continue to try to build a relationship with us'.[3] The White House recognised Laingen's positive contribution to engagement by extending what was only supposed to be his temporary position as Chargé d'Affaires. Although Vance would later decide against nominating Laingen as permanent ambassador, by October the State Department had resolved to ask the Iranians to accept another individual. The embassy was resuming normal consular business and tried to process the huge numbers of Iranian students requesting visas to attend American schools, colleges, and universities.

Many of Iran's ethnic minorities were also turning towards the embassy for visas. To support this, the consular section opened a new section in the embassy compound.[4] Unfortunately, US officials used their ability to grant visas in a manner that undermined some of the goodwill it could have generated. Having already given preferential treatment to well-placed members of the Shah's regime with good contacts in Washington, the competition for visas had meant that the only hope for many was to provide useful information to US officials.[5] In September, the US defence attaché decreed that visa referrals would 'only be handled to gain intelligence information useful to the United States'.[6]

All in all, the US embassy remained a little more optimistic. 'We thought that it was a mission achievable', notes Laingen, 'that there were enough signals; there was a sufficiently good atmosphere for us to continue to work to try to find a basis for a relationship with this new crowd.'[7] Some modest progress was being made on the arms supply programme. Conditions even appeared to be approaching whereby a delegation of Iranian military officers would travel to the US to sit down with senior officials from the Pentagon and go through the daunting amount of paper records that had been generated during the Shah era. Returning to the US for consultations in September, Laingen considered Washington slightly less optimistic about the state of bilateral relations, but found senior officials pleasantly surprised by the progress he reported. Although the US had no contact with Khomeini, Henry Precht and Bruce Laingen had managed to hold meetings with his key lieutenants, Ayatollah Montazeri and Ayatollah Behehsti, in October. Precht reported that both meetings had been relatively friendly.[8] Iranian oil exports to the US were also showing signs of recovery; the US was then getting almost as much crude oil as the previous year (700,000 versus 900,000 BPD), despite Iranian exports being down by a third.[9] October had also seen the highest-level discussion meeting between Yazdi and Vance on the sidelines of a gathering at the UN. The meeting had been a bruising affair.

After an opening lecture from Yazdi on the ills of US support for the Shah, the meeting got down to the basic issues both sides felt were more pressing. From the Iranian point of view, this boiled down to visas, the Shah and his assets, and the military spare parts it had paid for but not received. Vance responded that the consular section had expanded its offices and built the number of dedicated staff to around 70.[10] He also affirmed America's intention to resolve the military payments issue, which Yazdi angrily questioned. The Iranian delegation argued that if America had really accepted the Revolution and the new state of reality in Tehran, then they 'would have been much more aggressive in resolving that issue, that we would have been much more forthcoming in price considerations, contract resolutions, than we had signalled to them'.[11] Yazdi asked whether arms could be transferred to a third country, presumably either for resale or on transit. Official records of the meeting indicate that Vance reminded Yazdi that under the terms of bilateral agreements, US military equipment could not be transferred to third countries without prior approval.

On a more positive note, Vance affirmed that US policy was to sell Iran 'what it needed' in military equipment but that there might be some problems with classified military spare parts. Official records of the meeting indicate that Yazdi then began complaining that Bruce Laingen's comments to the head of the Iranian Ministry of the Interior in this regard constituted 'unwarranted interference'.[12] The conversation then moved on to the obligatory enquiries regarding the Shah's entry into the US, to which Vance affirmed his government's general disinclination to allow the Shah into America but offered no guarantees for the future. In relation to Iranian claims for the Shah's assets, Vance recommended, as Brzezinski would a few weeks later in Algiers, that the Iranians should take it up in the US courts.

On the one hand the meeting, which was more about symbolism than meaningful negotiation, was a lost opportunity. Vance had apparently been prepared to pass Yazdi the name of a new US ambassador, but was so angered by the Iranian's prolonged and venomous lecture on America's support for the Shah that he withheld it. The mild-mannered Vance was simply unprepared for what for Yazdi was a necessary act of revolutionary catharsis. Yet, at least the first hurdle in normal bilateral relations had been overcome. The next day US political-military officials, Yazdi, and an Iranian general tried again to sort out at least some of the mess which constituted US–Iranian military sales mechanisms.[13]

Yet the period from mid-September onwards saw some more worrying developments that tempered this sense of optimism. On the face of what it perceived to be improving relations between the Bazargan government and the US, the Iranian Left had begun to step up its anti-American propaganda in an apparent attempt to both derail engagement and undermine the Bazargan government.[14] The Tudeh utilised their broadcasting station, the National Voice of Iran, to rail against the prospect of resumed military deliveries. On 11 October, it broadcast a speech by Tudeh leader Nerredin Kianuri, who declared that until any such agreement was disregarded 'talk of the political independence of our country is still premature.'[15] The previous month, Ayatollah Montazeri had publicly criticised Bazargan for 'striking up a friendship with the United States'.[16] In the same month, Ayatollah Taleghani, a leading cleric believed to support cordial relations with the US, died of a heart attack. Like Shariatmadari, US officials had seen Taleghani as a possible counterbalance to Khomeini. The two had been involved in a bitter struggle that had seen Taleghani's two sons arrested in April. Laingen recollected that his disappearance was a 'particular loss in terms of the moderation we thought was building, even in the Revolutionary Council'.[17]

Engagement received another blow when the US Senate made another unhelpful and ill-timed interjection. This time it was a 'Meet the Press' interview by neoconservative Senator Henry Jackson. Jackson stated that the Iranian Revolution was doomed to failure and the country was about to break up.[18] Unsurprisingly, this was greeted with alarm by the Iranians and dismay by the embassy. Yazdi complained that Washington was attempting to undermine the Revolution and specifically working to destabilise the Kurdish areas.[19]

Letting the Shah into the US

The question of whether the Shah would be allowed into the US was a regular topic of conversation amongst US officials in Tehran. On 28 July, Bruce Laingen sent a memo warning of the dire consequences for US–Iranian relations should the Shah take up residence in America. Laingen said that some progress was being made in removing the deeply felt suspicion that Washington had not accepted the Revolution. The next 2–3 months would be 'crucial and possibly hopeful' but all would be undone should the Shah enter US soil. Should that happen, only 'luck' would prevent another physical assault on the compound. Laingen could offer no assurances that the Iranian armed forces would be then able to rescue US personnel as they had before in February.[20] Back in Washington, Charlie Naas put the case even more forcefully. Without hyperbole, Naas informed David Newsom that if the Shah were given asylum, Carter would either be 'greeting a lot of coffins at the airport or there would be a hostage situation'.[21]

The State Department had already started planning for the Shah's coming to America. The head of Iranian affairs at the State Department, Henry Precht, thought it was a bad but probably inevitable decision. Unlike those stuck in the US embassy in Tehran, Precht believed the fallout was manageable, and if he was going to come, better to get it over with sooner rather than later. In early August, he sent his assessment to Bruce Laingen:

> We have resisted intense pressure to allow him to come to the US because we did not wish to complicate the PGOI's problems or our efforts to construct a new relationship. Now with the new government firmly established and accepted, it seems appropriate to admit the shah to the US. The new government may not like it, but it is best to get the issue out of the way.[22]

In mid-August, US diplomats in Iran began receiving requests for information from members of the PGOI, who cited reports that the Shah had requested a US visa whilst in Mexico City. Laingen replied truthfully that he had no information on this and immediately cabled Washington for further clarification.[23] Warren Christopher cabled back to say that the story originated from a recent visit to the US by the Shah's oldest son, Reza. To do so, Reza had obtained a visa from Mexico City, but he had not requested visas for his parents. Christopher added that technically the Shah did not need a visa, having been issued one before he left Iran, though he advised Laingen not to inform the PGOI of this. Laingen informed the Iranian foreign ministry that the Shah's children should all be expected to reside in the US but his parents had not been issued a visa.[24]

On 30 September, Vance cabled the embassy in Tehran asking for information on the probable consequences of the Shah being allowed to the US for possibly life-saving medical treatment. Vance noted that this request followed pressure from David Rockefeller's office. They had informed Vance that Rockefeller had sent his personal physician to Mexico to examine the Shah, and a medical request that he be admitted to the US might follow.[25] On 20 October, the State Department learnt that the Shah had started chemotherapy as part of care for lymphoma 6 months ago. His situation was described as critical and in need of US medical support. The next day, Vance cabled Laingen with the bad news; the Shah would be permitted to enter the US on humanitarian grounds. Laingen should instruct Bazargan that this was not a political decision and the PGOI should provide 'necessary' security for American citizens in view of the 'special circumstances'.[26]

The Iranian reaction was one of extreme frustration but quiet acceptance. Yazdi suggested that the impact could be lessened if the Shah could be examined by Iranian doctors, to prove his cancer diagnosis, and if America could obtain assurances that the Shah would not speak to the press or participate in any political activity.[27] Laingen replied that he could guarantee neither. The State Department subsequently sent a few paragraphs of notes from the State Department's Medical Director describing the Shah's condition and a request to the Shah's representative that neither he nor his family engage in any political activities. They then agreed that Iranian doctors approved by the Iranian embassy in Washington could speak to doctors treating the Shah and exchange records but ruled out any direct access or examination.

As the embassy braced itself for a storm of protest, they were cautiously optimistic about the initial Iranian media coverage, which seemed to stress the Shah's grave medical condition rather than any conspiracy.[28] On 24 October, the US embassy reported that the 'reaction to the Shah's arrival in the US has been minimal'.[29] The embassy reported a small but orderly protest outside the embassy and no attempt to breach security, which they added had been slightly reinforced.

Meanwhile, the PGOI were getting desperate and informed US officials that they were coming under more pressure from hardliners. A representative from the Ministry of Foreign Affairs stated that if the Shah left the US immediately after he was released from hospital, the foreign ministry would be able to repair the damage, but otherwise 'there will be a crisis'.[30] The next day, Khomeini announced a huge march in Tehran against the 'asylum' given to the Shah by the US. The march was, however, routed away from the US embassy, offering some hope. The CIA noted, however, a breakaway protest at the embassy that was led by the Tudeh and other communist groups.[31]

Carter's refusal to heed his advice has subsequently, and rightly, been cited as one of the great missteps in US diplomacy with Iran.[32] The reasons commonly cited are the intense pressure he faced from the Shah's powerful allies.[33] Hamilton Jordan, Carter's chief of staff, highlighted domestic political considerations; if the Shah died outside the US, the Republicans would have another political stick to beat Carter: first in Congress during the ratification of SALT II, then during the upcoming presidential election.[34] Brzezinski also made the strategic argument that America's remaining allies would lose faith if the US was seen to abandon a former friend in his hour of need.

Whatever the cause, John Limbert summed up its effect: 'Washington destroyed its own effort to hold on in Iran.'[35] The decision was particularly egregious given that US officials inside Iran had started to see some modest improvements in the political landscape. Despite Laingen's personal dismay at the decision to allow the Shah entry into the US, he was still reasonably optimistic about the future. The week before the embassy was overrun, Laingen had noted the visit of US officials to the military supply offices HQ, with Revolutionary Guards looking on, as offering 'real support for our conclusion that things were going better'.[36] As the embassy surrendered to the militants, with Laingen on a visit to the foreign ministry, an 11-page confidential memo lay ready for him to sign informing Washington of the significance of the visit, describing the cooperation of the Revolutionary Guards and the military figures involved.

There is no doubt that letting the Shah into the US was a major and avoidable blunder that demonstrated wilful ignorance to the burden of history weighing on US–Iranian relations. It also marked a complete departure from the hard-headed realist approach to repairing America's position in Iran that Washington had committed itself to. On the other hand, Carter's more generous supporters might point to the fact that when Laingen had issued his memo advising against allowing the Shah into the US, he had only asked for a delay of 2–3 months. The Shah in fact arrived in New York almost exactly 3 months later. Laingen's reporting in August and September had also been markedly more optimistic in tone, therefore giving the impression that America had established a more resilient position in Iran than when Laingen had issued his original warning. Even after the decision to admit the Shah was taken, the scenes outside the embassy were relatively calm and the chaos many predicted did not immediately emerge.

Therefore, as costly as the episode was for American diplomacy, it did not alone lead to the seizure of the US embassy on 4 November. Of equal or even greater significance was Brzezinski's ill-fated decision to meet Bazargan and a number of the other PGOI officials on the margins of a diplomatic occasion in Algiers on 1 November. The critical factor here was that Bazargan did not have the express permission of Khomeini or the Revolutionary Council.

Handshake in Algiers

The occasion in Algiers was the anniversary celebration of the beginning of the Algerian Revolution. Yazdi and Bazargan were there as Iran's representatives, and at some point a picture was taken of Brzezinski shaking hands with

Bazargan, and Yazdi looking on. On the same day in Tehran, which was a Friday, Khomeini had sponsored a protest against the Shah's asylum in the US, which had ended without major incident. No newspapers are published on Friday in Iran and so the picture was only published on Saturday morning. Former US diplomat and hostage Victor Tomseth later claimed that it was this picture more than anything else that prompted the students to attack the embassy. According to Tomseth, 'their interpretation was that in effect U.S. policy was succeeding and we were actually making progress and trying to build a new relationship with post-Pahlavi Iran'.[37]

When Bazargan resigned after Khomeini refused to order the militants out of the US embassy, his resignation speech alluded to continual interference in his foreign policy but singled out the criticism he had received for meeting Brzezinski in Algiers. To Bazargan, the issue was symbolic of an increasingly dysfunctional and alien system of government. 'A prime minister who has to seek permission to meet ministers', he bluntly stated, was 'better off dead'.[38] He protested that he and his ministers had met with over 200 foreign representatives without express permission. In any case, he claimed that he had asked his Foreign Minister, Ebrahim Yazdi, to inform the 'imam', but that he had not done so. His protestation, that this was just a regular meeting unworthy of fanfare or hyperbole, was undoubtedly naive. Brzezinski, more than any other US politician, was widely distrusted in Iran and known to have supported a military coup in January 1979.

Yet the Algiers meeting is also illuminating in identifying some of the bureaucratic stresses within the Carter administration. Henry Precht recounts that his immediate attitude to a US delegation led by Brzezinski was 'anybody but Brzezinski'.[39] Precht's relationship with Brzezinski, and his aide Gary Sick, was extremely poor at this point. Even now the question of who initiated the meeting in Algiers, and whether Brzezinski was authorised to meet an Iranian delegation, is contested. Brzezinski, in his memoirs and in subsequent interviews, states outright that Bazargan had requested the meeting.[40] This version of events is supported by Gary Sick,[41] but strongly refuted by other US and Iranian sources, not least by the Iranian Foreign Minister, Ebrahim Yazdi, who accused Brzezinski of distorting events to 'lessen his own responsibility for the unfortunate political consequences of the act'.[42]

Another version of events is provided by the former US ambassador to Algiers, Ulric Haynes. Haynes contends that he was approached by Brzezinski and asked to set up a meeting with a high-ranking Iranian delegation, a course of action Haynes claims to have advised against. Brzezinski subsequently turned down Haynes' offer to accompany him, who unequivocally states that 'the attempt was on [Brzezinski's] side' and that he had 'absolutely no recollection of a first contact by the Iranians'. Furthermore, Haynes states that 'for the record, Brzezinski was not authorised to meet with Bazargan and Yazdi'.[43] Vance was apparently surprised by the

Brzezinski–Bazargan encounter, but his account fails to mention that the embassy in Tehran supported and helped organise the meeting. On 29 October, Chargé d'affaires Bruce Laingen, who had learnt about Brzezinski and Under Secretary Newsom's attendance from the wireless file, sent a cable to Newsom strongly advising they meet with Bazargan. Laingen described potential talks as 'very useful' and mentioned that he had broached the idea casually to Bazargan, who 'seemed very open to the idea'.[44]

Regardless of the factors that led to the meeting, it represented a severe political miscalculation.[45] Bazargan and Brzezinski unconsciously made the same fatal mistake in Algiers; they undermined the perception that Khomeini's world view would remain a permanent influence on Iranian foreign policy. It was, after all, Brzezinski who had won the argument back in January 1979, when Sullivan had forlornly pleaded with Carter to reach out to Khomeini. The Algiers meeting represented a continuation of that short-sighted decision. Ironically, Brzezinski left the meeting with renewed optimism that the provisional government could genuinely cooperate in containing the Soviet threat.[46] The two parties had apparently discussed additional intelligence sharing.[47]

On 3 November, more fuel was added to the fire when Radio Turkey aired an analysis predicting that within weeks CIA agents would conduct another coup, similar to Operation Ajax, to reinstall the Shah. On 4 November, a group of radical students seized the US embassy. Rather than rescue the US personnel, as they had back in February, the Bazargan government resigned. America's crushing embrace of the moderates, and dismissal of those it considered 'unworldly', had backfired.

'Think beyond the current imbroglio'

The hostage crisis remains the enduring example of Iran's rejection of international norms and ultimately cemented discourses of irrationality in the American consciousness. The *Washington Post* columnist Bill Gold wrote that 'The Ayatollah's call for all Moslems to join in a holy war against the United States leaves President Carter in the hopeless dilemma that is the fate of all who are called upon to deal rationally with irrational behavior'.[48] Three weeks into the crisis, Richard Nixon used his first live TV interview since his resignation to remark that America was dealing with 'irrational people and irrational leader'.[49] Carter himself was reported by apparently 'well-placed sources' to be spending hours reading intelligence reports that paint a psychological profile of Iran's Ayatollah Khomeini as 'irrational but very crafty'.[50]

The Carter administration's initial response was to continue along the Cold War 'realist' lines it had established. Carter was still determined and compelled (in an election year) to find and apply coercive levers against the Iranian leadership. On 9 November, five days after the embassy was seized by radical students, Paul Henze, a staff member in the NSC, underlined the need to 'think beyond the current imbroglio and not let emotions generated during it undermine our long term interests in this part of the world'.[51] Carter was also under pressure from Brzezinski to demonstrate 'resolve' and 'show the world that he is capable of handling a crisis with international implications'.[52]

For the next 13 months, the Carter administration grappled with the conflicting demands of domestic and geopolitical expediency. A key tool of US policy that reflected this tension, examined in detail here, were the economic sanctions levied against Iran by the US and its allies. In the face of Iran's continued defiance, however, the administration seemed to be moving towards an acceleration of military and economic pressure. The next chapter shows how the Soviet intervention in Afghanistan would arrest this movement towards increased confrontation and reinforce many of the premises discussed earlier in this book. Following one of the established themes of this book, this chapter also examines US assessments of Soviet and 'leftist' involvement in the hostage crisis and reassessments of the Soviet threat to Iran.

Differing perspectives of the hostage crisis in the Carter administration

The hostage crisis was viewed from different perspectives within the Carter administration. This reflected divergent responsibilities within the government, as well as the ideological and tactical differences that had already emerged within the US–Iran policy. Cyrus Vance and the State Department would remain committed to a diplomatic solution and continued efforts to maintain relations.[53] Hamilton Jordan, Carter's chief of staff and campaign manager, was obviously concerned with the domestic implications of the hostage crisis. Initially, the crisis was viewed as an opportunity; Jordan saw a chance to upstage Senator Kennedy's impending announcement that he would seek the Democratic nomination for the 1980 presidential election. 'It'll be over in a few hours', Jordan unsuspectingly told a colleague, 'but it could provide a nice contrast between Carter and our friend from Massachusetts in how to handle a crisis'.[54]

Two months before the crisis, Kennedy had led Carter amongst Democrats by 60 to 30 percent.[55] By mid-December, Carter's public stock had risen so meteorically that a veteran pollster described it as 'the largest increase in presidential popularity recorded in the four decades of the Gallup poll'.[56] This helped carry Carter to victory in the Iowa caucus on 21 January by a margin of 2 to 1.[57] It was an unsustainable rise, given the intractable nature of the crisis, and the defeats to Kennedy in the New York and Connecticut primaries on the 25th and 26th of March marked the beginning of the end of the 'rally round the flag' factor.

Brzezinski was less worried about domestic politics and the safety of the hostages than about the erosion of America's global credibility and position in the Persian Gulf.[58] Nor was he primarily engaged with negotiations with the Iranians for the safe return of the hostages. Brzezinski's refusal to meet with the families of the hostages, unlike Vance, reflected his belief that a scenario could emerge in which they would have to be sacrificed for the sake of America's 'national honour'.[59] In the immediate aftermath of the Soviet invasion, Brzezinski advised Carter that Soviet decisiveness would be contrasted with American restraint, 'Which will no longer be labelled as prudent but increasingly as timid'.[60] Because of his belief that America's national pride had been compromised, which in itself he believed to be a strategic threat, Brzezinski initially proposed an aggressive response to the hostage crisis. He took it upon himself, and his staff in the NSC, to initiate contingency plans for a military rescue.

The Secretary of Defense, Harold Brown, took a similar line to Brzezinski and advocated threatening Khomeini almost immediately with military reprisals.[61] Brown also shared Brzezinski's view that the crisis was an opportunity to reassert American global prestige and increase America's military presence in the region. If the hostages were harmed, Brown declared that the US should be prepared to occupy the Kharg Island oil terminal and destroy Iran's oil production facilities.[62] Carter broadly disagreed with Brown and Brzezinski and preferred a combination of economic sanctions, multilateral diplomatic pressure, and quiet negotiation. President Carter's preference for non-military measures naturally reflected his overriding concern for the safety of the 52 American captives.

To some extent, these differences reflected deeper disagreements on America's strategic posture and indeed the nature of the Soviet threat.[63] In the Pentagon and on the NSC staff, the view was held that the moderate Arab states would not openly call for a reassertion of US military power in the region but privately hoped for it. The State Department, whose responsibility it was for maintaining the complex diplomatic landscape in the region, held the opposite view. They judged that a more vigorous presence would be, in the words of William Odom, 'unwelcome and disruptive'.[64] Although Carter generally shared the State Department's emphasis on diplomacy in Iran, he would acquiesce with Brzezinski's vision of a greatly enhanced US power projection capability in the region.

Bureaucratic trauma

The US abruptly found itself confronting a major crisis with severe global and domestic implications without its entire Iranian-based diplomatic staff. In Iran, the wholesale resignation of the PGOI saw authority transferred by the Revolutionary Council to various individuals on an ad hoc basis. The CIA reported that the 'foreign policy bureaucracy is in chaos and the diplomatic corps suffers from serious morale problems'.[65] Nobody in

Washington was sure which individuals sat on the Revolutionary Council, let alone the relative influence or tensions within its members. All that was known was that Khomeini was the 'single most influential figure in the country'.[66]

The Revolutionary Council directed Abolhassan Bani-Sadr to take charge of the foreign affairs of the Islamic Republic.[67] Bani-Sadr, the son of an ayatollah, was widely respected as a major economic and political theoretician of the Islamic Revolution and, along with his rival Sadegh Ghotbzadeh, had been Khomeini's political strategist whilst in exile. He would last less than 2 weeks as head of the foreign ministry, replaced for opposing the hostage crisis. During this time, he concurrently held the unenviable position of finance minister. The economy was Bani-Sadr's strong ground, and few questioned either his expertise or the need for economic vitality in order to achieve the Revolution's goals. Consequently, it was in this area of policy that Bani-Sadr achieved most of his modest success as President.[68] The choice of Sadegh Ghotbzadeh as his replacement in the foreign ministry was reasonably good news from Washington's perspective. A committed anti-communist, Ghotbzadeh was reasonably well known to the State Department and had for some time had a good relationship with Richard Cottam. For this reason, and because Khomeini refused to meet any US officials, Cottam would become the principal contact between the State Department and the Iranian government for the first few months of the crisis.

Decoding Soviet-leftist involvement in the hostage crisis

Given the assumption that Khomeini and Moscow shared the basic desire to eliminate American influence from Iran, Soviet involvement in the crisis and its opportunity to benefit from it were immediate concerns for Washington. Broadcasts from Moscow Radio's World Service in Persian quickly supported the occupation of the US embassy on the grounds that it was filled with 'agents of the CIA and US imperialists'.[69] Iran's ambassador to Moscow, Mohammad Mokri, had reportedly received a warm reception after meeting with senior Soviet leaders to explain the situation as well as the 'stand of Imam Khomeini'.[70] Tehran Radio even reported that 'the decisive stands of the Iranian nation and the leader of the Islamic Revolution, Imam Khomeini, against the imperialist and Zionist plots have received a warm welcome from Soviet president Leonid Brezhnev and Foreign Minister Andrey Gromyko'.[71] In a *Le Monde* interview with Khomeini's grandson, it was claimed that the crisis opened the door for a 'tactical alliance' between the Islamic movement and the USSR.[72]

The Tudeh Party was a vocal supporter of the hostage crisis. Whilst the Tudeh's role in driving a wedge between the PGOI and the fundamentalists can be debated, there was no doubt that its goal had been completed.[73] Kianuri was quick to remind journalists, incorrectly as it happens, that 'the occupation began precisely when the Prime Minister Bazargan and Foreign Minister Yazdi were talking for hours in Algiers, without Imam Khomeini's permission, to Brzezinski, prime underminer of the Islamic Revolution'.[74] The crisis was also a vehicle for emphasising their common struggle against imperialism. In an 18 February interview, Kianuri said that the role of the students was 'very important' in defeating the attempts of the 'liberal bourgeoisie' under the government of Bazargan to divert the Revolution from its 'anti-imperialist' path.[75] Ganji also asserts that the Tudeh had played a significant role in the events that led up to the crisis, most notably by passing on to the clerics information about Brzezinski's meeting with Bazargan in Algiers that they had been given from Algerian communists.[76]

Any perception that the Tudeh could benefit from the crisis would appear extremely premature after the Soviet intervention. The party had welcomed the 1978 Marxist coup and continued to support the pro-Soviet regime in Kabul. At the same time, the new Tudeh leader, Kianuri, had tried to downplay Moscow's influence with the Tudeh.[77] The Soviet intervention in Afghanistan exposed this contradiction because the party was forced to defend Soviet action, which was universally unpopular amongst Iranians.

The other main leftist groups, the Feda'i and MEK, strongly supported the students occupying the embassy. John Stempel goes as far as to state that both played a significant role in the occupation and used the opportunity to increase their popularity domestically.[78] Khomeini was apparently aware that many of the students occupying the embassy were leftists.[79] One theory for his decision to throw his weight behind the hostage takers was that he did not want to appear less radical than the Left. Khomeini's immediate association with the crisis prevented the hostage takers from being labelled as communists or at least 'leftists'. The Supreme Leader was able to occupy the ground of the Left, using the embassy takeover to demonstrate the Iranian Revolution's anti-imperialist mission and solidarity with Third World people. This interpretation is used to explain the release of the black hostages and Sergeant Quarles' press conference statement condemning American imperialism.[80] Bani-Sadr and Bazargan would both later claim that leftists and communists had infiltrated the ranks of the 'Students Following the Imam's Line'.[81]

Paul Henze certainly approached the crisis as conveniently supportive of a leftist or Soviet agenda. In a memo to Brzezinksi four days into the crisis, Henze posited that 'It is in the long term interest of the left, much more than that of the religious fanatics, to have us out of Iran entirely; but it is very convenient for the left (whether they are manipulating or influencing the situation or not) to have the religious fanatics doing their work for them'.[82] Henze considered it highly suspicious that the espionage theme used as a pretext for the occupation of the embassy had been prominent 'amongst a whole series of anti-US themes in clandestine Soviet broadcasts to Iran in recent weeks'.[83]

Henze's analysis, which relied on supposition based on perceived rather than observable notions of Soviet influence, is illustrative of the cultural bias Gary Sick later described as interfering fundamentally with how the US assessed the balance of political forces in Iran.[84] Superficial labels such as 'fanatics' were substituted for a meaningful analysis of Iranian decision-making. Henze, a Horn of Africa specialist with little experience of Iranian affairs, found it strange that non-leftist radicals would be equally suspicious of US espionage. It seemed more plausible that they were being manipulated by an internal or external threat. Henze's analysis of Iran was characterised by two unhelpful and analytically shallow assumptions: that decision-making amongst the religious leadership was entirely irrational, and that the Left was in a position to inherit Iran. Both were demonstrated in this particular memo:

> Given the utterly irrational state of mind that dominates elements in Tehran, and the intense hatred of America by Khomeini, a seemingly rational action such as a naval blockade could conceivably provoke an Iranian invitation to the Soviets to come in to protect them. Khomeini could give such intervention his blessing with a doctrine of the 'lesser Satan'. The Iranian left, certainly capitalizing on current tensions to improve its position, could abet such a move.[85]

It is also clear that Henze perceived this process to have been progressing and 'the fact that we were on the way to re-establishing a military relationship and American business was still able to function was inimical to leftist objectives'. The logical response was to prevent 'leftist objectives' from being fulfilled by dispassionately viewing the crisis in its wider strategic context. Henze would also voice for the first time the notion that violent actions, however cathartic for the US, would only benefit 'the left' who 'will know to exploit such actions to our discredit and loss'. As already demonstrated, the notion of a monolithic 'leftist objective' flew in the face of the reality of an extremely fractious and divided political spectrum. Amongst the generalisations and assumptions that underpinned his analysis, he had at least one bit of sage advice: 'We are likely to hurt ourselves more than the Iranian fanatics by any violent actions.'[86]

The State Department's Iran working group agreed with Henze's later assessment but took a much more measured approach to Soviet subversion. Those closely involved with freeing the hostages were not preoccupied with the Soviets and did not frame their response within a close reference to how Moscow would react. Harold Saunders, head of the working groups, maintains that 'While Soviet subversive activities were constantly on our minds in a larger strategic context, the Soviet Union did not figure prominently in our management of the crisis'.[87] Carter himself was apparently not unduly concerned by the prospect of Moscow turning events to their advantage.[88]

The CIA was quickly tasked with establishing the possibility of Soviet involvement in the crisis and the extent to which it was attempting to benefit from the event. In early December, the agency produced an intelligence assessment that reported no evidence of direct or indirect Soviet involvement with the students occupying the embassy.[89] Soviet sources subsequently indicate that the Politburo was highly unsatisfied by the residency's lack of high-level sources in the Khomeini regime and its coverage of the hostage crisis in particular.[90]

Although not persuaded of a KGB hand in the actual crisis, there was still a general assumption that the Soviet Union would take advantage of the situation. Brzezinski noted that 'the Administration assumed that the Soviets relished our discomfort and sought to egg Iranian paranoia'.[91] The Soviets had, the CIA reported, 'tried to use the current crisis in US–Iranian relations to strengthen their ties to the Khomeini regime and improve their image as a defender of "anti-imperialist" Revolutionary movements'. The CIA judged that some tangible benefits were observable:

> There is little question that Soviet relations with Iran's rulers have improved as a result of the crisis in US–Iranian relations. Iran's hostility to the USSR eased perceptibly in mid November. Media attacks on the Soviets for their role in Afghanistan and destabilizing activities within Iran were muted, and the Tudeh Party has been allowed to play a more visible political role.[92]

After November 1979, policy-makers took a keener interest in the text of Soviet clandestine broadcasting, supplied by the CIA and Foreign Broadcast Information Service (FBIS), and made repeated complaints to Moscow regarding their content.[93] The USSR of course denied that it was responsible for NVOI broadcasts. Nevertheless, Soviet overt broadcasting continued to emphasise American military preparations, often in collusion with the Israelis, for direct action against Iran or support for internal Iranian counter-revolutionary groups opposed to Khomeini.

There is divided opinion as to whether the State Department's complaints resulted in a moderation of NVOI broadcasting. Henze opined that the 'the level and tone remains about the same as before the 9 November US protest'.[94] In contrast, the *Washington Post* on 22 November reported that the tone of broadcasts had shifted from encouraging the students that took over the embassy to urging the release of the hostages. It quoted one recent broadcast as saying that freeing the hostages would create 'the possibility of ending present tensions and the basis for clarifying our legitimate demands to world opinion'.[95] The paper linked this to a concurrent statement of non-interference by Gromyko. Officially, the Soviets supported the 9 November UNSC vote to reject the Iranian resolution calling for an investigation into the Shah. In doing so, they argued that the 'students' should first release the hostages in accordance to international law.

By January it was still unclear who exactly the hostage takers were. One theory was put to John L. Washburn, the night-shift chairman of the Iran hostage task force, in late January 1980 by an individual described as a 'cocky Texan' with good contacts in Iran. This individual advised that the core of students occupying the embassy were 'ringed by a Mujahedeen group'. They were described as 'increasingly radical in their internalizing Marxist outlook', and, as such, the result was an estrangement from a 'strictly Islamic ideal of state or government'. Khomeini, the State Department's source analysed, had moved against this by, amongst other tactics, preventing the mujahedeen presidential candidate, Rajavi, from running.[96] More recent studies indicate that the leftist connection ultimately amounted to the fact that several of the leaders of the students were close to a splinter group of the MEK.[97]

The US perceived in the hostage crisis a similar dilemma for the Soviet Union as had been presented by the Revolution itself. In both cases, the primary Soviet goal remained the prevention of a re-entry of the US into the Gulf, a preoccupation that guided Moscow's response to the Iranian Revolution, hostage crisis, and outbreak of the Iran–Iraq War. Moscow made great efforts to appear to be deterring a US military response, as much out of a desire to appear as the 'protector' of the Revolution as because of a genuine fear of such an eventuality.

As the hostage crisis quickly appeared increasingly intractable, however, Soviet rhetoric was not simply public posturing. Soviet fear of a US military intervention prompted Ambassador Dobrynin, acting on the behest of his superiors in Moscow, to communicate Moscow's position in a private letter to President Carter on 4 December 1979. The Soviets were concerned about the regional implications that a show of American force would have, particularly in Afghanistan. One week earlier, the Soviet Minister of Foreign Affairs, Andrei Gromyko, had urged mutual restraint and rational behaviour at his press conference in Bonn. Dobrynin went even further, emphasising the positive role Moscow was playing in the crisis, most specifically in communicating to the Iranian leadership the illegality of their action and their opinion that the release of the hostages would 'be met favourably in the world and not be detrimental to Iran'. It is clear that Carter was unimpressed; in the margin, he wrote 'Their public broadcasts are the opposite. No one knows if they're telling the truth here.' Dobrynin then warned the Americans that Moscow expected the US leadership to show 'restraint and composure'.[98]

The Soviets were not immune to some of the wider implications of the hostage crisis that ran contrary to their interests. Soviet sources also reveal a real fear for the diplomatic security of its own personnel in Iran.[99] Should the US choose to use force in Iran, the Soviet leadership would face the unappealing choice of appearing to be an ineffective supporter of the 'struggle against imperialism' or risking a major confrontation with the US on an issue not of their choosing.[100]

There are still those who are determined to portray the crisis as KGB instigated. Amir Taheri, a conservative journalist associated with a number of discredited conspiracy theories, insists that the hostage seizure was a Soviet-inspired plot to counter Brzezinski's efforts to organise radical Islam to better resist Soviet expansion.[101] Taheri's analysis is shared by some Shah-era monarchists, who continue to argue that the hostage crisis was orchestrated by the Soviets in order to prevent US–Iranian rapprochement and limit the Carter government's ability to react to the Soviet invasion of Afghanistan.[102] Another conservative author who has tried to finger KGB involvement is Kenneth Timmerman.[103] Timmerman alleged that Mohammed Musavi Kho'inha, the cleric whose advice the students sought in regard to Khomeini's reaction to the seizure, was a KGB agent. Babak Ganji correctly cites the lack of evidence for this assertion, but admits that Kho'inha had pro-Soviet and Tudeh sympathies and was close to the Soviet ambassador to Tehran, Vinogradov.[104] Others have pointed to the reported enrolment of several hostage takers, as well as Kho'inha, at Soviet and East German Universities.[105] Ganji also presents as circumstantial evidence the fact that an Egyptian journalist was able to meet some representatives of the hostage takers in the Soviet embassy. The final piece of 'evidence' is put forward by former CIA official Miles Copeland, who alleges in his book that Israeli intelligence had informed the CIA that the Mossad had identified significant numbers of the young hostage takers as being guided by older KGB agents.[106]

As intriguing as these theories are, they are not supported by verifiable evidence and in most cases say more about the ideological axioms of the authors than Soviet policy. Perhaps revealingly, two major studies of Soviet covert operations in the period written by former KGB agents Vasili Mitrokhin and Oleg Gordievsky make no mention of any involvement.[107] Three factors suggest that this was also the view of most members of the Carter administration. First, the State Department had been aware for some time that an attack on the embassy was a strongly possible result of the decision to allow the Shah entry in the US.[108] Second, as already noted, the CIA had reported no evidence of direct or indirect Soviet involvement. Third, nearly all those involved have written accounts of this period, or given interviews, and none has given credence to a Soviet hand in events. If we are to accept the version of events by the self-processed originator of the embassy seizure, Ebrahim Asgharzadeh, the Soviet embassy itself was only ruled out as the target by a majority vote of 3 to 2.[109]

The question of Soviet assistance in the event of a US military intervention

Should the US attack Iran, the question of whether the Soviets would intervene, with or without permission, was hotly debated in the Iranian and Western media. This is probably a good indicator that many Iranians believed such an attack could be imminent. The first hint of Soviet intentions came in late November with *Pravda* repeating Brezhnev's warning that the Soviet Union would not permit 'outside interference in Iran's internal affairs by anyone, in any form, and under any pretext'.[110] Given that this was simply a restatement of existing policy without any reference to the crisis in hand, and put together with other statements coming out of Russia repeating Carter's initial ruling out of military force, this was the Kremlin putting out a preliminary holding line.

Nevertheless, the Iranian ambassador to Moscow warmly welcomed the restatement and strongly hinted that Brezhnev had pledged his support in the event of a US military attack:

> Mr Brezhnev welcomed what I said warmly and with great joy, and signified his approval (or at least that was my understanding), indicating that the Soviet Union would not remain indifferent in the face of military intervention by America in Iran; and, several times during talks with the Soviet statesman, I felt that this was their approach.[111]

Soviet support was a problematic consideration for the Iranians. Here was an opportunity to deter US military and economic retaliation and even exploit American strategic anxieties. But there were ideological compromises and strategic risks associated with doing so. Tehran was loath to appear to be supporting a superpower agenda and anxious to demonstrate it could defend itself. What was hailed as the defining expression of Iranian anti-imperialism could also precipitate a reassertion of superpower influence in the region. Khomeini may have seen the hostage crisis as a useful vehicle for the consolidation of his theocratic vision, but nobody in Tehran wanted to see the crisis develop into a broader superpower conflict. The Iranian ambassador to Moscow, Mohammed Mokri, pointed out the danger: 'A confrontation between the Soviet Union and America, even if not military, means a sort of political crisis affecting all the Persian Gulf littoral states.'[112]

Bani-Sadr, who had replaced Yazdi as Foreign Minister on 12 November, was much less of a fan of the Soviets than Mokri. In an interview with *Le Monde,* he insisted that Iran wanted nothing to do with Soviet military assistance. He was careful, however, to remind the Americans that, in the event of a US military attack, the 'USSR could exploit its widespread influence in the Middle East'.[113] The Soviets never explicitly stated that they would intervene militarily in the event of a US attack on Iran, though they constantly warned them of any military escalation. Oblique references to 'protecting' Iran persisted, however, in the Iranian media. An editorial in *Ettela'at* exclaimed that 'In the opinion of our reporter Iran and the Soviet Union have begun a new chapter in political relations'.[114] It added that 'the foreign minister of the

Soviet Union officially announced that his country will protect Iran against any probable American attack'.[115]

Mokri was increasingly asked about the effect of the hostage crisis on Soviet–Iranian relations. Mokri refused to be drawn into publicly supporting a Soviet military role in Iran and, in a separate message broadcast on Tehran domestic radio, was keen to avoid Iranian policy to be appearing to conform to any Soviet agenda.[116] The following week, Mokri continued to hold the national sovereignty line by hinting only at a non-military role and insisting that Iran would not allow the Soviet Union to cross into Iran.[117]

It was clearly important for Iranian revolutionary credibility to avoid the country becoming, as Mokri stated in an interview with *ABC News* on 1 December, a 'site of superpowers' encounter'. It was, as Mokri articulated, a matter of national pride that 'we are capable to fight by ourselves and we do not allow any country to interfere in the domestic affairs of the country under the pretext of military aid'.[118] He reported that Khomeini himself had stated that Iran would not ask for Soviet troops to be sent to Iran's assistance. It was less clear whether Iran would refuse Soviet assistance of a much more limited nature, for instance the use of minesweeping vessels in the event of an American naval blockade.

A few weeks later, the CIA discovered that the Soviet General Command had drawn up contingency plans for an occupation of northern Iran in case of a US military attack.[119] Around the same time, on 1 December, the CIA reported a quote from a Fatah official, who claimed that Foreign Minister Gromyko had told a visiting Palestinian that 'we have informed Khomeini that we will not allow any US military aggression against Iran'. The CIA's judgement was that the Kremlin would condemn 'but probably will not confront the US military should they resort to a limited intervention in Iran'.[120] State Department Soviet experts, led by Marshall Shulman, added that Soviet leaders were not exploiting the hostage crisis because they recognised that America's reaction to an 'overtly unhelpful' Soviet role would have 'disastrous implications for US–Soviet relations'. The crisis was, in their view, preventing the Soviet Union from continuing its policy of presenting itself as the Revolution's protector. Nevertheless, Shulman warned that the US–Iranian confrontation was having a potentially dangerous effect on Soviet decision-making. The Soviets were becoming extremely concerned about instability in Iran, and their expectation of an imminent US intervention had probably led them to conclude that the advantages of direct involvement in Afghanistan outweighed the cost in terms of regional and US reactions.[121]

Tehran found it expedient at times to at least allude to a potential alliance with the Soviets in the event of a US military intervention, though they insisted no Russian troops would ever enter Iran. They were much clearer in their insistence that, following Western sanctions, Iran could and would turn to the Soviet Union and its allies as trading partners. Iranian officials noted with satisfaction the German Democratic Republic offer to meet Iran's need for food supplies in the event of an American 'economic siege'.[122]

The Iranians found themselves manipulating the Cold War paradigm, even boasting to the Americans in recognition that Soviet and Warsaw Pact states would be valuable allies in the face of US military and economic pressure. But there was also at least some sense of righteousness in diametrically reversing the strategic advantages America enjoyed during the Shah's era. On 22 November, over two and half weeks into the hostage crisis, an unnamed source quoted in a Spanish paper warned the US of Iran's ability to pass on sensitive US material still in Iran to the Soviets:

> We can do great harm to the US defence system by placing in the Soviet Union's hands the equipment found inside the US Embassy in Tehran and even one of the US F-14s which the United States sold our country during the old regime. It has cost the US many billion in protecting this latest model of aircraft against Soviet espionage.[123]

According to Rubinstein, it was an empty threat; Moscow had already obtained photographs of the F-14 Tomcat fighter aircraft, as well as samples of the AIM-54A Phoenix air-to-air missile, the improved version of the Hawk anti-aircraft missile, and other sophisticated weapons.[124]

The political dynamics of the oil embargo and assets freeze

Within ten days of the US embassy being seized, President Carter had initiated a set of economic sanctions that aimed to demonstrate his determination to extract a price for Iran's continued defiance. On 12 November, the President announced the first of his economic measures: an embargo of Iranian oil. At the start of November 1979, the US was still directly importing about 400,000 barrels of Iranian oil daily and another 200,000 to 300,000 indirectly.[125] The value of these imports to Iran was put at $13.8 million a day.[126] Senior Treasury officials Robert Carswell and Richard Davies were still fully aware that the nature of the world oil market essentially limited the effects of a single embargo to a reshuffling of the distribution chain.[127] Iran had plenty of willing customers for its oil, a fact quickly pointed out by the Iranian oil minister, Ali Akbar Moinfar, and America could easily find alternative supplies to Iranian oil by rerouting oil traffic through swap agreements.[128] The US essentially continued to swap Iranian oil via third parties or buy it once it had changed hands on the spot market. Rather than cause the Iranian economy difficulties, some oil analysts predicted that Iran could even benefit from higher spot market prices.[129] Although Washington recognised that the embargo would have little coercive impact, Carter felt it was politically important to eliminate the perception that oil would influence his response to the crisis.[130] Energy secretary, Charles Duncan, asserted:

'To the extent that the Iranians considered we were dependent on their oil, we want to tell them it is simply not true.'[131]

Moinfar subsequently claimed that the Revolutionary Council had already made the decision to stop oil exports to the US. Had they done so first, the economic effects would not have been different. The oil Iran refused to sell would be made available to other nations; the oil these countries normally purchased elsewhere would be available for export to the US.[132] Carter would, however, have been denied a symbolic victory.[133] As it was, Iran's subsequent cancelling of all contracts with US oil companies appeared meaningless.[134]

Executive Order 12170, which froze 12 billion dollars of Iran's assets, on 14 November, moved beyond political symbolism and established decisive collateral for the US. Yet, the freeze also illustrates the extent to which the sanctions supported much wider objectives than economic coercion. The text of the authorising executive order and accompanying public statements emphasised the need to protect US financial interests from an immediate mass withdrawal of Iranian assets.[135] Whilst the initial report to Congress on the freeze did refer to the need to protect US claimants, it was not widely expected to ensure Iran's debts would not be defaulted.[136] As the conflict dragged on, the frozen assets became increasingly tied up by claims lodged by creditors in courts across the US. After several months it was clear that any negotiated release of the hostages would have to be accompanied by some sort of financial settlement involving the assets and the claimants.[137] The Carter administration had thus established a $12 billion incentive for the Iranians to end the crisis.

The freeze undoubtedly placed more economic and political pressure on the Iranians than all the other economic and political measures combined.[138] Several aspects of the freeze, however, require further qualification when evaluating its effects and implications. First, the freeze was not constructed primarily to punish the Iranian leadership, but to protect US financial interests, and nor did Washington anticipate the eventual leverage it provided in the final negotiations.[139] A secondary point is that the effectiveness of this lever depended heavily on the cooperation of the banks and foreign governments.[140] US Treasury officials also acknowledge that the extraterritorial scope of the freeze threatened America's credibility in the eyes of foreign investors.[141] Some were even concerned that the offence some allies might take to the move could undermine the wider objective of coordinating Iran's economic and political isolation.[142]

The next step for Washington was to convince their closest European allies, who were also Iran's largest trading partners, to support economic sanctions. The US was undeniably asking Western Europe for a much greater economic sacrifice in response to a crisis that initially only marginally affected their interests. EEC exports to Iran had been steadily gaining ground in the first 11 months of 1979, with West Germany alone accounting for almost half their total value of $2.8 billion.[143] Whilst few new contracts were signed after the crisis erupted on 4 November, Europe's existing financial interests were not significantly damaged by it. At the start of 1980, Common Market trade with Iran was running at a rate of about $500 million a month and was still on an upward curve.[144] America's trade with Iran, in contrast, all but ended with the oil embargo, the financial freeze, and longshoremen's boycott of Iranian goods within 2 weeks of the crisis. American exports in January and February 1980 combined equalled a mere $1.8 million.[145]

On 10 December, Secretary of State Cyrus Vance travelled to Britain, Germany, France, Italy, and the NATO council in Brussels. With the White House conscious of Europe's eagerness to protect their investments, Vance was instructed to make clear to the Europeans that 'the alternative to peaceful sanctions was the unilateral US imposition of a blockade, including the possibility of mining'.[146] The Europeans feared that the Iranians could accept a Soviet offer of mine clearance, provoking a potential naval clash with US vessels and catastrophic escalation of East–West tensions. The threat of mining, which also risked sealing off international waters leading into the Persian Gulf, was thus an effective lever for maintaining Europe's interests in cooperating with less dangerous measures.[147] Vance left Europe labouring under the impression that the European allies had not only pledged support in the UN, but they had also agreed to impose sanctions in the event of a Soviet veto.[148]

The Soviet intervention in Afghanistan would, however, drastically modify both the mechanism and the strategic context for the sanctions. The geopolitical dynamics of the crisis had now been totally rearranged, and Soviet intentions in Iran and the response of the Iranian government to this apparent threat required a reassessment.

7
Viewing Afghanistan through the Prism of Iran

The key decision-makers in Washington and in the Soviet Union both viewed events in Afghanistan in the light of the situation in Iran and each other's perceived intentions there.[1] Moscow expected the US to intervene militarily in Iran, and this contributed to a broad pattern of threat perceptions that led to their decision to abandon its previously cautious policy in Afghanistan.[2] The Kremlin also feared that Washington, having been forced from Iran, was attempting to establish a new position in Afghanistan.[3] This theme was taken up in an article in *Pravda*:

> Since the Shah's regime in Iran collapsed, visitors from Western capitals have been incessantly roaming the Middle and Near East. They are engaged in a feverish search for 'a new foothold' in the region.[4]

Soviet intelligence had apparently concluded that Washington was planning an attack on Iran under the guise of releasing the hostages.[5] The Kremlin feared that a show of American force in the region would reassert US power in the Gulf and encourage the Afghan President, Hafizullah Amin, to further loosen his ties with Moscow. Deputy Foreign Minister Gregory Kornienko later admitted that forestalling such a move had influenced the decision to invade.[6]

Washington's vulnerability in this area had been identified in the earliest days of the Carter administration and enshrined in PD-16 and PD-18, both of which called for a strategic pivot towards the region.[7] The US response to the Afghan crisis has to be considered in the light of what some of Carter's advisors, particularly Brown and Brzezinski, saw as long-standing Soviet expansionist ambitions in the Persian Gulf.[8] Within hours of the crisis, Brzezinski told Carter, 'If the Soviets succeed in Afghanistan, and if Pakistan acquiesces, the age-long dream of Moscow to have direct access to the Indian Ocean will have been fulfilled'.[9] 'With Iran destabilised', he warned, 'there will be no firm bulwark in Southwest Asia against the Soviet drive to the Indian Ocean.'[10] Michael Oksenberg summed up the feeling in the National Security Council (NSC): 'this is a major watershed event' with 'profound implications for Soviet willingness to use military might to advance their interests'.[11] Fritz Ermath, a career analyst for the CIA at that time working in the NSC, warned that 'Next we shall very probably see civil strife in Iran with direct Soviet involvement'. The US would then have to decide 'under what conditions of Soviet involvement in Iran would we be prepared to put US forces into Iran'.[12] At a time of intense confrontation between Iran and America, the US ironically became increasingly preoccupied with Iran's security. Some US diplomats were quick to emphasise the connection between America's refusal to send the Iranian military vital spare parts and Iran's newly apparent vulnerability.[13]

At a Special Coordination Committee (SCC) meeting on 14 January, General Jones told a sober audience that for the first time Soviet fighter aircraft based in Afghanistan could reach the Straits of Hormuz, whilst armoured ground forces could reach the Arabian Sea via Baluchistan in 10–12 days.[14] Vance tried to inject a sense of caution to offset some of the more alarmist rhetoric. His chief Soviet advisor, Marshall Shulman, questioned the assumption that the Soviet action was an opportunist push towards the Persian Gulf provoked in part by Iran's vulnerability and America's diminished influence in the region. Shulman also publicly stated his view that the Soviet government invaded Afghanistan out of a broad fear of the creation of a crescent of militant, anti-Soviet nations on its southern border, not because it was seeking to gain control over Middle East oil.[15] Shulman's analysis of a primarily defensive Soviet motivation, although considered naive by many in the NSC, has been subsequently supported by multiple Soviet sources.[16] Indeed, it appears that the Soviet desire to stabilise the regime in Afghanistan was significantly motivated by its perception that the Iranian regime was implacably hostile to the Soviets, despite the hostage crisis, and that its aim was to 'weaken the Afghan regime, exert influence on the Muslim Republics in the Soviet Union, and prevent the spread of Communism in the region'.[17] The Soviets were thus motivated by the efforts of regional powers, including Iran and America, to support the Islamic insurgency.

In the end, however, it was the ascendant Brzezinski's view of Soviet intentions that led Carter to threaten direct military action following any attempt to 'gain control' of the Gulf.[18] Following the Soviet intervention, Brzezinski also began to exert more influence on America's response to the hostage crisis.[19] Brzezinski would, however, be forced to modify his view of US objectives in Iran and embrace Vance's emphasis on non-military policies.[20] Brzezinski recognised that a US military intervention in Iran would greatly increase domestic pressure on the leaders of America's regional allies.[21] Demonstrating America's resolve in Iran became much less important than cultivating regional allies in a reorganised anti-Soviet strategic alliance network. Brzezinski moved away from a major Iranian–American military confrontation, which risked splitting Islamic opposition to Soviet expansionism.[22]

The mutual threat approach

Initially, Carter and his advisors hoped that fear of Soviet aggression would mobilise those 'sensible' enough in Iran to end Iran's confrontation with America. Days after the Soviet intervention in Afghanistan, Brzezinski declared, 'I should think that every sober-headed Iranian – even the most anti-American ones – ought to ask themselves what do the events in Kabul portend for Tehran. There have been Soviet troops in Tehran before. Tehran could be next.'[23] Carter publicly outlined the need 'To persuade the Iranian leaders that the real danger to their nation lies to the North from Soviet troops in Afghanistan, and that the unwarranted Iranian quarrel with us hampers their response to this greater danger'.[24] The notion that the Soviet Union's invasion of Afghanistan would demonstrate in the clearest possible terms that Iran continued its confrontation with America at its peril was an instinctive and highly tempting analysis. Yet there were early signs that the Afghan crisis would not offer the US significant leverage. When asked by ABC News correspondent Frank Reynolds about the opportunity, Carter was quick to downplay the linkage to the American people:

> That may be a factor, but I think a minor factor. I understand that some of the European ambassadors did go to Qom with the purpose of talking to Khomeini after the Soviet invasion of Afghanistan, to remind Khomeini or his leaders there that this was a new and unprecedented threat to Iran, and that the resolution of the kidnapping of the hostages should be reconsidered under the new circumstances. But whether that has any affect on Khomeini, I just don't know.[25]

For Vance, Soviet intervention was a severe setback to what he had thought his primary goal would be as Secretary of State: improved East–West relations. Conversely, he saw a potentially positive effect on the crisis that would actually define his administration. The principal problem in the eyes of many in Washington was that Khomeini was impervious to geopolitical or strategic logic. Many in the State Department began, however, to believe that others in the Iranian government were fearful of Soviet aggression and could impress this upon Khomeini or the Revolutionary Council. Vance would later note: 'We received indications through our indirect channels that the Afghanistan invasion had stirred the interest of some of the Iranian leaders in a sign from us that would help them move Khomeini toward a resolution of the crisis.'[26]

Vance, when talking of indirect channels, was referring to Richard Cottam, who was then the main point of contact between the State Department and the Iranian government, and specifically Sadegh Ghotbzadeh. Speaking by phone, with Ghotbzadeh insisting on using code, Cottam asked Ghotbzadeh about the linkage between Afghanistan and the hostages and 'whether the argument could be made to Khomeini that once the hostage issue was over, Iran could assume a world role in opposing the Soviets'.[27] Ghotbzadeh replied that, although Afghanistan was important to him and others in the Revolutionary Council, 'it was not an effective argument with Khomeini'. According to Ghotbzadeh, he had already 'gotten into some trouble with the "party" because of his strong statement on Afghanistan'.[28] Khomeini was at the time much more preoccupied by internal threats and particularly his ongoing struggle with Ayatollah Shariatmadari. On 12 January, Iranian authorities in Tabriz raided the heavily fortified headquarters of the opposition MPRP, broadly loyal to Ayatollah Shariatmadari, arresting 11 supporters and 4 hours later executing them by firing squad.[29]

Despite Ghotbzadeh's downplaying any appeal to Khomeini on strategic grounds, his own enthusiasm for the Afghan linkage was seized upon by the State Department. At a tense NSC meeting, Vance declared: 'It is clear that the Iranians see the Soviet move into Afghanistan as a threat. This is where we must place the weight of our argument.'[30] Harold Saunders wrote that it was 'not without significance' that a 'key figure at the Iranian end of the channel was concerned about the implications of the Soviet invasion'.[31] Carter's Chief of Staff Hamilton Jordan had also expressed his belief that pressure was increasing on the Iranians to 'look to its interests vis-à-vis Afghanistan and the Soviets, and recognise that it badly needed a support that the US is willing to give if the hostage crisis can be resolved'.[32] This pressure would not, he told Carter, be 'effective on Khomeini or the militants, but it will strengthen the hand of the new president, or of the more sensible people around a failing Khomeini'.[33]

Ghotbzadeh seemed to be doing his best to galvanise some kind of response on Afghanistan. In an interview with *Le Figaro*, the Iranian Foreign Minister, who was himself about to contest the presidential elections, claimed he was 'very worried and alarmed' by the presence of Soviet tanks near the Afghan–Iran border.[34] He told reporters that the occupation of Afghanistan was a direct and intolerable threat to Iran.[35]

Just one day later, Ghotbzadeh walked back from his previous alarmist tone, probably in light of the political tensions he had outlined to Cottam. He now displayed little fear of an imminent Soviet invasion of Iran. Though insistent of Iran's deep opposition to Moscow's action, he noted that 'the question is not whether there are 20 km, 40 km or 100 km between the tanks and our border'.[36] Ghotbzadeh portrayed Iran as not unduly panicked by the external Soviet threat, but instead resolute in their diplomatic objection to what it maintained was an affront to the entire region.[37]

Apart from Ghotbzadeh, and with Bazargan, Yazdi, and Entezam out of the picture, it was difficult to see which 'sensible people' around Khomeini could be influenced regarding the situation in Afghanistan. The first elected President of the Islamic Republic, Abolhassan Bani-Sadr, was undoubtedly sensible and vocally supportive of the Afghan mujahedeen. The Soviets were clearly threatened enough by Bani-Sadr for the KGB to target him, along with Ghotbzadeh, for 'active measures'.[38] Yet Bani-Sadr had also been critical of Bazargan's engagement with America, particularly the Algiers meeting, and had alleged that Washington was supporting ethnic separatists.[39]

The CIA reported that Bani-Sadr did not believe Iran needed a close relationship with the US to deter any potential Soviet aggression against Iran. He had also rejected the possibility of military aid to Iran in the future. French intelligence, which knew Bani-Sadr well from his fifteen-year exile in Paris, described him to the CIA as a staunch advocate of a non-aligned foreign policy. As President, he would oppose an increased US security presence in the region and reject any mutual arrangements with US allies such as Egypt and Saudi Arabia. The CIA believed the new President advocated cordial relations with the US, but would be an unlikely facilitator of strategic alliance:

> Even if Bani-Sadr should become more concerned about the Soviet threat to Iran in the future, it is unlikely that he could openly align Iran with the US without facing major domestic criticism. Anti-Americanism is likely to remain a fundamental aspect of Iranian politics for some time and one that can easily be manipulated by Bani-Sadr's rivals against him. Moreover, Khomeini seems certain to continue to view the US as the greatest enemy of his vision of an Islamic government. The Ayatollah can remove Bani-Sadr from power at anytime.

The intelligence memorandum concluded that Bani-Sadr was unconcerned that Iran's support for the Afghan rebels would provoke Soviet reprisals against Iran and that the threat of guerrilla warfare was a sufficient deterrent. A quote from the Iranian President sums up his attitude: 'We do not intend to liberate ourselves from the hegemony of one of the two super powers only to fall under the yoke of another.'[40] As an alternative to superpower alignment, Bani-Sadr argued that Iran could and should procure the military and economic aid it required from Western Europe and Japan. In his view, the hostage crisis was a mistake because it would alienate Iran from these markets.

Other contacts inside Iran offered more hope. In February 1980, Hamilton Jordan met with an individual described only as a 'Mr S' but believed to be an influential member of the Revolutionary Council and very close to Khomeini. Jordan conceded Mr S's potential deviousness, but wrote that his concern for the Soviet threat, and belief that the hostage crisis had eroded Iran's ability to resist it, appeared genuine. Jordan quoted the Iranian as saying that 'I want them [the hostages] out so that we can turn our full anger and attention toward the Soviet Union'. The mysterious Iranian was even reported to be anxious to use the excuse of a small US diplomatic presence to reduce the Soviet embassy to a comparable size. After handing over intelligence on Soviet troop movements on Iran's north-west border, Jordan gushed that 'He loved it. He said, I will show this paper at the next meeting of the Council and tell everyone to get off their asses and prepare for attempted Soviet domination of Iran.'[41] Even at the height of a crisis in relations, the US was sharing intelligence with almost anyone who would listen. Mr S was not the first Iranian claiming influence over Khomeini and a conviction that the hostage crisis was a strategic error. He was also not the only official to reassure the US of a likely imminent resolution to the crisis.

Regardless of the CIA's assessment of Bani-Sadr and Cottam's conversations with Ghotbzadeh suggesting Khomeini would not link decision-making on the hostages to Soviet aggression in Afghanistan, the State Department still considered it a worthwhile strategy. Vance communicated Washington's post-Afghanistan strategy for the hostage crisis in two separate telegrams to Ghotbzadeh, Bani-Sadr, and his associate Ahmad Salamatian delivered via the Swiss ambassador to Iran, Erik Lang. The first telegram was a statement of America's position that had initially been sent in January but could not be verified as received in Tehran. It was a six-point statement outlining what America would offer in return for the safe and immediate release of the hostages. This included the facilitation of legal claims on the Shah's assets, an end to economic sanctions, a statement that the US 'understood the grievances felt by the people of Iran', and cooperation in a UN-sponsored forum to hear Iranian grievances. Crucially, however, it included an offer to discuss the 'current threat posed by the Soviet invasion of Afghanistan and to recommend to their government steps that the US and Iran might take in order to enhance the security of Iran, including the resumption of the supply of military spare parts by the United States to Iran'. The second statement went much further in emphasising the Soviet threat and presented information on Soviet troop movements and strength. It cautioned that Soviet moves were probably best interpreted as 'preparations for contingencies, rather than as signs of any decision in Moscow to undertake operations in the next months against Iran'. But the statement was clear: the Soviets were worried about instability and cross-border operations in Afghanistan and had shown their willingness to take any action they deemed necessary. To really hammer the point home, the telegram noted reports that Moscow still considered those parts of the 1921 Friendship Treaty which provided certain rights of military intervention in Iran to be valid. By way of a diplomatic and strategic opening, the telegram ended: 'Can the GOI confirm these reports, and if so, how does Iran interpret the Soviet position?[42] Unsurprisingly, this invitation met with no response.

There appeared no hope of persuading Khomeini of the benefits of strategic alliance, and those moderates who could appear further isolated when the clerically dominated Islamic Republican Party won control of the Majlis in March. Washington then largely gave up on Ghotbzadeh after the collapse of the Villalon–Bourget initiative and Ghotbzadeh's subsequent discrediting inside Iran.[43] Richard Cottam now posited that Ghotbzadeh's claim to be the main obstacle to communist influence in the new regime was perhaps self-serving. Ghotbzadeh was never fully trusted in the US, perhaps for good reason, but there is little reason to doubt his anti-communist credentials. In the spring of 1980, he told Moscow that it if it failed to withdraw troops from Afghanistan, Iran would give military assistance to the mujahedeen, and in July he ordered the Soviet embassy to cut its staff.

Much later it would be revealed that Ghotbzadeh was seen as such a threat by the Soviet Union that he was the target of sustained disinformation attacks by the KGB. Soviet agents passed onto Iranian contacts highly incriminating forged letters purporting to be from a US Senator. In July 1980, the Iranian ambassador in Paris was fed disinformation alleging that Ghotbzadeh was plotting with the Americans to overthrow Khomeini and claiming he had received $6 million in return for aiding the six embassy staff who were smuggled out with the assistance of the Canadian embassy.[44] Christopher Andrew suggests that it is likely that these allegations 'probably helped to bring about Ghotbzadeh dismissal in August'.[45]

Ghotbzadeh in any case had been unable to mobilise any real collective threat amongst the Iranian government. On 19 January 1980, he confirmed that Iran had taken 'no military measures to face up to the advance of Soviet tanks'.[46] Even by April 1980, Major General Shadmehr admitted that the military's response to Soviet manoeuvres and troop movements in the region of the Caucasus amounted to border guards 'watching their activities'.[47]

Ghotbzadeh continued his scathing attacks on the Soviet Union, most viscerally during a September interview in *Time*, but by that time he was speaking with the freedom of a man who knew his political career was sliding into the abyss.[48] The KGB would also continue to attack him long after he had been forced out of government, including a planted bogus CIA telegram, and would later claim some of the credit for his eventual arrest and execution in 1982.[49]

Analysing the Soviet military threat to Iran

The CIA was slow to predict that a major shift in Soviet policy in Afghanistan had occurred by early December. Even so, the Carter administration was very clear of the linkage between events in Iran and Afghanistan. In a mid-December SCC meeting on Iran, put together to discuss the latest developments in the hostage crisis, DCI Turner briefed participants on Soviet involvement in Afghanistan. The DCI started by observing that Soviet forces had remained stable in Afghanistan until recently, but now there was evidence of movement. Two new command posts had been created just north of the Afghan border and Soviet air assets appeared to be building up. The

DCI concluded, incorrectly, that the CIA 'did not see this as a crash build-up but rather as a steady planned build-up, perhaps related to Soviet perceptions of a deterioration of the Afghan military forces and the need to beef them up and some point'.[50] The Soviets, the CIA believed, had made a political decision to keep a pro-Soviet regime in power and to use military force to that end if necessary.[51]

What Turner did not know was that five days before this briefing, the final decision had been made in the Kremlin for a large-scale deployment of Soviet troops.[52] Turner was, in effect, simply repeating the findings of an Intelligence Community 'Alert Memorandum' from 14 September 1979. This report had stated: 'Soviet leaders may be on the threshold of a decision to commit their own forces to prevent the collapse of the regime and protect their sizeable stakes in Afghanistan.'[53] This memorandum had also made the judgement that, if Moscow ultimately did increase its military role, it was likely to do so only incrementally, by raising the number of military advisors and expanding their role in assisting the Afghan army in combat operations.[54] Turner, by mid-December, now believed there to be approximately 5,000 Soviet military advisors in Afghanistan, an increase of roughly 2,000 since the September Alert Memorandum. Whilst the CIA believed that the Soviets were preparing to directly intervene, militarily, to shore up a favourable position in Afghanistan, there was sharp disagreement as to the scale and role of Soviet troop involvement. Only a small minority of analysts argued that a large-scale Soviet invasion, of between 30,000 and 40,000 troops, was imminent.[55]

On 14 January, the NSC's pressman, Jerry Schecter, quoted a UPI report that a Soviet division of at least 10,000 troops had taken up positions along Iran's border within 'striking distance of Iran's oil fields'. To Schecter, the parallels between the Soviet build-up in Afghanistan and its relationship with the Tudeh were 'striking'. The CIA was asked to prepare a paper which would 'relate Afghanistan to Iran to show Soviet efforts with the Tudeh party'. Schecter asked, 'who is the Iranian Babrak Karmal; are the Soviets preparing an Iranian puppet?'[56]

There were compelling reasons why the similarity was not striking. Afghanistan had never been a US client state and pro-Soviet groups there had not been reduced to political or military insignificance, as they had in Iran under the Shah. The Iranian military had never, in any degree, been sympathetic to the Marxist cause. In contrast, it had been the Afghan army which had executed Mohammad Daoud Khan and effectively transferred power to People's Democratic Party of Afghanistan leader Nur Muhammad Taraki. The US embassy in Kabul characterised the DRA's outlook as 'generally indistinguishable from those of the Soviet Union and Cuba, and which do not take into account important US interests'.[57] The victory of the Islamists in Iran was, however, at the expense of America's most powerful regional client.

This was broadly the view that Marshall Shulman and Vance took. It was also the thrust of a CIA report of 15 January. It summarised the extent of Soviet ambitions thus:

> It is unlikely that the Soviet intervention in Afghanistan constitutes the pre-planned first step in the implementation of a highly articulated grand design for the rapid establishment of hegemonic control over all of Southwest Asia. Rather than signalling the carefully timed beginning of a premeditated strategic offensive, the occupation may have been a reluctantly authorised response to what was perceived by the Kremlin as an imminent and otherwise irreversible deterioration of its already established position in a country which fell well within the Soviet Union's legitimate sphere of influence.[58]

In contrast, the Defense Intelligence Agency (DIA) offered a highly alarmist commentary on the conventional military threat now facing Iran. 'The key motivation that propelled Moscow's move was to bring its long-standing strategic goals within reach. Control of Afghanistan would be a major step toward overland access to the Indian Ocean and to domination of the Asian sub-continent.'[59] The DIA made the threat to Iran explicit a few days later:

> Recent Soviet military activity in [excised] indicates Soviet Armed Forces in that area are in the early stages of preparation to take action in Iran. DIA believes these activities reflect intent to be prepared to intervene militarily in Iran, should the Soviet leadership elect that course of action. Assuming continued preparations, DIA believes Soviet forces will reach readiness for threat of war within the next few weeks.[60]

Few in the CIA disputed the need for a strong deterrence posture or enhanced security capability in region, but they broadly maintained the line that the balance of evidence suggested a reluctant and limited intervention aimed at consolidating the pro-Moscow regime in Afghanistan.[61] Exactly 3 weeks after Fritz Ermath recommended the US to consider its response to what he perceived as a Soviet ambition to control the Middle East, Carter drew his line in the sand. Pressed by Brzezinski for the need to send an unmistakable and explicit warning to the Soviets, Carter proclaimed his 'Doctrine':

> Let our position be absolutely clear: An attempt by any outside force to gain control of the Persian Gulf region will be regarded as an assault on the vital interests of the United States of America, and such an assault will be repelled by any means necessary, including military force.

Carter was essentially bluffing; the US military had little realistic capability of repelling a Soviet push into Iran, Pakistan, or even Turkey. A document known as the Wolfowitz report leaked to *New York Times* reporter Richard Burt affirmed the fact that US forces would not be able to repulse a Soviet push into northern Iran and, as such, the US should consider the use of tactical nuclear weapons in the event of a conflict in the region.[62] The Wolfowitz report concluded that the US could place only 20,000 US troops in theatre in the first 30 days of a conflict, whilst the Soviets could introduce 100,000.[63] The day before the leak, Vance had tried to play down some of the more alarmist rhetoric coming from, amongst others, Presidential Special Envoy Clark Clifford, who had recently stated that any Soviet intervention in the Persian Gulf would mean war. Vance felt that it was a mistake to 'draw lines' which could force the US to take a position it would later regret not being able to defend. He called Clark's verbosity 'more dramatic than necessary', asserting that he would have used 'different language'.[64]

Another of the hard chargers was Paul Henze. Henze had for some time worried about Soviet designs on Iran. Even before the Soviet intervention in Afghanistan he had lambasted the CIA and State Department, in several memos to Brzezinski, for not doing enough to gather evidence on Soviet covert operations in Iran or respond adequately to Soviet aggression in the Muslim world. In another memo on 11 April, he suggested that it was 'impossible to believe that the Soviets could resist temptation to take over most of Iran if the opportunity presented itself'.[65] According to Henze, the Soviets were now more likely to foment instability in Iran in order to get boots on the ground as a 'protecting power'. Brzezinski expected civil strife in Iran with direct Soviet involvement, a communist takeover in North Yemen, and increased Soviet efforts to destabilise Turkey and Pakistan.[66] The notion that 'The Soviets might see an intervention "to restore order" as attractive' had been raised by Richard Lehman, Chairman of the National Intelligence Council, even before Soviet troops entered Afghanistan.[67] Both Lehman and Henze warned that would have to be factored into any attempt by the US to destabilise the regime in response to the hostage crisis. This led Henze to believe that any US military response in Iran could not be limited to simply blockades or bombs and would have to entail the occupation of a 'sizeable part of the country'.[68]

The wide variety of responses was mirrored in the responses Washington received from some of its allies. The Europeans, though profoundly anxious for the implications of the interventions for East–West relations and détente, did not see Soviet ambitions in the region as starkly as many in the US.[69] The Israelis, who were gravely strategically and economically threatened by Soviet hegemony in the Persian Gulf, put their view of Soviet aggression forcefully: 'A single theme emerges strikingly from the Israeli analysis', a Defence Intelligence Agency report stated. 'A blatant Soviet drive toward the Persian Gulf has begun. Coming on the heels of the Iranian crisis, Israelis are concerned that the US may be unable, if not unwilling, to react forcefully to blatant provocation.'[70] Prime Minister Rabin, in a recent newspaper article, put the Israeli view simply: 'The Russians now pose the greatest danger to Israel's future.'[71]

With Sino–Soviet relations extremely hostile, an equally self-serving analysis was offered by the Chinese. Peking's view was that 'Soviet objectives in Afghanistan range far beyond the desire to control that country and represent an important step in the Kremlin's plan to gain direct access to the Indian Ocean and control Western oil supplies in the Persian Gulf Region'.[72] The Chinese also made an explicit Iranian linkage: 'The Soviet move came at this time in part because the Soviet Union saw that the United States was preoccupied with [the] crisis in Iran.'

In February, DCI Turner requested the Assistant National Intelligence Officer responsible for the USSR to produce a straw-man paper making what from the Soviet point of view might be the 'best case' for military intervention in Iran. This attempt to play devil's advocate was of little value, with the officer responsible trying in vain to simulate a level of recklessness and adventurism in the Politburo he clearly felt highly improbable. The report concluded that the Soviet Union would be most likely to intervene in order to prevent the state's disintegration but would be unable to do much to prevent 'fissiparous trends'.[73] The rest of the study simply restated observations of Iran's strategic importance that had underpinned US policy there for 30 years.

In mid-April, Brzezinski's daily report to the President included reference to 'possible shift in Soviet policy towards Iran' and that the 'Soviets are becoming increasingly disposed to use military force in northwest Iran'.[74] Brzezinski was basing his warning on a report by the Strategic Warning Staff, which had observed increasing Soviet clandestine political activity in the region and increasingly diminishing tolerance for turmoil on the Soviet border. 'If the Soviets decide to move, we might have no more than a few days of unambiguous warning', Brzezinski solemnly informed Carter. Seeking a modicum of balance to this stark warning, he added the caveat that 'Other elements of the Community are less alarmed, at least about the very near term, contending that the Soviets are still trying to posture politically and in propaganda for a more favorable relationship with Tehran'.[75]

A special national intelligence assessment of Soviet military options in Iran produced in August 1980 took a similar line, concluding that although the Soviets were taking steps to strengthen the ability of its forces to invade Iran, should Soviet leaders decide, they did not anticipate such a move.[76] Overall they viewed Soviet intentions as highly sensitive to both US military action and instability on the border, and preventing either or both was viewed as the most likely circumstances for a Soviet intervention. Should the Soviets decide to seize NW Iran, the CIA claimed to be able to provide at most a week's notice. A large-scale invasion of between 16 and 20 divisions would be visible approximately a month before. For the next few months at least, they expected Moscow to pursue its goals 'without direct use of military force'. In this context, instability in Iran remained an opportunity for Soviet subversive activities. The State Department's top intelligence officer specialising in Iran and Afghanistan, George Griffin, advised that the Soviet Union was 'constructing a better justification for a future attack on Pakistan, and perhaps Iran if subversion and cross-border thrusts do not produce the results they want'.[77]

Sanctions after Afghanistan: Cold War, transatlantic, and political dynamics

The immediate consequence of the Soviet intervention was the collapse of a United Nations framework for sanctions. Carter agreed to delay the vote for their adoption until the 13 January, but by then the announcement of a US grain embargo against the Soviets ended any illusion of Soviet cooperation. The predictable Soviet veto established much more problematic political and legal conditions for European sanctions.[78] Most of the EEC countries had laws similar to the US federal law United Nations Participation Act, which gives the President authority to enforce Security Council decisions. In the absence of a UN mandate, Carter could still impose sanctions using laws granting him emergency powers. Most European leaders, including West Germany and Britain, had no such authority and would have to pass specific legislation to adopt the financial and commercial restrictions mentioned in the vetoed UN sanctions.[79]

European diplomats also worried that sanctions were a tactical mistake, potentially weakening the position of moderate factions inside Iran who they believed were working towards the release of the hostages.[80] They also worried that Iran's economic collapse could invite Soviet interference or throw Iran into economic dependence on the Eastern bloc.[81] They noted Reza Salimi, Iran's finance minister, boasting that, in the event of a naval blockade, Iran had already arranged to ship all the supplies it required through the Soviet Union.[82] Washington was largely unconvinced, however, by the practical extent to which Iran could reconfigure its economy towards the Soviet bloc. A CIA analysis concluded, 'Despite publicity given by the Iranian Government to some recent trade deals with the USSR and East European countries, the Bloc does not represent an attractive alternative to Western goods or markets'. The report also concluded that the Soviet bloc only accounted for 5 percent of Iranian imports and would find it extremely difficult to replace the dominant position of the West in Iran's commercial relations.[83]

Meanwhile, the utility of the sanctions was being re-fashioned by Brzezinski's developing response to the Soviet intervention in Afghanistan. In Brzezinski's own words, the result was that 'during the next three months, the primary emphasis of our efforts was on gradually intensifying the sanctions while engaging in more direct and indirect negotiations'.[84] Military action, which was the main alternative to sanctions being considered, had to be ruled out.[85] Not only would military action offend the regional allies America needed to cultivate, Iran now appeared more visibly vulnerable to Soviet subversion and the possibility of future reconciliation had to be retained. As one US official explained, 'We do not want to put so much pressure on that it would lead to a disintegration of the country or to a permanent alienation between Iran and the United States'.[86]

Despite Brzezinski now appearing enthusiastic for sanctions as a non-military demonstration of American resolve, this did not reflect any increased optimism that they would have an effect in Tehran. The CIA delivered an equally pessimistic assessment of the value of sanctions: 'Our current economic pressures are unlikely to have any positive effect; their impact may be negative.'[87] This reassessment fitted closely with the advice Vance and Saunders had been receiving since the crisis began. At the same time, a new emphasis on negotiations was also provoked by the opening up of a new diplomatic channel with Iranian Foreign Minister Sadegh Ghotbzadeh and two intermediaries, Christian Bourget and Hector Villalon.[88] Together with UN Secretary General Waldheim, Villalon and Bourget urged the establishment of a special UN Commission to hear Iran's grievances and offer a suitably cathartic mechanism for the Iranians to release the hostages.

With the Iranians in agreement, and Bani-Sadr duly elected on 25 January, Washington was optimistic that it had finally found 'a firm commitment to resolve the crisis and negotiating partners who could negotiate with authority'.[89] During these negotiations, Ghotbzadeh had made it very clear that Khomeini was indifferent to US pressure.[90] Hamilton Jordan advised the President, 'Be quiet about sanctions. They are not a hopeful line anyway and are getting us crossways with our allies.'[91]

US hopes were quickly dashed. Khomeini refused the commission access to the hostages unless it first condemned America's crimes in Iran and the Third World.[92] Unable to do so under the terms of its charter, the Commission collapsed on 11 March. The affair left Ghotbzadeh, who had naively assured Khomeini that America would apologise before any movement was made on the hostages' release, damaged in both Iran and America.[93] Carter finally lost all patience when Villalon and Bourget inexplicably chose to forge a handwritten letter from Carter to Khomeini expressing his 'understanding' at Iran's actions and begging for the hostages to be released.[94] On 25 March, European leaders received a secret message from Carter outlining a timetable for tough new US measures to try to resolve the hostage situation. The timetable began with joint US–European sanctions and ended with a mid-May deadline for the Iranian government to release the hostages, after which the US would consider military options.[95]

This timetable was soon revised when the Carter administration perceived encouraging steps in Tehran and the imminent transfer of the hostages to government control. Carter later announced these positive developments on the morning of 1 April at the Wisconsin primary. As had happened before, America's hopes were dashed. Khomeini refused to force the militants to transfer the hostages to government control. In response, on 7 April, Carter announced a ban on exports to Iran and a break in diplomatic relations under Executive Order 12205. Carter stated, 'I am committed to the safe return of the American hostages and to the preservation of our national honor'.[96] This aspiration was eclipsed by the economic insignificance of the sanctions. US exports to Iran were only $1.4 million per month, compared to approximately $280 million per month in 1978.[97] Ronald Reagan, then the Republican front runner for the 1980 election campaign, wasted no time pointing this out: 'The drop in trade since this began has been so great that there really will be no impact on Iran at all.'[98]

April 1980 was a disastrous month for President Carter. His announcement of positive developments helped carry him to victory in Wisconsin and Kansas. The raising and subsequent dashing of America's collective hope destroyed one of Carter's few remaining assets: his promise not to play politics with the hostages. When Carter announced EO 12211 (banning all Iranian imports) on 17 April, he made it painfully obvious that Europe, if it wanted to avoid a US military response, had to come on board with a positive public statement supporting sanctions immediately.[99]

This ultimatum was misleading. Six days earlier, President Carter had already nominally agreed to launch Operation Eagle Claw, a military rescue of the hostages.[100] The day before announcing EO 12211, Carter signed the executive order authorising the mission for the 24th of April. Carter was admittedly operating under intense military and political pressures. By early May, temperatures in Iran would rise and available hours of darkness would drop; both these conditions would require major revisions in the plans and significantly increase all the risk factors.[101] Short of a significant change in the situation in Iran, this was the timetable dictating the rescue mission; European cooperation on sanctions had little bearing. Nevertheless, the EEC agreed on 22 April to enact sanctions.

Having agreed to a policy that most felt had little or no value beyond preventing military action and shoring up Western solidarity, Western leaders were privately shocked and dismayed by Carter's decision to launch the doomed rescue mission just days after the Luxembourg announcement. US officials explained their apparent duplicity by defining the rescue mission as 'an antiterrorist mission with humanitarian considerations'.[102] Carter had damaged a key accomplishment of the sanctions: transatlantic solidarity. Despite this, all of the EEC leaders dutifully pledged to still adopt the measures agreed in Luxembourg.

The Europeans still did not believe that they would compel the Iranians to release the hostages, but hoped they would prevent a US military intervention, which would threaten détente and security in the Persian Gulf. More broadly, they hoped to offset their refusal to support sanctions against the Soviets and to demonstrate their commitment to a transatlantic alliance at a time when they were also anxious about an impending American diversion from European security and resisting Washington's call for NATO to take a more active role in the Third World.[103] The US simply needed their support to demonstrate Carter's ability to organise an international response to the crisis and because sanctions without European cooperation would appear entirely toothless. In order to elicit this cooperation, they were able to manipulate some of the anxieties the Soviet intention and the hostage crisis had provoked in Europe. They did so by setting up a false choice between sanctions and military action.

The effects of the multilateral sanctions on the transatlantic alliance were thus partly contradictory. Although European cooperation eventually demonstrated solidarity, that unity was achieved through a certain degree of American duplicity and the manipulation of some underlining weaknesses within the transatlantic alliance. As Brzezinski would later admit: 'We were more likely to increase the chances of our allies joining us in sanctions against Iran if they became convinced that we were planning some sort of military action.'[104] The whole episode demonstrates, once again, the extent to which events in Iran and Afghanistan had become conflated.

The economic sacrifice Europe endured was still undeniably minimal; the sanctions were chiefly limited to contracts signed after 4 November. An estimated $10 billion would have been lost to Western European countries trading with Iran if the deals contracted before had been cancelled.[105] As Deputy Secretary of State Warren Christopher admitted: 'A large dose of realism is useful in evaluating another country's willingness to join in sanctions, especially in response to an episode that affects them only indirectly.'[106]

There is also little evidence to suggest that even substantially stronger EEC trade sanctions would have compelled the Iranian leadership to release the hostages any earlier. The Soviet veto of United Nations sanctions, and Iran's ability to import goods indirectly through third countries, ensured that Iran could source what it needed without facing severe economic difficulties.[107] The belief that the Iranian leadership could be coerced by economic pressure showed also a fundamental misunderstanding of who they were dealing with. The current Supreme Leader, Ali Khamenei, summed up Ayatollah Khomeini's response to economic sanctions thus:

> When those countries imposed sanctions on the Islamic Republic, the late Imam Khomeini expressed happiness in this regard and welcomed their action. The late Imam's reaction was quite meaningful, since because of those sanctions the Iranian people turned to their own resources and stood on their own two feet.[108]

Economic sanctions were perhaps most tactically useful as a substitute for actions that were potentially more damaging to Western interests. There are also indications that the Carter administration viewed Europe's cooperation as primarily symbolic. As one US official put it, the US was after 'form and not substance' of sanctions in order to 'isolate Iran diplomatically and put it under psychological pressure'.[109]

Symbolically they aimed to exact some economic cost to Iran's actions, but more importantly demonstrate American resolve to confront Iran without compromising wider regional strategies. Ultimately, it was not in America's interest for sanctions to critically destabilise the Iranian regime. Six months after Europe adopted sanctions, their tactical value was set forth in the transitional policy papers that outlined existing government policy. Prepared by the State Department in October 1980, the paper advised:

> Maintain our sanctions as part of a policy of doing no business with Iran, but permit our allies to resume trade and the provision of services to Iran to partly end Iran's isolation and allow some repair of sanctions/war/Revolution-caused damage to the economy.[110]

US perceptions of Iranian support for Afghans

In May 1979, Charles Naas had reported that the Iranian response to an appeal from Afghan rebels for more military assistance had been turned down by Khomeini personally. Instead, Khomeini promised 'humanitarian assistance'.[111] Naas added that other senior clerics, notably Ayatollah Rohani, were calling for a more active policy from the Iranian government but at this stage Khomeini was not interested.[112]

The Bazargan government, preoccupied with its own fragility, had little interest in devoting time or resources to the Afghans. Nor did they wish to provoke retaliatory Soviet interference in Iran's own internal conflicts. Foreign Minister Ebrahim Yazdi had met with Afghan officials during the Havana Non-Aligned Summit and later publicly confirmed that he had told the Afghans of Iran's intention not to interfere. Shortly before the Soviet intervention in Afghanistan, Abolhassan Bani-Sadr described as 'unfortunate' the Bazargan policy in Afghanistan.[113] To Bani-Sadr, Iran was not doing enough to help the Afghan rebels resisting the Soviet-supported Kabul government. He described Tehran's policy as not so much ineffective but 'weak and non existent'.[114] Though there is no doubting Bani-Sadr's antagonism to Soviet policy, it is also likely that Bani-Sadr already had one eye on the upcoming presidential elections 2 months later and was aware that his main rival, Sadegh Ghotbzadeh, would take a hard line on the Soviet Union.

Two months after making this statement, Bani-Sadr was elected President and Afghan policy became the responsibility of his government. The

US hoped that the escalation of the Afghan conflict following the direct involvement of Soviet troops would provoke an acceleration of Iranian support for the mujahedeen. In February 1980, the CIA provided the Iran working group with a profile of Bani-Sadr which suggested he appeared genuinely committed to supporting the Afghan insurgent movement.[115] The memorandum added that Bani-Sadr had promised training and weapons to the insurgents and, according to one statement, indicated that Iranian volunteers would be allowed to fight with the rebels. Nor was he concerned, in the CIA's opinion, by any potential Soviet military retaliation for doing so.[116]

Despite these and other bullish statements, there appeared little tangible evidence of an acceleration of support. It appeared that the central government was at best peripheral to Iranian support for Afghan insurgents. Even Khomeini, who as noted in Chapter 2 had lectured the Soviet ambassador about meddling in Afghanistan, did not issue anything approximating a call for arms. The State Department would later note their surprise at his reticence.[117] Instead, it was the religious figures and tribal leaders, mainly along the Afghan border, who had been giving support to the rebels, mostly independently. Amongst the many refugee camps that ran across Iran's eastern border, at least one Afghan source indicated that some of the refugees included former Afghan military personnel who were training insurgents with the tacit support of local Iranian authorities.[118] There were some reports that the religious leadership was providing some training and weapons support, but only of a very limited nature.[119] It was almost impossible, however, for US intelligence to distinguish between government and clerical authority in providing this aid.[120]

Foreign Minister Sadegh Ghotbzadeh outlined Iran's policy in Afghanistan in three simple terms. First, all Soviet troops must leave Afghanistan. Second, the 'insurgents' should be brought into a new government. Third, the Karmal regime cannot be recognised as Kabul's legitimate government but could participate in negotiations on the country's future as an 'interested party'.[121] In terms of their active support for the Afghan rebels, the CIA perceived that they had 'shown no sign of changing its policy of not giving any official support to the Afghan insurgent movement'.[122]

The Iranians remained not just distracted, but reluctant to risk Afghan or Soviet military retaliation on their poorly defended and tribally and ethnically fractious north-eastern border. They probably also recognised the need to not alienate the Soviet Union as the Carter administration was attempting to push through UN sanctions. For this reason, in early 1980, the CIA predicted that 'It is less likely that the Iranian government itself will openly back the insurgents in the near term'.[123] In May 1980, American intelligence described Iran's support for the insurgents as remaining 'largely symbolic'.[124] It judged the Iranian government as being too preoccupied with other problems and noted that even Afghans had 'publicly expressed dissatisfaction with the lack of significant Iranian support'.[125]

A less measured analysis was offered in a more extensive assessment of Iran's role in Afghanistan, in June, which judged Iranian involvement with the insurgents as 'certain to increase'.[126] The US continued to receive reports regarding Ghotbzadeh's bullish attitude to the Soviets. During a visit to Sweden in mid-June, he reportedly told his Swedish counterpart that Iran would do its best to 'create hell' for the Soviets in Afghanistan.[127] It was about this time that Ghotbzadeh publicly warned Moscow that if it did not withdraw, Iran would start arming the mujahedeen. The Soviet response was a savage KGB campaign against Ghotbzadeh that likely contributed to his downfall. By late June 1980, a CIA memorandum written by the Office of Political Analysis, in conjunction with the National Intelligence Officer for Near East/South Asia, reported that the Soviets were increasingly alarmed by Iran's role in Afghanistan. It also judged that Tehran 'provided important diplomatic support to the insurgents fighting the Soviets'.[128]

The differentiated attitude of the central government and the clergy, local officials, and elements of the Revolutionary Guard made it very difficult for the US to analyse Iran's overall strategy and capabilities in Afghanistan. It made it equally hard to judge the implications for US policy, regional stability, and Soviet–Iranian relations. The central government was perceived to have not 'lived up to its promises to provide material aid' but had continued to 'assert its willingness to do so if the Soviets do not withdraw from Afghanistan'.[129]

Until mid-June the Soviets generally refrained from commenting on Iran's support for insurgents, choosing to ignore them for the sake of improving their ties with the government. Although concerned, the Kremlin did not believe its chances of success or failure were significantly influenced by the relatively minor support Iran provided the rebels. In any case, the central Bani-Sadr government, with whom it had mostly cordial relations, was unable to prevent aid and shelter being provided to the Afghan rebels. In other words, the Soviets lacked any diplomatic leverage in Iran. The Afghans were still receiving aid from power bases outside the central government, which the CIA judged 'reflected the general consensus in Iran in support of the rebel cause'.[130] Washington broadly felt that the Soviets were unwilling to risk a significant deterioration of ties with Tehran, which would also lead to further alienation of the 'progressive' groups in Iran upon which Moscow's long-term Iran strategy still focussed.

Conclusion

The linkage between the hostage crisis and Afghanistan revolved around notions of threat perception. Washington hoped that fear of Soviet aggression would mobilise those 'sensible' enough in Iran to end Iran's confrontation with America. In the end, Khomeini's fear that the Revolution was not yet consolidated persuaded him not to intervene on the hostages' behalf.

It was equally clear that Khomeini did not fear US retaliation. A consensus then emerged in Washington that the hostages were being held according to a timetable dictated by domestic considerations and impervious to geopolitical considerations. Most Iranian specialists and former members of the Carter administration still acknowledge that the hostages were released only once the Iranian leadership had extracted the maximum political value from them.[131]

Iran was faced with few good policy alternatives in Afghanistan. The Iranian government had little interest in major instability, having already received an influx of up to 500,000 refugees. Nor did they desire a major conflict with the Soviet Union. As such, when a thousand Afghanis, together with Iranian supporters, stormed the Soviet embassy in Tehran on 9 January 1980, a withdrawal was very quickly negotiated by Iranian authorities.

The State Department still viewed a successful Soviet intervention in Afghanistan as provoking anxiety in Tehran. As long as the central government in Tehran and Qom was unable to re-impose its authority over the provinces, ethnically based demands for regional autonomy, and even secession, would continue. 'If the Soviets are able to install a reasonably stable regime in Kabul,' stated the Congressional Research Service's Afghanistan Task Force, 'the potential for inciting and supporting ethnic nationalism in Iran is substantial.'[132] The Iranians judged, however, that the consequences of aggressively seeking to destabilise the Afghan government were more risky. Whilst some support was given to the insurgents, it was both limited and largely irrelevant to the survival of the rebellion. The CIA and State Department generally understood Iran's pragmatic approach to events in Afghanistan, though it did little to change the wider perception of an irrational decision-making process.

8
US Policy and the Iran–Iraq War 1980–1981

Little attention has been paid to the Carter administration's response to the outbreak of the Iran–Iraq War. Carter himself makes only five passing mentions to the conflict in his memoirs. Nevertheless, within the limited scholarship reside some widely divergent interpretations. According to most former US officials, including Carter, Iraq's invasion provoked shock and disapproval.[1] To others, the initial phase of Iraqi victories provoked barely concealed satisfaction.[2] The Iranian government's allegation that America provided a 'green light' to Iraqi aggression continues to frame contemporary US–Iranian relations. Within this Machiavellian narrative lurks the possible origin of America's 'tilt' towards Iraq and the arms-for-hostages deals that evolved in the Iran–Contra scandal. In essence, therefore, there have been at least some suggestions that two of the most controversial episodes of the Reagan policy can be linked to the previous administration. This chapter argues in opposition to this suggestion. It charts US assessments of deteriorating Iran–Iraq relations after the Revolution and re-examines the nature of America's relationship with Iranian opposition groups which undoubtedly did encourage Iraq to attack the Islamic Republic.[3] Evaluating all the evidence, it shows that US officials were genuinely caught by surprise when hostilities broke out.

The anatomy of the 'green light' theory

Even before Iraq attacked Iran on 22 September 1980, the Iranian leadership had made it clear that it would consider America complicit in any attack by Iraq. Former President Bani-Sadr has alleged that in August 1980 his government obtained detailed accounts of several conversations between former Iranian generals and politicians, Iraqi representatives, and American and Israeli experts.[4] Bani-Sadr alleges that the US deliberately passed on intelligence that would encourage an Iraqi attack. Given that Bani-Sadr is still blamed by many Iranians for the military's lack of preparedness on the eve of Iraq's attack, he is not a perfect witness. Nevertheless, it is ironic that Iran's first elected President, who was impeached and barely escaped Iran with his life in 1981, has done so much to reinforce a theory held most dearly by the regime that ousted him.[5]

The case for American collusion appeared strengthened when in 1995 a memorandum surfaced written by Reagan's first Secretary of State, Alexander Haig. Apparently written in April 1981 whilst Haig was visiting US allies in the Middle East, Haig noted that 'It was also interesting to confirm that President Carter gave the Iraqis a green light to launch the war against Iran through Fahd'.[6] Both Haig and Carter subsequently refused to respond to questions arising from Haig's 'talking points'. Former Carter officials have without exception denied that any US encouragement was given to Iraq to invade Iran.

A slightly diluted variation of the 'green light' conspiracy is that, whilst not directly sanctioning the attack, the US encouraged it by passing intelligence to the Iraqis emphasising Iran's military vulnerability. According to Richard Sale, an investigative journalist working in Paris at the time and in contact with US officials and members of the Iranian opposition, the Pentagon sent doctored intelligence reports to Saddam via Iranian dissidents. These reports suggested that Iran's military was in disarray and that in Khuzestan and other provinces Iraqi forces would be greeted as liberators. Sale states that exiled former Prime Minister Shapour Bakhtiar told him personally that Iranian forces would be defeated in three days and many Iranian Arabs would rise in support.[7]

Another twist in the story is that Saddam met with CIA agents in Jordan to discuss plans for invading Iran. This theory is advanced by Saddam's biographer Said K. Aburish, who states that two meetings occurred. The first meeting is alleged to have occurred sometime in the summer of 1979, shortly before Saddam seized the presidency from General Ahmed Hassan al-Bakr. The second allegedly occurred in July 1980, with King Hussein himself acting as an intermediary between Saddam and the CIA agents.[8] A variation of this theory is provided by Bani-Sadr, who alleges that it was actually Brzezinski who met Saddam to assure him that Washington would not oppose the separation of Khuzestan (in south-west Iran) from Iran.[9] This version is moderated by Kenneth Timmerman, who states that Brzezinski was not present but the meetings were his idea.[10] Brzezinski was so outraged by Timmerman's book that he wrote a letter to the *Wall Street Journal* refuting any suggestion that the Carter administration 'in any fashion whatsoever, directly or indirectly, encouraged Iraq to undertake a military adventure against Iran'.[11]

Having consulted Brzezinski in the course of writing his own book, Gary Sick suggests there could be no tactical (vis-à-vis the hostages) or geopolitical rationale for encouraging an Iraqi attack. Sick admits that Brzezinski hoped the attack would put pressure on Iran to release the hostages, but he quickly changed his mind and encouraged Carter to oppose the Iraqi attack.[12] Hal Brands has more recently demolished the conspiracy theory by providing compelling evidence that Saddam believed Washington would strongly oppose his attack.[13] Given the difficulty US intelligence officials faced in persuading Saddam to accept intelligence after the Reagan administration fully 'tilted' towards Iraq, the extent to which they could influence Saddam's decision-making in 1980 is thus highly questionable.

It seems unthinkable that in an election year Carter would solicit actions that would further destabilise the Persian Gulf, distract attention from Soviet intervention in Afghanistan, and risk both the hostages' lives and rising oil prices. The Haig memo was written by an individual outside the government in 1980, and the exact circumstances in which he reached his interpretation remain unknown. Haig was apparently provided the information by Sadat and King Fahd of Saudi Arabia, and it is entirely plausible that they were trying to assign Carter some responsibility for a conflict they now asked Reagan to help fix. Other former US officials have suggested that the memo could represent some attempt at self-promotion by Haig.[14]

If the charge of direct American collusion is dismissed, the question of what America knew of Iraqi plans, and more importantly when, remains open. The majority of American officials plead ignorance; the Iraqi invasion was apparently greeted with unwelcome shock. Given the challenge to this narrative presented by Gasiorowski's analysis, discussed earlier in this book, as well as further documentary evidence uncovered here, it is necessary to explain what the US did know of Iraqi plans.[15] It is important to situate this within the wider context of US assessments and objectives in the region.

Analysing Iran–Iraq relations and the 'Kurdish problem'

The notion that most US analysts believed that Iraq was preparing to invade Iran as early as in late summer 1979 has already been critiqued in Chapter 5. The CIA nevertheless continued to receive reports of worsening Iran–Iraq relations throughout the rest of 1979 and into 1980. These were guided by the attempted assassination of Tariq Aziz, Khomeini's continued incitement to the Iraqi Shia, increasing border skirmishes, the ongoing hostage crisis, and aftermath of the Nuzhih plot. Relations rapidly deteriorated, particularly after June 1979, when Iraqi security forces arrested Ayatollah Muhammad Baqir al-Sadr on the eve of a scheduled trip to Tehran. Khomeini harshly criticised al-Sadr's house arrest, provoking Iraqi claims that Tehran was encouraging and exploiting internal divisions in Iraq. Despite this, there was some evidence that the Iraqi government was continuing to put out diplomatic feelers, inviting a delegation led by Bazargan to visit Iraq in July 1979.

Meanwhile, Iranian authorities were blaming Iraq for supporting Kurdish insurgents fighting for autonomy from the central government. The US began to closely monitor the Kurdish problem, which they saw as an easy gateway for Soviet meddling and a serious challenge to the authority of the moderate provisional government.[16] Quite apart from Washington's specific objectives in Iran, a Kurdish insurgency, and the resulting military response by Iran and other powers, had the potential to embroil Iran, Turkey, Iraq, Syria, and the Soviet Union into a regional conflict. The previous year had seen Iranian and Iraqi armed forces launching joint military 'pacification' operations in Kurdish areas. These operations were a direct consequence of the 1975 Algiers Accord, whereby the Shah agreed to end his support for the 1961–1975 Kurdish revolt in Iraq. With the collapse of the Pahlavi regime came the end of military cooperation. The Kurds once again became a source of considerable tension, particularly because of their belief that they could lever a degree of autonomy from the vulnerable post-revolutionary government. Whilst both countries still had an interest in keeping a lid on the national aspirations of their respective Kurdish populations, the Kurds now posed a far graver threat to the Islamic Republic than they did to the government in Baghdad. This sense of vulnerability was keenly felt in Tehran, and as bilateral relations deteriorated, the Iranian media increasingly alleged Iraqi involvement in the ongoing Kurdish revolt.[17] The tense atmosphere was further aggravated by violent clashes in Kurdish border areas, including attacks by the Iraqi air force on Iranian villages suspected of sheltering Iraqi Kurdish insurgents. In response, the Iranians provocatively welcomed the sons of a well-known Kurdish leader who had crossed the border seeking sanctuary.[18]

The situation with the Kurds and Arabs (who were also revolting with the suspected support of Iraq) was discussed in an 18 June meeting between Iranian Foreign Minister Ebrahim Yazdi and the US Chargé d'Affaires Charlie Naas. Yazdi explained that Iran had evidence that 'Iraqi support of these organizations continues and that relations between the two countries could not improve until it ceases'. Responding to a direct question from Naas, Yazdi stated that the PGOI 'does not know what might be bothering Iraq' and that 'certainly we have done nothing to bother them'.[19] Yazdi conceded that there was a potential 'spillover' effect from the Revolution amongst Iraqi Kurds and Shias, but categorically denied that this was being exploited. The Islamic Republic had a definite interest in the condition of religious centres in Najaf and Karbala, which he claimed were being threatened by the Iraqi government. According to Yazdi, it was this interest that had provoked Khomeini to protest the arrest of Ayatollah al-Sadr.

The US had retained some good contacts with the Kurds, having only reluctantly abandoned their support for the Peshmerga when the Shah unexpectedly cut them off in March 1975. The Peshmerga's leader, Mustafa Barzani, had been allowed entry to the US for medical treatment.[20] Barzani died in Washington in March 1979, but his entourage remained important figures in Kurdish politics and became important sources of information on Kurdish and regional affairs. One such individual was Mohammed Dosky, a Kurd from a prominent family in northern Iraq with an American wife. In May 1979, Dosky was operating as a Kurdistan Democratic Party (KDP) representative in Washington and in contact with David Reuther, who worked on Iraq policy for the State Department. Dosky advised that Khomeini had resented the conditions of his exile in Iraq and was not 'particularly disposed toward Baghdad'.[21]

Dosky's view was that Iraq's overriding goal was to persuade the new government in Tehran to live up to the conditions of the Algiers Accord. He suggested that Baghdad would attempt to emphasise Iraq's ability to stir up factional tensions within Kurdish parties, alleging that Iraq was supporting a force loyal to Jalal Talabani, which had recently clashed with the Barzani faction. He put out the view that Iraq was using Kurdish groups not out of a sense of opportunism, or as a prelude to the coming conflict, but in order to consolidate agreements made with the Shah.

A detailed CIA study of the 'Kurdish problem' was completed on 1 August 1979. It reported little hope for Kurdish autonomy but noted that if the Iranian government failed to gain control over areas taken over by Kurds, it would be compelled to suppress their demands and thereby incite other Kurdish groups in neighbouring countries, particularly Iraq.[22] An alternative view was provided by the US defence attaché in Tehran. Having spoken at length to a colleague just returned from a secret five-day trip to western Iran, he informed Washington that the situation was being grossly exaggerated by the Iranian press. The attaché stated that 'It appears that there has been an attempt by someone or some group in the government, possibly even Khomeini, to purposefully magnify and distort the situation in Kurdistan in an attempt to rally mass opinion or at least provide sufficient justification for major and more drastic decisions'.[23] His conclusion was that the Kurds posed no threat to the central government, but the Iranian regular and irregular military was in no position to effectively pacify them in their own region.

The US started to make other enquiries regarding Iraqi support for the Kurds, not least because they were still in search of intelligence they could provide the Iranians as proof of their goodwill. In Beirut the CIA station received information from contacts in Fatah that the Palestine Liberation Organization (PLO) had confirmed that Iraq was indeed supporting the Kurds. The same sources claimed that Saddam Hussein himself was directly involved in supervising these operations and had even sent high-ranking Iraqi officers to train and organise Kurdish fighters.[24] The CIA may have taken the claim of Saddam's personal supervision with a pinch of salt, but the agency could assume that the PLO had reasonably good information. A high-level member of the KDP's politburo, Kerim Hissami, was known to be in contact with a PLO representative in Baghdad. Hissami was also known to have headed a KDP delegation that had visited Lebanon to meet PLO leaders.[25]

On 8 September, Vance sent a memo to the US interest section in Baghdad soliciting information on the Iraqi version of events. Unsurprisingly, this proved fruitless, so the US turned to Turkey. The US ambassador in Ankara, Ronald Spiers, requested a meeting to discuss the matter with the director of Turkey's Ministry of Foreign Affairs, responsible for the Middle East. The Turkish official offered no hard evidence of Iraqi support but considered it probable. Spiers was told that the Turkish government did not have a clear idea of what game Iraq was playing vis-à-vis the Kurds.[26]

The CIA next proposed establishing a relationship with Sardar Jaff, a Kurd from a prominent family in Kirkuk. Jaff had been an associate of the Barzani faction, which had received considerable assistance from the Shah before 1975. After the Revolution, he was forced to flee to Baghdad, where he established a reasonably good relationship with the Iraqi government. Despite some reservations about his reliability, in late September the CIA agreed to underwrite his flight from Baghdad to Bonn if he agreed to report back any information he acquired. Jaff's statement was unequivocal: the Iraqi government had been helping the Kurds 'tremendously', offering Kurdish organisations 'carte blanche to obtain assistance from Iraq'.[27]

According to Jaff, Iraq was the only foreign sponsor of the Kurds, and Saddam was extremely angry with the Kremlin for not supplying weapons for him to provide to the Kurds.[28] Of significance to later events, CIA agents in Bonn and Paris also believed that during his trip to Europe, Jaff had met with Bakhtiar. The inability of the CIA to establish a link between the Soviet Union and the Kurds was troubling to some in the administration. National Security Council (NSC) staffer Paul Henze railed against both the CIA and the State Department for reporting that there was no evidence for Soviet support.[29]

Another area for which Iran cited Iraqi meddling was in Khuzestan. Like in Kurdish areas, allegations of Iraqi support for Arab organisations in Khuzestan went back to the period of confrontation between Iraq and the Shah. At that time, dissident organisations such as the National Liberation Front of Arabistan were allegedly allowed to establish offices in Basra and Baghdad. The State Department made enquiries with the Kuwaitis regarding Iraq's involvement in Khuzestan. In a meeting between the political chief of the US embassy in Kuwait and a senior Kuwait advisor for the Ministry of Foreign Affairs, it became apparent that the Kuwaitis took it for granted that there was some Iraqi involvement. The US political chief posited whether 'Kuwait might take the further step of encouraging Iraq to curtail its rumored activities in Khuzestan'. The Kuwaitis replied that this was unlikely.[30]

In the period before the hostage crisis, the picture of Iran–Iraq relations was confusing. The US was confident that Iraq was supporting the Kurds, though its motivation was not entirely clear. At the same time, Saddam had begun to play on the anxieties the Iranian Revolution had provoked in the Arab world. Over the autumn of 1979, he began raising the issue of Iran's 1971 seizure of the three Tunbs from the UAE. In February 1980, Saddam would use the issue as a platform to unveil his 'Arab National Charter', which represented a bold assertion of his leadership of the Arab world.[31]

By early November 1979, members of the PGOI were increasingly worried about deteriorating relations with Iraq. The CIA had been alerted to this just days before the hostage crisis by Abbas Amir-Entezam, who had recently returned to Tehran before taking up a permanent ambassadorship in Stockholm. Despite Cave's apparent warning in the October briefing, a CIA cable in early November 1979 said that the Iraqis hoped 'to settle its differences with Iran through negotiations'.[32] Their preference would be to deal with the moderate Bazargan government, but the Iraqis were concerned by its lack of authority and Saddam Hussein was understood to be unwilling to negotiate with the clerics. Saddam, like most other countries, perceived a dual government in Iran. He recognised that the Bazargan government understood the need for correct relations with Iraq, but considered Khomeini implacably hostile towards Iraq. Saddam's policy was remarkably similar to Washington's insofar as he saw a proper relationship with the Bazargan government as the best means of supporting their struggle against more radical elements. One policy initiative suggested by Precht was to approach the Iraqis on the basis of a mutual interest in avoiding actions that would further undermine the moderates. Precht, who was well aware of Iraqi support for the Kurds, advised that the Iraqis be reminded of the damage the ethnic rebellions were inflicting on the provisional government. Baghdad could then hopefully be persuaded to take steps to 'reduce pressure on the Bazargan government'.[33] The demise of the moderates would profoundly change Saddam's decision-making calculus.

In another apparent case of symmetry between the US and Iraq, the Iranian moderates feared a backlash from their efforts to defuse relations with Iraq. In October, Yazdi met with Saddam Hussein on the margins of the non-aligned conference in Havana. Yazdi reassured Saddam on all the major issues of concern to Iraq: Iran was not agitating the Shia population in Iraq, had no territorial designs over Bahrain, and was not seeking to export the Revolution abroad. They agreed to further meetings to discuss the issue, but Yazdi returned to strong criticism in the Iranian media for meeting Saddam. Yazdi and other moderates became acutely afraid that any public statements in support of this aim would invite further criticism.

US–Iraqi relations and Iran–Iraq tensions

The hostage crisis consolidated clerical power and prompted mass resignation of the Bazargan government, which had attempted to improve bilateral relations. Baghdad was aware that Khomeini was poorly disposed towards them, and Saddam was broadly unwilling to do business with him. Tehran was conscious that America's and Iraq's interests correlated now more than ever. Brzezinski in his weekly report to the President, dated 21 December, reported a similar feeling:

> I have checked with Cy Vance, and he agrees with the notion that it might be useful for Jim Schlesinger to pay a personal visit to Iraq early in 1980 and to engage the Iraqi leaders in a wider discussion.[34]

Brzezinski's view crystallised further after the Soviet intervention in Afghanistan. From early 1980, both Iraqi and American leaders indicated a growing coincidence of interests in their public statements.[35] Following a speech by Saddam denouncing the Soviet invasion of Afghanistan, Brzezinski began thinking about the practical steps he could take to bring Iraq into his vision of a reordered regional realignment. Saddam's attempt to position himself as the leader of the Arab world, encapsulated in his announcement on 8 February of the pan-Arab 'National Charter', encouraged the view that a degree of cooperation with Iraq was necessary to maintain Arab support against the Soviets in Afghanistan. Following statements that neither country was fundamentally opposed together in areas of mutual interest, by February 1980 the US and Iraq had publicly agreed to cooperate on an informal basis.[36]

Iraq's importance to the region's dynamics lay first in Egypt's diplomatic isolation, rendering Iraq the most powerful Arab country opposing Israel. More pressingly, as Iran's most potent regional threat, those Arabic countries anxious about Iranian intentions and capabilities were drawn towards it. As the border dispute between Iran and Iraq erupted in frequent skirmishes, King Hussein of Jordan, on 9 April, urged all Arabs to support Iraq. Soon after, Hussein's effort to mediate a rapprochement between Iraq and Saudi Arabia was realised. On 10 April, US Under Secretary of State David Newsom publicly declared that 'The United States is prepared ... to resume diplomatic relations with Iraq at any time'.[37] Following the release of the transcript of a meeting between Saddam Hussein and US ambassador April Glaspie on 25 July 1990, it appears that Saddam took the decision to accept this offer during the 2 months before Iraq's invasion of Iran. According to Saddam, the decision was postponed 'when the war started ... to avoid misinterpretation'.[38]

These diplomatic manoeuvrings were not unnoticed in Tehran, where talk of American retaliation had become a national preoccupation. The combination of escalating violence on the Iran–Iraq border, a failed US military rescue attempt on 24 April, continued unrest amongst the Kurds, and the knowledge of exiled Iranian dissidents travelling freely between Iraq and the West led to a predictable outcome. It became immediately apparent that if the Iraqis did launch an attack, America would be charged as its accomplice. On 25 August, *Keyhan*, the hard-line tribune of the regime, quoted sources confirming the hand of the 'Great Satan':

Although the part played by America and by its dependent elements in the Iraqi Ba'athist Government's provocations is evident, the joint American–Iraqi plan to attack Iran simultaneously in the south and the west was foredoomed.[39]

Even before the failed rescue attempt, some in Iran suspected America would use Iraq as a proxy for its retaliation against the hostage taking. On 10 April, Carter noted in his diary that 'The Iranian terrorists are making all kinds of crazy threats to kill the American hostages if they are invaded by Iraq – whom they identify as an American puppet'.[40] Carter admits that the increasing likelihood of an Iraqi attack formed part of the rationale for risking the hostages' lives by attempting a rescue attempt.

Warnings of an Iraqi military attack

Recently uncovered documentary evidence confirms that in April, the Defense Intelligence Agency (DIA) had received intelligence suggesting that the chances of that attack had risen considerably. The DIA now reported that 'the situation is presently more critical than previously reported'. The source put the chance of an imminent Iraqi attack at about 50 percent.[41] Two days later, a separate CIA intelligence memorandum reported that 'Evidence indicates that Iraq had probably planned to initiate a major military move against Iran with the aim of toppling the Khomeini regime'. As well as stating that the situation was 'moving uncontrollably toward war', the report confirmed that the Iraqis had tried to use Kuwait as intermediaries for obtaining 'United States support or approval' for an attack.[42] These two analyses provoke legitimate questions as to why senior US officials responsible for Persian Gulf affairs maintain that the US had at most 24 hours' notice of the Iraqi attack.[43]

The warnings were disseminated, but the most likely explanation why they were not acted upon is that those who doubted they amounted to compelling evidence won the argument. In effect, they were right. Only in early July did US observers note the movement of Iraqi assets out of garrison with war-related 'basic loads' of ammunition and certain extra equipment typically left behind in garrison during exercise deployments. In the first week of September, Iraqi troops had successfully moved into a disputed pocket of territory that had been awarded to Iraq under the 1974 Algiers Accord but never evacuated by the Iranians. Iranian sources frequently cite this date, the 4th of September, as the beginning of hostilities. On 17 September, a CIA intelligence memorandum reported significantly increased Iraqi troop movements on the border and stated that 'the intensification of border clashes between Iran and Iraq has reached a point where a serious conflict is now a distinct possibility'.[44] The agency noted the extreme risks associated with a major Iraqi offensive in Khuzestan, warning that it would involve Iraq in a 'costly and protracted conflict'. Another report indicated that Saddam had been emboldened by the relative ease by which Iraqi forces had dislodged Iranian troops from the disputed border territory. In fact, however, these small pieces of terrain had only contained Iranian gendarmerie, not regular Iranian forces.[45]

Nevertheless, as Wayne White notes, 'the outbreak of war did, in fact, come as a surprise to most of us because a decent portion of Iraq's ground forces were still in garrison. The hasty movement of the remaining units up to the front immediately after the beginning of major hostilities was the activity that tended to nudge me toward the abrupt scenario in which Saddam ordered the attack before all military preparations had been completed.'[46] When the invasion did occur on 22 September, it was unclear whether Saddam had simply fallen into a rage following a smaller skirmish. The ongoing war of words and a tendency on both sides to posture for domestic and international audiences made detaching Saddam's intentions from rhetoric a difficult undertaking. Ambassador Nathaniel Howell, then Director of the State Department's Office of Lebanon, Jordan, Syrian Arab Republic, and Iraq Affairs, describes a common view of Saddam's intentions:

> We all watched Saddam's actions and rhetoric closely but most people I knew tended to believe he was posturing. So far as I am aware, I was the first official to act on that judgment. The evening before the invasion began, I sent a cable to USINT Baghdad instructing them to advise American contractors working on a refinery to evacuate to Kuwait. The war began before the evacuation could be carried out. I took this action with the knowledge of my superiors but not on the basis of any decision within the USG.[47]

US relations with Iranian dissidents

Soon after Iran came under attack, Khomeini declared that 'We are at war with America' and that 'the hand of the US has appeared from the sleeve of Iraq'.[48] There was political utility in declaring a hidden US hand, but his conviction also reflected his misguided view of relations between US intelligence and Iranian dissidents. With a pressing need for intelligence on internal Iranian affairs, the US had established a line of communication with these exiles even before the hostage crisis. The State Department generally disapproved of these contacts, but the CIA saw them as useful sources of intelligence.[49] One report, which detailed a second request by Bakhtiar to meet with high-level US officials, stated that the US position was clear: the US would not 'fund, assist, or guide his movement, but were providing the channel as a means by which he could provide us information on his intentions and capabilities'.[50] A corollary of Washington's refusal to support the nascent Iranian opposition, coalescing around the Shah's last Prime Minister

Shapour Bakhtiar, was that they approached Iraq for assistance.[51] Gary Sick writes that 'The leaders in Iran were no doubt aware that the United States was maintaining contact with a number of Iranian exiles in Europe, some of whom were independently providing advice and encouragement to Saddam Hussein to invade Iran'.[52]

Another figure known to be both actively plotting against the Khomeini regime and encouraging Saddam to attack the Islamic Republic was General Oveissi, the former Chief of Staff of the Iranian armed forces. Oveissi's presence in Baghdad was reported in *Washington Post* on 20 May 1980, and the *New York Times* reported a subsequent visit to Washington on 19 June. The *Post* reported that Oveissi was 'preparing an exile army to invade Iran from seven points'. The CIA was also well aware of Bakhtiar's frequent visits to Baghdad. There is no evidence to suggest, as some have, that either or both were encouraging Iraq to attack on behalf of the US.[53] In fact, there is no evidence that either had any influence on Iraqi decision-making. Yet it would seem plausible that if the Iranian opposition groups were aware and involved with Iraqi plans, and they maintain that they were, then so was US intelligence.

The Nuzhih plot greatly increased the Iranian government's paranoia. The plot occurred on the night of 9 July, with an attempt by several hundred active and retired Iranian paratroopers to initiate a coup d'état against the Islamic Republic. The Iranian authorities had, however, been tipped off: some allege by Iraqi intelligence, who recognised the damage the subsequent purge would inflict upon the Iranian military.[54] Bakhtiar was helping to fund both of the chief instigators of the coup, Colonel Muhammad Baqir Bani-Amir and Colonel Ataullah Ahmadi. This money was in turn provided by Iraqi intelligence, which was aware of the plot but not involved in its planning. In order to bolster the confidence of the coup leaders, Bakhtiar informed them that the US had given its blessing. He was lying; the US knew nothing about the Nuzhih operation and would have likely opposed it on the grounds that it would endanger the lives of the hostages.[55] Yet, once the coup was foiled, it was for the Iranians the final *casus belli* for American complicity in any Iraqi attack.

Responding to the Iraqi invasion

Once hostilities broke out, the Carter administration's response was guided by four key concerns: the hostage crisis, oil supplies, the Soviet threat, and America's strategic alliance network. The US was unsure of the implications for them all. Nat Howell was charged with drafting the State Department's official policy position, to be announced by Warren Christopher. There was no clear consensus; some argued that 'Iran is the strategic choice' and others leaned towards saving positions in the Arab world.[56] The resulting document took a middle ground, reiterating America's opposition to the acquisition of territory by force but emphasising the need to maintain right of passage by non-belligerents in the Gulf.

If there was an immediate practical tilt towards Iraq, it was seen mostly in terms of the energy policy. It was an election year and oil prices were certain to be a political issue. Iranian retaliatory strikes had, by the first week, caused the suspension of Iraqi oil exports.[57] This concern had been voiced in earlier documents discussing the potential for conflict between Iran and Iraq. It also appears to have been discussed with the Saudis. Once hostilities did break out, the Saudis went some way to ameliorate the loss in production by significantly increasing their own output.[58] Yet, as a senior source in the Energy Department confirms, the US also took active steps to make sure that Iraq's ability to export through the Gulf was unimpaired and could be quickly restored after the cessation of hostilities, primarily by expediting the purchase and early placement of single-point mooring buoys in the Gulf. To facilitate these purchases, an Iraqi official was granted a visa to visit Houston, where he was advised on buying and positioning the appropriate equipment by a member of US intelligence.[59] As it turned out, they had only limited effect, given the scale of Iranian retaliatory strikes. Nevertheless, in part because of the increased production of Saudi Arabia and other non-OPEC producers, the feared spike in oil prices did not materialise.

Beyond energy policy, the implications for the hostage crisis loomed largest. It appears that Iraq had hoped that the fighting would be confined to the border area, and had retained most of its troops in garrison. Baghdad had not banked on Iran's response of total war. Washington hoped that immediate, but fairly limited, Iraqi successes would persuade the Iranians to reach a settlement on the hostages. Brzezinski was himself convinced that the Iranians would have little choice but to acquiesce in an arms-for-hostages deal. This hope soon faded.[60] The conflict immediately plunged an already chaotic Iranian decision-making process into a state of panicked distraction. The Iranians believed that Iraq was acting as America's proxy, and once they were able to source most of the military equipment they required from Israel, the Soviet Union, and European arms dealers, they were not in the mood to look favourably on the hostage issue. The US eventually managed to persuade Israel from selling arms to Iran while Americans were held hostage in Tehran, but CIA sources indicated that European arms dealers were providing it with weapons with or without government approval.[61] Privately, Brzezinski and other high-level US officials suspected that the Begin government would continue to covertly support Iran, in part because they recognised Israel's fear of Iraq greatly surpassed that of Iran, but also because Brzezinski suspected that Begin hoped for Carter's electoral defeat.[62]

Perhaps the most decisive US intervention in the early days of the war was the steps Washington took to prevent Iraq from mounting attacks against Iran from neighbouring Gulf countries. Just days into the conflict, US intelligence reported that Iraqi MIG-23 aircraft, a small number of helicopters, and even transporters carrying Iraqi special forces were attempting to land in Kuwait, Bahrain, Dhahran, the UAE, and Oman. It was soon clear that, with the probable exception of Oman and Ras al-Khaimah, the Gulf states had not permitted their territory to be used, and most made frantic attempts to dissuade the Iraqi aircraft from landing; Bahrain even physically blockaded its runways. Saddam's precise intentions were unclear; certainly the bases offered the opportunity to mount air strikes against targets in south-central and south-eastern Iran, but sustained operations outside Iraqi territory would require substantial additional operational support. The presence of Iraqi Special Forces may have suggested commando operations around Bandar Abbas or a potential invasion of Abu Musa and the Greater and Lesser Tunbs, both of which would have drawn Iranian troops away from the main fighting in Khuzestan. The political implications were clearer; by drawing in the Gulf states, Saddam could demonstrate to Iran that it faced a broad Arab front. Unfortunately for Saddam, Iraqi aircraft failed to land, or were quickly sent packing, in all the Gulf states apart from Oman and Ras al-Khaimah.[63]

US officials had been caught off-guard by this development and were clearly horrified. Faced with a potential spread of the conflict into the wider Gulf region, including states where the US had security arrangements, Carter and his senior advisors quickly resolved to bring all possible pressure to bear on Oman and Ras al-Khaimah to not to allow Iraq the use of their territory to attack Iran.[64] Carter was in a strong position to force them to back down, given the opposition of virtually all other Gulf states to Iraq's actions, and a recent agreement with Oman that substantially strengthened economic relations and allowed US access to virtually every military facility inside Oman. After a series of telephone conversations between the White House, Sultan Qaboos, and Sheik Sakr, the Iraqis were swiftly sent on their way.[65] The episode represented a constructive intervention by Washington and further contradicts the 'green light' conspiracy. It also demonstrates that if there was any initial tilt towards Iraq, it was extremely limited and almost exclusively confined to assistance to Iraq's energy sector. On 28 September, Secretary of State Muskie met with the Iraqi Foreign Minister Sa'dun Hammadi and outlined US opposition to 'any escalation of the conflict'. Despite Hammadi's claim that Iraq's objectives were limited, on the same day, Warren Christopher outlined Washington's objection to the 'dismemberment of Iran'.[66] This was also privately communicated to the Iraqi leadership via a backchannel that had been established via Jordan, with King Hussein embracing his role as intermediary with enthusiasm. Early on in the war, Nick Veliotes, then US ambassador to Jordan, was told by King Hussein that Saddam was contemplating annexing oil-rich Khuzestan, which he argued would benefit the West as the oilfields would be protected from the Soviets. Veliotes replied that 'the US was unalterably opposed to any efforts to dismember Iran'; shortly afterwards, he was instructed to 'tell

Hussein that the US would not tolerate Iraqi efforts to widen the war by using airbases in the Gulf to attack Iranian targets'.[67]

This is not to say, however, that the US still hoped that modest Iraqi gains would equate to leverage on the hostage issue. This hope would soon fade, as Iran was able to source the necessary resources it needed to keep fighting. On 11 October, the Iraqi government severed diplomatic relations with Syria, Libya, and North Korea, all of whom were supplying Iran with weaponry.[68] More ominously for the US, Moscow began to move closer towards both Iran and Syria, signing an official treaty of alliance with the Syria, which contained a clause stressing the importance of the Iranian revolution. Thus, although Iran was diplomatically isolated in the UN, and would soon demonstrate a more urgent interest in the return of its frozen 12 billion dollars of assets, the initial hope for an arms-for-hostages deal passed. Brzezinski concluded that 'the Iran–Iraq war created less of an opportunity for negotiation than we may have though'.[69]

A shift in US strategy

As the Iraqi offensive quickly faltered, most regional parties started pushing for a settlement.[70] Iran and Iraq refused. The US was forced to reconsider its policy position. The drain on Iran's resources was beginning to mobilise some urgency on the hostage crisis, but there was no sense of a dramatic change in Iran's negotiating position. Indeed, it appears that the most significant progress had been made shortly before Iraq's intervention, with the approach of Sadegh Tabatabai.[71] The demands made by Tabatabai were not substantially different to previous ones, but for the first time the US was dealing with a representative who was a relative of Khomeini.[72] The consensus emerged in Washington that the Iraqi invasion had disrupted the momentum behind this initiative but that eventually Iran's economic and political isolation would convince the Iranians to settle the hostage issue.[73]

The view that the conflict offered only limited active leverage on the hostage crisis dovetailed with the view that Iran's military would regroup and the conflict would remain a stalemate.[74] Brzezinski now advised Carter that Iraq had 'bitten off more than it can chew' and predicted a war of attrition. Although the implications of this were still unclear, there were still strategic interests to protect and even opportunities to exploit. Brzezinski believed the threat to regional security offered the US a unique opportunity to consolidate its security position in a manner 'even a few weeks ago would not be possible'.[75] In particular, the Saudis and other Gulf Arab states became anxious to see a heightened US military presence and enhance their own defences by purchasing more US hardware. The Saudis were declared accomplices in Iraq's invasion and, fearing retaliatory attacks by Iran, urgently requested the deployment of American AWACS planes and further intelligence sharing arrangements. This prompted a dispute between Brzezinski and Brown, who both supported strong support for the Saudis, and Muskie and Christopher, who feared that further US intervention on behalf of the Arabs could provoke Soviet retaliation.[76] In the end, Brzezinski won the argument and the AWACS were deployed. Nevertheless, technical issues and problems with the Saudi command and control structure delayed their effectiveness for the early part of the war.[77]

A week after Iraqi troops had poured over the border into western Iran, and as the US hostages were approaching almost a year in captivity, Brzezinski began to contemplate a tilt back towards Iran:

> While reinforcing our position in Saudi Arabia, and while not clashing with Arab aspirations (and thus while not openly opposing Iraq), we should actively seek new contacts with Iran to explore the possibility of helping it just enough to put sufficient pressure on Iraq to pull back from most, if not all, of its current acquisitions. Only by attempting to do this can we make the needed effort to safeguard Iran from Soviet penetration or internal disintegration.

Although Brzezinski talked of seeking new contacts with Iran, the US simply did not have the capability to find them. Washington did make a last attempt to revive the arms-for-hostages deal, with Gary Sick preparing an inventory of non-lethal Iranian spare parts valued at $150 million.[78] In reality, however, most involved were not optimistic that Iran would release the hostages anytime soon.[79] The extent of the 'tilt' back towards Iran simply meant a much more strict posture of neutrality and public support for Iran's security. In a speech in Pennsylvania on 15 October, Carter affirmed America's commitment to the 'proposition that the national security and integrity of Iran is in the interest of national stability. We oppose any effort to dismember Iran.'[80] The Carter administration began to actively try and prevent arms shipments to Iraq. They were, however, unable to prevent significant amounts of arms reaching Iraq from Jordan, despite appeals to Amman. The Saudis also continued to expand their assistance to Iraq.[81] Nevertheless, the US had moved away from Iraq enough for Saddam to claim in December that it was supporting 'Iran's "aggression" against Iraq'.[82]

There was one unexpected boon for the US. As the conflict went on, it became apparent that, despite Carter's broadly neutral posture, there was an opportunity to manoeuvre Egypt out of its isolation: a consequence of the peace it had made with Israel. Some in Washington felt responsibility for Egypt's reduced influence and were eager to exploit the opportunity for Cairo to re-ingratiate itself with the Arab world. The opportunity lay in Iraq's growing need for Soviet-origin weapons, which Egypt was eventually able to provide. In return, Iraq led the way in re-integrating Egypt into the Arab world.[83]

US policy and the Soviet threat

As border skirmishes intensified in April 1980, the CIA had begun to assess how Moscow would react to the outbreak of hostilities. One intelligence memorandum circulated in April suggested a probable tilt towards Iran in the event of a war. This assessment was influenced by Moscow's apparent support for Tehran's position on the hostage crisis. Although long and generous supporters of Iraq, the CIA concluded that 'the long history of Soviet–Iraqi relations has shown the Iraqis to be unreliable and resistant to Soviet efforts to meddle in Iraqi internal affairs'.[84] The report's authors also suggested that Iran would be inclined to accept Soviet support, overcoming both ideological and historical hostility to their northern neighbour. The report was in some respects an accurate prediction; on 4 October, the Soviet ambassador to Iran, Vladimir Vinogradov, met Iranian Prime Minister Raja'i and offered Soviet military equipment to Iran. Raja'i made Vinogradov's offer public in order to encourage the rift in Soviet–Iraqi relations. Despite his claims that he had refused Soviet arms, within days, Moscow was assisting Libya, North Korea, Syria, and Vietnam to supply arms to Iran. It was even reported by Israeli media that an Iranian delegation had travelled to Moscow to purchase US weapons captured by the Soviet Union and transferred to the USSR.[85]

Both superpowers were clearly uncertain how each other would react to the conflict. In the early days, Soviet arms carriers en route to Iraq were closely monitored for clues to the Kremlin's thinking. When one in the Indian Ocean turned around, it was taken as a sign that they were as uncertain of how to respond as Washington.[86] Both superpowers saw the conflict as potentially enhancing their adversary's position by providing the necessary justification for projecting their military power. The Americans feared the crisis would overshadow the Soviet intervention in Afghanistan and split Arab resistance to it. The Soviets mirrored this concern with their fear that the Iran–Iraq conflict would split the Arab world and overshadow the significance of the Arab–Israeli conflict, which was hitherto Moscow's traditional vehicle of influence in the Middle East. Both were concerned about the effects of the war on Iran's internal political dynamics. Both were disadvantaged by the accompanying consolidation of the clerical position inside Iran and sought to encourage the ascendancy of favoured secular alternatives. Neither was successful in doing so.

The Soviet Union's geographic proximity to Iran and the concerns it had regarding its own sizeable Muslim demographic appear to constitute a significantly more immediate threat from the consolidation of radical theocracy in Iran. The dynamic was slightly different from the US perspective, yet Washington's claim over the Gulf as a sphere of influence went some way to replicating the Soviet Union's closer proximity. On the other hand, an Iranian victory portended a fundamental reorientation of the balance of power in the region that neither Washington nor Moscow considered acceptable. This symmetry reinforced the posture of neutrality both sides adopted for the first two years of the conflict. There was continued fear that Iran would seek to improve relations with the opposing superpower in order to better resist Iraqi forces.

Also driving this fear, particularly in Moscow, was the fact that Iraq relied on Soviet-origin military hardware whilst Iran's military was broadly configured to use American equipment. With little question of the US resuming arms shipments to Iran, Moscow, which was still supplying Iraq before its attack, appeared to have greater leverage. The intelligence memorandum released just days before the start of hostilities noted that Moscow would be conscious that shutting off supplies to Iraq, which it did, could push Iraq further towards the West.[87] The US correctly predicted that Moscow would be highly dissatisfied with Iraq's action.

The US was also troubled by Saudi opposition to Washington's embargo on arms to Iraq. The Kingdom even took tentative steps towards improving relations with Moscow in the hope that the Kremlin could be persuaded to drop its own embargo. The Saudis also began strengthening its security ties with France, Iraq's second major arms supplier and critical of Washington's militarisation of the Gulf and abandonment of détente. To make matters worse, the Saudis made some positive noises about Brezhnev's December call for the use of force by great powers to be banned in the Gulf. It appears most likely, however, that this was connected to the Saudis' desire to see Soviet arms reach Iraq via Saudi Arabia.[88]

Concluding remarks

Iraqi fears of aggressive Khomeinism, and the promise of lucrative territorial gains in provinces believed to be friendly to Iraq, and not foreign manipulation, appear by far the most reasonable explanation for the outbreak of war. The hostage crisis, the Soviet invasion of Afghanistan, and Iraq's growing rift with the Soviet Union encouraged a warming in US–Iraqi relations. Nevertheless, the US continued to offer a future strategic relationship with Iran if they released the hostages.[89]

It is highly unlikely that the US was ever in possession of any clear evidence of Saddam's intention to invade Iran. Although the Carter administration drastically underestimated the scale of Saddam's plans, the disorganised and apparently impetuous nature of the invasion, with much of the Iraqi army still in garrison, and occurring in the context of border skirmishes and aggressive propaganda, muddied the waters for US observers. If the US was, as Cave contends, passing on warnings (verified or doctored) of advanced Iraqi war preparations as early as 1979, the Iranians did not act upon it. Conscious of being labelled pro-American, and unwilling to detail their secret dealings with US intelligence officials, it is possible that the Bazargan government would not have informed Ayatollah Khomeini's office.

The administration's initial hope was for Iraqi forces to make limited gains; almost exclusively because of the leverage it could offer the US on the hostage crisis. At the same time, they moved quickly to try and protect Iraq's oil-producing capacity. Of far greater significance to the latter concern was Saudi Arabia's decision to increase its own oil production. Both goals reflected pressing domestic concerns just weeks before the US public would go to the polls. Within little more than a week, the Iraqi offensive had begun to stall, and, with Iran able to source weapons from elsewhere, albeit at a premium, the initial hopes that Iran would be compelled to resolve the hostage crisis rescinded. Interestingly, the failure of the Iraqi military to exploit their early successes appears to have been blamed on Baghdad's ineptitude rather than credited to the surprising resilience and cohesion of the Iranian military.[90] The danger then was that the conflict would spread to Saudi Arabia, Syria, or Jordan and that Iran and Syria would move closer towards the Soviet Union. Washington had already been instrumental in preventing the entanglement of some Gulf states. By October 1980, Brzezinski advised Carter to oppose the Iraqi occupation of Iran, because of the danger that it would encourage Soviet penetration.[91] The policy that emerged was characterised by a desire to preserve all options, whilst trying to avoid actions that would undermine the Carter Doctrine or establish an opening for the Soviet Union. The impetus for America to adjust its policy of neutrality, and take a definitive position on which side to back, came in 1982, when the Iranian military threatened to overrun Iraq.

Conclusion

Reflections on the Soviet threat in Iran

Many US officials had anticipated Soviet subversion and opportunism as the Shah's regime collapsed; they then expected the Kremlin to exploit the security vacuum created by Iran's chaotic revolutionary transition. Brzezinski informed Carter in March 1979 that the Soviet Union 'could become the major strategic winner in the Persian Gulf as a result of the downfall of the Shah. In a prolonged period of change in Iran, the Soviet would be increasingly inclined to provide backing for those forces which they considered sympathetic to their own interests.'[1] The Islamic Revolution had convinced many in the Carter administration that pro-Western regimes in countries like Saudi Arabia, North Yemen, and Pakistan could be brought down by revolutionary Islamic movements and that the small communist groups in these countries could take advantage of the political and social crisis and take power, perhaps with Soviet assistance.[2]

In fact, the hawks in the Carter administration exaggerated Soviet regional ambitions, entirely misread Soviet motivations for intervening in Afghanistan, and unduly fretted about Iran's vulnerability to Soviet expansionism. Soviet policy in Iran demonstrated that even in a country of critical and economic importance, close to the Soviet orbit, and with a well-established group of leftist movements, Moscow was realistic about its limited ability to enhance its influence in the region. Khomeini had swiftly isolated Iran's pro-Soviet Tudeh Party and made no effort to temper his harsh anti-communism or hostility to Moscow's policies in neighbouring Afghanistan. The Soviets failed to protect the Tudeh party, let alone position them into influence. In addition, Iranian authorities openly blamed Moscow for instigating the growing ethnic and political insurrection inside Iran. Exactly 1 month before the US hostages were seized, Brezhnev admitted to his East German counterpart, Erich Honecker: 'Our initiatives with regard to the development of good neighbourly relations with Iran are currently not gaining any practical results.'[3]

With little capability to influence events in Iran, the general objective of Soviet policy was to prevent a re-entry of the US into the Gulf. The Kremlin issued strong warnings against any American military intervention, hoping also to ingratiate itself with the regime by portraying Moscow as the Revolution's protector. Soviet-controlled covert broadcasting inside Iran and the pro-Soviet Tudeh stoked anti-Americanism, constantly raised the spectre of a US-inspired counter-revolution, and attacked any perceived attempt by the Bazargan government to repair relations with the US. The Kremlin appeared unsure of how to extract any potential benefits from the hostage crisis without endangering its own interests inside Iran and its relationship with Washington.

This book has shown that these obstacles were often understood by US analysts. It thus identifies a paradox; perceptions of the Soviet threat in Iran featured heavily in US strategic planning, yet contemporary assessments by intelligence professionals and area specialists often downplayed Soviet influence. One CIA assessment of Soviet prospects in June 1979 concluded that the Soviets had 'not benefited directly' from the Revolution and 'it is unlikely that the Soviets will score dramatic gains in the Middle East in the foreseeable future'. Assessments routinely talked about potential Soviet destabilising activities; however, even this desire was acknowledged to be highly circumscribed by geopolitics. In September, Harold Saunders wrote a memo to Vance suggesting that Moscow's desire to mount subversive actions in Iran, such as supporting Kurdish revels in Iran, was highly constrained by their fear of 'chaos on their borders and the implications for spreading instability in the region'.[4] By mid-October 1979, the State Department was reporting that most colleagues agreed that Moscow had effectively given up on Iran and was 'Laying back waiting for social Revolution'.[5] It appears that US policy was increasingly being driven by the perception of Soviet ascendancy, the unravelling of détente, and the resulting hardening of domestic opinion on Cold War issues, rather than the rather more sober analysis being produced by US regional experts.

The Soviet intervention in Afghanistan made the US much less willing to risk actions that might drive Iran towards Moscow or render it vulnerable to Soviet penetration. Brzezinski also saw military action as jeopardising the organisation of Islamic opposition to Soviet expansionism.[6] This book has shown that this central objective, and attendant tensions within the Western Alliance, shaped both the scope and timing of the sanctions enacted by Washington and its allies. The eventual doomed rescue mission was largely the result of intense electoral pressures. The situation in Afghanistan demonstrated the extent to which both sides viewed each other's intentions in light of growing instability in Iran. Again, the State Department and CIA produced a number of analyses doubting that Moscow had Iran in its sights and would intervene even in the event of US military action. The problem facing those like Marshall Shulman, who presented a more benign analysis of Soviet intentions, was that whether the original motivation was defensive or offensive, the Soviets were in a position to achieve both objectives.[7] America's humiliation by a regime in Iran unable to even defend itself from its smaller neighbour was contrasted to the Kremlin's willingness to defend and even expand their interests in the region by intervening in Afghanistan. In the last days of his presidency, Carter signed two Presidential Directives – PD-62 on 'Modifications in U.S. National Security' and PD-63 on 'Persian Gulf Security Framework'. PD-62 warned that 'Given the increased risk of major local and regional conflict involving key U.S. interests in the 1980s we must increase the priority given to readiness in defense resource allocations'.[8] America was still far from having the capability to defend its vital interests in Europe, East Asia, and the Persian Gulf simultaneously. Nevertheless, Carter had overseen a process that would eventually see America dramatically increase its capacity to project power in the region.[9]

There were some significant similarities in the objectives of both superpowers in Iran. Both wanted to contain the characteristics of the Iranian Revolution that challenged their interests in the region. Yet both also hoped not to drive Iran into the arms of the other. Both were aware of the factions in Iran which supported closer relations but neither was able to manoeuvre them into positions of influence. Indeed, it was their perceived association with these factions that contributed to their alienation. Both viewed clerical dominance as unsustainable in the long term. Perhaps most importantly, both suffered from the burden of Iran's historical experience at the hands of superpowers.

Final days of the Carter administration

The prevalent opinion in the US in January 1979 had been that a Khomeini government would likely 'dissolve shortly of its own incompetence if nothing else'.[10] By the time the State Department provided the incoming Reagan administration with a 3-year projection of the situation in Iran, they believed it 'Quite likely that a regime dominated by clerics will survive during this period'.[11] The clerics 'will lose power one day', they advised, 'but it will not be a complete or sudden loss'. It should not, they concluded, 'be counted out as a major, competing force for a long time'.[12]

Nevertheless, they cautioned that efforts to destabilise Khomeini's position, especially through the support of exiled groups, would be counterproductive. None of these groups, the State Department observed, had 'real support among any significant part of the Iranian public and many, by associating themselves with Iraq and/or attacking Khomeini when criticising the clerics, have alienated even potential supporters'.[13] They included, as a cautionary warning, a recent report they had received from an exiled pro-monarchist group, complete with a comprehensive dissection of its analytical frailties and self-serving conclusions.

By linking Iran's stability to America's Cold War interests, the Cold War mentality on this occasion contributed to a sensible prescription. They advised the Reagan team that stability within the Iranian leadership was the most effective way of safeguarding Western access to Gulf oil and resisting Soviet expansion. The degeneration into chaos or even civil war was still seen as almost the only scenario in which the Tudeh and other leftist groups might seize power. Whilst the experts within the outgoing Carter administration believed this 'unlikely in the near term, such a development could lead to a Soviet intervention in Iran'.[14] It was because of this, and because they generally viewed no alternative group capable of maintaining stability, that they advised against supporting dissident Iranian groups. It would be a lesson that later US administrations would fail to learn.

The legacy of US–Iranian relations 1979–1981

The legacy of the Carter administration's failure to normalise relations with post-revolutionary Iran has mainly been understood in terms of the disastrous and long-term consequences of the hostage crisis for US–Iranian relations. A much smaller literature cites the conflated crises in Iran and Afghanistan as the catalyst for the US to begin shifting strategic priorities away from the North-east Asian and European theatre and in favour of the Persian Gulf.[15] There has been comparatively little research into how the Carter administration attempted to build a new relationship with post-revolutionary Iran. In addressing this gap, this book has challenged the narrative presented by Ayatollah Khamenei and other leading figures in post-revolutionary Iran. Khamenei's revolutionary discourse emphasises both resistance to (and victimhood against) Washington's bullying and aggressive opposition to its very existence. According to this narrative, the Islamic Republic bravely and divinely survives intact despite an immediate and sustained conspiracy to destroy it. As well as forming part of the two duelling narratives that are central to the current impasse in US–Iranian relations, this version of events also provides a specific justification for the hostage crisis. It allows the regime to frame what amounted to an egregious act of political opportunism as a defensive action that legitimately eliminated the US embassy as a site for counter-revolutionary plots.

The view that Washington immediately set out to destabilise post-revolutionary Iran is regularly repeated in Iran's official and semi-official media, often in order to blame internal discord on ongoing US-inspired conspiracies against Iran. A February 2009 editorial in *Keyhan*, a hard-line newspaper widely considered to be the public mouthpiece of the Supreme Leader, summed up the regime's narrative of the West's policy since the 1979 Revolution: 'Since the first day of the victory of the Islamic Revolution, Western powers, led by America, launched a project to abolish the revolution, or at least suppress it.'[16]

The political utility of this narrative for suppressing dissent was demonstrated when hundreds of thousands of Iranians took to the streets in 2009 to protest what they considered to be the fraudulent re-election of President Mahmoud Ahmadinejad. When the protests expanded into a broad movement demanding respect for basic political freedoms, the regime, as well as deploying brutal force against the protestors, mounted a concerted propaganda campaign to depict them as agents of America's latest conspiracy to destroy the Revolution. In her recent study of competing discourses of legitimacy since the 2009 crisis, Maaike Warnaar repeatedly shows how hardliners characterised the 2009 protests as an externally supported 'attempted coup' very much in line with the West's Iran policy since the 1979 Revolution.[17]

The origins of the US–Iranian confrontation are complex, but the essential feature of the relationship is mutual distrust. Both sides hold tightly to their respective grievances, some based on fact, others based on myth. The sense in Iran that Washington never really accepted the Revolution has been woven into a durable and multifaceted national narrative. Whilst it is impossible to know whether Supreme Leader Ayatollah Khamenei really believes that Washington refused to accept the Revolution, this book has shown that the narrative he has consistently presented flies in the face of all the evidence. The Carter administration made no attempt to prevent the Revolution from succeeding in 1979 and actively sought good relations with post-revolutionary Iran. The US accepted the Revolution, and as Carter prepared to leave office in the end of 1980, analysts in the State Department advised the incoming Reagan government not to engage in counter-revolutionary activities. It was a tragic irony, therefore, that during the 1981 Algiers Accord (which formally resolved the hostage crisis), Iran put great effort into extracting an assurance from Washington that the US government would not attempt to overthrow the Islamic Republic. Although this concession was framed as an achievement by Iranian diplomats, this book highlights how much of a Pyrrhic victory it was.

Yet the US narrative of the origins of the US–Iranian confrontation also suffers from myopia. Washington had certainly not sought to clash with the new leadership in Iran, but US policy-makers failed to learn the lessons of why Iran policy had failed in the first place. In early 1979, the lesson of America's relationship with the Shah should have been that any regime considered by its public to be either created by, or at least dependent on, America will be fundamentally fragile. Nevertheless, US policy-makers continued to try and identify moderates in Iran who they believed wanted a relationship with the US and could potentially wrestle control of Iran's foreign policy away from those identified as fanatics. US officials were convinced that sooner or later clerical rule would prove unsustainable: that fanatical clerics could not rule a modern country. The binary categorisation of Iran's leaders into 'moderate' and 'fanatic' occurred very quickly after the Revolution and remains a feature of American political discourse.

It has been an American tendency, seen recently with tragic consequences in Iraq, to choose favourites and try to anoint them as the new elites of a country.[18] Washington tends to prefer secular, Western-educated politicians who appear to be congenial to US interests. This was the case in Iran in 1979 and would be again during Iran–Contra. A covert action document written in January 1986 by Reagan's National Security Advisor John Poindexter illustrates that many of same themes that had guided US engagement in 1979 remained at the core of the Reagan administration's attempt to restore a strategic alliance with 'moderates' in Iran. The document, signed by President Ronald Reagan, outlined the following aim:

> The USG will act to facilitate efforts by third parties and third countries to establish contact with moderate elements within and outside the government of Iran by providing these elements with arms, equipment and relayed material in order to enhance the credibility of these elements in their effort to achieve a more pro-US government in Iran by demonstrating their ability to obtain requisite resources to defend their country against Iraq and intervention by the Soviet Union.[19]

What is evident from an analysis of Washington's approach to repairing relations after 1979 is an effort to restore the pre-existing geopolitical foundations of its relationship with Iran. Reflecting on the starting point for the 'new' US policy, Assistant Secretary of State Harold Saunders summed it up neatly: 'Keeping Iran out of the Soviet orbit had seemed critical to American strategists since World War II.'[20] From a revolutionary standpoint, however, this Cold War mindset was a self-evidently failed and anachronistic framework for US–Iranian relations. An engagement strategy pinned on an anti-communist alliance failed for four clear reasons. First, it was not perceived with sufficient alarm by a wide enough base in Iran's political system. Second, it represented the acceptance of terms similar to the Shah's relationship with the US. Third, it would require a degree of American participation in Iranian affairs which the Iranians found politically unacceptable. Fourth, it toxified the group of Iranian elites the US hoped to engage, making them easy targets for those on both the Left and religious Right who actively hoped to eliminate US influence in the Gulf.

Henry Precht would later acknowledge that America's acceptance of the Revolution could not be demonstrated 'just because it believed it was anti-communist and needed American security guarantees'.[21] Khomeini spoke in March 1979 of the US relationship with the Shah as simply designed 'to protect itself and its bases from the Soviet Union'. Khomeini described this iniquitous relationship as high treason to the homeland.[22] It was not particularly surprising that his followers, as well as leftists active in Iran, viewed with extreme suspicion any suggestion that the Bazargan government was forming a strategic alliance with America. Even many so-called moderates, such as Deputy Prime Minister Sadegh Tabatatai, felt that Iran was still being treated as a pawn in superpower politics:

> Soviet Union is striving to create a corridor to the Gulf of Oman by way of Baluchistan, on Iran's border zone, whilst America itself wishes to erect a barbed wire fence around the Persian Gulf.[23]

The Iranians perceived the threats of both superpowers, but not from a mindset that saw cooperation with either as necessary to confronting them. Iran's self-sufficiency, and thus detachment from the Cold War paradigm, was the long-term strategy for securing Iran's national sovereignty for the first time in its recent history. Rather than reaching out to the US for security guarantees, the new regime needed time and space to reconfigure and reassert its own foreign policy agenda. Behind the failure to embed American threat perceptions in Iran's new foreign policy orientation also lay contrasting conceptions of power. Khomeini believed that Iran's revolutionary example was so potent a force of attraction that Iran could mainly rely on *dawat* (calling) and *tabligh* (dissemination, advertisement) to advance a cultural and spiritual hegemony. Khomeini thus felt Iran had no need for a strategic relationship with the US that furnished him with advanced weaponry.[24] US policy-makers simply saw the region as an arena for material superpower competition. They could not appreciate the notion that its relationship with the Shah had undermined Iranian sovereignty or even increased its vulnerability to threats not explicitly shared by Washington.

The Carter administration's failure to engage Iran in 1979 was partly the result of a disconnect between America's reading of the Revolution's impact on US strategy, which was imbibed with Cold War ideology and orthodox assumptions about diplomacy and statecraft, and the radical change to Iran's political orientation and position in the international system that many of Iran's new leaders believed their Revolution had achieved. America's goals in Iran were specific: a working anti-Soviet relationship; the resumption of intelligence activities directed against the Soviet Union; the release of the hostages; cooperation in Afghanistan; a strategic relationship with other regional US allies; and the eventual moderation of Iran's apparent destabilisation of the Gulf monarchies.

Though Iran also had specific aims, such as the delivery of materials it had paid for, what it wanted, and continues to want, included more abstract notions of respect and acceptance. In other words, its expectations of its foreign relations transcended matters of military and economic mutual interest. Whether or not America could ever overcome the burden of history through which many Iranians viewed American intentions is impossible to judge. But the reality was that Washington had not even persuaded many moderate Iranians that it had accepted the Revolution or ceased 'interfering' in Iran.[25] After making vague statements about accepting the Revolution, neither Carter nor any high-level official made favourable references to the Islamic Republic. One of Laingen's last requests was for an official at under-secretary level or above to travel to Tehran to assist their effort to persuade Iran of Washington's serious intention to adjust to the realities of a post-Shah Iran. Laingen wrote: 'We would welcome the allied support in our efforts to enhance our credentials with the new Iranian leadership that a senior visitor could bring to bear.'[26] It fell on deaf ears.

Thirty years after the Islamic Revolution, a new US President would attempt to engage Iran. Like Carter, Barack Obama entered the White House with a mandate to redefine US foreign policy and whitewash the dark record of his predecessor. In March 2009, the 44th US President asserted his acceptance of the Revolution by publically reaching out to the Iranian government in his 2009 Nowruz message.[27] Then, as in 1979, US overtures were driven in part by concerns regarding America's ability to manage regional instability. Obama's engagement was organised around the principle of encouraging regional stability with an emphasis on cooperation in areas of mutual concern. As in 1979, there was little substance to US engagement beyond these vaguely articulated principles.

As had occurred in 1979, a domestic power struggle erupted in Iran with the US identified with the losing faction. In one sense, Obama had learned the lessons of 1979; he refused to publically align America with the Green Movement. The Obama administration recognised that aligning itself with the apparently more moderate group would simply damage the Iranian reform movement further and allow hardliners to once again portray the US as undermining Iranian sovereignty. In a departure from the previous Bush administration's refusal to negotiate with Iran's government and active support for groups hoping to topple it, Obama appeared to take the attitude that the US would have to deal with whichever group emerged from the power struggle. The brutality with which the Iranian regime broke the protests made engagement a far harder sell for Obama. The Arab Spring phenomenon that began in December 2010 was another nail in the coffin for US diplomacy. The unprecedented challenge it posed to the authority of authoritarian regimes across the Middle East and North Africa, and the fall of leaders in Tunisia, Egypt, Libya, and Yemen, provoked paranoia and defiance amongst America's undemocratic allies in the region. As in 1979, these allies harboured serious doubts as to whether Washington would stand by them and provide the security guarantees they felt they had been promised. The Saudis in particular made no effort to hide their alarm at the prospect of any US–Iranian rapprochement, as they had ever since the Iranian Revolution.

The Saudis, in their self-appointed role as counter-revolutionary vanguard, framed the Arab Spring as a vehicle for Iran to expand its regional influence. When protests spread to Bahrain, the Saudis moved troops and armour into their tiny neighbour, scuttling a mediation effort by the US between the Bahraini regime and its opposition. The justification for crushing the pro-democracy movement in Bahrain was that the opposition there was nothing more than an Iranian proxy attempting to establish a Shia-dominated regional order.[28] Although not directly endorsing this analysis, powerful voices in Washington, particularly in Congress, shared the Saudis' contention that Iran remained the greatest threat to regional stability. The Obama administration, already in re-election mode, felt vulnerable to the charge that it had been insufficiently robust in slowing Iran's nuclear programme. Once again, those advocating engagement in the US were undermined by domestic politics and the anxieties of regional allies. The legacy of the events discussed in this book has been that speaking in anything other than belligerent terms when talking about Iran remains politically toxic.

The trauma of America's earliest experience with revolutionary Iran continues to frame contemporary relations. The hostility Iran's ascendant radical leadership had demonstrated towards America was seen in Washington as a violation of normative state behaviour and evidence of an inability to define or protect Iran's national interest. The idea that the regime would commit acts deliberately aimed at sabotaging relations with the US was inexplicable. The view of a hostile and irrational Iran, whose leaders were unwilling or ideologically unable to pursue a foreign policy based on the national interest, has now embedded itself in an influential strata of America's political elite.[29] Surveying the first two years of America's experience with post-revolutionary Iran, it might appear quite reasonable to question the rationality of those who had come to dominate Iranian foreign policy. Iran's decision to prolong the 444-day hostage crisis was an illegal, violent, and unprovoked violation of all diplomatic norms. Moreover, it contributed to Iran's international isolation and indirectly encouraged a devastating attack by Iraq. Bruce Riedel, a senior analyst for the CIA at the time, recollects his view at the time being that 'The Iranian regime isn't in the least bothered by having multiple enemies'.[30]

The Carter administration doubted Iran's rational credentials largely because they considered Iran's clerical leadership unable to define its national interest. On closer inspection, the claim that Iran displayed a casual disregard for its own security and indifference to making powerful enemies does not quite stand up to scrutiny. As much as the hostage crisis was an egregious act of criminality that permanently damaged Iran's international reputation, American analysts concurrently perceived an infuriatingly pragmatic Iranian foreign policy in its response to the Soviet intervention in Afghanistan. Khomeini lectured the Soviet ambassador about meddling in Afghanistan, but did not issue anything approximating a call for arms.[31] This was for good reason; Iran had little interest in major regional instability, having already received an influx of up to 500,000 refugees. Nor did Iran wish to provoke a confrontation with the Soviets, particularly when it needed Eastern bloc trade to offset Western sanctions and following

Moscow's neutrality in the Iran–Iraq War. Thus, when a thousand Afghanis, together with Iranian supporters, stormed the Soviet embassy in Tehran on 9 January 1980, a withdrawal was very quickly negotiated by Iranian authorities. The CIA described Iran's support for the insurgents as remaining 'largely symbolic' because 'Tehran probably does not want to let the Afghan issue interfere with its efforts to increase trade and economic contacts with the Soviets'.[32] The sources indicate a real sense of disappointment amongst US officials that Iran was not being more active in providing support to the Afghan rebels or taking anything other than a rhetorical position against the Soviet intervention. Indeed, those who question Iran's rational credentials fail to adequately explain why Iran was willing to agree to a secret arms-for-hostages deal with both the Reagan administration and Israel. In 1979, the Shah's last Prime Minister, Shapour Bakhtiar, admitted that Khomeini's 'obvious irrationality' was of great help in his efforts to organise an opposition movement in exile.[33] Since then, the characterisation of Iranian rationality has been pervaded by ideological axioms and seized upon by a variety of political agendas. The tenor of the public debate over Iran's rationality has become increasingly more visceral and politically motivated.

Decoding the psychological, political, and social dynamics of post-revolutionary Iran was a task that the US diplomatic or intelligence community was educationally and culturally poorly equipped to undertake. Trained to perceive power and influence through a secular lens, instinctively they reached out to the mostly Western-educated nationalist leaders who dominated the Bazargan provisional government. They struggled to identify suitable interlocutors at alternative levels of Iranian society and, although recognising the influence of clerical elites, could neither connect with their world view nor conceptualise the framework in which their discourse operated.[34] The US thus constructed less of a coherent engagement strategy than a set of guiding principles constructed according to what it perceived as mutual strategic, political, and economic interests. It was an approach that implicitly imposed America's view of Iran's needs, which, when not accepted, was treated as evidence of irrationality.

Despite the failure to normalise bilateral relations, the Carter administration continued to view this objective as vital and, more importantly, achievable. Support for opposition groups or military threats, they also counselled, would 'make an eventual rapprochement with Iran more difficult'.[35] As such, the government advised the next administration to 'continue to recognise the Revolution and follow a policy of restraint and non-interference to allow the present power struggle to work out'. This was despite the fact that the hostages had been in captivity for a year. At worst, they confided, the US could rely on the fact that 'extremists in Iran are non communist'.[36]

The Carter administration was slow to react to fast-moving political events in Iran, but deserves credit for accepting a revolution that had removed one of its closest allies.[37] US policy was flawed not because it was malevolently anti-Iranian, extremist, or attempting regime change, charges that are persistently levelled at it by the Iranian government and could perhaps characterise the policies of some of Carter's successors. It could be argued, however, that the basis of continued American failure to restore relations had still been laid. The Carter administration had not sought a confrontation with Iran, but they had simply failed to recognise the nature of the new regime or read its pattern of behaviour.

Appendix

A note on primary sources

The book draws upon extensive use of US primary documents, which are drawn from four main sources: the embassy documents obtained following its seizure by the Iranian students and subsequently released in multiple volumes; material available at the National Security Archive (NSA) in Washington; material available at the Carter Library in Atlanta; and those documents published online by the Declassified Document Reference System (DDRS).

The digitalised NSA collection *Iran: The Making of US Policy, 1977–1980* is searchable by keyword, date, and origin, and this represents an invaluable source for the researcher. I give particular thanks to the staff at the National Security Archive, and in particular Malcolm Byrne, who, in addition to advising me of the location of unpublished sources of interest, also provided me with documents produced for conferences organised solely or jointly by the archive. Some of these briefing books are now available via the Carter–Brezhnev Project website.

In the case of the Carter Library, the Brzezinski Donated Collection has served to increase the number of documents available from the National Security Council (NSC). The DDRS has in turn far fewer State Department sources, instead being dominated by NSC and CIA documents. The CIA's Freedom of Information website (www.foia.cia.gov) has also been a useful source of the agency's intelligence estimates, reports, and memorandums, albeit often quite heavily redacted. The website is keyword and date searchable, but documents are not given unique identifying numbers, which makes for rather limited citations.

During my research I surveyed well over a thousand documents from the sources mentioned above. Overall, this book directly cites over 150 of these primary documents (a list of these documents appears in the appendix). Unsurprisingly for a study of US diplomacy, the largest share of primary documents originate from the State Department – mostly in the form of traffic to and from the embassy in Tehran. The CIA and the NSC contribute the next highest proportion. During the course of my research I found that Pentagon sources comprised a clear minority of the available documentation in all of the collections I surveyed. As an indication, a search for Department of Defense sources within the NSA's digital collection *Iran: The Making of US Policy, 1977–80* yields just 65 records from a collection that exceeds 3,680 (and only 18 after February 1979).[1] In comparison, a search for Department of State yields over 2,300 sources.

The wider availability of State Department sources is partly due to the fact that more of these documents were in the public domain anyway, having been looted from the US embassy and subsequently published in multiple volumes by the Iran hostage takers. A substantial part of the NSA's digital collection is harvested from these volumes. It is also due to a significant reduction in the Pentagon's interests in Iran after the Revolution.[2] Amongst the sources surveyed, this study found no evidence to suggest that the occupants of the Office of the Defense Attaché, headed by Colonel Leland J. Holland, differed from their embassy colleagues in their analysis of events in Iran. In particular, they were equally optimistic, at least initially, that positive relations should and could be formed, and saw the moderates as broadly pro-American.[3] Nevertheless, Military Intelligence was frank about the conditions in early March, which they described, in similar terms to Sullivan's, as 'Chaos and little central authority'.[4]

I am grateful to have received the personal recollection of 12 former Carter officials, many of them on several occasions over a period of 5 years. A list can be found in the appendix. Without exception, those I spoke to offered detailed, and in some cases quite moving, observations that both supported and greatly enriched my reading of the documentation. The events being discussed occurred well over 30 years ago, and it is to their credit that, without exception, all those interviewed freely admitted that memories of certain events were hazy or simply missing. Some, like Bill Quandt, Nick Veliotes, or Nat Howell, were not directly responsible for Iran policy at the time, but provided fascinating insights into the wider bureaucratic and policy environment. Even if the reader observes relatively few citations drawn from these interviews, they were nevertheless critical in gaining an overall picture of policy-making and implementation during this period.

For some, Iran policy represented a traumatic episode in their lives; Bruce Laingen and John Limbert spent 444 miserable days in captivity, whilst Charlie Naas endured the earlier violent seizure of the US embassy in February 1979. Charlie Naas spent the remainder of his time in Tehran wondering when they would next 'come over the wall', only to watch it happen to his replacement just a few months after his departure. Speaking to Naas, who recalled how he continues to regularly mull over the events in 1979, taught me not to underestimate the psychological strain put upon those at the coalface of American diplomacy. Those back in Washington involved in the laborious and frustrating process of trying to free their comrades faced different but still emotionally demanding pressures. There is always the potential in these circumstances for emotion to cloud objective reflection. At no point did I consider any of the testimonies to be self-serving. Inline with good scholarly practice, however, no assertions of fact are based on testimony alone. Cross-checking their information was made easier by the fact that nearly all had provided detailed accounts of the period on other occasions. John Limbert, Gary Sick, and Harold Saunders had already written highly regarded accounts of their experiences.

Notes

Introduction

1. 'Victory for Khomeini as Army Steps Aside', 11 February 1979, BBC News.
2. (Untitled), Thomas Kent, Associated Press, 11 February 1979.
3. 'The Iranian Revolution: An Oral History with Henry Precht, Then State Department Desk Officer,' *Middle East Journal*, Vol. 58, No. 1 (Winter 2004), 29–30.
4. James Gerstenzang (untitled), Associated Press, 12 February 1979.
5. John Limbert, *Negotiating with Iran: Wrestling the Ghosts of History* (United States Institute of Peace Press, 2009), 89. Limbert was a former official at the US embassy in Tehran, where he was held captive during the hostage crisis. In November 2009, he was appointed as the first-ever US Deputy Assistant Secretary of State for Iran.
6. This includes two-time former President Hashemi Rafsanjani, former Chief Commander of the Revolutionary Guard Mohsen Rezaie, and former Foreign Minister Ali Akbar Velayati. See James Blight, Janet M. Lang, Hussein Banai, Malcolm Byrne, John Tirman, and Bruce Riedel, *Becoming Enemies U.S.–Iran Relations and the Iran–Iraq War*, 1979–88 (Rowman & Littlefield Publishers, 2012), 259.
7. For example, John Lancaster, 'Head Iranian Cleric Rejects Talks with U.S.; Remarks Reflect Deepening Power Struggle with Moderates', *Washington Post*, 17 January 1998.
8. Scott Peterson, 'Inside the Mind of Iran's Khamenei', *Christian Science Monitor*, 4 December 2012.
9. Quoted in John Lancaster, 'Head Iranian Cleric Rejects Talks with U.S.'
10. 'The Iranian Revolution: An Oral History with Henry Precht', 16.
11. Interview with Gary Sick, 25 May 2012.
12. Interview with Henry Precht, 14 May 2012.
13. Sick, *All Fall Down: America's Fateful Encounter with Iran* (Random House, 1985), 7.
14. Interview with Charlies Naas, 11 May 2012.
15. Michael Hunt, *Ideology and U.S. Foreign Policy* (Yale University Press, 1987), 105–107. My thanks to Luca Tardelli, whose doctoral research on this topic was presented at a PhD FPA workshop in November 2011.
16. Richard Cottam, 'US and Soviet Responses to Islamic Political Militancy', in Nikki R. Keddie and Mark J. Gasiorowski, eds, *Neither East nor West: Iran, the Soviet Union, and the United States* (Yale University Press, 1990), 274.
17. 'The Barzagan Government One Month Later and Prospects for the Future', Cable State, Sullivan to Department of State, 17 March 1979, NSADC: IR02382.
18. Quoted in Limbert, *Negotiating with Iran*, 91.
19. Barry Rubin. 'American Relations with the Islamic Republic of Iran, 1979–1981', *Iranian Studies*, Vol. 13, No. 1/4 (1980), 311.
20. Limbert, 91.
21. 'Khomeyni Meets Soviet Envoy', Tehran Domestic Service, 24 March 1979, FBIS-MEA-79-060.
22. William Beeman, *The Great Satan versus the Mad Mullahs: How the United States and Iran Demonize Each Other* (Greenwood Press, 2005), 13–17.

23. 'Guidance', Cable State, Christopher to Laingen, 156833, 18 June 1979, NSADC: IR02690.
24. Murray, *US Foreign Policy and Iran*, 21, 26.
25. Bill, *The Eagle and the Lion*, 286–288; Scott Armstrong, 'Iran Documents Give Rare Glimpse of CIA Enterprise', *Washington Post*, 31 January 1982.
26. 'Military Sales to Iran', cable Tehran, Laingen to US State Department, 07430, 17th July 1979, NSADC: IR02762.
27. Quoted in ABC News Transcripts: 'World News Tonight', 11 May 1980.
28. Christian Emery, 'The Transatlantic and Cold War Dynamics of Iran Sanctions, 1979–1980', *Cold War History*, Vol. 10, No. 3 (2010), 371–396.
29. BBC Worldwide Monitoring Service, Sunday 22 March 2009.
30. See Gary Sick, *All Fall Down*; James Bill, *The Eagle and the Lion: The Tragedy of American–Iranian Relations* (Yale University Press, 1988); Richard Cottam, *Iran and the United States: A Cold War Case Study* (University of Pittsburgh Press, 1988); Ofira Seliktar, *Failing the Crystal Ball Test* (Greenwood Publishing Group, 2000). Bruce Jentleson, ' "Discrepant Responses to Falling Dictator": Presidential Belief Systems and the Mediating Effects of the Senior Advisory Process', *Political Psychology,* Vol. 11, No. 2 (1990), 370.
31. See Warren Christopher, ed., *American Hostages in Iran: Conduct of a Crisis* (Yale University Press, 1985); Russell Moses, *Freeing the Hostages* (University of Pittsburgh Press, 1996); David Farber, *Taken Hostage: The Iran Hostage Crisis and America's First Encounter with Radical Islam* (Princeton University Press, 2005).
32. See Alexander Moens, *Foreign Policy under Carter*; Seliktar, *Failing the Crystal Ball Test*. For foreign policy analysis literature on the hostage crisis, see Steve Smith, 'Policy Preferences and the Bureaucratic Position: The Case of the American Hostage Mission', *International Affairs*, Vol. 61, No. 1 (1984–1985), 9–25; Steve Smith, 'Groupthink and the Hostage Rescue Mission', *British Journal of Political Science*, Vol. 15, No. 1 (1985), 117–123; Betty Glad, 'Personality, Political and Group Process Variables in Foreign Policy Decision Making: Jimmy Carter's Handling of the Iranian Hostage Crisis', *International Political Science Review*, Vol. 10, No. 1 (1989), 35–91.
33. Michael Donovan, 'National Intelligence and the Iranian Revolution', *Intelligence and National Security*, Vol. 12, No. 1 (1997), 143–163. Robert Jervis, *Why Intelligence Fails: Lessons from the Iranian Revolution and the Iraq War* (Cornell University Press, 2010); 'Iran: Intelligence Failure or Policy Stalemate?', *Working Group Report No. 1*, Institute for the Study of Diplomacy, Edmund A. Walsh School of Foreign Service, Georgetown University, 23 November 2004.
34. Christopher Hemmer, 'Historical Analogies and the Definition of Interests: The Iranian Hostage Crisis and Ronald Reagan's Policy toward the Hostages in Lebanon', *Political Psychology,* Vol. 20, No. 2 (June 1999), 267–289; David Brulé, 'Explaining and Forecasting Leaders' Decisions: A Poliheuristic Analysis of the Iran Hostage Rescue Decision', *International Studies Perspectives*, Vol. 6, No. 1 (2005), 99–113; David Patrick Houghton, *US Foreign Policy and the Iran Hostage Crisis* (Cambridge University Press, 2001).
35. Joshua Muravchik, *The Uncertain Crusade: Jimmy Carter and the Dilemmas of Human Rights Policy* (London: Hamilton Press, 1986), 212.
36. Robert Strong, *Working in the World: Jimmy Carter and the Making of American Foreign Policy* (Baton Rouge: Louisiana State University Press, 2000), 66.
37. Moens, 145–147.
38. Kaufman, 160.

39. Bill, 255–258.
40. Ansari, 81.
41. See, for example, Brzezinski, *Power and Principle: Memoirs of the National Security Adviser, 1977–1981* (Farrar, Straus & Giroux, 1983); Christopher, ed., *American Hostages in Iran*; Robert E. Huyser. *Mission to Tehran* (Harper and Row, 1986); Hamilton Jordan. *Crisis: The Last Year of the Carter Presidency* (Putnam, 1982); John Stempel, *Inside the Iranian Revolution* (Indiana University Press, 1981); William Sullivan, *Mission to Iran: The Last US Ambassador* (Norton, 1981); Cyrus Vance, *Hard Choices: Critical Years in America's Foreign Policy* (Simon and Schuster, 1983).
42. William E. Odom, 'The Cold War Origins of the US Central Command', *Journal of Cold War Studies*, Vol. 8, No. 2 (2006), 52–53, 56–57; Olav Njølstad, 'Shifting Priorities: The Persian Gulf in US Strategic Planning in the Carter Years', *Cold War History*, Vol. 4, No. 3 (2004), 21–55.
43. See James Goode's review of Seliktar's book in *International Journal of Middle East Studies*, Vol. 33, No. 4 (2001), 648–649.
44. Sick, *All Fall Down* (1985); Bill, *The Eagle and the Lion* (1988); Cottam, *Iran and the United States* (1988).
45. Barry Rubin, 'American Relations with the Islamic Republic of Iran, 1979–1981', *Iranian Studies*, Vol. 13, No. 1/4 (1980), 308; Bill, 421–422; Cottam, *Iran and the United States*, 192–197; Seliktar, *Failing the Crystal Ball Test*, 125–127; Murray, 28.
46. Quoted in 'The US and Iran Part III – The Hostage Crisis', *PRI's The World*, 27 October 2004.
47. Letter from L. Bruce Laingen to *New York Times*, 'Iran Hostage Crisis: Notes to a Post-Script', 13 January 1983.
48. William J. Daugherty, 'A First Tour Like No Other', CSI Publication, 1996.
49. Quoted in Jimmy Carter, *Keeping Faith: Memoirs of a President* (William Collins and Sons, 1982), 438.
50. Rubin. 'American Relations with the Islamic Republic of Iran, 1979–1981', 308.
51. Kenneth Pollack, *Persian Puzzle: The Conflict between Iran and America* (Random House 2004), 146.
52. Cottam,192–197.
53. Blight et al., *Becoming Enemies*.
54. Interview with Ambassador John Limbert, 18 May 2012.
55. Blight et al., 238.
56. Ibid., 238–289, 258.
57. Ibid., 257–258.
58. Ibid., 241.
59. Mark Gasiorowski, 'US Intelligence Assistance to Iran, May–October 1979', *Middle East Journal*, Vol. 6, No. 4 (2012), 613–627.
60. Martin Sicker, *The Bear and the Lion* (Praeger Publishing, 1984); Muriel Atkin, 'Myths of Soviet–Iranian Relations', in Keddie and Gasiorowski, *Neither East nor West*, 100–111; Shireen T. Hunter, 'The Soviet Union and the Islamic Republic of Iran', in Hafeez Malik, ed., *Soviet–American Relations with Pakistan, Iran and Afghanistan* (St Martin's Press, 1987).
61. Ervand Abrahamian, *Radical Islam: The Iranian Mojahadedin* (IB Tauris, 1989); Maziar Behrooz, *Rebels with a Cause: The Failure of the Left in Iran*, (IB Tauris, 1999); Stephanie Cronin, ed., *Reformers and Revolutionaries in Modern Iran: New Perspectives on the Iranian Left* (Routledge, 2004).
62. Victor Nemchenok, 'In Search of Stability amid Chaos: US Policy toward Iran, 1961–63', *Cold War History*, Vol. 10, No. 3 (2010), 341–369; Andrew Warne,

'Psychoanalyzing Iran: Kennedy's Iran Task Force and the Modernization of Orientalism, 1961–3', *The International History Review*, 2013 (online preview).
63. Warne, 2.
64. Sick, 9.
65. Michael Latham, *Modernization as Ideology: American Social Science and 'Nation Building'* in the Kennedy Era (University of North Carolina Press, 2000), 209. See also Nemchenok, 343.
66. Barry Rubin, *Paved with Good Intentions* (Penguin, 1981), 106–107; Bill, *The Eagle and the Lion*, 151; James Goode, 'Reforming Iran during the Kennedy Years'. *Diplomatic History*, Vol. 15, No. 1 (Winter 1991), 573–574.
67. Warne, 14.
68. 'Letter from the Ambassador to Iran (Holmes) to the Acting Assistant Secretary of State for Near Eastern and South Asian Affairs (Meyer)', 27 August 1961, 234–242 in US DoS, FRUS, 1961–1963: Vol. XVII, 235, 238.
69. The circumstances of Amini's resignation are described by Nemchenok, 356–358.
70. Ali Ansari, *Confronting Iran*, 48.
71. 'Memorandum for the Record – Minutes of Meeting of the Special Group (CI)', 5 November 1962, quoted in Nemchenok, 359.
72. Warne, 2–3.
73. Ansari, 48.
74. Sick, 10.
75. Quoted in Ansari, 53.
76. Bill, 171, 179.
77. Robert Litvak, *Détente and the Nixon Doctrine: American Foreign Policy and the Pursuit of Stability, 1969–1976* (Cambridge University Press, 1986), 9.
78. Ibid., 1.
79. Ibid., 83.
80. Robert Dallek, *Nixon and Kissinger: Partners in Power* (Harper Collins, 2007), 300.
81. Sick, 13.
82. Litvak, *Détente and the Nixon Doctrine*,140–141.
83. Sick, *All Fall Down*, 13.
84. For a recent and highly detailed narrative of Nixon–Shah relations, see Andrew Scott Cooper, *The Oil Kings: How the US, Iran and Saudi Arabia Changed the Balance of Power in the Region* (One World, 2011). See also Roham Alvandi, 'Nixon, Kissinger and the Shah: The Origins of Iranian Primacy in the Persian Gulf', *Diplomatic History*, Vol. 36, No. 20 (2012), 337–372.
85. Ansari, 63.
86. Mottahedeh, *The Mantle of the Prophet: Religion and Politics in Iran* (Pantheon, 1985), 331.
87. Ansari, 331.
88. Mottahedeh, 331.
89. See 'Iran: Intelligence Failure or Policy Stalemate?'.
90. Ibid, 6.
91. Bill, 211.

1 The Collapse of US Policy 1977–1979

1. Sick, 28.
2. Interview with Zbigniew Brzezinski, 'Carter Presidency Project', Miller Center of Public Affairs, University of Virginia, 18 February 1982.

3. William E. Odom, 'The Cold War Origins of the US Central Command', *Journal of Cold War Studies*, Vol. 8, No. 2 (2006), 58.

4. Interview with William Odom, 'Carter Presidency Project', Miller Center of Public Affairs, University of Virginia, 18 February 1982.

5. Odom; Olav Njølstad, 'Shifting Priorities: The Persian Gulf in US Strategic Planning in the Carter Years', *Cold War History*, Vol. 4, No. 3 (2004), 21–55.

6. Interview with William Odom, 'Carter Presidency Project'.

7. Thomson and Utgoff to Brzezinski, 8 July 1977, Zbigniew Brzezinski collection: Subject File, Box 24, 'Meetings PRC 7/8/77' folder, JCL.

8. Odom, 58.

9. Interview with William Odom, 'Carter Presidency Project'.

10. Frank Ninkovich, *The Wilsonian Century: US Foreign Policy since 1900* (Chicago University Press, 1999), p. 248.

11. Andrew Scott Cooper, 'Bad Romance: The Curious Case of the Shah and the Neocons', PBS Frontline: Tehran Bureau, 12 July 2012.

12. Ibid.

13. This view was captured vividly in Arthur Schelinger Jr's seminal book *The Imperial Presidency* (Houghton Mifflin Company, 1973).

14. Report for the Secretary of Defense on the Implementation of the United States Foreign Military Sales Program in Iran, 19 September 1977, NSADC: IR01227.

15. 'Annual Policy and Resource Assessment for Iran – Part One', Cable Tehran, 02930, 5 April 1977, NSADC: IR01159.

16. Cooper, *The Oil Kings*.

17. Sick, 15–20.

18. 'Annual Policy and Resource Assessment for Iran – Part One', Cable Tehran, 02930, 5 April 1977, NSADC: IR01159.

19. Kenneth R. Timmerman, 'Fanning the Flames: Guns, Greed and Geopolitics in the Gulf War', *The Iran Brief*, 1986–1988, chapter 5.

20. James A. Phillips, 'The Iranian Revolution: Long-Term Implications', *Heritage Backgrounder* #89. See also William Branigin, 'Iran Cancels Arms Orders with U.S.', *Washington Post*, 10 April 1979.

21. Seliktar, 54.

22. Sullivan, 224–236, 259–260; Carter, 445; Vance, 335–339, Brzezinski, 380–389; Sick, 138–156; Cottam, 186; Bill, 405–423; Mehran Kamrava, *Revolution in Iran: The Roots of Turmoil* (Taylor & Francis, 1990), 42–45; Thornton, 265; Ganji, 1, 100–117.

23. 'Human Rights Emphasis Stalled Iran Policy at Crucial Time, Book Says', Associated Press, 2 November 1981.

24. Seliktar, 55; Erwin Hargrove, *Jimmy Carter as President Leadership and the Politics of the Public Good* (Louisiana State University, 1988), 164.

25. 'Recent Events in Iran', State Department Memo, Patricia Derian to Roy Atherton, 5 December 1977, DDRS: CK3100009091.

26. John Gilbert, 'Jimmy Carter's Human Rights Policy and Iran: a Re-Examination, 1976–79', *Concept: An Interdisciplinary Journal of Graduate Studies*, Vol. 31, (2008); James Bill, 'Iran and the Crisis of 78', *Foreign Affairs*, Vol. 57, No. 2 (1978), 329; Kaufman, 4; Donnette Murphy, *US Foreign Policy and Iran: American–Iranian Relations since the Islamic Revolution* (Routledge, 2009), 14–16.

27. James Bill, 'Iran and the Crisis of 78', 329.

28. Ibid.
29. Nikki Keddie, *Modern Iran: Roots and Results of Revolution* (Yale University Press, 2003), 215.
30. Hong Kong AFP – 5 December 1979. FBIS-MEA-79-236 on 6 December 1979.
31. Cited in Rubin, *Paved with Good Intentions* (Penguin, 1981), 195.
32. Kaufman, 4.
33. Seliktar, 54–55.
34. 'The Iranian Revolution: An Oral History with Henry Precht, Then State Department Desk Officer Henry Precht', *Middle East Journal*, Vol. 58, No. 1 (Winter 2004), 10.
35. Bill, *The Eagle and the Lion,* 407.
36. Ibid., 408.
37. 'Iran in the 1980s', Report, CIA, 1 August 1977. DDRS: CK3100225219.
38. Quoted in Carter, 438.
39. David Gibbs, 'Does the USSR Have a Grand Strategy?', *Journal of Peace Research*, Vol. 24, No. 1 (1987), 368.
40. 'Annual Policy Assessment', Cable, US embassy, Kabul, to US Department of State, 01765, 9 March 1976. NSADC: AF00210.
41. Steve Galster introductory essay to the National Security Archive microfiche collection *Afghanistan: The Making of US Policy, 1973–1990.*
42. 'Afghanistan in 1977: An External Assessment', Cable, Theodore Elliot (US embassy, Kabul) to US State Department and multiple US embassies, 30 January 1978. NSADC: AF00259.
43. Scott Armstrong, 'Iran Crisis Finally Forces Itself on Vance', *The Washington Post*, 28 October 1980.
44. The Iranian Revolution: An Oral History with Henry Precht.
45. 'Assessment of the Political Situation in Iran', Report, Defense Intelligence Agency, 1 September 1978, NSADA: IR01497.
46. Scott Armstrong, 'Iran Crisis Finally Forces Itself on Vance'.
47. Sick, 4.
48. 'Iran: Intelligence Failure or Policy Stalemate?', 2.
49. Ibid., 9.
50. Ibid.
51. US House of Representatives, Permanent Select Committee on Intelligence, *Iran. Evaluation of US Intelligence Performance Prior to November 1978*, Staff Report, Washington, DC, January 1979.
52. Sick, 72.
53. Sullivan, 191–192.
54. Vance, 329.
55. Henry Precht (A reply to James Goode's Review of Ofira Seliktar), 'Failing the Crystal Ball Test: The Carter Administration and the Fundamentalist Revolution in Iran', *International Journal of Middle East Studies*, Vol. 33, No. 4 (2001), 667–668.
56. Scott Armstrong, 'Iran Crisis Finally Forces Itself on Vance'.
57. Ibid.
58. Brzezinski, 397.
59. Brzezinski, 372, 397; Sick, 72; Bruce Jentleson, '"Discrepant Responses to Falling Dictator": Presidential Belief Systems and the Mediating Effects of the Senior Advisory Process', *Political Psychology*, Vol. 11, No. 2 (1990), 370.
60. Interview with Charlie Naas, 11 May 2012.

2 Framing the Revolution as a Cold War Crisis

1. Leffler, *For the Soul of Mankind*, 313.
2. Richard Lehman, 'The US Stake in Iran', Brzezinski Country File, Box 30, 'Iran 21-27/11 1979, JCL.
3. Statement by the Chairman of the Joint Chiefs of Staff before the Senate Armed Services Committee, 25 January 1979.
4. Richard Cottam, 'Goodbye to America's Shah', *Foreign Policy*, 16 March 1979.
5. *New York Times*, 11 January 1979.
6. 'Changes in the Middle East: Moscow's Perceptions and Options', *Intelligence Report*, CIA, June 1979, NSADC: IR02628.
7. These early hopes would be widely reflected on in the US media. See Scott Armstrong, 'Iran Crisis Finally Forces Itself on Vance', *Washington Post*, 29 October 1980; Haynes Johnson, 'Carter; Changes in Carter's Views Reflect Harsh Realities of 1980', *Washington Post*, 13 January 1980.
8. Quoted in Christopher Wren, 'Brezhnev Appeals to Carter on Arms', *New York Times*, 19 January 1977.
9. Betty Glad, *An Outsider in the White House: Jimmy Carter, His Advisors, and the Making of American Foreign Policy* (Cornell University Press, 2009), 43.
10. Transcript of discussion taken from 'SALT II and the Growth of Mistrust', Carter–Brezhnev critical oral history conference, Musgrove, St Simons Island, Georgia, 7–9 May, 1994.
11. This included Brzezinski, Brown, Vance, Gelb, as well as Dobrynin, Viktor Sukhodrev, former interpreter and aide to Leonid Brezhnev, and Andrei Gromyko, and other high-level former members of the Soviet Ministry of Foreign Affairs.
12. Transcript of discussion taken from 'SALT II and the Growth of Mistrust'.
13. 'Soviet–US Relations: A Six Month Report', Department of State. Bureau of Intelligence and Research, 15 August 1977, NSADC: SE00506.
14. James G. Blight and Janet M. Lang, 'When Empathy Failed Using Critical Oral History to Reassess the Collapse of U.S.–Soviet Détente in the Carter–Brezhnev Years', *Journal of Cold War Studies*, Vol. 12, No. 2 (Spring 2010), 58–59.
15. Ibid, 60, 71.
16. Gloria Duffy, 'Crisis Mangling and the Cuban Brigade', *International Security*, Vol. 8, No. 1 (1983), 67.
17. John Dumbrell, Review of Auten, Brian J., *Carter's Conversion: The Hardening of American Defense Policy* (University of Missouri Press, 2008), H-Diplo, H-Net Reviews, June 2009.
18. Odom, 52–3; Njølstad, 21–55.
19. Duffy, 71.
20. Blight and Lang, 'When Empathy Failed', 59–61.
21. Leo Sartori, 'Will SALT II Survive?', *International Security*, Vol. 10, No. 3 (1985/86), 148.
22. George Lenczowski, 'The Arc of Crisis: Its Central Sector', *Foreign Affairs*, Vol. 47, No. 4 (1979), 796.
23. Auten, 286.
24. Westad, 288; Halliday, 'The Iranian Revolution and Great Power Politics', 246.
25. Moses, 85; Sick, 'Military Options and Constraints', 343.
26. Brzezinski to Carter, 2 December 1978, NSC Weekly Report No. 81, Zbigniew Brzezinski Collection, Weekly Reports, Box 41, 'Weekly Reports 71–81' folder, JCL.

27. Scott Armstrong, 'Iran Crisis Finally Forces Itself on Vance', *Washington Post*, 29 October 1980.
28. Brzezinski provides President Jimmy Carter with National Security Council (NSC) Weekly Report No. 84. Memo. White House. Issue Date: 12 January 1979. 'Arc of Crisis'. NSA.
29. National Security Council (NSC) Weekly Report No. 84. Memo. Brzezinski to Carter, 12 January 1979, NSADC: CK3100543545.
30. 'US Policy toward Iran', Statement by Assistant Secretary Saunders before the subcommittee on Europe and the Middle East of the Committee on Foreign Affairs, House of Representatives, 96th Cong., 1st session, 17 January 1979, NSADC: IR02110.
31. 'Memo on Consultative Security Framework for the Middle East', State Department Memo, 17 February 1979, DDRS: CK3100105244.
32. 'An Interview with Kissinger', *Time*, 15 January 1979, 29.
33. George Lenczowski, 'The Arc of Crisis: Its Central Sector', *Foreign Affairs*, Vol. 57, No. 4 (1979), 816–818.
34. 'The Crumbling Triangle', *Economist*, 8 December 1978, p. 12.
35. Brzezinski to Carter, 'Consultative Security Framework for the Middle East', 3 March 1979, Box 3, '4/79' folder, JCL.
36. 'Changes in the Middle East: Moscow's Perceptions and Options', Intelligence Report, CIA, *c.* June 1979, NSADC: IR02628.
37. 'Memo on Consultative Security Framework for the Middle East'.
38. 'Is Turkey Susceptible to the Iranian Sickness?', Paul B. Henze to Zbigniew Brzezinski, NSC, 15 December 1978, DDRS: CK3100151950.
39. 'Memo on Consultative Security Framework for the Middle East'.
40. http://ankara.usembassy.gov/uploads/images/V7MIea8CEsOMQ0WsODuhAA/ 30t7299.pdf.
41. R. K. Ramazani, 'Security in the Persian Gulf', *Foreign Affairs*, Vol. 57, No. 4 (Spring 1979), 822.
42. 'Memo on Consultative Security Framework for the Middle East'.
43. Tehran International Service – 15 June 1979, 'Tehran Reports on Remarks by Envoy to USSR', FBIS-MEA-79-120 on 20 June 1979.
44. See Strobe Talbot, *Endgame: The Inside Story of SALT II*, (Harper Collins, 1979), 156–61. Also James A. Phillips. 'The Iranian Revolution: Long-Term Implications', 15 June 1979, *Heritage Backgrounder* #89.
45. 'Iran: Khomeini's Prospects and Views', Intelligence Memorandum, CIA. National Foreign Assessment Center, 19 January 1979, NSADC: IR02131.
46. 'Iran: Arafat's Visit Intended to Garner Support for PLO', Defense Intelligence Commentary, *c.* 23 February 1979, NSADC: IR03590.
47. 'Changes in the Middle East: Moscow's Perceptions and Options'.
48. Carter, 237.
49. Garthoff, 725.
50. Conference Transcript for 'US–Soviet Relations and Soviet Foreign Policy toward the Middle East and Africa in the 1970's', The Norwegian Nobel Institute, Lysebu, 1–3 October, 1995.
51. Robert Moss, 'Who's Meddling in Iran', *New Republic* 12 February 1978, Vol. 179, No. 23, pp. 15–18.
52. 'Opposition Demonstrations in Iran: Leadership, Organization, and Tactics', Memorandum, CIA, 21 December 1978, NSADC: IR01952.
53. 'Soviet Involvement in the Iranian Crisis', Intelligence Report, CIA, National Foreign Assessment Center, 1 March 1979, NSADC: IR02357.

54. 'Assessment of Soviet Posture and Intentions Regarding Situation in Iran', Cable State, 296841, Vance to multiple embassies, 23 November 1978, NSADC: IR01798.
55. Sicker, *The Bear and the Lion*, p. 110.
56. Khomeini Interview in Beirut Monday Morning, 1st January 1979, FBIS-MEA-79-011
57. 'Brezhnev Letter to Carter Regarding the Situation in Iran', letter, 17 November 1978, DDRS: CK3100073474.
58. *Pravda*, 21 January 1979.
59. 'NVOI Scores Bakhtiar Policy', FBIS-MEA-79-023 on 1 February 1979.
60. 'Soviet MFA Iranian Desk Officer Discusses Iran', Cable Moscow, 01105, Toon to US State Department, 13 January 1979, NSADC: IR02076.
61. 'Tehran Radio Cites USSR, PRC Attitudes on US Policy', FBIS-MEA-79-028 on 8 February 1979.
62. 'Changes in the Middle East: Moscow's Perceptions and Options'.
63. Ibid.
64. Quoted in Dilip Hiro, *Iran under the Ayatollahs*, 283.
65. 'Changes in the Middle East: Moscow's Perceptions and Options', Intelligence Report, CIA, *c.* June 1979, NSADC: IR02628.
66. Francis Fukuyama, 'The Soviet Threat to the Persian Gulf', March 1981, Rand Corporation Paper Series, 1.
67. Sicker, *The Bear and the Lion*, 140.
68. Roger. Howard, *Iran Oil: The New Middle East Challenge to America*. (IB Tauris, 2007), 17.
69. National Security Council (NSC) Weekly Report No. 84. Memo. Brzezinski to Carter, 12 January 1979, DDRS: CK3100543545.
70. Limbert, 91.
71. 'The Hostage Crisis in Iran 1979–81', State Department draft report on the 1979–1981 hostage crisis in Iran. 8 January 1981. DDRS: CK3100135327.
72. Email from Henry Precht, 3 August 2010.
73. 'Departing Impressions of Iran', Cable Tehran, 02615, 5 March 1979, NSA: IR02363.
74. 'Meeting with Bazargan', Cable Tehran, Laingen to Department of State, 08970, 12 August 1979, NSADC: IR02876.
75. Ganji, 131.
76. 'The Barzagan Government One Month Later and Prospects for the Future', Cable State, Sullivan to Department of State, 003016, 17 March 1979, Documents from the US Espionage Den, v. 14:30-36, NSADC: IR02382.
77. Brzezinski to Carter, 2 December 1978, NSC Weekly Report No. 81, JCL, Zbigniew Brzezinski Collection, Weekly Reports, Box 41, 'Weekly Reports 71–81' folder.
78. Howard, 17.
79. Mottahedeh, 330.
80. For scholarship on the Left, see Abrahamian, 'Communism and Communalism in Iran: The Tudah and the Firqah-I Dimukrat', *International Journal of Middle East Studies*, Vol. 1, No. 4 (October, 1970): 291–316; Sepehr Zabih, *The Communist Movement in Iran* (Berkeley: University of California Press, 1966). For later works, see Ervand Abrahamian, *Radical Islam: The Iranian Mojahedin* (IB Tauris, 1989); Sepehr Zabih, *The Left in Contemporary Iran* (Hoover Press Publication, 1986); Homa Katouzian, 'Khalil Maleki: The Odd Intellectual Out', in Negin Nabavi, ed., *Intellectual Trends in Twentieth-Century Iran* (University Press

of Florida, 2003), 24–52; Mohsen M. Milani, 'Harvest of Shame: Tudeh and the Bazargan Government', *Middle Eastern Studies*, Vol. 29, No. 2 (1993), 307–320; Maziar Behrooz, *Rebels with a Cause: The Failure of the Left in Iran* (IB Tauris, 2000).

81. See Ervand Abrahamian, *Iran between Two Revolutions* (Princeton University Press, 1982), 534; Assef Bayat, 'Shari'ati and Marx: A Critique of an "Islamic" Critique of Marxism', *Journal of Comparative Poetics*, No. 10 (1990), 19–41; Ali Rahnema, *An Islamic Utopian: A Political Biography of Ali Shari'ati* (IB Tauris, 2000); Mangol Bayat, 'Iran's Real Revolutionary Leader', *Christian Science Monitor*, 24 May 1977; Mehbi Abed, 'Ali Shariati: The Architect of the 1979 Islamic Revolution of Iran', *Iranian Studies*, Vol. 19, No. 3/4 (1986), 229–234.

82. R. K. Ramazani, 'Iran's Foreign Policy: Contending Orientations', *Middle East Journal*, Vol. 43, No. 2 (Spring 1989), 203.

83. 'Iran: Communist Activities (an Intelligence Estimate)', CIA, National Foreign Assessment Center, February 1979, NLC-6-29-4-1-9.

84. Rubin, 'American Relations with the Islamic Republic of Iran, 1979–1981', 311.

85. Kurzman, *The Unthinkable Revolution in Iran*, 146; Behrooz, *Rebels with a Cause*, 59, 68, 73; Abrahamian, *Radical Islam: The Iranian Mojahedin*, 171.

86. 'Soviet Involvement in the Iranian Crisis', Intelligence Report, CIA, National Foreign Assessment Center, 1 March 1979, NSADC: IR02357.

87. Eric Rouleau, 'Khomeini's Iran', *Foreign Affairs*, Vol. 59, No. 1 (1980), 18.

88. 'The Opposition to the Shah', Memorandum, Brzezinski to Carter, White House, 3 November 1978, NLC-6-29-2-5-7.

89. 'Iran: Communist Activities (an Intelligence Estimate)'.

90. 'The Tudeh Party: A Vehicle of Communism in Iran', Report, CIA, 18 July, 1949, http://www.foia.cia.gov.

91. Melvyn Leffler, *Origins of the Cold War* (Routledge, 1994), 96.

92. Ibid., 83.

93. 'Iran: Communist Activities (an Intelligence Estimate)'.

94. Behrooz, 364.

95. 'Iran: Communist Activities (an Intelligence Estimate)'.

96. Howard, 17.

97. The full text of new material is available from www.nytimes.com/library/world/mideast/041600iran-cia-index.html.

98. Stephen Kinzer, *All the Shah's Men: An American Coup and the Roots of Middle East Terror* (Wiley, 2007), 205–206.

99. 'Iran: Communist Activities (an Intelligence Estimate)'.

100. Ibid.

101. Sicker, *The Bear and the Lion*, 86.

102. Abrahamian, *Radical Islam*, 116.

103. Sicker, *The Bear and the Lion*, 97.

104. Roger Benjamin and John Kautsky, 'Communism and Economic Development', *American Political Science Review*, Vol. 62, No. 1 (1968), 122.

105. Brenda Shaffer, 'Partners in Need: The Strategic Relationship of Russia and Iran', Policy Paper No. 57 (2001), Washington Institute for Near East Policy, 8.

106. Keddie, *Neither East Nor West: Iran, the Soviet Union, and the United States*, 5.

107. Kishawarz, *I Condemn* (Tehran: Rawaq Publications, n.d.), 79–80.

108. Maziar Behrooz, 'Tudeh Factionalism and the 1953 Coup in Iran', *International Journal of Middle East Studies*, Vol. 33, No. 3 (2001), 376.

109. Ibid., 377.

110. Javadzadeh, Abdy, 'Borrowing Ideology: Marxists Becoming Muslims during the 1979 Revolution in Iran', Paper presented at the annual meeting of the American Sociological Association, Montreal Convention Center, Montreal, Quebec, Canada (10 August 2006), 25.
111. 'Iran: Communist Activities (an Intelligence Estimate)'.
112. Ervand Abrahamian, 'Iran in Revolution: The Opposition Forces', *MERIP Reports*, No. 75/76 (March–April 1979), 8.
113. 'Iran in the 1980s', Intelligence Report, Central Intelligence Report, 1 August 1977, DDRS: CK3100225218.
114. Nathan Coombs, 'The Excess of the Left in Iran' – review of *Rebels with a Cause: The Failure of the Left in Iran*, by Maziar Behrooz on CultureWars.org, 17 July 2008.
115. Negin Nabavi, 'The Changing Concept of the "Intellectual" in Iran of the 1960s', *Iranian Studies*, Vol. 32, No. 3 (1999), 336–338.
116. Mottahedeh, 291. For the intellectuals' perception of the Tudeh in the 1940s, see Homa Katouzian, *Sadeq Hedayat: The Life and Literature of an Iranian Writer* (London, 1991), 162–163. Jalal Al-e-Ahmad, who has come to be considered the 'leading spokesman for the non-establishment Iranian intelligentsia', has been written about extensively. See Michael Hillmann, 'Cultural Dilemmas of an Iranian Literary Intellectual,' in *Iranian Culture: A Persianist View* (London, 1990), 119–144; Brad Hanson, 'The Westoxication of Iran: Depictions and Reactions of Beh-rangi, Al-e Ahmad and Shariati', *International Journal of Middle East Studies*, Vol. 15, No. 1 (February 1983): 1–23; Mehrzad Boroujerdi, *Iranian Intellectuals and the West: The Tormented Triumph of Nativism* (New York, 1996), 65–76; Ali Gheissari, *Iranian Intellectuals in the 20th Century* (University of Texas Press, 1997), 88–92. For a discussion of Maleki, see Homa Katouzian, *Musaddiq and the Struggle for Power* (London, 1990), 95–113.
117. Mottahedeh, 290. Maleki and his disciple Al-e-Ahmad would, with Dr Mozzafar Baghai, form the 'Toilers Party', dedicated to supporting the newly ascendant Mossadeq. The Toilers Party would itself soon split into various irreconcilable factions. One faction joined Baghai in opposing Mossadeq and the other joined with Maleki in his support for Mossadeq's policies. This latter group became known as the Third Force in 1952 and it was the dominant left-wing element in the National Front.
118. 'Assessment of the Internal Politics Scene in Iran', Memorandum, Saunders to Vance, 17 August 1978, NSADC: IR01476.
119. 'Soviet Involvement in the Iranian Crisis'.
120. Ibid.
121. Kurzman, 146.
122. 'Soviet Academic Discusses Iran', Cable Moscow, 01045, Toon to US State Department, 12 January 1979, NSADC: IR02073.
123. 'French Paper on Increasing Communist Infiltration', *Le Figaro*, 26 January 1979, FBIS-MEA-79-022 on 31 January 1979.
124. Ibid.
125. Email correspondence with Henry Precht, 6 May 2009.
126. 'Iran: Communist Activities (an Intelligence Estimate)',
127. 'Soviet designs seen behind Kianuri Tudeh appointment', *Le Monde*, Paris, 31 January 1979, FBIS-MEA-79-023 on 1 February 1979.
128. My thanks to Dr Siavush Randjbar-Daemi for sharing his considerable insights on this period.

129. Interview reported in 'Iran: Communist Activities (an Intelligence Estimate)'.
130. 'Iran: Communist Activities (an Intelligence Estimate)'.
131. Ganji, 133.
132. Annabelle Sreberny and Ai Mohammadi, *Small Media, Big Revolution: Communication, Culture and the Iranian Revolution* (University of Minnesota Press, 1994), 160.
133. For a brief description of Rahman Hatefi's record during this period, see Hossein Shahidi, *Journalism in Iran: From Mission to Profession* (Routledge, 2007), 18.
134. 'Brzezinski Daily Report to Carter', 5 March 1979, JCL- 1-9-8-21-0.

3 US–Iranian Elite Interactions and the Pathologies of Engagement

1. David Armstrong's *Revolution and World Order* (Oxford University Press, 1993), 1.
2. Raymond Aron, *Peace and War: A Theory of International Relations* (Weidenfeld and Nicolson, 1966), 101; Fred Halliday, *Revolution and World Politics: The Rise and Fall of the Sixth Great Power* (Palgrave MacMillan, 1999), 134–137.
3. S. J. Dehghani Firouz Abadi, 'Emancipating Foreign Policy: Critical Theory and Islamic Republic of Iran's Foreign Policy', *The Iranian Journal of International Affairs*, Vol. 20, No. 3 (2008): 1–26; Takeyh, *Guardians of the Revolution*.
4. Steven Walt, *Revolution and War* (Cornell University Press, 1996), 30–33. I am also indebted to Luca Tardelli's unpublished paper 'The US political elite and the sources of American foreign policy towards the Russian and Iranian revolutions'.
5. Ruhi Ramazani, 'Ideology and Pragmatism in Iran's Foreign Policy', *Middle East Journal*, Vol. 8, No. 4 (2004), 7.
6. Ansari, *Confronting Iran*, 128.
7. Dorraj Manochehr, 'Populism and Corporatism in Post-Revolutionary Iranian Political Culture', in Samih K. Farsouh and Mehrdad Mashayekhi (eds), *Political Culture of the Islamic Republic* (Routledge, 1992); Ansari, *Confronting Iran*; Brenda Shaffer, ed., *The Limits of Culture: Islam and Foreign Policy* (MIT Press, 2006), Anoushiravan Ehteshami and Mahjoob Zweiri, *Iran's Foreign Policy: From Khatami to Ahmadinejad* (Garnet Publishing Limited, 2008).
8. Anoush Ehteshami, 'Iran's International Relations: Pragmatism in a Revolutionary Bottle', in The Middle East Institute (ed.), *The Iranian Revolution at 30* (Washington, DC: The Middle East Institute, 2009), 129.
9. Stephen D. Krasner, *Sovereignty: Organized Hypocrisy* (Princeton University Press, 1999), 7.
10. See Alexander L. George (ed), *Avoiding War: Problems of Crisis Management* (Westview Press, 1991); Robert Jervis, 'Hypothesis on Misperception', *World Politics*, Vol. 20, No. 3 (April 1968), 454
11. Ralph K. White, *Fearful Warriors: A Psychological Profile of U.S.–Soviet Relations* (New York: Free Press, 1984), 160–161. See also Bright and Lang, 'When Empathy Failed', 38–39; Blight et al., *Becoming Enemies*, chapter 1.
12. Murray, 21, 26,
13. Jordan, *Crisis*, 28; Murray, 27.
14. 'Liberation Movement of Iran (LMI) – Views on Politics in Iran', Memorandum of Conversation Tehran, 25 May 1978, NSADC: IR01399.
15. Gasiorowski, 'US Intelligence Assistance to Iran, May–October 1979', 616–620.
16. Sick, 232. See NSADC documents IR00397, IR00401, and IR00430.
17. Gasiorowski, 616.

18. 'Contact with Sadegh Ghotbzadeh in November 1977', Confidential, Memorandum State, Henry Precht to Robert B. Mantel, 17 January 1979, NSADC: IR021200.
19. Bill, *The Eagle and the Lion*, 267.
20. [CIA Agent Vernon Cassin's Assessment of Bani Sadr Case] Cable Tehran, DCI, 54174, 9 September 1979, NSADC: IR03012.
21. See documents from the US Espionage Den. v. 25: 34.
22. US Espionage Den v. 25: 34, 38–39. Also '[Political Opposition in Iran]' Confidential, Memorandum of Conversation Tehran, Lambrakis to State Department, 12 June 1978, NSADC: IR01417.
23. 'Liberation Movement of Iran (LMI) – Views on Politics in Iran', Memorandum of Conversation Tehran, 25 May 1978, NSADC: IR01399.
24. Ganji, 87.
25. 'Assessment of Soviet Posture and Intentions Regarding Situation in Iran', Cable State, Vance to all near Eastern and Asian embassies, 296841, 23 November 1978, NSADC: IR01798.
26. 'Cottam on Khomeini, Liberation Movement (LMI) and National Front (INF)', Cable Tehran, Sullivan to Vance, 00066, 2 January 1979, NSADC: IR02002.
27. 'Further Report of Richard Cottam', Cable State, Vance to Embassy Tehran, 004510, 7 January 1979, NSADC: IR02021.
28. 'Assessment of Soviet Posture and Intentions Regarding Situation in Iran'. See also 'Political/Security Report November 26', Cable Tehran, 26 November 1978, NSADC: IR01804.
29. 'Iran: Khomeini's Prospects and Views', intelligence memorandum, CIA, 19 January 1979, NSADC: IR02131.
30. David Harris, *The Crisis: The President, the Prophet, and the Shah – 1979 and the Coming of Militant Islam* (New York: Little, Brown, and Company, 2004), 155.
31. 'The Iranian Revolution: An Oral History with Henry Precht, Then State Department Desk Officer,' *Middle East Journal*, Vol. 58, No. 1 (Winter 2004), 22.
32. Ganji, 93.
33. Interview with Precht, 21 May 2008.
34. 'Conversation with Ibrahim Yazdi, Advisor to Khomeini', 12 December 1978, at Dominique's Restaurant [Memorandum for the Files], secret, memorandum, Henry Precht, 13 December 1978, Department of State, NSADC: IR01919.
35. 'Cottam on Khomeini, Liberation Movement (LMI) and National Front (INF)'.
36. Kurzman, 157.
37. Bill, 256.
38. 'The Iranian Revolution: An Oral History with Henry Precht', 23.
39. 'USG Policy Guidance', Cable State, Sullivan to Vance, 10 January 1979, DDRS: CK3100503552.
40. Interview with Gary Sick, 25 May 2012.
41. Sick, 143.
42. Ibid.
43. Ibid., 144.
44. Ibid., p. 141.
45. 'LMI Wants US to Push; Conflict with Moderates Shaping Up', memo, US Embassy Tehran to Secretary of State, Washington, 22 January 1979, NSADC: IR02148.
46. Sick, 150.
47. Bill, 290–393.
48. Brzezinski, 390–392.

49. Beeman, 13–17.
50. Zbigniew Brzezinski provides President Jimmy Carter with NSC Weekly Report No. 84. Memo. White House. Issue date: 12 January 1979. 'Arc of Crisis'. NSA.
51. Jervis, 'Hypothesis on Misperception', 466.
52. Zbigniew Brzezinski's memo to President Carter (NSC Weekly Report No. 87), 2 February 1979.
53. Murray, 27.
54. 'Khomeyni says he hopes to "guide," but not be President', Khomeini interview with *Le Monde*, 10 January 1979, FBIS-MEA-79-008 on 11 January 1979. Khomeini repeated this statement almost verbatim in an interview with Rome's *L'Espresso* – 28 January 1979.
55. Keddie, 240.
56. 'Khomeini Comments on Islamic Republic, Gas, Oil', *L'Espresso*, 28 January 1979, FBIS-MEA-79- 027 on 7 February 1979.
57. 'Iran: Understanding the Shi'ite Islamic Movement', Cable Tehran, Sullivan to Vance, 01691, 3 February 1978, NSADC: IR01298.
58. Janet Afary and Kevin B. Anderson, *Foucault and the Iranian Revolution: Gender and the Seductions of Islamism* (University of Chicago Press, 2005), 70–71.
59. Mottahedeh, 373.
60. Keddie, 232.
61. Afary and Anderson, 71–72.
62. Luca Tardelli, Unpublished paper presented at the LSE Foreign Policy Workshop, 22 November 2011.
63. Zbigniew Brzezinski's memo to President Carter (NSC Weekly Report No. 87), 2 February 1979.
64. 'Iran: Khomeini's Prospects and Views', intelligence memorandum, CIA, 19 January 1979, NSADC: IR02131.
65. 'Policy towards Iran', briefing memorandum, State Department, Saunders to Vance, 5 September 1979, NSADC: IR02996.
66. Keddie, 243.
67. 'Iran: Communist Activities (an Intelligence Estimate)'.
68. 'Iran – Prospects for Bazargan Government', alert memorandum, CIA, Turner to NSC, 1 March 1979, NSADC: IR02356.
69. Sullivan, 273–274.
70. 'The Iranian Revolution: An Oral History with Henry Precht', 19.
71. 'Iran: Communist Activities (an Intelligence Estimate)'.
72. 'Soviet Involvement in the Iranian Crisis'.
73. J. P. Smith, 'Iran's Radicals Key to Oil Exports, US Aides say', *Washington Post*, 14 February 1979. Phillips, James A. 'The Iranian Oil Crisis', The Heritage Foundation Backgrounder #76, 28 February 1979.
74. 'Soviet Involvement in the Iranian Crisis'.
75. James A. Philips, 'The Iranian Oil Crisis'.
76. Mohsen M. Milani, 'Harvest of Shame: Tudeh and the Bazargan Government', *Middle Eastern Studies*, Vol. 29, No. 2 (1993), 307.
77. 'NVOI Defend Soviet Union in Radio Broadcast', Tehran Domestic Service, 16 May 1979. As published in FBIS-MEA-79-103.
78. Memo for David Aaron from Situation Room, NSC, 12 March 1979, NLC-1-10-1-2-6.
79. Ervand Abrahamian, *Tortured Confessions*, 201.

80. 'Assessment of Soviet Posture and Intentions Regarding Situation in Iran', Cable State, 296841, Vance to multiple embassies, 23 November 1978, NSADC: IR01798.
81. 'Iran: Communist Activities (an Intelligence Estimate)'.
82. Email correspondence with Henry Precht, 6 May 2009.
83. Chief of the Oriental Institute's Middle Asia Section, Yuriy Gankovskiy, had privately admitted to a US counterpart that the Tudeh were 'very weak' in January 1979.
84. 'Tudeh Party Leader Interviewed on Current Situation', An-Nahar Al-'Arabi Wa Ad-Duwali (Paris), 4 June 1979. As published in FBIS-MEA-79-110 on 6 June 1979.
85. 'Iran Briefing', Cable State, Vance to multiple embassies, 267001, 12 October 1979, NSADC: IR03266.
86. Ibid.
87. 'Soviet Involvement in the Iranian Crisis'.
88. 'Soviet Reaction to the Iranian Crisis, *Soviet Report*, Vol.1, No. 2, December 1979. The Center for Strategic and International Studies.
89. 'Iran and the USSR after the Shah', Memorandum, CIA, National Foreign Assessment Center, 17 August 1979, NSA: IR02906.
90. 'Iran – Prospects for Bazargan Government', alert memorandum, CIA, Turner to NSC, 1 March 1979, NSA: IR02356.
91. 'Anti-US Statements by National Voice of Iran (NVA)', Brzezinski collection: File Iran: 11/1-14/79 Box 29, JCL; 'The President's Comments on Persian-Language Broadcasting and Related Issues', Memorandum, NSC, Henze to Brzezinski, 6 February 1979, DDRS: CK3100143708; 'VOA Broadcasting', memorandum, Reinhardt to Brzezinski, 9 February 1979, DDRS: CK3100144133; 'Iran – The Psychological Problem and Some Solutions', Memorandum, International Communications Agency. Office of Near Eastern and South Asian Affairs, Curran to Office of the Director, 9 February 1979, NSA: IR02268.
92. Text of the Algiers Accord's 'General Principles' agreed on 18 January 1981. See http://www.parstimes.com/history/algiers_accords.pdf.
93. Interview with Charlies Naas, 11 May 2012.
94. Hunt, *Ideology and US Foreign Policy*, 105–107.
95. 'Iran: Khomeini's Prospects and Views', intelligence memorandum, Central Intelligence Agency, National Foreign Assessment Center, 19 January 1979, NSADC: IR02131.
96. 'Iran: Arafat's Visit Intended to Garner Support for PLO', Defense Intelligence Commentary, *c.* 23 February 1979, NSADC: IR03590.
97. Ansari, 57.

4   Putting Engagement into Practice

1. For recent criticism of this trait, particularly during America's nation-building project in post-Saddam Iraq, see Christian Caryl, 'The U.S. spent billions promoting democracy in Iraq. Now the official verdict is in: It was all for nothing', *Foreign Policy*, 5 March 2013.
2. Bill, 255–258.
3. Interview with Henry Precht, 14 May 2012.
4. *New York Times,* 11 January 1979.
5. *New York Times,* 15 January 1979.
6. Vance, 134–135.
7. *New York Times,* 20 January 1979.

8. For list of agenda topics, see http://www.lib.umich.edu/govdocs/pdf/nscmeet7. pdf.

9. 'Visit' (Charg Laingen Proposes That Under Secretary Cooper Make a Short Official Visit to Iran), Cable Tehran, Laingen to US State Department, 11523, 2 November 1979, NSADA: IR03456.

10. Interview with Gary Sick, 25 May 2012.

11. Interview with Charlies Naas, 11 May 2012.

12. Interview with Gary Sick, 25 May 2012.

13. Sick, *'All Fall Down'*, 187.

14. 'The Iranian Revolution: An Oral History with Henry Precht', 29–30.

15. Email from Precht, 6 May 2009.

16. 'Policy towards Iran', briefing memorandum, State Department, Saunders to Vance, 5 September 1979, NSADC: IR02996.

17. 'Reporting Subjects', Cable State, Christopher to US embassy, 168047, 29 June 1979, NSADC: IR02724.

18. William A. Philips, 'Iran, the United States and the Hostages: After 300 days', Heritage Foundation, 29 August 1980.

19. Beeman, *The 'Great Satan' vs. the 'Mad Mullahs'*, 19.

20. Bill, 290–293.

21. Bowden, 156.

22. 'Message for Ambassador Sullivan', Cable State, Vance to United Kingdom embassy, 18 February 1979, NSADC: IR02315.

23. Seliktar,143.

24. Athens Elevtherotipia, 7 February 1979; 'Bazargan Interviewed in Tehran by Greek Paper', FBIS-MEA-79-028 on 8 February 1979.

25. David Menashri, *Iran: A Decade of War and Revolution* (Holmes and Meier, 1990), 97.

26. Carter, 452.

27. Carter, 460

28. 'The Iranian Revolution: An Oral History with Henry Precht', 30.

29. Interview with Charlie Naas, 11 May 2012.

30. 'The Barzagan Government One Month Later and Prospects for the Future', Cable State, Sullivan to Department of State, 003016, 17 March 1979, NSADC: IR02382.

31. Thomas Thornton to David Aaron, 'Message to the Vice President on Afghanistan', 23 March 1979, NSC memorandum, Brzezinski donated material, country file, Box 1, 'Afghanistan 1/77-3/79', NLC-6-1-1-12-0.

32. Gilles Dorronsoro, *Revolution Unending: Afghanistan, 1979 to the Present*, CERI series in Comparative Politics and International Studies (C. Hurst & Co., 2005), 98.

33. 'Soviet Activities in Afghanistan', Charles Naas to Deputy Prime Minister Amir Entezam, 16 May 1979; Documents prepared for Carter–Brezhnev Project Conference, 'Global Competition and the Deterioration of U.S.–Soviet Relations, 1977–1980,' Fort Lauderdale, FL, 23–26 March 1995.

34. 'Meeting with Prime Minister Bazargan', Cable Tehran, Laingen to Department of State, 08970, 12 August 1979, NSADC: IR02876.

35. Thomas Thornton to David Aaron, 'Message to the Vice President on Afghanistan', 23 March 1979, NSC memorandum, Brzezinski donated material, country file, Box 1, 'Afghanistan 1/77-3/79', NLC-6-1-1-12-0.

36. Sick noted that Morteza Bazargan was 'extremely naïve, but well meaning, He has no experience of foreign policy'.

37. 'Meeting with Morteza Bazargan', NSC memorandum, Gary Sick to David Newsom, 25 May 1979, NSADC: IR02610.
38. Interview with Charlies Naas, 11 May 2012.
39. Mahmood T. Davari, *The Political Thought of Ayatullah Murtaza Mutahhari: An Iranian Theoretician of the Islamic State* (Routledge, 2005), 74.
40. Rouleau, 18.
41. 'Montazeri: US behind Leftist Organisations in Iran', Paris, *Al-Mustaqbal*, 16 June 1979.
42. Montazeri Interview with *Ar-Ra'y al-Am* (Kuwait), FBIS-MEA-79-182 on 18 September 1979.
43. Quoted in 'The US and Iran Part III – The Hostage Crisis', *PRI's The World*, 27 October 2004.
44. Cottam, 208.
45. 'The Iranian Revolution: An Oral History with Henry Precht', 30.
46. 'Letter from Foreign Minister Yazdi to Secretary of State Vance', 20 May 1979, NSADC: IR02583.
47. Foreign Affairs Oral History Program, Association for Diplomatic Studies, Interview with Ambassador Bruce Laingen. Dates: 9 January, 7 April, 25 August 1992; 17 February, 27 May 1993.
48. Email from Charlie Naas, 22 April 2010.
49. Interview with Charlie Naas, 11 May 2012.
50. 'US–Iran Relations', Cable State, 6 June 1979, Department of State, Current Foreign Relations, NSADC: IR02648.
51. Foreign Affairs Oral History Program, Interview with Ambassador Bruce Laingen.
52. David Lamb, *The Africans* (Random House, 1982), 46.
53. Crawford Young and Thomas Turner, *The Rise and Decline of the Zairian State* (University of Wisconsin Press, 1985), 31.
54. Tehran International Service, 7 June 1979, 'Tehran Discusses Reasons for Refusing US Ambassador'.
55. 'Amir-Entezam Statement', Cable State, Christopher to US Embassy Tehran, 163650, 24 June 1979, NSADC: IR02714.
56. Foreign Affairs Oral History Program, Interview with Ambassador Bruce Laingen.
57. 'Threat Assessment: Iran', report, Department of Defense, Office of Security, Threat Analysis Group, 14 June 1979, NSADC: IR02682.
58. Email from Ambassador Bruce Laingen, 23 April 2010.
59. 'USG–PGOI Relations', Christopher to US embassy Tehran, 139729, 1 June 1979, NSADC: IR02633.
60. Sick, 188.
61. 'The Iranian Scene; Implications for US Interests', 1979, Cable Tehran, Naas to US State Department, 05951, 8 June 1979, NSADC:IR02660.
62. The American Posture in Iran: 1. Changing Circumstances', Cable Tehran, 30 May 1979, NSADC: IR02623.
63. Quoted in Ganji, 136.
64. 'The Iranian Scene; Implications for US Interests'.
65. Stempel, 211.
66. Seliktar, 126.
67. Sick, 200.
68. Seliktar, 126–127.
69. 'Irano–Iraq Relations', Cable Tehran, 06378, 19 June 1979. Documents from the US Espionage Den v. 10:80. Author's interview with Naas, 22 April 2010.

70. Bill, 276–283.
71. National Security Council (NSC) Weekly Report No. 84. Memo. Brzezinski to Carter, White House, 12 January 1979, DDRS: CK3100543545.
72. 'The Gulf Arabs and Iran', CIA report, 8 December 1978, 'Iran: 12/78-1/79', Brzezinski donated country file, box 29, NLC-6-29-3-10-0, JCL.
73. Seliktar, 133.
74. Sick, 188.
75. Ganji, 141.
76. 'The Barzagan Government One Month Later'.
77. 'The Iranian Scene; Implications for US Interests', 1979, Cable Tehran, Naas to US State Department, 05951, NSADC: IR02660.
78. 'Guidance' (General Guidance for Chargé Laingen's Embassy Priorities), Cable State, Christopher to Laingen, 156833, 18 June 1979, NSADC: IR02690.
79. 'The Iranian Scene; Implications for US Interests'.
80. 'USG–PGOI Relations'.
81. Interview with Henry Precht, 10 May 2012.
82. 'USG–PGOI Relations'.
83. 'Policy towards Iran'.
84. 'Guidance' (General Guidance for Chargé Laingen's Embassy Priorities).
85. Sick, 188.
86. 'Meeting with Radical Movement Leader Rahmatollah Moghaddam-Maraghei', Cable Tehran, Laingen to US State Department, 11460, 30 October 1979, NSADC: IR03431.
87. Brzezinski, 518, 565.
88. 'Departing Impressions of Iran', Cable Tehran, 02615, 5 March 1979, NSA: IR02363.
89. 'Changes in the Middle East: Moscow's Perceptions and Options', Intelligence Report, CIA, *c*. June 1979, NSA: IR02628.
90. Chief of the Oriental Institute's Middle Asia Section Yuriy Gankovskiy had privately admitted to a US counterpart that the Tudeh were 'very weak' in January 1979.
91. 'Tudeh Party Leader Interviewed on Current Situation', An-Nahar Al-'Arabi Wa Ad-Duwali (Paris), 4 June 1979, FBIS-MEA-79-110.
92. 'Iran Briefing', Cable State, Vance to multiple embassies, 267001, 12 October 1979, NSA: IR03266.
93. Author's interviews with Henry Precht and Harold Saunders (Washington, DC, May 2008).
94. Tehran Domestic Service, 10 June 1979, 'Mokri Meets with Khomeyni', FBIS-MEA-79-113 on 11 June 1979.
95. 'Iran: Communist Activities (an Intelligence Estimate)'.
96. Tehran Domestic Service, 9 June 1979, ' Iranian Ambassador to USSR Describes Relations', FBIS-MEA-79-113. On 9 June 1979.
97. Tehran Domestic Service, 10 June 1979, 'Mokri Meets with Khomeyni', FBIS-MEA-79-113 on 11 June 1979.
98. Tehran Domestic Service, 12 June 1979, 'Khomeyni Asks USSR Not to Supply Arms, Interfere in Afghanistan', FBIS-MEA-79-115.
99. 'Paris Magazine Publishes Interview with Islamic Republican Party Leader', *Al-Mustaqbal* (Paris), 16 June 1979.
100. 'Islamic Fundamentalism and the Soviet Union', UK delegation to NATO, State Department, 30 July 1979, NSA: IR02796.

101. 'Tehran Broadcasts Anti-Soviet Programs', *Al-Hawadith* (London), 25 May 1979.
102. 'Iran and the U.S.S.R. after the Shah', memorandum, CIA, National Foreign Assessment Center, 17 August 1979, DDRS: CK3100219663.
103. Aryeh Yodfat, *The Soviet Union and Revolutionary Iran* (Croom Helm, 1984), 61.
104. 'Iran and the U.S.S.R. after the Shah'.
105. 'Kurds, Iran, etc.', Henze to Brzezinski, NSC, memo, 4 September, 1979, DDRS: CK3100528462.
106. Quoted in *Pravda*, 29 August 1979.
107. Yodfat, 63.
108. Ibid., 63.
109. Alexander Bovin, *Nedelya*, 3–9 September 1979.
110. 'Soviet Policy toward Iran', Cable Moscow, Toon to US State Department, 22156, 17 September 1979, NSA: IR03083.
111. Ibid.
112. Phillips, James A., 'The Iranian Revolution: Long-Term Implications', The Heritage Foundation Backgrounder #89, 15 June 1979.
113. Ibid.
114. Seliktar, 143.
115. 'Military Sales to Iran', Cable Tehran, Laingen to US State Department, 07430, 17 July 1979, NSADC: IR02762.
116. Ganji, 137.
117. Letter from William Proxmire (Dem-Wisconsin) to President Carter, 28 August 1979, DDRS: CK3100536018
118. Foreign Affairs Oral History Program, Interview with Ambassador Bruce Laingen.
119. Seliktar, 143.
120. Vance, 368.
121. 'Military Sales to Iran'.
122. Ibid.
123. Interview with Naas, 11 May 2012.
124. Ibid.
125. 'Meeting with Prime Minister Bazargan'.
126. Alexander Moens, *Foreign Policy under Carter: Testing Multiple Advocacy Decision Making* (Westview Press, 1990), 140; Carter, *Keeping Faith*, 435.

5 The CIA and Engagement

1. 'US–Iran Relations', Cable State, 6 June 1979, US Department of State, NSADC: IR02648.
2. William J. Daugherty, 'A First Tour Like No Other', CSI publication, 1996.
3. Ibid.
4. For a study of this conflict, see Dilip Hiro, *Iran under the Ayatollahs*, Routledge, 1985, 139–144.
5. 'Assessment of Internal Political Scene in Iran', memorandum, State Department, Saunders to Vance, 17 August 1978, NSADC: IR01476. See also Donovan, 'National Intelligence and the Iranian Revolution', 146.
6. These meetings are described in Documents from the U.S. Espionage Den, v. 55:22-51.
7. Documents from the US Espionage Den, v. 55:26.
8. Documents from the US Espionage Den, v. 55:34.
9. Ibid.

10. Documents from the US Espionage Den, v. 55:35.
11. Documents from the US Espionage Den, v. 55:63-64.
12. Keddie, *Roots of Revolution*, 242.
13. Hiro, 139–143.
14. 'Alleged Extremist Activities and Plans for Shariatmadari-Backed Political Stance', Cable CIA, 482081, 25 July 1979, NSADC: IR02780.
15. Hiro, 142.
16. Ibid., p. 143.
17. Ibid., p. 142.
18. Keddie, p. 249.
19. Documents from the US Espionage Den, v. 55:3.
20. Bill, *The Eagle and the Lion*, 290.
21. Bowden, 179–181.
22. Gasiorowski, 'US Intelligence Assistance to Iran', May–October 1979', 616–618.
23. Thomas Thornton to David Aaron, 'Message to the Vice President on Afghanistan', 23 March 1979, NSC memorandum, Brzezinski donated material, country file, Box 1, 'Afghanistan 1/77-3/79', NLC-6-1-1-12-0.
24. 'Soviet Activities in Afghanistan', Charles Naas to Deputy Prime Minister Amir Entezam, 16 May 1979; Documents prepared for Carter–Brehnev Project Conference, 'Global Competition and the Deterioration of U.S.–Soviet Relations, 1977–1980', Fort Lauderdale, FL, 23–26 March 1995.
25. Gasiorowski, 616–618.
26. Interview with Naas, 12 May 2012.
27. Telephone interview with Bruce Laingen, 23 April 2010.
28. Foreign Affairs Oral History Program, Interview with Ambassador Bruce Laingen.
29. Gasiorowski, 619.
30. Email from George Cave, 27 September 2012.
31. Bill, 291.
32. 'Perseverance and Honor: Interview with Abbas Amir-Entezam', published in *Payvand*, 24 February 2006.
33. Gasiorowski, 619–620.
34. Ibid.
35. 'Policy towards Iran', briefing memorandum, Saunders to Vance, 5 September 1979, NSADC: IR02996.
36. 'Views on Iran's Political Situation; Includes Proposed Questions for Laingen's Meeting with Iranian Foreign Minister Yazdi', letter, Precht to Laingen, 13 September 1979, NSADC: IR03063.
37. Gasiorowski, 622–624.
38. Ibid.
39. Interview with Henry Precht, 21 May 2008.
40. 'Continuation of the Steps Taken to Begin an Intelligence Relationship with the Bazargan Government', Cable, 515885, 19 September 1979, CIA, NSADC: AF00651.
41. Gasiorowski, 616–620.
42. Bill, 146, 401–402.
43. 'Abbas Amir-Entezam Concern about Iranian Relations with Iraq', Secret, Cable CIA, 543216, 31 October 1979, NSADC: IR03446.
44. Email from George Cave, 27 September 2012.
45. Gasiorowski, 616–620.

46. Email from Wayne White, 20 January 2012; Interview with Gary Sick, 25 May 2012.
47. Email from Henry Precht, 30 July 2010.
48. Ibid.
49. Email to author, 20 January 2012.
50. 'Perseverance and Honor: Interview with Abbas Amir-Entezam', published in *Payvand*, 24 February 2006.
51. Hiro, 180.
52. Saunders, 54.
53. Ibid., 280.

6   Re-evaluating US Policy after the Hostage Crisis

1. Foreign Affairs Oral History Program, Ambassador Bruce Laingen.
2. Interview with Ambassador John Limbert, 18 May 2012.
3. Foreign Affairs Oral History Program, Ambassador Bruce Laingen.
4. Saunders, 55.
5. Bill, 287–288.
6. Ibid., 288.
7. Foreign Affairs Oral History Program, Interview with Ambassador Bruce Laingen.
8. Bill, 279.
9. 'Policy towards Iran', briefing memorandum, Saunders to Vance, 5 September 1979, NSADC: IR02996.
10. Saunders, 55.
11. Foreign Affairs Oral History Program, Interview with Ambassador Bruce Laingen.
12. 'Secretary's Meeting with Foreign Minister Yazdi', Cable State, US Department of State to US Embassy Tehran, 009006, 4 October 1979, NSADC: IR03213.
13. Sick, 189.
14. Milani, 'Harvest of Shame', 307.
15. NVOI broadcasts are transcribed in File 'Iran: 11/1-14/79', Box 29, JCL.
16. FBIS-MEA-79-182 on 18 September 1979.
17. Foreign Affairs Oral History Program, Interview with Ambassador Bruce Laingen.
18. Bill, 285.
19. Ibid., 292.
20. 'Shah's Desire to Reside in the US', Secret, Cable Tehran, 07930, 28 July 1979, NSADC: IR02788.
21. Interview with Charlie Naas, 11 May 2012.
22. 'Planning for the Shah to Come to the United States', Letter State, Precht to Laingen, 2 August 1979, NSADC: IR02827.
23. 'Inquiry from PGOI Concerning Shah', Cable Tehran, 16 August 1979, NSADC: IR02892.
24. 'Inquiry from PGOI Concerning Shah', Cable Tehran, 19 August 1979, NSADC: IR02912.
25. 'Shah of Iran', Cable State, 29 September 1979, NSADC: IR03180.
26. 'The Shah's Illness', Cable State, 21 October 1979, NSADC: IR03344.
27. 'The Shah's Illness', Cable Tehran, 21 October 1979, NSADC: IR03345.
28. 'Media Reaction on Shah's Trip to U.S.', Cable Tehran, 11255, 24 October 1979, NSADC: IR03376.
29. 'The Shah in the US', Cable Tehran, 24 October 1979, NSADC: IR03379
30. 'The Shah in the US', Cable Tehran, 31 October 1979, NSADC: IR03441.

31. 'Ayatollah Khomeini Calls for Clergy and Students to Confront the U.S. Until It Releases the Shah', CIA Intelligence Report, 2 November 1979, NSADC: IR03465.
32. See, for example, the discussion amongst former scholars and practitioners in *Becoming Enemies*, 257–259.
33. See Bill, chapter 9.
34. Kaufman, 194–195.
35. John Limbert, keynote speech at 'One Term President, Long-Term Legacy: Jimmy Carter and Iran', Conference at Durham University, 19 October, 2012.
36. Foreign Affairs Oral History Program, Interview with Ambassador Bruce Laingen.
37. 'The Iran Hostage Crisis: An Interview with Victor Tomseth Conducted by David Taboua', 26 December 2009, Maryland Digital Cultural Heritage.
38. 'Text of Bazargan's Resignation Speech', Tehran Domestic Radio, 8 November 1979.
39. Interview with Precht, 21 May 2008.
40. Brzezinski, 475–476.
41. Sick, 222.
42. Bill, 294.
43. Moses, 368.
44. 'Provisional Government of Iran Delegation to Algiers', Cable Tehran, Laingen to Newsom, 11422, 29 October 1979, NSADC: IR03420.
45. Bill, 294.
46. Interview with Gary Sick, 25 May 2012.
47. Brzezinski, 475–476.
48. Bill Gold, 'As Others See Us', *Washington Post*, 26 November 1979.
49. Reported in *New York Times*, 27 November 1979, p. 11.
50. *U.S. News & World Report*, 3 December 1979, 'Washington Whispers'.
51. 'Thoughts on Iran', memorandum, Henze to Brzezinski, National Security Council, 9 November 1979, DDRS: CK3100504698.
52. Brzezinski, 480; Jordan, 53.
53. Steve Smith, 'Policy Preferences and Bureaucratic Position: The Case of the American Hostage Rescue Mission', *International Affairs*, Vol. 61, No. 1 (1984–1985), 9–25.
54. Jordan, 19.
55. Edward Walsh, 'Rivals Doubt Carter Will Retain Poll Gains after Iran Crisis', *Washington Post*, 17 December 1979.
56. Ibid.
57. Carter, 482; Moses, 108.
58. Leffler, 328; Brzezinski, 484–485.
59. Brzezinski, 480.
60. 'Reflections on Soviet Intervention in Afghanistan', Memorandum, Brzezinski to Carter, White House, 26 December 1979, DDRS: CK3100098563.
61. Sick, 205; Thornton, 448; Ganji, 158.
62. Ganji, 158.
63. Shortly after the hostage crisis began, the influential NSC staff member Paul Henze sent a memo to Brzezinski suggesting a much more vigorous and visible re-establishment of American power in the Muslim world. He also implicitly criticised the State Department's Soviet expert Marshall Shulman for repeating the 'soothing words of Dobrynin' as evidence of Soviet policy. See 'The US and the

Islamic World', memorandum, Henze to Brzezinski, National Security Council, 27 November 1979, DDRS: CK3100155679.

64. Odom, 56–57.
65. 'Iran: Bani-Sadr's Foreign Policy Views', Intelligence memorandum, CIA, 5 February 1980, DDRS: CK3100160311.
66. Ibid.
67. Behrooz, 'Trends in the Foreign Policy of the Islamic Republic of Iran, 1979–1988',17–19.
68. Hiro, 150.
69. Ganji, 163.
70. 'Tehran Radio: Brezhnev, Gromyko Support Khomeyni's Stand', as published in FBIS-MEA-79-219 on 9 November 1979.
71. Ibid.
72. *Le Monde*, 30 November 1979.
73. Ganji, 154; Mohsen Milani, *The Making of Iran's Islamic Revolution: From Monarchy to Islamic Republic* (Westview Press, 1994), 153.
74. 'Tudeh's Kianuri on Embassy Takeover, Relations with Khomeini', *MERIP Reports*, No. 86, 'The Left Forces in Iran' (March–April 1980), 24.
75. Quoted in R. K. Ramazani, 'Iran's Revolution: Patterns, Problems and Prospects', *International Affairs (Royal Institute of International Affairs 1944–)*, Vol. 56, No. 3 (Summer 1980), 454.
76. Ganji, 149.
77. For an interview with Kianuri, see 'Tudeh's Kianuri on Embassy Takeover, Relations with Khomeini', *MERIP Reports*, No. 86, 'The Left Forces in Iran' (March–April 1980), 24–25.
78. Stempel, 226.
79. Farber, 158.
80. Ibid.
81. Ganji, 154.
82. 'Thoughts on Iran'.
83. Ibid.
84. Sick, 167.
85. 'Thoughts on Iran'.
86. Ibid.
87. Saunders, 93.
88. Ibid., 13–14, 372.
89. 'Soviet Efforts to Benefit from the US–Iran Crisis', Intelligence Estimate, National Foreign Assessment Center, CIA, 1 December 1979, DDRS: CK3100219671.
90. Christopher Andrew and Vasili Mitrokhin, *The Mitrokhin Archive II* (Allen Lane, 2005), 187.
91. Moses, 372–373.
92. 'Soviet Efforts to Benefit from the US–Iran Crisis'.
93. 'Soviet Clandestine Broadcasting in Iran', memorandum, Henze to Brzezinski, NSC, 15 November 1979, NLC-6-29-7-1-6.
94. Ibid.
95. 'Soviet-Based Radio Urges Hostages' Release in Iran', Anonymous, *Washington Post*, 22 November 1979.
96. 'Conversation with (Redacted)', Memorandum State, Washburn to Precht, 27 January 1980, DDRS: CK3100112384.
97. Ganji, pp. 152–153.

98. Letter from Ambassador Dobrynin to President Carter, 4 December 1979, DDRS: CK3100497366.
99. The KGB station chief in Tehran, Leonid Shebarshin, feared that the Soviet embassy would be attacked after Afghanistan. See Andrew and Mitrokhin, 184.
100. 'Soviet Reaction to the Iranian Crisis'.
101. Amir Taheri, 'America Can't Do a Thing', *New York Post*, 2 November 2004.
102. Houchang Nahavandi, a former minister of the Shah who opposed his departure in favour of bolstering the military, makes this argument in an interview with Jamie Glazov, 'The Last Shah of Iran', *FrontPageMagazine.com*, 6 March 2006. Also in Houchang Nahavandi, *Iran, the Clash of Ambitions* (Aquilion, 2006).
103. Kenneth Timmerman, 'Fanning the Flames: Guns, Greed, and Geopolitics in the Gulf War', syndicated by New York Times Syndication Sales, 1987, published in book form as *Ol ins Feuer* (Orell Fssl, 1988), 117.
104. Ganji, 154–155.
105. Ibid.; Christos Ioannudes, *America's Iran* (University Press of America, 1984); Seliktar, 158.
106. Miles Copeland, *The Game Player* (Aurum Press, 1989), 256.
107. Christopher Andrew and Oleg Gordievsky, *KGB: Inside Story of Its Foreign Operations from Lenin to Gorbachev* (Hodder & Stoughton, 1990).
108. For this view, see 'Planning for the Shah to Come to the United States'.
109. Mark Bowden, *The Atlantic*, December 2004. Online.
110. Quoted in Ganji, 164.
111. '*Keyhan* Comment on USSR Reaction to US Intervention', *Keyhan* (Tehran), 21 November 1979.
112. Ibid.
113. 'Bani-Sadr Discusses Possible Soviet Aid', *Le Monde* (Paris), 24 November 1979, FBIS-MEA-79-230 on 28 November 1979.
114. 'Ambassador Meets Gromyko; USSR to "Protect" Iran', *Ettela'at* (Tehran), 27 November 1979, FBIS-MEA-79-236 on 6 December 1979.
115. Ibid.
116. 'Moscow Envoy on Situation', Tehran Domestic Service, 20 November 1979.
117. *Ettela'at* (Tehran), 27 November 1979, FBIS-MEA-79-236 on 6 December 1979.
118. 'USSR Envoy on Soviet Position'.
119. Ibid.
120. 'Soviet Efforts to Benefit from the US–Iran Crisis'. Also 'USSR Envoy on Soviet Position', Tehran, 1 December 1979, published in FBIS-MEA-79-233 on 3 December 1979.
121. 'Possible Conclusions of a Soviet Policy Review,' memorandum from Shulman to Vance, 4 December 1979. Documents prepared for Carter–Brezhnev Project Conference 'Global Competition and the Deterioration of U.S.–Soviet Relations, 1977–1980', Fort Lauderdale, FL, 23–26 March 1995.
122. 'Moscow Envoy on Situation'.
123. 'Source Discusses Blocking of Hormuz Strait', *El Pais* (Madrid), 22 November 1979.
124. Rubinstein, 601.
125. Robert B. Cullen, Associated Press, 6 November, 1979; Milton R. Copulos and James A. Phillips, 'The Iranian Dilemma: Energy and Security Implications', Heritage Foundation Background Briefing No.105, 16 November 1979. US imports of Iranian oil were higher in November 1979 than in the same month of any other previous year (Energy Information Administration statistics).

126. Hossein Alikhani, *Sanctioning Iran: Anatomy of a Failed Policy* (IB Tauris, 2001), 67.
127. Carswell and Davies, 'Economic and Financial Pressures', in Christopher, 176.
128. Jonathan C. Randal, 'U.S., Iran Declare Halt to Oil Trade', *Washington Post*, 13 November 1979.
129. Ibid.; W. A. Bachman, 'U.S. Shaping Strategy to Offset Iranian Crude Loss', *Oil & Gas Journal*, 3 December 1979.
130. Jordan, 54; Carter, 461; Carswell and Davies, 176.
131. 'Iran: The Test of Wills', *Time*, 26 November 1979.
132. 'What If Iran Ended U.S. Oil Sales?', *U.S. News & World Report*, 19 November 1979.
133. Carswell and Davies, 255.
134. 'Pressure on the Ayatollah', *Washington Post*, 13 November 1979; Carswell and Davies, 176.
135. The threat was made by acting Iranian foreign and finance minister, Abolhassan Bani-Sadr, on 13 November. In July 1981, Fernand St Germain, chairman of the House Committee on Banking, Finance and Urban Affairs, confirmed that plans to enact a freeze in the event of a threatened withdrawal of Iranian assets predated the hostage crisis. See 'Iran, the Financial Aspects of the Hostage Settlement Agreement', Committee on Banking, Finance and Urban Affairs, House of Representatives, 97th Congress, 1st Session, July 1981.
136. Moses, 328. For other studies of this motivation, see Benjamin Cohen, *In Whose Interest? International Banking and American Foreign Policy* (Yale University Press, 1986), and Karin Lissakers, 'Money and Manipulation', *Foreign Policy*, No. 44 (Fall 1981), 107–126; Khosrow Fatemi, 'The Iranian Revolution: Its Impact on Economic Relations with the United States', *International Journal of Middle East Studies* Vo.12, No. 3 (1980), 303–317.
137. Carswell, 249.
138. Moses, 338.
139. Ibid.
140. Carswell, 264; see also Hoffman, 235–280.
141. Christopher, 24–25; Carswell, 328.
142. Moses, 113.
143. Robert McCartney, 'Europeans Discuss Iran Sanctions', Associated Press, 17 May 1980.
144. Bradley Graham, 'Europe to Impose Sanctions on Iran Despite Britain', *Washington Post*, 21 May 1980.
145. Philip Shehadi, 'Economic Sanctions and Iranian Trade', *MERIP Reports*, No. 98 (July–August 1981), 15–16.
146. Sick, 241.
147. Carter, 466.
148. Sick, 242.

7   Viewing Afghanistan through the Prism of Iran

1. Ganji, 169.
2. Leffler, 333; Vladislav Zubok, *A Failed Empire: The Soviet Union in the Cold War from Stalin to Gorbachev* (The University of North Carolina Press, 2007), 262; Z. Hilali, 'The Soviet Decision-Making for Intervention in Afghanistan and

Its Motives', *The Journal of Slavic Military Studies*, Vol. 16, No. 2 (2003), 122; Hiro, 284.
3. Leffler, 333; Zubok, 262.
4. Vsevolod Ovchinnikov, '*Pravda* on Lord Carrington's "Gallop around Asia"', Moscow Home Service, 21 January 1980.
5. Hiro, 284.
6. 'US–Soviet Relations and Soviet Foreign Policy toward the Middle East and Africa in the 1970's', Conference Reader Edited by Odd Arne Westad, Norwegian Nobel Institute, Lysebu, 1–3 October 1995.
7. Odom, Njølstad.
8. Andrew Hartman, '"The Red Template": US Policy in Soviet-Occupied Afghanistan', *Third World Quarterly*, Vol. 23, No. 3 (2002), 468; Richard K. Betts, *Nuclear Blackmail and Nuclear Balance* (Brookings Institution Press, 1987), 188.
9. 'Reflections on Soviet Intervention in Afghanistan', Brzezinski to Carter, 26 December 1979, DDRS: CK3100098563.
10. Ibid.
11. 'Afghanistan', memorandum, NSC, Oksenberg to Brzezinski, 29 December 1979, Brzezinski donated collection, Country File, Box 1, 'Afghanistan: 4–12, 79', JCL.
12. 'NSC on Afghanistan', National Security Council memorandum, NSC026, 2 January 1980, Declassified documents prepared for 'A Critical Oral History Conference', The Woodrow Wilson Center, 25–26 July 2005.
13. Haynes Johnson, 'Carter; Changes in Carter's Views Reflect Harsh Realities of 1980', *Washington Post*, 13 January 1980.
14. Summary of Conclusions, 'SCC Meeting on U.S. Strategy for South West Asia and Persian Gulf', 14 January 1980, Documents prepared for Carter–Brezhnev Project 'The Intervention in Afghanistan and the Fall of Détente', Lysebu, Norway, 17–20 September 1995.
15. Hilali, 122.
16. Hartman, 468–469.
17. Soviet source quoted in Westad, 315.
18. Carol R. Saivetz, 'Superpower Competition in the Middle East and the Collapse of Détente', in Odd Arne Westad (ed.) *The Fall of Détente*, 90.
19. Moses, 85; Sick, 343.
20. Brzezinski, 480; Jordan, 53.
21. 'Moslem Emotions and Anti-American Sentiments. Back to Basics', memorandum, Rentcshler to Brzezinski, 3 December 1979, DDRS: CK3100143598.
22. Brzezinski, 84.
23. Associated Press, 31 December 1979.
24. State of the Union Address, 23 January 1980.
25. 'Carter Interview with Frank Reynolds', White House Internal Transcript, 31 December 1979, Box 17, JCL.
26. Vance, 400.
27. 'Memorandum of Conversation between Richard Cottam and Sadeg Ghotbzadeh', Iran: Update, January 1980, Brzezinski Country File NLC-6-32-6-8-6.
28. Ibid.
29. Ibid.
30. 'NSC on Afghanistan', Minutes from National Security Council meeting, 2 January 1980, The Carter Administration and the 'Arc of Crisis' 1977–1981, Declassified documents prepared for 'A Critical Oral History Conference', The Woodrow Wilson Center, 25–26 July 2005.

31. Quoted in Moses, 120.
32. 'What Can We Do about the Hostages?', Memorandum White House, Jordan to Jimmy Carter, 22 January 1980, Box 34B, File: Iran, 1/80, JCL.
33. Ibid.
34. 'Qotbzadeh Interview', Paris AFP, 19 January 1980.
35. Ibid.
36. 'Qotbzadeh Interview', Paris Domestic Service, 20 January 1980, as published in FBIS-MEA-80-014-S on 21 January 1980.
37. Ibid.
38. Andrew and Mitrokhin, 184.
39. 'Bani Sadr: "We Will Not Kill Hostages" ', *Al Hawadith* (London). 16 November 1979.
40. 'Iran: Bani-Sadr's Foreign Policy Views', Intelligence memorandum, CIA, 5 February 1980, DDRS: CK3100160311.
41. Draft report from HJ to JC of conversation with an Iranian contact close to the govt, February 1980 (precise date unknown), Hamilton Jordan Confidential File, Box 34B, 1977–80, Iran: 11/79-03/80, JCL.
42. 'Telegram to Ambassador Lang', Telegram State, 3 February 1980, Hamilton Jordan Confidential File, Box 34B, 1977–80, Iran: 11/79-03/80, JCL.
43. For details of the affairs, see Moses, 156.
44. Andrew and Mitrokhin, 185.
45. Ibid.
46. 'Qotbzadeh Interview', Paris AFP, 19 January 1980.
47. 'Chief of Staff Gen Shadmehr Notes Soviet Troop Movements', Tehran Domestic Service, 17 April 1980.
48. 'An Interview with Ghotbzadeh', *Time*, Monday, 1 September 1980.
49. Andrew and Mitrokhin, 185.
50. 'Minutes of Special Coordination Meeting', Stansfield Turner, 17 December 1979, Carter–Brezhnev Project, Box 5, National Security Archive.
51. Ibid.
52. Leffler, 331–333.
53. Doug MacEachin, Janne E. Nolan, and Kristine Tockman, 'The Soviet Invasion of Afghanistan in 1979: Failure of Intelligence or of the Policy Process?', Institute for the Study of Diplomacy, Edmund A. Walsh School of Foreign Service, Georgetown University, Group Report, No. 111 (26 September 2005), 4.
54. Ibid., 4.
55. Ibid., 6.
56. 'SCC Working Group on Iran and Afghanistan: Public Posture', Memorandum NSC, Schecter to Brzezinski, 14 January 1980, Carter–Brezhnev Project, Box 5, National Security Archive unpublished material.
57. 'President Amin's Desire for Better Relations', Cable, Blood (US Embassy Kabul) to State Department, 07645, 23 October 1979, NSADC: AF00706.
58. 'Soviet Union and Southwest Asia', Intelligence memorandum from DCI Turner, 15 January 1980, http://www.foia.cia.gov/.
59. 'The Soviet Invasion of Afghanistan', Defense Intelligence Summary, c. February 1980, NSA: AF00849.
60. 'USSR: A Military Option', Defense Intelligence Agency, 5 February 1980, NSA: SE00532.
61. This judgement was repeated in a subsequent study entitled 'A Soviet "Best Case" for Military Intervention in Iran' presented on 19 February 1980.

62. Richard Burt, 'US Sees Need for Nuclear Arms to Repel Soviet Attack on Iran', *New York Times*, 2 February 1980.
63. As reported in Ibid. For a useful study of these issues, see Kenneth N. Waltz, 'A Strategy for the Rapid Deployment Force', *International Security*, Vol. 5, No. 4 (Spring, 1981), 49–73.
64. Quoted in Joseph Kraft, 'Administration has Doctrine of Confusion', *Sarasota Herald-Tribune*, 6 February 1980.
65. 'Iran and the Soviets', memorandum, NSC, Henze to Brzezinski, 11 April 1980, DDRS: CK3100469805.
66. Leffler, 336.
67. 'US Stake in Iran'.
68. Ibid.
69. Lundestad, 208–212.
70. 'Israel Is Extremely Gloomy about Afghanistan', Defense Intelligence Summary, January 1980, NSADC: AF00744.
71. Ibid.
72. Afghanistan: Soviet Invasion and US Responses', Carter–Reagan Transitions Papers Collection, unpublished, Box 1, 1980–81, RECNO: 81, Department of State Briefing Paper, National Security Archive.
73. 'A Soviet "Best Case" for Military Intervention in Iran', Intelligence memorandum, CIA, 19 February 1980, The Carter Administration and the 'Arc of Crisis' 1977–1981, Declassified documents prepared for 'A Critical Oral History Conference', The Woodrow Wilson Center, 25–26 July 2005.
74. Brzezinski's Daily Report to Carter, White House, 14 April 1980, NLC-1-15-1-8-5, JCL.
75. Ibid.
76. 'Soviet Military Options in Iran', Special National Intelligence Estimate, CIA, 21 August 1980, http://www.foia.cia.gov.
77. 'Moscow's Afghan Strategy', Cable, Griffen (US Embassy Kabul) to US State Department, 02445, 28 August 1980, NSADC: AF01036.
78. It is likely that some had supported the resolution in the knowledge that the Soviets would veto it anyway.
79. John M. Goshko, ' "Allies" Laws May Limit Cooperation on Iran Sanctions', *Washington Post*, 18 January 1980.
80. Robert McCartney, 'Europeans Discuss Iran Sanctions', Associated Press, 17 May 1980; 'How To Be a Good Ally without Putting Oneself Out', *Economist*, 19 April 1980.
81. Carswell, 253; Sick, 248; Ganji, 180; Robert R. Bowie, 'The Atlantic Alliance', *Daedalus*, Vol. 110, No. 1 (Winter, 1981), 62; Leonard Downie, Jr, 'Allies Plan Limits to Their Support of U.S. Sanctions', *Washington Post*, 18 January 1980.
82. 'Mo'infar, Salimi on EEC Decision', AFP (Paris), 23 April 1980.
83. 'National Intelligence Daily', CIA, 30 April 1980, http://www.foia.cia.gov.
84. Brzezinski, 484; Moses, 88; Ganji, 180.
85. Baldwin, 260.
86. Robert Cullen, 'US, Allies to Postpone New Sanctions against Iran', Associated Press, 22 January 1980.
87. 'The Hostage Situation', Memo from DCI Turner, CIA, 9 January 1980, Brzezinski's Country Files, 1977–1981, NLC-6-30-6-3-3.
88. For a description of this initiative, see Saunders, 114–125.
89. Ibid., 120.

90. Moses, 337.
91. 'What Can We Do about the Hostages?'
92. Saunders, 132.
93. Moses, 156.
94. Sick, 272; Saunders, 134.
95. Leonard Downie, Jr, 'Allies Had Hoped to Prevent Use of Force by U.S.; Joining Sanctions Seen as Inducement', *Washington Post*, 24 April 1980.
96. Robert Cullen, 'Immediate, Tangible Results from New Sanctions Aren't Likely', Associated Press, 8 April 1980.
97. Alikhani, 79.
98. William M. Welch, 'Reagan Calls Iran Sanctions More of Same', Associated Press, 7 April 1980.
99. Quoted in Natalino Ronzitti, *Rescuing Nationals Abroad through Military Coercion and Intervention on Grounds of Humanity* (Martinus Nijhoff, 1985), 43.
100. Despite planning and training for Operation Eagle Claw having started almost immediately after the crisis began, the first realistic capability for a rescue mission was not reached until the end of March.
101. Holloway Report, 17, http://www.gwu.edu/~nsarchiv/NSAEBB/NSAEBB63/doc8.pdf.
102. John M. Goshko and Don Oberdorfer, 'The Options Now; Future Course of the Confrontation Is More Complicated and Dangerous', *Washington Post*, 26 April 1980.
103. Lundestad, 209–212; Minton Goldman, 'President Carter, Western Europe, and Afghanistan in 1980: Inter-allied Differences over Policy Toward the Soviet Invasion', in Herbert D. Rosenbaum and Alexej Ugrinsky, eds, *Jimmy Carter: Foreign Policy and Post-Presidential Years* (Greenwood Press, 1994), 23; Downie, Jr, 'Allies Plan Limits to Their Support of U.S. Sanctions'.
104. Brzezinski, 487.
105. 'European Community Nations Impose Sanctions on Iran; Britain Modifies Stand', Facts on File, *World News Digest*, 23 May 1980, 378.
106. Christopher, 8.
107. Hiro, 323.
108. Sadjadpour, *Reading Khamenei: The World View of Iran's Most Powerful Leader*, 11.
109. Quoted in ABC News Transcripts: *World News Tonight*, 11 May 1980.
110. State Department: Iran Transitional Paper: #1, 4 December 1980, Carter–Brezhnev Project, Box 5, National Security Archive.
111. 'Limited Iranian Response to Afghan Rebel Appeal', Cable, Naas to US Embassy Pakistan, 05246, 21 May 1979, NSADC: AF00554. See also Bradsher, *Afghanistan and the Soviet Union*, 101. Also Male, *Revolutionary Afghanistan*, 161–162.
112. 'Limited Iranian Response to Afghan Rebel Appeal'.
113. 'Bani Sadr: "We Will Not Kill Hostages" '.
114. Ibid.
115. 'Iran: Bani-Sadr's Foreign Policy Views'.
116. Ibid.
117. 'Afghanistan: Soviet Invasion and US Responses'.
118. 'Iran: Views on Afghanistan', CIA, National Foreign Assessment Center, 1 February 1980, http://www.foia.cia.gov.
119. Ibid.
120. 'Impact of Iranian and Afghan Events on South Asia', National Foreign Intelligence Center, Intelligence Assessment, 7 January 1980, http://www.foia.cia.gov.

121. 'Afghanistan: Iran's Role in the Crisis', Intelligence memorandum, CIA, 27 June 1980, The Carter Administration and the 'Arc of Crisis' 1977–1981.
122. 'Iran: Views on Afghanistan'.
123. Ibid.
124. 'Iran: Situation Report', Intelligence memorandum, CIA, 20 May 1980, http://www.foia.cia.gov.
125. Ibid.
126. 'Iran: Views on Afghanistan'.
127. 'Noon Notes', National Security Council memo, Situation Room to Brzezinski, 18 June 1980, NLC-1-15-7-24-1.
128. 'Iran: Views on Afghanistan'.
129. Ibid.
130. Ibid.
131. Harold Saunders, 44–45; Sick, 206; Vance, 375–377; Bill, 296–297; Farber, 182; Haughton, 10; Baqer Moin, *Khomeini: Life of the Ayatollah* (IB Tauris, 1999), 227–228.
132. 'Afghanistan: Soviet Invasion and U.S. Responses'.

8 US Policy and the Iran–Iraq War 1980–1981

1. Sick; Cottam; Carter; Jordan.
2. Chubin and Tripp, *Iran and Iraq at War* (Westview Press, 1991); Stephen C. Pelletiere, *The Iran–Iraq War: Chaos in a Vacuum* (Praeger, 1982), 43.
3. Sasan Fayazmanesh, Graig Unger, Dilip Hiro, and journalists Robert Parry and Richard Sale allege US collusion with these groups.
4. Abol Hassan Bani-Sadr, *My Turn to Speak: Iran, the Revolution and Secret Deals with the U.S.* (Brassey's, 1991), 70.
5. Dilip Hiro uses Bani-Sadr's account to write that 'By supplying secret information, which exaggerated Iran's military weakness, to Saudi Arabia for onward transmission to Baghdad, Washington encouraged Iraq to attack Iran'. Dilip Hiro, *The Longest War* (Routledge, 1991), 71.
6. The document was discovered by journalist Robert Parry amid records from a Congressional investigation into the early history of the Reagan administration's contacts with Iran. Parry published the memo in 1995 on Consortiumnews.com in 1995.
7. Private email correspondence (17 October 2010).
8. PBS interview with Said K Aburish: http://www.pbs.org/wgbh/pages/frontline/shows/saddam/interviews/aburish.html.
9. Larry Everest, 'Fueling the Iran–Iraq Slaughter', Z-Net, 5 September 2002. See also Bani-Sadr, 70.
10. Kenneth R Timmerman, *The Death Lobby: How the West Armed Iraq* (Houghton Mifflin, 1991), 76.
11. *Wall Street Journal*, 18 June 1991.
12. Gary Sick, *October Surprise* (Times Books, 1992), 106–107.
13. Hal Brands, 'Saddam Hussein, the United States, and the Invasion of Iran: Was There a Green Light?', *Cold War History*, Vol. 2, No. 2 (2012), 319–343.
14. See various discussions in Blight et al., *Becoming Enemies*.
15. Gasiorowski, 'US Intelligence Assistance to Iran, May–October 1979'.
16. See, for example, 'The Kurdish Problem in Perspective', CIA Report, 1 August 1979, NSADC: IR02818.

17. Ibid., 64. See also Menshari, 101.
18. Hiro, *The Longest War*, 27.
19. 'Iranian–Iraqi Tensions', Cable Tehran, 06292, Naas to State Department, 18 June 1979, NSADC: IR02687.
20. David A. Korn, 'The Last Years of Mustafa Barzani', *Middle East Quarterly*, Vol. 1, No. 2 (2004), 13–27.
21. 'Kurdish Views on Iraq and Iran', memorandum, Department of State, Office of the Executive Secretary, 9 May 1979, NSADC: IR02540.
22. 'The Kurdish Problem in Perspective'.
23. 'Conditions in Western Iran', Secret, Cable Tehran, 09447, 26 August 1979, NSADC: IR02929.
24. 'Iraqi Support for Iranian Kurds', Cable Beirut, 54572, CIA, 6 September 1979, NSADC: IR02997.
25. See 'Status of the Kurdish Movement in Iran', CIA Report, 17 October 1979, NSADC: IR03308.
26. 'Turkish Views on Kurdish Troubles in Iran', Cable Ankara, 06618, 10 September 1979, in Documents from the US Espionage Den, v. 31, 123–124.
27. 'Intelligence Information on Sadar Jaf', Cable CIA Station Bonn, 85112, 5 October 1979, US Espionage Den, v. 32, 46.
28. 'Information on Catomic/19 Meeting with Sadar Jaf', Cable CIA Station Bonn, 85221, 10 October 1979, Espionage Den, vol. 32, 47–49.
29. Henze to Brzezinski, 'Kurds, Iran, etc.', NSC, memo, 4 September 1979, DDRS: CK3100528462.
30. 'Iraqi–Iranian and Kuwaiti–Iranian Relations', Cable Kuwait, 02807, 11 June 1979, NSADC: IR02668.
31. F. Gregory Gause III, 'Iraq's Decisions to Go to War, 1980 and 1990', *Middle East Journal*, Vol. 56, No. 1 (2002), 65.
32. 'Abbas Amir-Entezam Concern about Iranian Relations with Iraq', Cable CIA, 543216, 31 October 1979, IR03446.
33. 'Policy Initiatives – Talks with [Permanent Representatives]', Memorandum State, 31 October 1979, NSADC: IR03276.
34. Memorandum, Zbigniew Brzezinski to the President, 'NSC Weekly Report #122', Top Secret, 21 December 1979.
35. Thornton, 518.
36. Ibid., 519.
37. David Newsom, 'US–Persian Gulf Relationship', Department of State Bulletin, August 1980, 62. See also Thornton, 521.
38. The transcript, which was released by Iraq, was published in the *New York Times*, 23 September 1990, 19. See also Sick, *October Surprise*, 106–107.
39. As published in: Daily Report, South Asia, FBIS-SAS-80-172, 3 September 1980.
40. Carter, 506.
41. 'Iraq Goads Iran', Defense Intelligence Agency cable, Intelligence Information Report, 01113, 9 April 1980, NSADC: G00021.
42. 'Possible Iranian–Iraqi Conflict', CIA memorandum, 11 April 1980, NSADC: HN01992.
43. Email from Wayne White, 4 April 2011. Gary Sick, Charlie Naas, and Henry Precht repeated White's sentiment in correspondence with this author.
44. Iran–Iraq Conflict [Attached to Forwarding Memorandum], CIA Alert Memorandum, 17 September 1980, NSADC: HN01999.
45. Email from Wayne White, 3 March 2012.

46. Email from Wayne White, 20 January 2012.
47. Email from Nat Howell, 5 May 2010.
48. Ganji, 207.
49. Gasiorowski, 'The Nuzhih Plot and Iranian Politics', 649.
50. 'Run-down on SDRap/SD Pepper Operations', Cable CIA, 19 October 1979, NSADC: IR03326.
51. 'SD Pepper/1 Reports that Shahpour Bakhtiar Wants American Aid for His Movement', Secret, Cable CIA, 534442, 18 October 1979, NSADC: IR03309.
52. Sick, *October Surprise*, 107.
53. For this claim, see Sasan Fayazmanesh, *The United States and Iran: Sanctions, Wars and the Policy of Dual Containment* (Routledge, 2008), 21.
54. Gasiorowski, 'The Nuzhih Plot and Iranian Politics', 645–666.
55. Ibid., 652.
56. Email from Nat Howell to author, 5 May 2010.
57. Ganji, 209; Thornton, 523.
58. See Zbigniew Brzezinski to the President, 'NSC Weekly Report #156', Secret, 3 October 1980.
59. This account was provided by a former senior official closely involved in US energy strategy at the time. They wish to remain anonymous.
60. Thornton, 522.
61. United States Embassy in Israel Cable from Samuel W. Lewis to the Department of State, 'Conversation with [Excised]', 12 December 1980.
62. Brzezinski, 279. See also Thornton, 524.
63. Oman's sympathy towards Iraq was well known, but Qaboos' motivation is still unclear. What is clear is that he had been a close friend of the Shah and was probably convinced by Saddam that one decisive attack could bring the Revolution down. In Ras al-Khaimah, Emir Sheik Sakr had apparently taken the decision without notifying the federal government, much to the alarm of other UAE leaders, but probably saw an opportunity to fulfil Ras al-Khaimah's specific claim on one of the disputed islands.
64. Sick, 106.
65. Email from Sick, 31 January 2012.
66. Ganji, 210.
67. Email from Veliotes, 19 January 2012.
68. Ganji, 212.
69. Brzezinski, 504.
70. Jordan was increasingly making hugely lucrative financial gains from the diversion of trade to the Jordanian port of Aqaba.
71. Haughton, 141.
72. Moses, 255.
73. Ibid., 269; Saunders, 290–291.
74. Ibid., 281.
75. Zbigniew Brzezinski to the President; Conference Reader, 64.
76. Ganji, 209.
77. See Zbigniew Brzezinski to the President; also email from Nat Howell, 5 May 2010.
78. Sick, 313–314; Dumbrell, 171.
79. Sick, 313.
80. Quoted in Thornton, 524.
81. Ganji, 213–214.
82. CWIHP Conference Timeline, 3.

83. Howell's email to author, 5 May 2010.
84. 'Possible Iranian–Iraqi Conflict'.
85. Ganji, 212; Thornton, 523.
86. Howell's email to author, 5 May 2010.
87. Iran–Iraq Conflict [Attached to Forwarding Memorandum], NSADC: HN01999.
88. Ganji, 212.
89. 'Telegram to Ambassador Lang', 3 February 1980, Jimmy Carter Library, Hamilton Jordan Confidential File, Box 34B, 1977–80, Iran: 11/79-03/80.
90. Moses, 281–282.
91. Sick, 106–107.

Conclusion

1. 'Brzezinski daily report to Carter', 5 March 1979, JCL-1-9-8-21-0.
2. Njølstad, 47–48.
3. 'Stenographic Minutes of Meeting in Berlin', Brezhnev to Honecker, 4 October 1979, Documents prepared for Carter–Brezhnev Project conference 'The Intervention in Afghanistan and the Fall of Détente', Lysebu, Norway, 17–20 September 1995.
4. 'Policy towards Iran', briefing memorandum, State Department, Saunders to Vance, 5 September 1979, NSA: IR02996.
5. 'Update on Iran', Cable Brussels, Giltman to US Embassy London, Mission to NATO, 07205, 19 October 1979, NSA: IR03327.
6. Brzezinski, 484–485.
7. 'Afghanistan: Soviet Invasion and U.S. Responses', 10 January 1980, Congressional Research Service, Afghan Group, Foreign Affairs and National Defense Division, NSA: AF00789.
8. PD-62, 'Modifications in U.S. National Strategy', 15 January 1981, JCL, Presidential Directives collection.
9. Njølstad,43–48.
10. 'Forecast: Cloudy for Iran', State Department memo, Airgram, A-1, McGaffey to US State Department, 6 January 1979, NSADC: IR02016.
11. 'Political Scenario for Iran over the Next 3–5 Years', Iran Transition Paper No. 1, State Department, 4 December 1980, Carter–Reagan Transition Papers, NSA.
12. Ibid.
13. 'Political Scenario for Iran over the Next 3–5 Years'.
14. Iran Transition Paper No. 2, November 1980 (exact date unknown), Carter–Reagan Transition Papers, Unpublished, Box 1, 1980–1981, NSA.
15. Odom, 'The Cold War Origins of the US Central Command', 52–53, 56–57; Njølstad, 'Shifting Priorities', 21–55.
16. Quoted in Maaike Warnaar, 'Competing Discourses of Legitimacy among the Iranian Political Elite', working paper presented at British Society for Middle Eastern Studies Conference, LSE, November 2012.
17. Ibid.
18. See Blight et al., *Becoming Enemies*, 128. For recent criticism of this trait, particularly during America's nation-building project in post-Saddam Iraq, see Christian Caryl, 'The U.S. Spent Billions Promoting Democracy in Iraq. Now the Official Verdict Is In: It Was All for Nothing', *Foreign Policy*, 5 March 2013.
19. 'Covert Action Finding Regarding Iran', John M. Poindexter to President Ronald Reagan (prepared by Oliver North), 17 January 1986, NSADC: IC02181.

20. Harold Saunders, 54.
21. Henry Precht, 'Ayatollah Realpolitik', *Foreign Policy*, No. 70 (Spring 1988), 117.
22. 'Khomeyni Meets Soviet Envoy', Tehran Domestic Service, 24 March 1979, FBIS-MEA-79-060.
23. Tehran, *AYANDEGAN*, 3 July 1979, FBIS-MEA-79-132.
24. Arshin Adib-Moghaddam, 'Manufacturing War: Iran in the Neoconservative Imagination', *Third World Quarterly*, Vol. 28, No. 3 (2007), 635–653.
25. See, for example, the CIA's profile of Bani-Sadr, 'Iran: Bani-Sadr's Foreign Policy Views', Intelligence Memorandum, CIA, 5 February 1980, DDRS: CK3100160311.
26. 'Visit', Cable Tehran, Laingen to US State Department, 11523, 2 November 1979, NSADC: IR03456.
27. In contrast, President G. W. Bush has addressed only the Iranian people in his Nowruz message and identified the government within an 'axis of evil'.
28. Trita Parsi, *A Single Role of the Dice: Obama's Diplomacy with Iran* (Yale University Press, 2012), 227.
29. 'Manufacturing War: Iran in the Neoconservative Imagination', 636.
30. Quoted in Blight et al., *Becoming Enemies*, 72.
31. 'Afghanistan: Soviet Invasion and US Responses', RECNO: 81, Department of State Briefing Paper, Carter–Reagan Transitions Papers Collection, unpublished, Box 1, 1980–1981, NSA.
32. 'Iran: Situation Report', Intelligence Memorandum, CIA, 20 May 1980, http://www.foia.cia.gov.
33. Ian Murray, 'Former Prime Minister of Iran Waits Expectantly in Paris for Fall of the Khomeini Regime', *Times*, 14 November 1979.
34. Murray, 26; see also Beeman, 49.
35. 'Political Scenario for Iran over the Next 3–5 Years'.
36. Iran Transition Paper No. 2, November 1980.
37. The same can more or less be said of Obama's response to the Egyptian Revolution.

Appendix

1. Many of which are simply notices of pending FOIA requests yet to be processed by the DoD.
2. Erich Von Marbod, Deputy Director, Defense Security Assistance Agency, negotiated the Memorandum of Understanding of 3 February 1979, which restructured the US foreign military sales programme with Iran and reduced Iran's military purchases by $6 billion.
3. See, for example, 'Sitrep for Period 17–18 March 1978', Cable Tehran, US Embassy Iran, Office of the Defense Attaché, 18 March 1979, NSADC: IR02383.
4. 'Iran: Chaos and Little Central Authority', Defense Intelligence Commentary, 2 March 1979, NSADC: IR03590.

Interviews

- Henry Precht, Washington, 21 May 2008, 25 May 2012 (plus follow-up emails)
- Harold Saunders, Washington, 20 May 2008
- Gary Sick, Columbia, NYC, 24 April 2007, 25 May 2012 (plus follow-up emails)
- William B. Quandt, Charlottesville, VA, 6 May 2008
- Nathaniel Howell, Charlottesville, VA (multiple interviews between 18 April and 10 May 2008, plus follow-up emails)
- Charlie Naas, 11 May 2010 (multiple emails since April 2010)
- Bruce Laingen, 23 April 2010 (telephone interview)
- Wayne White (multiple emails over January–March 2012)
- Nick Veliotes (email 19 January 2012)
- John Limbert, Arlington, VA, 18 May 2012
- George Cave, 27 September 2012 (email)

My thanks also to Dr Malcolm Byrne, Professor Ruhi Ramazani, Professor Melvyn Leffler, Professor Richard Bulliet, Professor Ali Ansari, Dr Toby Dodge, Dr Siavush Randjbar-Daemi, and Professor Lawrence Potter for offering their time and insights.

List of Documents

Pre-1976

1. 'The Tudeh Party: A Vehicle of Communism in Iran', Report, Central Intelligence Agency, 18 July 1949. http://www.foia.cia.gov.
2. 'Measures to Organize a Separatist Movement in Southern Azerbaijan and Other Provinces of Northern Iran', Decree of the CC CPSU Politburo to Mir Bagirov CC Secretary of the Communist Party of Azerbaijan, Cold War International History Project. Source: GAPPOD AzR, f. 1, op. 89, d. 90, ll. 4–5. Obtained by Jamil Hasanli. Translated for CWIHP by Gary Goldberg.

1976

3. 'Annual Policy Assessment', Cable, US Embassy Kabul to US Department of State, 01765, 9 March 1976, NSA Digital Collection: AF00210.

1977

4. 'General Brown's Trip to Tehran', National Security Council memorandum, Bill Quandt to Gary Sick, 22 March 1977, DDRS, Document Number: CK3100129078.
5. 'Annual Policy and Resource Assessment for Iran – Part One', Cable Tehran, 02930, 5 April 1977, NSA Digital Collection: IR01159.
6. 'Iran in the 1980s', Report, Central Intelligence Agency, 1 August 1977. DDRS, Document Number: CK3100225219.
7. Report for the Secretary of Defense on the Implementation of the United States Foreign Military Sales Program in Iran, 19 September 1977, NSA Digital Collection: IR01227.
8. 'Recent Events in Iran', State Department Memorandum, Patricia Derian to Roy Atherton, 5 December 1977, DDRS, Document Number: CK3100009091.

1978

9. 'Afghanistan in 1977: An External Assessment', Cable, Theodore Elliot (US Embassy Kabul) to US State Department and multiple US embassies, 00820, 30 January 1978, NSA Digital Collection: AF00259.
10. 'Iran: Understanding the Shi'ite Islamic Movement', Cable Tehran, Sullivan to Vance, 01691, 3 February 1978, Documents from the US Espionage Den, v. 12-A:39-46, NSA Digital Collection: IR01298.
11. 'Liberation Movement of Iran (LMI) – Views on Politics in Iran', Memorandum of Conversation Tehran, 25 May 1978, Documents from the US Espionage Den, v. 24:6-9, NSA Digital Collection: IR01399.
12. 'Assessment of the Internal Politics Scene in Iran', Memorandum, Saunders to Vance, 17 August 1978, NSA Digital Collection: IR01476.

13. 'The Opposition to the Shah', Memorandum, Brzezinski to Carter, White House, 3 November 1978, Brzezinski donated material, Country File, NLC-6-29-2-5-7, Jimmy Carter Library.
14. 'Brezhnev Letter to Carter Regarding the Situation in Iran', Letter, 17 November 1978, DDRS, Document Number: CK3100073474.
15. 'Assessment of Soviet Posture and Intentions Regarding Situation in Iran', Cable State, Vance to all Near Eastern and Asian embassies, 296841, 23 November 1978, Documents from the US Espionage Den, v. 48:89-93, NSA Digital Collection: IR01798.
16. 'The Gulf Arabs and Iran', CIA Report, 8 December 1978, 'Iran: 12/78-1/79', Brzezinski donated, Country File, Box 29, NLC-6-29-3-10-0, Jimmy Carter Library.
17. 'Conversation with Ibrahim Yazdi, Advisor to Khomeini', 12 December 1978, at Dominique's Restaurant [Memorandum for the Files], Secret, Memorandum, Henry Precht, 13 December 1978, Department of State, Documents from the US Espionage Den, v. 18:115-119, NSA Digital Collection: IR01919.
18. 'Is Turkey Susceptible to the Iranian Sickness?', Memorandum to Zbigniew Brzezinski from Paul B. Henze, National Security Council, 15 December 1978, DDRS, Document Number: CK3100151950.
19. 'Opposition Demonstrations in Iran: Leadership, Organization, and Tactics', Intelligence Memorandum, Central Intelligence Agency, 21 December 1978, NSA Digital Collection: IR01952.

1979

20. 'Khomeini's Lieutenants in Iran', Intelligence Memorandum, Central Intelligence Agency, National Foreign Assessment Center, January 1979, 'Iran: 12/78-1/79', Box 29, NLC-6-29-3-21-8.
21. 'Cottam on Khomeini, Liberation Movement (LMI) and National Front (INF)', Cable Tehran, Sullivan to Vance, 00066, 2 January 1979, Documents from the US Espionage Den, v. 24:44-46, NSA Digital Collection: IR02002.
22. 'Forecast: Cloudy for Iran', State Department memo, Airgram, A-1, McGaffey to US State Department, 6 January 1979, Documents from the US Espionage Den, v. 63:32-36, NSA Digital Collection: IR02016.
23. 'Further Report of Richard Cottam', Cable State, Vance to Embassy Tehran, 004510, 7 January 1979, Documents from the US Espionage Den, v. 10:126-127, NSA Digital Collection: IR02021.
24. 'USG Policy Guidance', Cable State, Sullivan to Vance, 10 January 1979, DDRS, Document Number: CK3100503552.
25. National Security Council (NSC) Weekly Report No. 84, Memo, Brzezinski to Carter, White House, 12 January 1979, DDRS, Document Number: CK3100543545.
26. 'Soviet Academic Discusses Iran', Cable Moscow, 01045, Toon to US State Department, 12 January 1979, Documents from the US Espionage Den, v. 48:117-118, NSA Digital Collection: IR02073.
27. 'Soviet MFA Iranian Desk Officer Discusses Iran', Cable Moscow, 01105, Toon to US State Department, 13 January 1979, Documents from the US Espionage Den, v. 48:119-125, NSA Digital Collection: IR02076.
28. 'US Policy toward Iran', Statement by Assistant Secretary Saunders before the Subcommittee on Europe and the Middle East of the Committee on Foreign

Affairs, House of Representatives, 96th Cong., 1st session, 17 January 1979, NSA Digital Collection: IR02110.

29. 'Contact with Sadegh Ghotbzadeh in November 1977', Memorandum State, Henry Precht to Robert B. Mantel, 17 January 1979, Documents from the US Espionage Den, v. 18:98-99, NSA Digital Collection: IR02120.

30. 'Iran: Khomeini's Prospects and Views', Intelligence Memorandum, Central Intelligence Agency, National Foreign Assessment Center, 19 January 1979, NSA Digital Collection: IR02131.

31. 'LMI Wants US to Push; Conflict with Moderates Shaping Up', Memo, US Embassy Tehran to Secretary of State, Washington, 22 January 1979, Documents from the US Espionage Den, v. 10:109-111, NSA Digital Collection: IR02148.

32. Zbigniew Brzezinski's memo to President Carter (NSC Weekly Report No. 87), 2 February 1979, 'Arc of Crisis', National Security Archive.

33. 'The President's Comments on Persian-language Broadcasting and Related Issues', Memorandum, National Security Council, Henze to Brzezinski, 6 February 1979, DDRS, Document Number: CK3100143708.

34. 'VOA Broadcasting', Memorandum, Reinhardt to Brzezinski, 9 February 1979, DDRS, Document Number: CK3100144133.

35. 'Iran – The Psychological Problem and Some Solutions', Memorandum, International Communications Agency, Office of Near Eastern and South Asian Affairs, Curran to Office of the Director, 9 February 1979, Documents from the US Espionage Den, v. 1-6:558-559, NSA Digital Collection: IR02268.

36. 'Iran: Communist Activities (an Intelligence Estimate)', Central Intelligence Agency, National Foreign Assessment Center, February 1979, NLC-6-29-4-1-9, Jimmy Carter Library.

37. 'Message for Ambassador Sullivan', Cable State, Vance to United Kingdom Embassy, 042077, 18 February 1979, NSA Digital Collection: IR02315.

38. 'Iran: Arafat's Visit Intended to Garner Support for PLO', Defense Intelligence Commentary, *c.* 23 February 1979, NSA Digital Collection: IR03590.

39. 'Memo on Consultative Security Framework for the Middle East', State Department Memorandum, 28 February 1979, DDRS, Document Number: CK3100105244.

40. 'Evening Report – 28 February 1979', Memorandum to Zbigniew Brzezinski from Paul B. Henze, National Security Council, 28 February 1979, DDRS, Document Number: CK3100496495.

41. 'Soviet Involvement in the Iranian Crisis', Intelligence Report, Central Intelligence Agency, National Foreign Assessment Center, 1 March 1979, NSA Digital Collection: IR02357.

42. 'Iran – Prospects for Bazargan Government', Alert Memorandum, Central Intelligence Agency, Turner to NSC, 1 March 1979, NSA Digital Collection: IR02356.

43. 'Iran: The Leftist Challenge to the Bazargan Government', Intelligence Report, 5 March 1979, NSA Digital Collection: IR02366.

44. 'Brzezinski Daily Report to Carter', 5 March 1979, NLC-1-9-8-21-0.

45. 'Departing Impressions of Iran', Cable Tehran, 02615, 5 March 1979, NSA Digital Collection: IR02363.

46. 'The Barzagan Government One Month Later and Prospects for the Future', Cable State, Sullivan to Department of State, 003016, 17 March 1979, Documents from the US Espionage Den, v. 14:30-36, NSA Digital Collection: IR02382.

104. 'The Shah in the US', Cable Tehran, 31 October 1979, NSA Digital Collection: IR03441.
105. 'Ayatollah Khomeini Calls for Clergy and Students to Confront the U.S. [Until It Releases the Shah]', CIA Intelligence Report, 2 November 1979, NSA Digital Collection: IR03465.
106. 'Visit' (Charg Laingen Proposes That Under Secretary Cooper Make a Short Official Visit to Iran), Cable Tehran, Laingen to US State Department, 11523, 2 November 1979, Documents from the US Espionage Den, v. 16:165, NSA Digital Collection: IR0346.
107. 'Thoughts on Iran', Memorandum, Henze to Brzezinski, National Security Council, 9 November 1979, DDRS, Document Number: CK3100504698.
108. 'Soviet Clandestine Broadcasting in Iran', Memorandum, Henze to Brzezinski, National Security Council, 15 November 1979, NLC-6-29-7-1-6, Jimmy Carter Library.
109. 'The US and the Islamic World', Memorandum, Henze to Brzezinski, National Security Council, 27 November 1979, DDRS, Document Number: CK3100155679.
110. 'US Stake in Iran', National Intelligence Council, Richard Lehman, 27 November 1979, Jimmy Carter Library, Brzezinski Country File, 1977–81, Iran: 11/21-27/79, Box 30.
111. 'Soviet Efforts to Benefit from the US–Iran Crisis', Intelligence Estimate, National Foreign Assessment Center, Central Intelligence Agency, 1 December 1979, DDRS, Document Number: CK3100219671.
112. 'Moslem Emotions and Anti-American Sentiments. Back to Basics', Memorandum, National Security Council, Rentschler to Brzezinski, 3 December 1979, DDRS, Document Number: CK3100143598.
113. Letter from Ambassador Dobrynin to President Carter, 4 December 1979, DDRS, Document Number: CK3100497366.
114. 'Minutes of Special Coordination Meeting', Stansfield Turner, 17 December 1979, Carter–Brezhnev Project, Box 5, National Security Archive unpublished material.
115. 'Reflections on Soviet Intervention in Afghanistan', Memorandum, Brzezinski to Carter, White House, 26 December 1979, DDRS, Document Number: CK3100098563.
116. 'Afghanistan', Memorandum, National Security Council, Oksenberg to Brzezinski, 29 December 1979, Brzezinski donated collection, Country File, Box 1, 'Afghanistan: 4–12, 79', Jimmy Carter Library.
117. 'Carter Interview with Frank Reynolds', White House Internal Transcript, 31 December 1979, Box 17, Jimmy Carter Library.

1980

118. 'Memorandum of Conversation between Richard Cottam and Sadeg Ghotbzadeh', Iran: Update, January 1980, Brzezinski Country File, NLC-6-32-6-8-6.
119. 'Israel Is Extremely Gloomy about Afghanistan', Defense Intelligence Summary, January 1980, NSA Digital Collection: AF00744.
120. 'NSC on Afghanistan', National Security Council memorandum, NSC026, 2 January 1980, The Carter Administration and the 'Arc of Crisis' 1977–1981, Declassified Documents prepared for 'A Critical Oral History Conference', Woodrow Wilson Center, 25–26 July 2005.

141. 'National Intelligence Daily', Central Intelligence Agency, 30 April 1980, http://www.foia.cia.gov.
142. 'Iran: Situation Report', Intelligence Memorandum, Central Intelligence Agency, 20 May 1980, http://www.foia.cia.gov.
143. 'Noon Notes', National Security Council memo, Situation Room to Brzezinski, 18 June 1980, NLC-1-15-7-24-1.
144. Brzezinski Daily Report for Carter, 17 June 1980, NLC- 1-15-7-18-8.
145. 'Afghanistan: Iran's Role in the Crisis', Intelligence Memorandum, Central Intelligence Agency, 27 June 1980, The Carter Administration and the 'Arc of Crisis' 1977–1981, Declassified Documents prepared for 'A Critical Oral History Conference', Woodrow Wilson Center, 25–26 July 2005.
146. 'Soviet Military Options in Iran', Special National Intelligence Estimate, Central Intelligence Agency, 21 August 1980, http://www.foia.cia.gov.
147. 'Moscow's Afghan Strategy', Cable, Griffen (US Embassy Kabul) to US State Department, 02445, 28 August 1980, NSA Digital Collection: AF01036.
148. 'Iran–Iraq Conflict', CIA Alert Memorandum, 17 September 1980, NSA Digital Collection: N01999.
149. Iran Transition Paper No. 2, November 1980 (exact date unknown), Carter–Reagan Transition Papers, Unpublished, Box 1, 1980–81, National Security Archives.
150. State Department: Iran Transitional Paper: #1, 4 December 1980, Carter–Brezhnev Project, Box 5, National Security Archive unpublished material.
151. 'Political Scenario for Iran over the Next 3–5 Years', Iran Transition Paper No. 1, State Department, 4 December 1980, Carter–Reagan Transition Papers, unpublished, Box 1, 1980–81, National Security Archive.
152. United States Embassy in Israel Cable from Samuel W. Lewis to the Department of State, 'Conversation with [Excised]', 12 December 1980.

1981

153. 'The Hostage Crisis in Iran 1979–81', State Department draft report on the 1979–1981 hostage crisis in Iran, 8 January 1981, DDRS, Document Number: CK3100135327.
154. 'Afghanistan: Soviet Invasion and US Responses', RECNO: 81, Department of State Briefing Paper, Carter–Reagan Transition Papers, unpublished, Box 1, 1980–81, National Security Archive.
155. PD-62, 'Modifications in U.S. National Strategy', 15 January 1981, Presidential Directives collection, Jimmy Carter Library.

Bibliography

Books

Abrahamian, Ervand. *Iran between Two Revolutions*, Princeton University Press, 1982.
Abrahamian, Ervand. *Radical Islam: The Iranian Mojahedin*, IB Tauris, 1989.
Abrahamian, Ervand. *Tortured Confessions*, University of California Press, 1999.
Afary, Janet & Anderson, Kevin B. *Foucault and the Iranian Revolution: Gender and the Seductions of Islamism*, University of Chicago Press, 2005.
Alerassool, Mahvash. *Freezing Assets: The USA and the Most Effective Economic Sanction*, Macmillan with St Martin's Press, 1993.
Alexander, Yonah & Nanes, Allan (eds). *The United States and Iran: A Documentary History*, University Publications of America, 1980.
Alikhani, Hossein. *Sanctioning Iran: Anatomy of a Failed Policy*, New York: IB Tauris, 2001.
Allison, Graham. *Essence of Decision: Explaining the Cuban Missile Crisis*, Little Brown, 1971.
Andrew, Christopher & Gordievsky, Oleg. *KGB: Inside Story of Its Foreign Operations from Lenin to Gorbachev*, Hodder & Stoughton, 1990.
Andrew, Christopher & Mitrokhin, Vasili. *The Mitrokhin Archive II*, Allen Lane, 2005.
Ansari Ali, *Confronting Iran: The Failure of American Foreign Policy and the Next Great Crisis in the Middle East*, Hurst, 2006.
Arjomand, Said Amir. *The Turban for the Crown: Islamic Revolution in Iran*, Oxford University Press, 1988.
Aron, Raymond. *Peace and War: A Theory of International Relations*, Weidenfeld and Nicolson, 1966.
Atkin, Muriel. 'Myths of Soviet–Iranian Relations', in Nikki R. Keddie & Mark J. Gasiorowski, eds, *Neither East nor West: Iran, the Soviet Union, and the United States*, Yale University Press, 1990, pp. 100–111.
Auten, Brian J. *Carter's Conversion: The Hardening of American Defense Policy*, University of Missouri Press, 2008.
Bakhash, Shaul. *The Reign of the Ayatollahs*, Basic Books, 1984.
Baldwin, James. *Economic Statecraft*, Princeton University Press, 1985.
Beeman, William O. *The Great Satan vs the Mad Mullahs: How the United States and Iran Demonize Each Other*, University of Chicago Press, 2005.
Behrooz, Maziar. 'Trends in the Foreign Policy of the Islamic Republic of Iran, 1979–1988', in Nikki R. Keddie & Mark J. Gasiorowski, eds, *Neither East nor West: Iran, the Soviet Union, and the United States*, Yale University Press, 1990, pp. 19–35.
Behrooz, Maziar. *Rebels with a Cause: The Failure of the Left in Iran*, IB Tauris, 1999.
Behrooz, Maziar. 'Iranian Revolution and the Legacy of the Guerrilla Movement', in Stephanie Cronin, ed, *Reformers and Revolutionaries in Modern Iran: New Perspectives on the Iranian Left*, RoutledgeCurzon, 2004.
Bennigsen, A. *Muslim National Communism in the Soviet Union: A Revolutionary Strategy for the Colonial World*, Chicago University Press, 1980.
Bennigsen, A. *Mystics and Commissars, Muslims of the Soviet Empire: A Guide*, Hurst, 1985.

Bennigsen, A. & Broxup, M. *Islamic Threat to the Soviet State*, Palgrave Macmillan, 1982.

Betts, Richard K. *Nuclear Blackmail and Nuclear Balance*, Brookings Institution Press, 1987.

Bill, James A. *The Eagle and the Lion: The Tragedy of American–Iranian Relations*, Yale University Press, 1988.

Blight, James, Lang, Janet M., Banai, Hussein, Byrne, Malcolm, Tirman, John & Riedel, Bruce. *Becoming Enemies: U.S.–Iran Relations and the Iran–Iraq War, 1979–88*, Rowman & Littlefield, 2012.

Bodanski, Yossef. *Bin Laden: The Man Who Declared War on America*, Prima Lifestyles, 2001.

Boroujerdi, Mehrzad. *Iranian Intellectuals and the West: The Tormented Triumph of Nativism*, Syracuse University Press, 1996.

Bowden, Mark. *Guests of the Ayatollah: The First Battle in America's War with Militant Islam*, Atlantic Monthly Press, 2006.

Bradsher, Henry S. *Afghanistan and the Soviet Union*, Duke University Press, 1983.

Brighi, Elisabetta & Hill, Christopher. 'Implementation and Behaviour', in Steve Smith, Amelia Hadfield & Tim Dunne, eds, *Foreign Policy: Theories, Actors, Cases*, Oxford University Press, 2008.

Brumberg, Daniel. *Reinventing Khomeini: The Struggle for Reform in Iran*, University of Chicago Press, 2001.

Brzezinski, Zbigniew. *Power and Principle: Memoirs of the National Security Adviser, 1977–1981*, Farrar, Straus & Giroux, 1983.

Burhaneddin, Yassin. *Vision or Reality: The Kurds in the Policy of the Great Powers, 1941–1947*, Lund University Press, 1995.

Carswell, Robert & Davies, Richard J. 'The Economic and Financial Pressures', in Warren Christopher, ed, *American Hostages in Iran: Conduct of a Crisis*, Yale University Press, 1985a, pp. 172–200.

Carswell, Robert & Davies, Richard J. 'Freeze and Sanctions' and 'Crafting the Financial Settlement', in Warren Christopher, ed, *American Hostages in Iran: Conduct of a Crisis*, Yale University Press, 1985b, pp. 173–200.

Carter, Jimmy. *Keeping Faith: Memoirs of a President*, William Collins and Sons, 1982.

Christopher, Warren, Saunders, Harold H. & Sick, Gary. *American Hostages in Iran: Conduct of a Crisis* (A Council on Foreign Relations book), Edited by Warren Christopher, Yale University Press, 1985.

Chubin, Sharam, 'The Soviets and the Gulf: Changing Priorities in the 1980s', in Rosemary Hollis, ed, *The Soviets, Their Successors and the Middle East: Turning Point*, St Martin's Press, 1993.

Cohen, Benjamin. *In Whose Interest? International Banking and American Foreign Policy*, Yale University Press, 1986.

Cooper, Andrew Scott. *The Oil Kings: How the US, Iran and Saudi Arabia Changed the Balance of Power in the Region*, One World, 2011.

Copeland, Miles. *The Game Player*, Aurum Press, 1989.

Cottam, Richard. *Foreign Policy Motivation: A General Theory and a Case Study*, University of Pittsburgh Press, 1977.

Cottam, Richard. *Iran and the United States: A Cold War Case Study*, University of Pittsburgh Press, 1988.

Cottam, Richard. 'US and Soviet Responses to Islamic Political Militancy', in Nikki R. Keddie & Mark J. Gasiorowski, eds, *Neither East nor West: Iran, the Soviet Union, and the United States*, Yale University Press, 1990.

Crenshaw, Martha. *Terrorism in Context*, Penn State Press, 1995.

Dallek, Robert. *Nixon and Kissinger: Partners in Power*, HarperCollins, 2007.

Daneshvar, Parviz. *Revolution in Iran*, Macmillan, 1996.

Davari, Mahmood T. *The Political Thought of Ayatullah Murtaza Mutahhari: An Iranian Theoretician of the Islamic State*, Routledge, 2005.

Dorraj, Manochehr, 'Populism and Corporatism in Post-Revolutionary Iranian Political Culture', in Samih K. Farsouh & Mehrdad Mashayekhi, eds, *Political Culture of the Islamic Republic*, Routledge, 1992.

Dorronsoro, Gilles. *Revolution Unending: Afghanistan, 1979 to the Present* (CERI Series in Comparative Politics and International Studies), Hurst, 2005.

Doxey, Margaret. *Economic Sanctions and International Enforcement*, Oxford University Press, 1971.

Dreyfus, Robert. *Devil's Game: How the United States Helped Unleash Fundamentalist Islam*, Henry Holt, 2006.

Dumbrell, John. *The Carter Presidency: A Re-evaluation*, Manchester University Press, 2005.

Eagleton, Jr, William. *The Kurdish Republic of 1946*, Oxford University Press, 1963.

Ehteshami, Anoushiravan & Zweiri, Mahjoob. *Iran's Foreign Policy: From Khatemi to Ahmadinejad*, Garnet Publishing, 2008.

Emery, Christian, 'Reappraising the Carter administration's response to the Iran-Iraq War', in Nigel Ashton and Bryan Gibson (eds.) *The Iran-Iraq War: New International Perspectives*. Routledge, 2012.

Engdahl, William. *A Century of War: Anglo-American Oil Politics and the New World Order*, Pluto Press, 1992.

Farber, David. *Taken Hostage: The Iran Hostage Crisis and America's First Encounter with Radical Islam*, Princeton University Press, 2005.

Fischer, Michael. *Iran: From Religious Dispute to Revolution*, University of Wisconsin Press, 2003.

Ganji, Babak. *Politics of Confrontation: The Foreign Policy of the USA and Revolutionary Iran*, IB Tauris, 2006.

Garthoff, Raymond. *Detente and Confrontation: American–Soviet Relations from Nixon to Reagan* (Revised edition), Brookings Institution Press, 1994.

Gasiorowski, Mark. 'Security Relations between the United States and Iran', in Nikki R. Keddie & Mark J. Gasiorowski, eds, *Neither East nor West: Iran, the Soviet Union, and the United States*, Yale University Press, 1990, pp. 145–165.

Gheissari, Ali. *Iranian Intellectuals in the 20th Century*, University of Texas Press, 1997.

Girardet, Edward. *Afghanistan: The Soviet War*, Palgrave Macmillan, 1986.

Goldman, Minton. 'President Carter, Western Europe, and Afghanistan in 1980' in Herbert D. Rosenbaum & Alexej Ugrinsky, eds, *Jimmy Carter: Foreign Policy and Post-Presidential Years (Contributions in Political Science)*, Greenwood Press, 1994, pp. 19–34.

Gonzales, Nathan. *Engaging Iran*, Praeger, 2007.

Gregory Gause, F. *The International Relations of the Persian Gulf*, Cambridge University Press, 2010.

Haig, Alexander. *Caveat: Realism, Reagan and Foreign Policy*, Macmillan, 1984.

Halliday, Fred. *Ideology in the Middle East and Pakistan*, Palgrave Macmillan, 1988.

Halliday, Fred. 'The Iranian Revolution and Great Power Politics', in Nikki R. Keddie & Mark J. Gasiorowski, eds, *Neither East nor West: Iran, the Soviet Union, and the United States*, Yale University Press, 1990, pp. 246–264.

Halliday, Fred. *Revolution and World Politics: The Rise and Fall of the Sixth Great Power*, Palgrave MacMillan, 1999.

Harris, David. *The Crisis: The President, the Prophet, and the Shah – 1979 and the Coming of Militant Islam*, Little, Brown, 2004.

Herrmann, Richard. 'The Role of Iran in Soviet Perceptions and Policy, 1946–1988', in Nikki R. Keddie & Mark J. Gasiorowski, eds, *Neither East nor West: Iran, the Soviet Union, and the United States*, Yale University Press, 1990, pp. 63–99.

Hillmann, Michael. *Iranian Culture: A Persianist View*, University Press of America, 1990.

Hiro, Dilip. *Iran under the Ayatollahs*, Routledge and Kegan Paul, 1985.

Hoffman, John E. 'The Bankers Channel', in Warren Christopher, ed, *American Hostages in Iran: Conduct of a Crisis* (A Council on Foreign Relations book), Yale University Press, 1985, pp. 235–280.

Hooglund, Eric. 'Iran and Central Asia', in Anoushiravan Ehteshami, ed, *From the Gulf to Central Asia: Players in the New Great Game*, University of Exeter Press, 1998, pp. 114–128.

Houghton, David Patrick. *US Foreign Policy and the Iran Hostage Crisis*, Cambridge University Press, 2001.

Howard, Roger. *Iran Oil: The New Middle East Challenge to America*, IB Tauris, 2007.

Hunt, Michael H. *Ideology and U.S. Foreign Policy*, Yale University Press, 1987.

Hunter, Shireen T. 'The Soviet Union and the Islamic Republic of Iran', in Hafeez Malik, ed, *Soviet–American Relations with Pakistan, Iran and Afghanistan*, St Martin's Press, 1987.

Huyser, Robert E. *Mission to Tehran*, Harper and Row, 1986.

Ioannudes, Christos. *America's Iran*, University Press of America, 1984.

Jervis, Robert. *Perception and Misperception in International Politics*, Princeton University Press, 1976.

Jordan, Hamilton. *Crisis: The Last Year of the Carter Presidency*, Putnam, 1982.

Kamrava, Mehran. *Revolution in Iran: The Roots of Turmoil*, Taylor & Francis, 1990.

Karpat, Kermal. *Political and Social Thought in the Contemporary Middle East*, Praeger, 1982.

Katouzian, Homa. *Musaddiq and the Struggle for Power*, I. B. Tauris, 1990.

Katouzian, Homa. *Sadeq Hedayat: The Life and Literature of an Iranian Writer*, Palgrave Macmillan, 1992.

Katouzian, Homa. 'Khalil Maleki: The Odd Intellectual Out', in Negin Nabavi, ed., *Intellectual Trends in Twentieth-Century Iran*, University Press of Florida, 2003, pp. 24–52.

Kaufman, Scott. *Plans Unravelled: The Foreign Policy of the Carter Administration*, Northern Illinois University Press, 2008.

Keddie, Nikki R. *Roots of Revolution: An Interpretive History of Modern Iran*, Yale University Press, 1981.

Keddie, Nikki, R. *Modern Iran: Roots and Results of Revolution*, Yale University Press, 2003.

Keddie, Nikki R. *Modern Iran: Roots and Results of Revolution* (updated edition), Yale University Press, 2006.

Kenndy-Pipe, Caroline. *The Origins of the Cold War*, Palgrave Macmillan, 2007.

Keppel, Gilles. *Roots of Radical Islam*, Saqi Books, 2005.

Khalizad, Zalmay & Benard, Cheryl. *The Government of God: Iran's Islamic Republic*, Columbia University Press, 1984.

King, P. H. *The United Nations and the Iran–Iraq War*, Ford Foundation, 1987.

Kinzer, Stephen. *All the Shah's Men: An American Coup and the Roots of Middle East Terror*, Wiley, 2003.

Kishawarz, *I Condemn*, Rawaq Publications, n.d.

Kurzman, Charles. *The Unthinkable Revolution in Iran*, Harvard University Press, 2004.

Kuzichkin, Vladimir. *Inside the KGB: My Life in Soviet Espionage*, trans. Thomas B Beattie, Pantheon Books, 1990.

Lamb, David. *The Africans*, Random House, 1982.

Latham, Michael. *Modernization as Ideology: American Social Science and 'Nation Building' in the Kennedy Era*, University of North Carolina Press, 2000.

Ledeen, Michael & Lewis, William. *Debacle: The American Failure in Iran*, Alfred A. Knopf, 1981.

Leffler, Melvyn. *Origins of the Cold War*, Routledge, 1994.

Leffler, Melvyn. *For the Soul of Mankind: The United States, the Soviet Union, and the Cold War*, Hill and Wang, 2007.

Limbert, John, *Negotiating with Iran: Wrestling the Ghosts of History*, United States Institute of Peace Press, 2009.

Litwak, Robert. *Détente and the Nixon Doctrine: American Foreign Policy and the Pursuit of Stability, 1969–1976*, Cambridge University Press, 1984.

Losman, Donald. *International Economic Sanctions: The Cases of Cuba, Israel and Rhodesia*, University of New Mexico Press, 1979.

Lundestad, Geir. *Empire by Integration: The United States and European Integration, 1945–1997*, Oxford University Press, 1998.

Lundestad, Geir. *The United States and Western Europe since 1945*, Oxford University Press, 2003.

Male, Beverley. *Revolutionary Afghanistan: A Re-appraisal*, Croom Helm, 1982.

McCain, Morrs. 'Thinking South: Soviet Strategic Interests in Iran, Afghanistan and Pakistan', in Hafeez Malik, ed., *Soviet–American Relations with Pakistan, Iran and Afghanistan*, St Martin's Press, 1987, pp. 39–53.

McGwire, Michael, *Military Objectives in Soviet Foreign Policy*, Brookings Institution Press, 1987.

Menashri, David. *Iran: A Decade of War and Revolution*, New York: Holmes and Meier, 1990.

Mirsepassi, Ali. 'The Tragedy of the Iranian Left', in Stephanie Cronin, ed., *Reformers and Revolutionaries in Modern Iran: New Perspectives on the Iranian Left*, RoutledgeCurzon, 2004, pp. 229–249.

Moens, Alexander. *Foreign Policy under Carter: Testing Multiple Advocacy Decision Making*, Westview Press, 1990.

Mohsen Milani, *The Making of Iran's Islamic Revolution: From Monarchy to Islamic Republic*, Westview Press, 1994.

Moin, Baqer. *Khomeini: Life of the Ayatollah*, IB Tauris, 1999.

Moses, Russell Leigh. *Freeing the Hostages: Re-examining US–Iranian Negotiations and Soviet Policy, 1979–81*, University of Pittsburgh Press, 1996.

Mottahedeh, Roy. *The Mantle of the Prophet: Religion and Politics in Iran*, Pantheon Books, 1985.

Muravchik, Joshua. *The Uncertain Crusade: Jimmy Carter and the Dilemmas of Human Rights Policy*, Hamilton Press, 1986.

Murray, Donnette. *US Foreign Policy and Iran: American–Iranian Relations since the Islamic Revolution*, Routledge, 2009.

Nahavandi, Houchang. *Iran, the Clash of Ambitions*, Aquilion, 2006.

Nasr, Vali. *The Shia Revival*, Norton, 2006.

Ninkovich, Frank. *The Wilsonian Century: U.S. Foreign Policy since 1900*, University of Chicago Press, 1999.

Parsi, Trita. *Treacherous Alliance: The Secret Dealings of Israel, Iran, and the United States*, Yale University Press, 2007.

Parsi, Trita. *A Single Role of the Dice: Obama's Diplomacy with Iran*, Yale University Press, 2012.

Parsons, Antony. *The Pride and the Fall: Iran, 1974–1979*, Jonathan Cape, 1984.

Pollack, Kenneth. *The Persian Puzzle: The Conflict between Iran and America*, Random House, 2004.

Rahnema, Ali. *An Islamic Utopian: A Political Biography of Ali Shari'ati*, IB Tauris, 2000.

Ramazani, R. K. *The United States and Iran: The Patterns of Influence*, Praeger, 1982.

Rodinson, Maxime. *Marxism and the Modern World*, Monthly Review Press, 1981.

Ro'I, Yaacov. *The USSR and the Muslim World: Issues in Domestic and Foreign Policy*, Unwin Hyman, 1984.

Ronzitti, Natalino. *Rescuing Nationals Abroad through Military Coercion and Intervention on Grounds of Humanity*, Martinus Nijhoff, 1985.

Rowe, David. *Manipulating the Market: Understanding Economic Sanctions, Institutional Change and Political Unity of White Rhodesia*, University of Michigan Press, 2001.

Rubin, Barry. *Paved with Good Intentions*, Penguin, 1981.

Rubinstein, Alvin Z. *Soviet Policy toward Turkey, Iran and Afghanistan*, Praeger, 1982.

Sachedina, Abulaziz. 'Ali Shariati: Ideologue of the Iranian Revolution', in John L. Esposito, ed., *Voices of Resurgent Islam*, Oxford University Press, 1983.

Sadjadpour, Karim. *Reading Khamenei: The World View of Iran's Most Powerful Leader*, Carnegie Endowment for International Peace, 2008.

Saghafi-Ameri, Nasser. 'Iranian Foreign Policy: Concurrence of Ideology and Pragmatism', Online article, The Middle East Institute, January 29, 2009. http://www.mei.edu/content/iranian-foreign-policy-concurrence-ideology-and-pragmatismSaivetz, Carol. 'Superpower Competition in the Middle East and the Collapse of Détente', in Odd Arne Westad, ed., *The Fall of Détente*, Scandinavian University Press, 1997, pp. 72–94.

Saunders, Harold. 'Diplomacy and Pressure', in Warren Christopher, ed., *American Hostages in Iran: The Conduct of a Crisis*, Yale University Press, 1985a, pp. 72–102.

Saunders, Harold. 'The Crisis Begins', in Warren Christopher ed., *American Hostages in Iran: Conduct of a Crisis*, Yale University Press, 1985b, pp. 35–71.

Seliktar, Ofira. *Failing the Crystal Ball Test*, Greenwood Publishing, 2000.

Semati, Mehdi. *Media, Culture and Society in Iran: Living with Globalization and the Islamic State*, Routledge, 2007.

Shaffer, Brenda (ed). *The Limits of Culture: Islam and Foreign Policy*, The MIT Press, 2006.

Sick, Gary. *All Fall Down: America's Fateful Encounter with Iran*, Random House, 1985a.

Sick, Gary. 'Military Options and Constraints', in Warren Christopher, ed., *American Hostages in Iran: Conduct of a Crisis*, Yale University Press, 1985b, pp. 144–172.

Sicker, Martin. *The Bear and the Lion*, New York: Praeger Publishing, 1984.

Sreberny-Mohammadi, Annabelle & Mohammadi, Ali. *Small Media, Big Revolution: Communication, Culture and the Iranian Revolution*, University of Minnesota Press, 1994.

Stempel, John D. *Inside the Iranian Revolution*, Indiana University Press, 1981.

Strong, Robert. *Working in the World: Jimmy Carter and the Making of American Foreign Policy*, Louisiana State University Press, 2000.

Sullivan, William. *Mission to Iran: The Last US Ambassador*, New York: Norton, 1981.

Takeyh, Ray. *Hidden Iran: Paradox and Power in the Islamic Republic*, Times Books/Henry Holt, 2006.

Talbott, Strobe. *Endgame: The Inside Story of SALT II*, HarperCollins, 1979.

Thornton, Richard C. *The Carter Years: Toward a New Global Order*, Paragon House, 1992.

Timmerman, Kenneth. 'Fanning the Flames: Guns, Greed, and Geopolitics in the Gulf War', *The Iran Brief*, 1986–1988, published in book form as *Ol ins Feuer*, Orell Füssli, 1988.

Vance, Cyrus. *Hard Choices: Critical Years in America's Foreign Policy*, Simon and Schuster, 1983.

Varasteh, Manshour. 'The Soviet Union and Iran, 1979–89' , in Anoushiravan Ehteshami & Manshour Varasteh, eds, *Iran and the International Community*, Routledge, 1991, pp. 46–59.

Walt, Steven. *Revolution and War*, Cornell University Press, 1996.

Westad, Odd Arne (ed.). 'The Road to Kabul', in *The Fall of Détente*, Scandinavian University Press, 1997, pp. 119–125.

Westad, Odd Arne. *The Global Cold War*, Cambridge University Press, 2005.

Yodfat, Aryeh Y. *The Soviet Union and Revolutionary Iran*, St Martin's Press, 1984.

Young, Crawford & Turner, Thomas. *The Rise and Decline of the Zairian State*, University of Wisconsin Press, 1985.

Zabih, Sepehr. *The Communist Movement in Iran*, University of California Press, 1966.

Zabih, Sepehr. *The Left in Contemporary Iran*, Hoover Press, 1986.

Zonis, Marvin. *Majestic Failure: The Fall of the Shah*, University of Chicago Press, 1991.

Zubok, Vladislav M. *A Failed Empire: The Soviet Union in the Cold War from Stalin to Gorbachev*, University of North Carolina Press, 2007.

Articles

Abadi, S. & Dehghani Firouz, J. 'Emancipating Foreign Policy: Critical Theory and Islamic Republic of Iran's Foreign Policy', *The Iranian Journal of International Affairs*, 2008, 20(3): 1–26.

Abed, Mehbi. 'Ali Shariati: The Architect of the 1979 Islamic Revolution of Iran', *Iranian Studies*, 1986, 19(3/4): 229–234.

Abrahamian, Ervand. 'Communism and Communalism in Iran: The Tudah and the Firqah-I Dimukrat', *International Journal of Middle East Studies*, 1970, 1(4): 291–316.

Akhavi, Shahrough. 'Soviet Perceptions of the Iranian Revolution', *Iranian Studies*, 1986, 19(1): 3–29.

Akhavi, Shahrough. 'Islam, Politics and Society in the Thought of Ayatollah Khomeini, Ayatollah Taliqani and Ali Shariati', *Middle Eastern Studies*, 1988, 24(4): 404–431.

Alvandi, Roham. 'Nixon, Kissinger and the Shah: The Origins of Iranian Primacy in the Persian Gulf', *Diplomatic History*, 2012, 36(20): 337–372.

Bayat, Assef. 'Shari'ati and Marx: A Critique of an "Islamic" Critique of Marxism', *Alif: Journal of Comparative Poetics*, 1990, 10 ('Marxism and the Critical Discourse'): 19–41.

Behrooz, Maziar. 'Iran's Fadayan 1971–1988: A Case Study in Iranian Marxism', *JUSUR*, 1990, 6: 1–39.

Behrooz, Maziar. 'Tudeh Factionalism and the 1953 Coup in Iran', *International Journal of Middle East Studies*, 2001, 33(3): 363–382.

Benjamin, Roger W. & Kautsky, John H. 'Communism and Economic Development', *The American Political Science Review*, 1968, 62(1): 122.

Biener, Hansjoerg. 'The Arrival of Radio Farda: International Broadcasting to Iran at a Crossroads', *Middle East Review of International Affairs*, 2003, 7(1): 13–22.

Bill, James A. 'Iran and the Crisis of 78', *Foreign Affairs*, 1978, 57(2): 323–342.

Bowie, Robert, 'The Atlantic Alliance', *Daedalus*, 1981, 110(1) ('U.S. Defense Policy in the 1980s') pp. 23–40.

Brulé, David. 'Explaining and Forecasting Leaders' Decisions: A Poliheuristic Analysis of the Iran Hostage Rescue Decision', *International Studies Perspectives*, 2005, 6(1): 99–113.

Carswell, Robert. 'Economic Sanctions and the Iran Experience', *Foreign Affairs*, 1981–1982 60 (2): 247–265.

Caryl, Christian. 'The Democracy Boondoggle in Iraq', *Foreign Policy*, 5 March 2013. http://www.foreignpolicy.com/articles/2013/03/05/the_democracy_boondoggle_in_iraq.

Chubin, Shahram. 'The Soviet Union and Iran', *Foreign Affairs*, 1983, 61(4): 921–949.

Cottam, Richard. Review of *American Hostages in Iran: The Conduct of a Crisis* by Warren Christopher, Harold H. Saunders & Gary Sick and *All Fall Down: America's Tragic Encounter with Iran* by Gary Sick, *International Journal of Middle East Studies*, 1987, 19(2): 251–255.

Dabashi, Hamdi. 'The End of Islamic Ideology', *Social Research*, 2000, 67(2): 475–518.

Dankert, Pieter, 'Europe Together, America Apart', *Foreign Policy*, 1983–1984, 53: 18–33.

Daugherty, William J. 'A First Tour Like No Other', *Studies in Intelligence* (Spring 1998): 1–45.

Dawisha, Karen. 'Soviet Decision-Making in the Middle East: The 1973 October War and the 1980 Gulf War', *International Affairs (Royal Institute of International Affairs 1944–)*, 1980–1981, 57(1): 43–59.

Donovan, Michael. 'National Intelligence and the Iranian Revolution', *Intelligence and National Security*, 1997, 12(1): 143–163.

Drury, Cooper. 'Revisiting Economic Sanctions Reconsidered', *Journal of Peace Research*, 1998, 35(4): 497–509.

Dufft, Gloria. 'Crisis Mangling and the Cuban Brigade', *International Security*, 1983, 8(1): 67–87.

Emery, Christian, 'The transatlantic and Cold War dynamics of Iran sanctions, 1979–1980', *Cold War History*, 2010, 10 (3): 371–396.

Fatemi, Khosrow. 'The Iranian Revolution: Its Impact on Economic Relations with the United States', *International Journal of Middle East Studies*, 1980, 12(3): 303–317.

Freedman, Lawrence. 'The Atlantic Crisis', *International Affairs (Royal Institute of International Affairs 1944–)*, 1982, 58(3): 395–412.

Galtung, Johan. 'On the Effects of International Economic Sanctions: With Examples from the Case of Rhodesia', *World Politics*, 1967, 19(3): 378–416.

Gasiorowski, Mark. 'US Intelligence Assistance to Iran, May–October 1979', *Middle East Journal*, 2012, 6(4): 613–627.

Gibbs, David. 'Does the USSR Have a Grand Strategy? Re-interpreting the Invasion of Afghanistan', *Journal of Peace Research*, 1987, 24(1): 365–379.

Gilbert, John. 'Jimmy Carter's Human Rights Policy and Iran: A Re-examination, 1976–79', *Concept: An Interdisciplinary Journal of Graduate Studies*, 2008, 31. Online

Glad, Betty. 'Personality, Political and Group Process Variables in Foreign Policy Decision Making: Jimmy Carter's Handling of the Iranian Hostage Crisis', *International Political Science Review*, 1989, 10(1): 35–91.

Hakimian, H. 'Industrialization and the Standard of Living of the Working Class in Iran, 1960–1979', *Development and Change*, 1988, 19: 3–32.

Halliday, Fred. 'Counter-Revolution and Revolt in Iran', 17 July 2009, http://www.opendemocracy.net/article/iran-s-tide-of-history-counter-revolution-and-after.

Hanson, Brad. 'The Westoxication of Iran: Depictions and Reactions of Beh-rangi, Al-e Ahmad and Shariati', *International Journal of Middle East Studies*, 1983, 15(1): 1–23.

Hartman, Andrew. ' "The Red Template': US Policy in Soviet-Occupied Afghanistan', *Third World Quarterly*, 2002, 23(3): 468–469.

Hass, Richard. 'Sanctioning Madness', *Foreign Affairs*, 1997, 76(6): 74–85.

Hemmer, Christopher. 'Historical Analogies and the Definition of Interests: The Iranian Hostage Crisis and Ronald Reagan's Policy Toward the Hostages in Lebanon', *Political Psychology*, 1999, 20(2, June): 267–289.

Hershberg, Jim. 'The War in Afghanistan and the Iran Contra Affair: Missing Link?' *Cold War History*, 2003, 3(3): 23–48.

Hilali, Z. 'The Soviet Decision-Making for Intervention in Afghanistan and Its Motives', *Journal of Slavic Military Studies*, 2003, 16(2): 113–144.

Houghton, David Patrick. 'Reinvigorating the Study of Foreign Policy Decision-Making: Toward a Constructivist Approach', *Foreign Policy Analysis*, 2007, 3(1): 24–45.

Imam, Zafar. 'Soviet Treaties with Third World Countries', *Soviet Studies*, 1983, 35(1): 53–70.

Jentleson, Bruce. ' "Discrepant Responses to Falling Dictator": Presidential Belief Systems and the Mediating Effects of the Senior Advisory Process', *Political Psychology*, 1990, 11(2): 370.

Karasapan, Ömer. 'Turkey and US Strategy in the Age of Glasnost', *Middle East Report*, 1989, 160: 4–10, 22.

Kindleberger, Charles. 'US Foreign Economic Policy, 1776–1976', *Foreign Affairs*, 1977, 55(2): 395–417.

Laird, Robbin. 'France, Germany, and the Future of the Atlantic Alliance', *Proceedings of the Academy of Political Science*, 1991, 38(1) ('The New Europe: Revolution in East–West Relations'): 50–59.

Legvold, Robert. 'The Super Rivals: Conflict in the Third World', *Foreign Affairs*, 1979, 57(4): 755–778.

Lenczowski, George. 'The Arc of Crisis: Its Central Sector', *Foreign Affairs*, 1979, 57(4): 796–820.

Lieber, Robert J. 'Energy, Economics and Security in Alliance Perspective', *International Security*, 1980, 4(4): 139–163.

Lindsay, James. 'Trade Sanctions as Policy Instruments: A Re-examination', *International Studies Quarterly*, 1986, 30(2): 153–173.

Lissakers, Karin. 'Money and Manipulation', *Foreign Policy*, 1981, 44: 107–126.

Lorentz, John H. Review of *The Government of God: Iran's Islamic Republic* by Cheryl Benard and Zalmay Khalilzad, *Iranian Studies*, 1989, 22(2/3): 161–163.

Milani, Mohsen M. 'Harvest of Shame: Tudeh and the Bazargan Government', *Middle Eastern Studies*, 1993, 29(2): 307–320.

Moss, Robert. 'Who's Meddling in Iran', *New Republic*, 1978, 179: 15–18.

Nabavi, Negin. 'The Changing Concept of the "Intellectual" in Iran of the 1960s', *Iranian Studies*, 1999, 32(3): 333–350.

Nemchenok, Victor V. 'In Search of Stability amid Chaos: US Policy toward Iran, 1961–63', *Cold War History*, 2010, 10(3): 341–369.

Njølstad, Olav. 'Shifting Priorities: The Persian Gulf in US Strategic Planning in the Carter Years', *Cold War History*, 2004, 4(3): 21–55.

Odom, William E. 'The Cold War Origins of the U.S. Central Command', *Journal of Cold War Studies*, 2006, 8(2): 52–82.

Olcott, Martha Brill. 'Soviet Islam and World Revolution', *World Politics*, 1982, 3(4): 487–504.

Oyos, Matthew M. 'Jimmy Carter and SALT II: The Path to Frustration', *American Diplomacy*, 1996, 1(2) (e-journal).

Pape, Robert A. 'Why Economic Sanctions Do Not Work', *International Security*, 1997, 22(2): 90–136.

Precht, Henry. 'Ayatollah Realpolitik', *Foreign Policy*, 1988, 70: 109–128.

Precht, Henry. 'The Iranian Revolution: An Oral History With Henry Precht, Then State Department Desk Officer', *Middle East Journal*, 2004, 58(1): 9–31.

Ramazani, R. K. 'Security in the Persian Gulf', *Foreign Affairs*, 1979, 57(4): 821–835.

Ramazani, R. K. 'Iran's Revolution: Patterns, Problems and Prospects', *International Affairs (Royal Institute of International Affairs 1944–)*, 1980, 56(3): 443–457.

Ramazani, R. K. 'Iran: Burying the Hatchet', *Foreign Policy*, 1985, 60(Fall): 52–74.

Ramazani, R. K. 'Iran's Foreign Policy: Contending Orientations', *Middle East Journal*, 1989, 43(2): 202–217.

Reisman, Michael. 'The Legal Effect of Vetoed Resolutions', *American Journal of International Law*, 1980, 74(4): 904–907.

Roosevelt, Jr, Archie. 'The Kurdish Republic of Mahabad', *Middle East Journal*, 1947, 1(3): 247–269.

Rouleau, Eric. 'Khomeini's Iran', *Foreign Affairs*, 1980, 59(1): 1–20.

Rubin, Barry. 'American Relations with the Islamic Republic of Iran, 1979–1981', *Iranian Studies*, 1980, 13(1/4) ('Iranian Revolution in Perspective'): 307–326.

Rubinstein, Alvin. 'The Soviet Union and Iran under Khomeini', *International Affairs*, 1981, 57(4): 599–617.

Saikal, Amin. 'Soviet Policy toward Southwest Asia', *Annals of the American Academy of Political and Social Science*, 1985, 481 ('Soviet Foreign Policy in an Uncertain World'): 104–116.

Sartori, Leo. 'Will SALT II Survive?', *International Security*, 1985–1986, 10(3): 147–174.

Shehadi, Philip. 'Economic Sanctions and Iranian Trade', *MERIP Reports*, 1981, 98: 15–16.

Smith, Steve. 'Policy Preferences and Bureaucratic Position: The Case of the American Hostage Rescue Mission', *International Affairs*, 1984–1985, 61(1): 9–25.

Smith, Steve. 'Groupthink and the Hostage Rescue Mission', *British Journal of Political Science*, 1985, 15(1): 117–123.

Waltz, Kenneth N. 'A Strategy for the Rapid Deployment Force', *International Security*, 1981, 5(4): 49–73.

Warne, Andrew. 'Psychoanalyzing Iran: Kennedy's Iran Task Force and the Modernization of Orientalism, 1961–3', *International History Review*, 2013, 35(2): 396–422.

Newspapers and magazines

Armstrong, Scott. 'Iran Crisis Finally Forces Itself on Vance', *Washington Post*, 29 October 1980.

Armstrong, Scott. 'Iran Documents Give Rare Glimpse of CIA Enterprise', *Washington Post*, 31 January 1982.

Armstrong, Scott. 'Carter's Strange Account of the Iran Mess', *Washington Post*, 7 November 1982.

Bayat, Mangol. 'Iran's Real Revolutionary Leader', *Christian Science Monitor*, 24 May 1977.

Behrooz, Maziar. 'The Red Rose: A Biography of Khosrow Golesorkhi', *The Iranian*, 20 March 2003.

Behrooz, Maziar. 'Iran's Guerrillas: The Legacy of Iran's Guerrilla Movement', *Iranian.com*, 13 September 2004.

Bovin, Aleksandr. *Nedelya*, 3–9 September 1979. Editorial.

Bowden, Mark. 'Among the Hostage-Takers', *Atlantic*, December 2004.

Branigin, William. 'Iran Cancels Arms Orders with U.S.', *Washington Post*, 10 April 1979.

Burt, Richard. 'US Sees Need for Nuclear Arms to Repel Soviet Attack on Iran', *New York Times*, 2 February 1980.

Cullen, Robert. 'US, Allies to Postpone New Sanctions against Iran', *Associated Press*, 22 January 1980.

Cullen, Robert. 'Immediate, Tangible Results from New Sanctions Aren't Likely', Associated Press, 8 April 1980.

Demchenko, P. 'The USSR and Iran: Horizons of Co-operation', *Pravda*, 6 April 1979.

Downie Jr, Leonard. 'Allies Plan Limits to Their Support of U.S. Sanctions', *Washington Post*, 18 January 1980.

Downie Jr, Leonard. 'Allies Had Hoped to Prevent Use of Force by U.S.; Joining Sanctions Seen as Inducement', *Washington Post*, 24 April 1980.

Emery, Chris. 'Obama Faces Reality in Iran', *Guardian*, 14 June 2009.

Falk, Richard. 'Trusting Khomeini' (op-ed), *New York Times*, 16 February 1979.

Goshko, John M. 'Allies' Laws May Limit Cooperation on Iran Sanctions', *Washington Post*, 18 January 1980.

Goshko, John M. & Oberdorfer, Don. 'The Options Now; Future Course of the Confrontation Is More Complicated and Dangerous', *Washington Post*, 26 April 1980.

Graham, Bradley. 'Europe to Impose Sanctions on Iran Despite Britain', *Washington Post*, 21 May 1980.

Henderson, David. 'Why Economic Sanctions Don't work', *Hoover Digest*, no. 4 (1998).

Hoagland, Jim. 'Reactions to Shah's Crisis Called a Broad Failure', *Washington Post*, 25 January 1979.

Johnson, Haynes. 'Carter; Changes in Carter's Views Reflect Harsh Realities of 1980', *Washington Post*, 13 January 1980.

Keegan, John. 'The Ordeal of Afghanistan', *Atlantic Monthly*, November 1985.

Kraft, Joseph. 'Administration Has Doctrine of Confusion', *Sarasota Herald-Tribune*, 6 February 1980.

Markham, James M. 'Iran Crisis Undermining US in Gulf Area', *New York Times*, 8 February 1979.

McCartney, Robert. 'Europeans Discuss Iran Sanctions', Associated Press, 17 May 1980.

McCombs, Phil. 'New Case of International Terrorism; Reminder of Vulnerability', *Washington Post*, 23 July 1980.

Meyer, Cord. 'The Kremlin's Work in Iran', *Washington Post*, 10 February 1979.

Moubayed, Sami. 'Roots of the Kurdish Struggle Run Deep', *Asia Times*, 3 November 2007.

Mullin, Dennis. 'Khomeini's Chaos: Report from the Scene', *U.S. News & World Report*, 13 August 1979.

Petrossian, Vahe. 'Dilemmas of the Iranian Revolution', *World Today*, January 1980.

Randal, Jonathan C. 'US, Iran Declare Halt to Oil Trade', *Washington Post*, 13 November 1979.

Schlesinger, James. 'Fragmentation and Hubris', *National Interest*, Fall 1997.

Smith, J. P. 'Iran's Radicals Key to Oil Exports, US Aides Say', *Washington Post*, 14 February 1979.

Smith, Terence. 'Putting the Hostages' Lives First', *New York Times Magazine*, 17 May 1981.

Taheri, Amir. 'America Can't Do a Thing', *New York Post*, 2 November 2004.

Walsh, Edward. 'Rivals Doubt Carter Will Retain Poll Gains After Iran Crisis', *The Washington Post*, 17 December 1979.

Weisskopf, Michael. 'Executed in Iranian Crackdown; Iranian Executions Spur Riots; Fighting in Tabriz Matches Backers of Rival Ayatollahs', *Washington Post*, 13 January 1980.

Welch, William M. 'Reagan Calls Iran Sanctions More of Same', Associated Press, 7 April 1980.

'The Crumbling Triangle', *Economist*, 8 December 1978, p. 12.

'Kissinger's Critique (Continued)', *Economist*, 10 February 1979, p. 31.

'Russians Using PLO as Khomeini Link', *Telegraph*, 1 March 1979.

'Pressure on the Ayatollah', *Washington Post*, 13 November 1979.

'What If Iran Ended U.S. Oil Sales?', *U.S. News & World Report*, 19 November 1979.

'Soviet-Based Radio Urges Hostages Release in Iran', *Washington Post*, 22 November 1979.

'Iran: The Test of Wills', *Time*, 26 November, 1979.

'Carter Would Fight for Persian Gulf; Seeks to Resume Draft Registration', *Washington Post*, 24 January 1980.

'How to Be a Good Ally without Putting Oneself Out', *Economist*, 19 April 1980.

'Stunned Allies React to Aborted Hostage Rescue Effort', Associated Press, 25 April 1980.

'European Community Nations Impose Sanctions on Iran; Britain Modifies Stand', *Facts on File World News Digest*, 23 May 1980.

'Exiles Plan Assault on Iran', *Christian Science Monitor* (Boston, MA), 19 June 1980.

'An Interview with Ghotbzadeh', *Time*, Monday, 1 September 1980.

'Human Rights Emphasis Stalled Iran Policy at Crucial Time, Book Says', Associated Press, 2 November 1981.

Letter from L. Bruce Laingen to *New York Times*, 'Iran Hostage Crisis: Notes to a Post-Script', 13 January 1983.

'The US and Iran Part III – The Hostage Crisis', *PRI's The World*, 27 October 2004.

'The Last Shah of Iran', *FrontPageMagazine.com*, 6 March 2006.

Reports

Copulos, Milton R. & Phillips, James, A. 'The Iranian Dilemma: Energy and Security Implications', Heritage Foundation, background briefing no. 105 (16 November 1979), p. 55.

Cosser, Ralph A. 'Iran: Soviet Interests, American Concerns', McNair Papers Number 11, The Institute for National Strategic Studies, National Defense University, July 1990. p. 44.

Foreign Affairs Oral History Program, Association for Diplomatic Studies. Interview with Ambassador Bruce Laingen. Dates: 9 January, 7 April, 25 August, 1992; 17 February, 27 May 1993.

Fukuyama, Francis. 'The Soviet Threat to the Persian Gulf', March 1981, Rand Corporation Paper Series.

Holloway Report. http://www.gwu.edu/~ nsarchiv/NSAEBB/NSAEBB63/doc8.pdf.

'Iran: Intelligence Failure or Policy Stalemate?', Working Group Report No. 1, Institute for the Study of Diplomacy, Edmund A. Walsh School of Foreign Service, Georgetown University, 23 November 2004.

Katzman, Kenneth. 'The People's Mojahedin Organization of Iran', US State Department Report presented to Committee on Foreign Affairs, House of Representatives, Washington, DC, November 1992, 6p. Doc. call no.: M-U 42953-1 no. 92-824F.

MacEachin, Doug, Nolan, Janne E. & Tockman, Kristine. 'The Soviet Invasion of Afghanistan in 1979: Failure of Intelligence or of the Policy Process?', Institute for the Study of Diplomacy, Edmund A. Walsh School of Foreign Service, Georgetown University, Group Report, No. 111, 26 September 2005.

Official Journal of the European Communities, no. C115/ 2021, 18 May 1981.

Phillips, James A. 'The Iranian Oil Crisis', Heritage Foundation Backgrounder #76, 28 February 1979.

Phillips, James A. 'The Iranian Revolution: Long-Term Implications', Heritage Foundation Backgrounder #89, 15 June 1979.

Phillips, James A. 'Iran, the United States and the Hostages: After 300 Days', Heritage Foundation, 29 August 1980.

Sadjadpour, Karim. 'Reading Khamenei: The World View of Iran's Most Powerful Leader', Carnegie Endowment for International Peace, 2008, p. 11.

Shaffer, Brenda. 'Partners in Need: The Strategic Relationship of Russia and Iran', Policy Paper no. 57, Washington Institute for Near East Policy, 2001, p. 8.

Shultz, S. R. B. '51–52 Tower Commission Report'.

'Soviet Reaction to the Iranian Crisis', Soviet Report, Vol. 1, No. 2, The Center for Strategic and International Studies, December 1979.

'Soviet Union – Military Presence in the Third World', Country Studies Series by Federal Research Division of the Library of Congress, 1989.

US House of Representatives, Permanent Select Committee on Intelligence. 'Iran. Evaluation of U.S. Intelligence Performance Prior to November 1978', staff report, Washington, DC, January 1979.

'US Policy toward Iran', January 1979, Hearing before the Subcommittee on Europe and the Middle East of the Committee on Foreign Affairs, House of Representatives, 96th Cong., 1st session.

Unpublished material

Carter Presidency Project: Interviews with Zbigniew Brzezinksi, Madeleine K. Albright, Leslie Denend, William Odom, 18 February 1982, Miller Center of Public Affairs, University of Virginia. p. 31 (full transcript).

'Changes in the Middle East: Moscow's Perceptions and Options', CIA Intelligence Estimate, 29 May 1979. Unpublished collection of documents prepared by Malcolm Byrne, National Security Archives.

Conference Reader compiled by Christian F. Ostermann and Mircea Munteanu. 'Towards an International History of the War in Afghanistan', 29–30 April 2002, Washington, DC.

Javadzadeh, Abdy. 'Borrowing Ideology: Marxists Becoming Muslims during the 1979 Revolution in Iran', 10 August 2006, Paper presented at the annual meeting of the American Sociological Association, Montreal Convention Center, Montreal, Quebec, Canada.

Tardelli, Luca. 'The US Political Elite and the Sources of American Foreign Policy towards the Russian and Iranian Revolutions', 22 November 2011, Foreign Policy Workshop, LSE.

'The Carter Administration and the "Arc of Crisis" 1977–1981, Declassified Documents Prepared for 'A Critical Oral History Conference', Woodrow Wilson Center, 25–26 July 2005. Organised by The Cold War International History Project and National Security Archive in cooperation with the Middle East Program, WWICS.

'The Intervention in Afghanistan and Fall of Détente', 1995 Nobel Symposium Conference Reader (unpublished), Oslo, Norway, National Security Archive.

'US–Soviet Relations and Soviet Foreign Policy toward the Middle East and Africa in the 1970's', Conference Reader edited by Odd Arne Westad, 1–3 October 1995, The Norwegian Nobel Institute, Lysebu. Transcribed by Gail Adams Kvam. My thanks to Malcolm Byrne for providing this material.

Index

Printed and bound by CPI Group (UK) Ltd, Croydon, CR0 4YY